The Limits of Culture

The BCSIA Studies in International Security book series is edited at the Belfer Center for Science and International Affairs at Harvard University's John F. Kennedy School of Government and published by The MIT Press. The series publishes books on contemporary issues in international security policy, as well as their conceptual and historical foundations. Topics of particular interest to the series include the spread of weapons of mass destruction, internal conflict, the international effects of democracy and democratization, and U.S. defense policy.

A complete list of BCSIA Studies in International Security appears at the back of this volume.

The Limits of Culture

Islam and Foreign Policy

Brenda Shaffer, editor

BCSIA Studies in International Security

The MIT Press
Cambridge, Massachusetts
London, England

This book was typeset in Palatino by Wellington Graphics and was
printed and bound in the United States of America.

Library of Congress Cataloging-in-Publication Data

The limits of culture : Islam and foreign policy / Brenda Shaffer (ed.).
p.   cm. — (BCSIA studies in international security)
Includes bibliographical references.
ISBN 0-262-19529-1 (hc : alk. paper) — ISBN 0-262-69321-6 (pbk. : alk. paper)
1. International relations and culture. 2. Islamic countries—Foreign relations. I. Shaffer,
Brenda. II. Series.

JZ1251.L55 2005
327'0917'67—dc22   2004057937

10 9 8 7 6 5 4 3 2 1

Contents

Acknowledgments

In recent decades, area studies and international relations specialists have conducted and published research with little dialogue between their respective fields, especially concerning the impact of culture on states. In my own academic training, I have crossed the hallway a number of times between humanities and social sciences. When students have asked me which emphasis to put in their studies, knowing that my own training has been in both regional and theoretical aspects of international relations, I always have to answer that you need both forms of training. On the one hand, I believe that for a researcher to understand a specific case, one has to be immersed in the language, geography, and ruling power structure of a specific state. Without having extensive case-specific knowledge, the researcher will not see the nuances of the behavior of the case and may get caught up in a state's declared rhetoric about its own behavior. On the other hand, a researcher only trained in area studies may be limited by this training into considering only the specifics of a case and not see the general principles that may be having a greater effect on a state's decisions.

The Limits of Culture: Islam and Foreign Policy represents an attempt to reap the benefits of the knowledge of both of the disciplines of regional studies and international relations. The assembled authors in this book are experts in different fields of international relations and regional studies. While possessing different backgrounds and training, all were tasked with the same research question: does local culture frequently explain a state's foreign policy decisions? Or, is culture just one among many factors that have varying influences on a state's foreign policy?

In international relations theory, the role assigned to culture varies greatly between different schools of thought within the discipline. Neither a good debate nor an informative dialogue, however, is currently on-going within the discipline of international relations. Each camp feels completely certain in its position. When I initiated this project on culture and foreign policy, realist colleagues asked me why I was beating a dead horse, being so sure that local culture is rarely a significant factor in a state's foreign policy preferences and that this fact has been clearly proven. Constructivist colleagues also were surprised by this research question, when it is clear to them that culture is an unquestionable part of a state's behavior and its very existence. In the policy world, culture, and especially history, is regularly attributed an important role in affecting political outcomes. Culture is an important variable in the formal training programs of government policy analysis and has thus had a huge impact on their work. Decision-makers are consumers of newspapers more than international relations journals, and journalists tend to emphasize cultural, especially religious and historical factors in their analyses of states' foreign policies. All this, without questioning and looking empirically to see if that emphasis on culture is in any way justified. I hope this book will spur debate and dialogue within in the international relations discipline, between regional/historical studies and international relations, and between the academic and policy spheres.

The Limits of Culture: Islam and Foreign Policy is the result of a two-year research project that was conducted under the auspices and sponsorship of the Belfer Center of Science and International Affairs (BCSIA) at the Kennedy School of Government at Harvard University. It is my pleasure to thank a number of people that played crucial roles in the research project and subsequently, this book. First and foremost, I would like to thank Professor Graham Allison, who gave me the opportunity to lead this research project and encouraged me to research this topic for which he knew I had a passion; over the years he has been a kind colleague and good friend, and I appreciate his support and guidance. Next, I would like to acknowledge each of the chapter authors of this book, all of whom are outstanding professionals in their different fields and who together were able to provide a very unique look at culture and foreign policy. Dr. Steven E. Miller provided consistent support, excellent feedback and suggestions at different stages of the manuscript, and he formulated my own main points—much better than I could have done. Arman Grigorian encouraged me to research the topic of the impact of culture and foreign policy through our conversations on the Caucasus, and especially by saying to me in one of our many academic (and not so academic) arguments, "you idiot, Turkey and Russia are not historical enemies—they are just bordering states of relatively the same power." I am grateful to Sean Lynn-Jones for suggesting the book's title and for his excellent comments on the book at various stages of the writing and research. John Grennan was an outstanding research assistant from the project's inception and indexer in the final stages of the book. Professor Michael Desch generously gave much appreciated feedback and advice on the book's manuscript. I would like to thank Susan Lynch for her research assistance and her outstanding editing ability. Avinoam Idan taught me about geographic factors in the Caucasus and Central Asia—I greatly value our research partnership. Jane Greenhood and Arthur Hughes, through their generosity and kindness, made it possible for me to conduct this research in Cambridge. Harvey Kruger and the Harry S. Truman Research Institute for the Advancement of Peace at the Hebrew University of Jerusalem supported my research while I worked on this book and I am grateful. Finally, I would like to thank Yehuda and especially Yael and Omri Shaffer, my teenage twins, for their constant interest in my work, their philosophical questions, and their excellent jokes.

Brenda Shaffer
Cambridge, Massachusetts
August 2005

Chapter 1

Introduction:
The Limits of Culture

Brenda Shaffer

Culture—and especially religion as a form of culture—has gained popularity in the second half of the twentieth century as a key explanation of states' and other political entities' foreign policies. Policymakers and journalists frequently use culture as a variable to explain and predict alliances and lines of conflict. Diplomats and government analysts are trained to learn the culture of the place that they will serve or research in order to understand a state's anticipated behavior. Moreover, in the 1990s, a plethora of works appeared in mainstream international relations publications that set up culture as an independent variable and used it to explain a number of foreign policy choices. Even John Mearsheimer and Stephen Walt—prominent realists who often dismiss cultural factors—invoked the culturalist argument in their critique of U.S. policy toward Iraq on the eve of the 2003 war. In claiming that cooperation was not likely to have taken place between Saddam Hussein and the al-Qaeda terrorist network, they argued that conflicting culturally-based identities make it hard to imagine the forging of cooperation between the "secular" regime of Saddam Hussein and the "Islamic fundamentalist" al-Qaeda, despite the fact that they share a common enemy.[1]

States need legitimacy; humans who are affected by culture are central actors in the decision-making process in states and constitute the publics of states. Thus, assuming that all things are equal, culture can be assumed to play a role in foreign policy decision-making. All things are not equal, however, and policy choices have costs, benefits, and trade-offs. Pursuit of both culturally-based and materially-based interests often

---

1. John J. Mearsheimer and Stephen M. Walt, "Keeping Saddam in a Box," February 2, 2003, *New York Times.*

conflict, and regimes must determine which interest receives priority. To conclude that culture is the main driving force behind a state's policy choices, a significant number of cases should be identifiable where the culturally-based goal collides with basic material interests of either the state or its ruling elite in such matters as state preservation, security, prosperity, or regime preservation, but the commitment to the culturally-based goal overrides. In other words, if culture is a predominant factor in a state's foreign policy, then the decision-making elite would frequently accord it precedence even when this action would be significantly costly to the state in a material way. If few cases, however, are found in which material interests are subordinated to the pursuit of cultural interests, international relations theory should rethink the serious role that it has attributed to culture in recent years.

This book examines the impact of culture on the foreign policies of states. It will explore the question: does local culture frequently explain a state's foreign policy decisions? In other words, if a researcher knows the primary collective culture of the residents of a state, does it significantly contribute to the ability of the researcher to assess the foreign policy decisions of a state, such as the coalitions and alignments that it will build and the lines of conflict that will be formed with neighboring states, or is culture just one among many factors that have varying influences on a state's foreign policy?

Culture is an extremely controversial term, and few have been able to formulate a working definition that is precise and exclusive enough in order that it may serve as a clear independent variable that can be examined.[2] In this book, culture will be defined as the force or group of forces that determines a predominant self-identity of a specific and sizeable collective of people.[3] Under this definition, culture encompasses the factors of religion, ethnicity, history, and civilization. In this study, the impact of ideology will also be analyzed together with the term culture, because ideology can determine the identity of a collective and is a non-material interest. The main dichotomy of interests here is material versus non-

---

2. For a thorough discussion of different definitions of culture, see Markus Fischer's chapter in this book.

3. Strategic culture will not be included in this study. Strategic culture may be affected by culture, but it is neither a form of culture nor is it a source of a collective's identity. For more on strategic culture, see Alastair Iain Johnston, "Thinking about Strategic Culture." *International Security*, Vol. 19, No. 4 (Spring 1995), pp. 32–44; Alastair Iain Johnston, *Cultural Realism: Strategic Culture and Grand Strategy in Chinese History* (Princeton, N.J.: Princeton University Press, 1988); Stephen Peter Rosen, "Military Effectiveness: Why Society Matters," *International Security*, Vol. 19, No. 4 (Spring 1995), pp. 5–31.

material cultural and ideological interests.[4] Moreover, this book will examine the impact of specific local cultures on state foreign policies. In contrast, many of the previous works that have delved into the question of culture and foreign policy have meshed the question of the impact of local culture together with that of universal norms on foreign policies.[5] Universal norms and cultures are very different types of variables than particular indigenous cultures. In addition, since there are many material benefits that can be derived from observance of universally declared norms, it is difficult to say if compliance reflects cultural interests or material interests.

In addition, this book will analyze the role of culture in the foreign policy of states and not of non-state actors.[6] In researching the impact of culture on foreign policy, it is essential to distinguish between the actions of an individual human and those of the state. This book assumes that human beings and groups of humans are often driven by culture. The human is a unique animal that may sacrifice his life due to emotions like jealousy or the desire for glory. The state, however, makes decisions in a different way than either the individual human or the aggregate views of the humans who participate in the decision-making process. Furthermore, the state possesses additional interests to those of the individuals residing in the state.

In examining the relationship between culture and foreign policy, this book represents a comparative analysis of the foreign policies of a number of states of the Caspian region and Central Asia in the first ten years following the Soviet breakup (1991–2001).[7] Many surmised that the Caspian region would be a highly likely case where culture—especially in

---

4. National interest can be composed of both material and non-material interests, such as culture and ideology. In many of the previous works that look at the question of culture and foreign policy, national interest was erroneously used to connote material interests.

5. Judith Goldstein and Robert O. Keohane, eds., *Ideas and Foreign Policy: Beliefs, Institutions and Political Change* (Ithaca, N.Y.: Cornell University Press, 1993); and Peter J. Katzenstein (ed.), *The Culture of National Security: Norms and Identity in World Politics* (New York: Columbia University Press, 1996).

6. The state possesses interests and considerations that affect its policies and are different than those of non-states, precisely due to one of the important characteristics of statehood: it possesses a clearly defined territory, is sovereign, and monopolizes the use of force in the territory that it rules.

7. The Caspian region encompasses the Caspian Sea's littoral states (Russia, Iran, Azerbaijan, Kazakhstan, and Turkmenistan) as well as neighboring states that are part of the energy, trade, and transport network of the Caspian Basin (Georgia, Turkey, and Uzbekistan) and the security context of the greater region (Armenia, Pakistan, Afghanistan, the Kyrgyz Republic, and Tajikistan).

the forms of ethnicity and religion—would play an important role in the foreign policies of the states of the region.[8] This book puts special emphasis on examining the foreign policies of three self-proclaimed "Islamic Republics"—Iran, Pakistan, and Taliban Afghanistan—presumably the strongest cases for the cultural argument. All three of these states, in declaring themselves "Islamic republics," formally articulated that Islam serves as the guiding force of their state policies and the state should serve as an instrument of Islam. It is reasonable to assume that if culture were a leading factor in the formation of foreign policy choices, it would appear in the preferences of these three states. Analysis of the Caspian region sheds further light on the role of Islam in the foreign policy of states: since both Muslims and non-Muslims populate the region, it is possible to examine whether or not Islam serves as a basis for coalitions and lines of cooperation between Muslim-populated states.

The findings in this book include:

STATES AND RULING REGIMES DO NOT NECESSARILY GET CAUGHT IN THEIR OWN RHETORIC. The cases presented here show that even the most culturally and ideologically articulate states in the international system, such as the Islamic Republic of Iran, can conduct policies on a regular basis that completely contradict their formal cultural identification, dictates, and consequent state ideology—without domestic retribution. In fact, the case evidence in this book shows that not only can states conduct policies that contradict their official culture, but, at times, states use certain cultural rhetoric to endow their decisions with legitimacy even when this rhetoric is in defiance of the officially articulated culture of the state. For instance, Iranian officials have on many occasions praised Tehran's "cultural ties" with Armenia at the expense of its ties with Shi'i Azerbaijan with little public retribution.

OFFICIAL STATE CULTURE DOES NOT NECESSARILY LIMIT FOREIGN POLICY OPTIONS. Leaders can stretch identities wide enough to allow a large

---

8. A significant number of books and articles published on the region in the early 1990s stressed the importance of culture, especially ethnic identity and politics, in the anticipated political outcomes in the region. For example, many of these early works on Central Asia and Azerbaijan stressed political rivalry in the region between Iran and Turkey, assuming that these two Muslim powers would be the main sources of influence in the region, due to the Muslim background of the residents of the region. See, for instance, Ahmed Rashid, *The Resurgence of Central Asia: Islam or Nationalism* (London and New Jersey: Zed Books, 1994); Rajan Menon and Henry J. Barkey, "The Transformation of Central Asia: Implications for Regional and International Security," *Survival*, Vol. 34, No. 4 (Winter 1992–93), pp. 68–89. In addition, journalist accounts especially tended to frame the conflicts in the region in cultural terms. See, for instance, Serge Schmemann, "Ethnic Battles Flaring in Former Soviet Fringe," *New York Times*, May 24, 1992.

variety of foreign policy options, including ones that seemingly contradict the articulated state identity. One of the methods used by regimes to escape potential political retribution from their citizenry is to recreate the content of their cultural identities that will allow them the legitimacy to pursue preferred political options. For instance, many of the regimes in Central Asia often succeed in reconciling their desire for domestic Islamic legitimacy for their regimes with their very pro-Western policies by creating a distinction between the dictates of "good Islam" or "real Islam," and "bad Islam" or "false Islam." Good and real Islam, as interpreted by these regimes, is one of tolerance of foreigners and other religions and is locally rooted, reflecting local (non-Arab) traditions. In contrast, bad and false Islam, as interpreted by Central Asia's leaders, is led by foreign Muslims and is intolerant toward non-Muslims.

OFFICIALLY ARTICULATED STATE CULTURE IS NOT NECESSARILY THE CULTURAL FACTOR THAT INFLUENCES FOREIGN POLICY. In the cases where cultural influences on foreign policy were detected, these influences were connected not to the officially articulated culture of the state, but to subtle cultural influences that most likely would be spotted by only a regional specialist looking at the state, such as the prevalent cultural practice in Central Asia to refrain from reporting bad news or potential consequences, especially to one's superiors.

CULTURAL AFFINITY DOES NOT NECESSARILY TRANSLATE INTO POLITICAL ALLIANCES OR CLOSE COOPERATION. None of the case evidence presented in this book corroborates the statement that cultural affinity leads to greater security cooperation or lower propensity to conflict. In fact, the lines of cooperation, designation of threats, and camps connected to conflicts displayed neither impact of cultural affinity nor lack thereof. Furthermore, the cases presented here raise questions as to the direction of the causal relationship between culture and foreign policy. In this volume, Douglas Blum postulated that some cultural choices are influenced by the existence of a strategic alliance or cooperation, while Ido Oren and Robert Kauffman suggested that changes in cultural views and security ties by alliances may go hand in hand. Moreover, in many states, the prevailing culture possessed by the people differs from the security strategy employed by the ruling regime.

RELIGIOUS IDENTITY SHOULD NOT BE ASSUMED TO BE THE PRIMARY CULTURAL INFLUENCE AFFECTING A REGIME'S IDENTITY OR BEHAVIOR. In the cases examined in this study, no correlation was found between common religious affinity and perception of threat, tendency to form alliances and strategic cooperation, or lines of conflict. This was especially true of the actions of the Islamic Republic of Iran in the region. Also, common religious identity can be amplified by a regime as a source of conflict (leadership rivalry, conflict over interpretation of doctrine, succession issues) or can be broken down into divisive sub-identities (such as Shi'i or Sunni) to legitimize policy choices.

REGIME TYPES THAT ALLOW CULTURALLY-BASED MINORITIES, SUCH AS ETHNICALLY-BASED DIASPORAS, TO HAVE SIGNIFICANT INFLUENCE ON POLICY FORMATION ARE ESPECIALLY CONDUCIVE TO CULTURAL INFLUENCES ON FOREIGN POLICY. Through the activities of domestic lobbies acting to promote their perception of the interests of co-ethnics abroad, cultural goals are sometimes promoted in opposition to a government's strategic priorities, especially in a governmental system like that of the United States, which permits the legislative branch to influence foreign policy significantly. In regimes where foreign policy was not controlled by a central actor, more opportunity for promotion of culturally-based interests seems to exist. This was found in the case of Iran, where ideological islands in the regime can promote culturally-based policies in defiance of the more materially-based preferences of the state executive. In this study, the authoritarian, centralized states analyzed were found to be the most likely to stray from their officially articulated cultures in their foreign policy choices. A powerful example in this study is the Islamic Republic of Iran. Additionally, in September 2002, Kazakhstan and Uzbekistan successfully negotiated an expansive territorial compromise on their common border that left thousands of their co-ethnics and citizens outside of their state borders in contradiction to their ethnically-based, nationalistic state cultures. This was greatly facilitated by the lack of vocal political opposition that could have made this move domestically costly.

POLICY DILEMMAS BETWEEN MATERIAL INTERESTS AND CULTURAL INTERESTS ARE ESPECIALLY ACUTE IN STATES THAT IDENTIFY WITH TRANS-STATE IDEOLOGIES (such as Islam, communism). The interests of the state face an inherent clash with the promotion of the interests of groups outside its borders. Moreover, these universal ideologies are often centered in specific states, such as Islam in Saudi Arabia, creating potential clashes between the state when it promotes its own interests and other states that nominally identify with the universal identity based there.

STATES MAY NOT TAKE THEIR OWN RHETORIC SERIOUSLY, BUT OTHERS TAKE THEIR RHETORIC SERIOUSLY. While the states examined in this study often acted in defiance of their official culturally-based rhetoric, they often took the culturally-based rhetoric of their opponents seriously. Azerbaijanis believe that Yerevan's and Moscow's close military cooperation is fostered by their common Christian Orthodox background, regardless of the fact that the Azerbaijanis clearly see that shared religious affinity does not aid neighboring Georgia in its relations with Moscow. An additional example is that U.S. policymakers take Iran's Islamic rhetoric seriously, and many policymakers believe this Islamic solidarity serves as the basis for Tehran's foreign policy preferences (see Ali Ansari's chapter in this volume). Consequently, Tehran's rhetoric affected Washington's views of its policy options toward Iran, including routes of cooperation.

CULTURE SEEMS TO HAVE MORE INFLUENCE IN INSTANCES WHERE DECISION-MAKERS DO NOT HAVE COMPREHENSIVE INFORMATION ON FOR-EIGN POLICY DILEMMAS AND THE ANTICIPATED TRADE-OFFS OF THEIR ACTIONS, OR WHEN THEY LACK SUFFICIENT INFORMATION TO JUDGE THE EX-TENT OF A CONFLICT BETWEEN MATERIAL INTERESTS AND CULTURAL ONES. If the decision-maker is not fully aware of the material costs of promoting a cultural goal, the inclination is to promote it. Moreover, culture can have an impact when a small amount of people control the flow of infor-mation on certain topic. For instance, the cultural views of a diplomat abroad can shape the information that flows to decision-makers, depriv-ing them of the ability to discern material costs of a decision.

The emerging foreign policies of the Caspian states, the coalitions that they have formed, and the failure of some of the most ideologically articulate states in the international system, such as the Islamic Republic of Iran, to promote their cultural interests when it was detrimental to the state's other interests, all provide a significant challenge to the culturalist argument. In the case of the Muslim-populated states of the Caspian re-gion—including the Islamic Republics of Iran and Pakistan—culture seems to give us little explanation for the foreign policies of these states, especially in the choices of alliance partners and in spheres affecting their critical security interests. Accordingly, culture's role as foreign policy in-put must be analyzed on a case-by-case basis. Moreover, policymakers should be careful not to use culture as the default explanation unless spe-cific case evidence corroborates this determination.

This study also specifically provides knowledge and understanding of the Caspian region, which is of rising importance in geopolitical terms: the Caspian region is awash with oil and gas, a large number of U.S. troops are deployed in the area, and U.S. bases have been established there to maintain the anti-terrorism effort and other operations in Af-ghanistan, Iraq, and other Muslim-populated states. Moreover, the terri-tories of many of the states of the region are used for U.S. flyovers into the Middle East and beyond. Serious conflicts that raged in the area in the early 1990s, killing tens of thousands and turning millions into refugees, can easily reignite.[9] Understanding the dynamics of the Caspian region is essential to understanding how to resolve those conflicts successfully and

---

9. Among the serious conflicts that have raged in the region: the Nagorno-Karabagh

prevent their reemergence from threatening the important achievements in the area during the first decade of independence from the Soviet Union.

Culture in International Relations Theory

In the second half of the twentieth century, culture became a mainstream explanation in international relations theory of states' foreign policy preferences.

During the World War II period, the U.S. military called upon cultural anthropologists to profile the cultures of Germany and Japan in order to explain and anticipate their state policies.[10] The development of international relations theory in the postwar period was highly influenced by the compelling example of Nazi Germany—a powerful state whose ideology seemed to be the driving force behind its foreign policy decisions.[11]

In the post–World War II period, many U.S. universities established departments and centers of regional studies. The founding of these area studies departments reflected the belief that each state is very different and the way to understand a place or state is to immerse oneself in study of a specific region—learning its language, culture, and particular historical experience. Experts and policymakers on certain states were generally trained in area studies departments, learning the peculiarities of a state or region. Government analysts are trained to see culture as an important input in the foreign policy of states (see Roger Kangas's chapter in this volume). Terms like "national character" appeared frequently in this period in international relations discussions.[12]

Beginning in the 1990s, many works in mainstream international relations scholarship appeared which accorded culture a major role in explaining the actions of states and other actors in the international system.

---

conflict between Azerbaijan and Armenia; Abkhaz and South Ossetian civil wars in Georgia; and Tajikistan's civil war.

10.   See Michael Desch, "Culture Clash: Assessing the Importance of Ideas in Security Studies," *International Security*, Vol. 23, No. 1 (Summer 1998), p. 144.

11.   One of the most outstanding examples of Nazi Germany's preference for ideological considerations over material interests was Hitler's decision in the spring of 1944, over the objections of Germany's military leadership, to allocate trains to transport the Jews of Hungary to extermination camps in Poland, thus denying their use for supplying Germany's troops on the Eastern Front.

12.   Desch, p. 145.

In this period, many international relations theorists promoted culture as an independent variable and used it to explain a number of foreign policy choices: alliance partners (Michael Barnett, Thomas Risse-Kappen, and Samuel Huntington); use or non-use of weapons (Jeffrey Legro); choice of military doctrine (Elizabeth Kier); or economic behavior (Samuel Huntington and Lawrence Harrison).[13] Among the major international relations paradigms, the constructivist paradigm attaches the most importance to culture as a variable in the international discipline relations, and its adherents published a number of works in this period promoting the importance of culture in foreign relations outcomes.[14]

Samuel Huntington and his civilization paradigm, as well as various specialists on Islam and Muslim history, were important academic forces that emphasized the importance of culture in explaining the actions of states, especially those of Muslim-populated states.[15] The latter had a huge impact on the way policymakers and journalists view the policies and conflicts in Muslim-populated states, while less so on international relations debates. Samuel Huntington propelled the role of culture in the

---

13.   See Katzenstein, *The Culture of National Security: Norms and Identity in World*; Michael N. Barnett, "Identity and Alliances in the Middle East," in Katzenstein, *The Culture of National Security*; Shibley Telhami and Michael Barnett, *Identity and Foreign Policy in the Middle East* (Ithaca, N.Y.: Cornell University Press, 2002); Thomas Risse-Kappen, "Collective Identity in a Democratic Community: The Case of NATO," in Katzenstein, *The Culture of National Security*; Samuel Huntington, *The Clash of Civilizations and the Remaking of World Order* (New York: Touchstone, 1997); Jeffrey W. Legro, *Cooperation Under Fire: Anglo-German Restraint during World War II* (Ithaca, N.Y.: Cornell University Press, 1995); Elizabeth Kier, *Imagining War: French Military Doctrine Between the Wars* (Princeton, N.J.: Princeton University Press, 1997); and Lawrence E. Harrison and Samuel P. Huntington, eds., *Culture Matters: How Values Shape Human Progress* (New York: Basic Books, 2000).

14.   See Yosef Lapid and Friedrich V. Kratochwil, eds., *The Return of Culture and Identity in IR Theory* (Boulder, Colo.: Lynne Rienner, 1996); R.B.J. Walker, ed., *Culture, Ideology, and World Order* (Boulder, Colo.: Westview, 1984); Jongsuk Chay, ed., *Culture and International Relations* (New York: Praeger, 1990); Katzenstein, ed., *The Culture of National Security*; Valerie M. Hudson, *Culture and Foreign Policy* (Boulder, Colo.: Lynne Rienner, 1997); Dominique Jaquin-Berdal, Andrew Oros, and Marco Verweij, eds., *Culture in World Politics* (New York: St. Martin's, 1998); Ted Hopf, "The Promise of Constructivism in International Relations Theory," *International Security*, Vol. 23, No. 1 (Summer 1998), pp. 171–200; Ted Hopf, *Social Construction of International Politics: Identities and Foreign Policies, Moscow, 1955 and 1999* (Ithaca, N.Y., Cornell University Press, 2002); and Alexander Wendt, "Anarchy is What States Make of It: The Social Construction of Power Politics," *International Organization*, Vol. 46, No. 2 (Spring 1992), pp. 391–425.

15.   The most prominent Islamic history specialist was Bernard Lewis, who wielded significant influence over how policymakers depict Muslim-populated states.

foreign policy of states to the center stage of both academic and wider debates. In his article *The Clash of Civilizations*,[16] he states clearly: "The great divisions among humankind and the dominating source of conflict will be cultural. Nation states will remain the most powerful actors in world affairs, but the principle conflicts of global politics will occur between nations and groups of different civilizations."[17]

He further concludes that: "The most important conflicts of the future will occur among the cultural fault lines separating these civilizations from one another,"[18] and that "a civilization is a cultural entity."[19]

Critiques of Huntington appeared all over the globe, especially in the Muslim world. Most critics attacked Huntington's prediction of clashes or took issue with his emphasis on the civilization unit of identity.[20] Few argued, however, with his idea that culture plays an important role in determining foreign policies.[21] In fact, some prominent realists who critiqued his theory, such as Robert Jervis, praised the fact that Huntington had succeeded in drawing attention to culture and religion in international relations as factors that "deserve—indeed demand—more consideration."[22] In many of the critiques which appeared in political science mainstream journals, *The Clash of Civilizations* was praised precisely for its emphasis of culture. Stephen Shulman wrote in *The Journal of Politics* on Huntington that "he redresses one of the most glaring weaknesses of lib-

---

16.   Samuel P. Huntington, "The Clash of Civilizations?" *Foreign Affairs,* Vol 72, Number 3 (Summer 1993), pp. 22–49.

17.   Ibid, p. 22.

18.   Ibid, p. 25.

19.   Ibid, p. 23.

20.   Richard Rosecrance, "Review: Samuel Huntington's *The Clash of Civilizations and the Remaking of World Order,*" *American Political Science Review,* Vol. 92, Issue 4 (December 1998), pp. 978–980. Rosecrance's criticism focuses on the lack of support that civilization should serve as the main unit of analysis, pointing to wars within civilizations, economic cooperation between members of different civilizations that can build important links, and the fact that many "cultural conflicts" take place within the borders of states. Rosecrance ends with recognition that culture is impacting international relations and that Huntington is right to suggest that Western states will have to find means of accommodating Chinese civilization "within a more pluralistic society of nations."

21.   The most important exception among the critics of Huntington's *Clash of Civilizations* is Fouad Ajami, who criticized the view that culture determines foreign policy. He stated clearly, "States avert their gaze from blood ties when they need to; they see brotherhood and faith and kind when it is in their interest to do so." Fouad Ajami, "The Summoning," *Foreign Affairs,* Vol. 72, No. 4, (September–October 1993), pp. 2–9.

22.   See Robert Jervis, Review of *The Clash of Civilizations and the Remaking of World Order,*" *Political Science Quarterly,* Vol. 112, No. 2 (Summer 1997), pp. 307–308.

eralism and realism alike: neglect of the cultural sources of cooperation and conflict."[23] Moreover, many of Huntington's most vocal protagonists in the Muslim world emphasized in their critiques the importance of culture as a main factor in international relations. Iran's President Mohammed Khatami led in this field, promoting a "Dialogue of Civilizations," and, at his urging, the United Nations enthusiastically declared 2001 to be the year of the "Dialogue of Civilizations."[24] The basis of this campaign is that while cultures create different politics between states, through dialogue they need not clash.

In light of the growing number of works in mainstream international relations and security studies theory propounding the importance of the factor of culture, Michael Desch published a major article in *International Security* chronicling the growth of the preponderance of the culturalist argument.[25] Desch concludes, "The best case that can be made for these new cultural theories is that they are sometimes useful as a supplement to realist theories."[26] Desch's article was juxtapositioned in the same volume of *International Security* with an article by Ted Hopf that presented the constructivist view on the importance of culture in the foreign policy outcomes of states.[27] Hopf writes, "The identity of a state implies its preferences and consequent actions."[28]

Following the breakup of Yugoslavia and the Soviet Union, cultural explanations played a prominent role in the analysis of the conflicts that emerged in the Balkans and the post-Soviet sphere, especially those that were actually read by policymakers.[29] Historians and area specialists

---

23. Stephen Shulman, Review of *The Clash of Civilizations and the Remaking of World Order*," *The Journal of Politics*, Vol. 60, No. 1 (February 1998), pp. 304–306.

24. See Conference Report of the International Conference on the Dialogue of Civilizations sponsored by the United Nations and the United Nations University, July 31–August 3, 2001, Kyoto and Tokyo. This report defines civilization as "cultural characteristics of a certain time or place and in this sense can well be replaced by the term 'culture'." In addition, the "A Framework for Action" document promoted by the United Nations suggests that "dialogue of civilizations can and should be developed into a new paradigm of international relations." (http://www.unu.edu/dialogue/FrameworkForAction.pdf).

25. Desch, "Culture Clash: Assessing the Importance of Ideas in Security Studies," pp. 141–170.

26. Desch, p. 142.

27. Ted Hopf, "The Promise of Constructivism in International Relations Theory," *International Security*, Vol. 23, No. 1 (Summer 1998), pp. 171–200.

28. Ibid., p. 175.

29. See, for example, U.S. Deputy Secretary of State Strobe Talbott, in discussing the Balkans and the Caucasus in 1998, referred to "the eruption of medieval struggles over

were the prominent researchers explaining the Caspian region—especially the "Islamic Republics" like Iran—to the outside world and to policymakers in the post–Soviet period, while few social scientists published during that period on the region's foreign policy.[30] This region and the conflicts that raged there have frequently been used as cases to illustrate the claims of proponents of cultural theories.[31] The protagonists of the conflicts in the Caucasus were identified by outside analysts in cultural, predominately religious terms ("Christian Armenia" versus "Shi'i Muslim Azerbaijan"; Chechen fighters were described as "Islamic militants") even in places where religious differences were not the main factor contributing to the emergence of the conflicts.

The September 11, 2001, terrorist attacks on the United States triggered a heightened resurgence of emphasis on culture and, especially, of religion in foreign policy research and among the press and policymakers. The events appeared to vindicate those who argued that culture is a leading factor in states' foreign policies, especially in the case of Islam's role in the foreign policies of Muslim-populated states. In the aftermath of September 11, analysts scrambled to try to understand the basic tenets of Islam and what the *Quran* had to say relevant to foreign policy issues as diverse as the use of nuclear weapons, peacekeeping missions, and warfare during the holy month of Ramadan, assuming that religious doctrine was the basis of the foreign policy choices of a number of Muslim-populated states. This rush among researchers to view religion and culture as the key explanations was understandably fostered by the fact that the terrorists used Islam and its struggle against the West to justify

---

blood and culture." Address at Bucharest University, Bucharest, Romania, March 19, 1998.

30.   From a search of the articles which appeared between 1990 and 1999 in major political science and international relations journals (*American Political Science Review, American Journal of Political Science, Comparative Politics, Foreign Affairs, International Organizations, International Security, Journal of Conflict Resolution, World Politics, Political Science Quarterly,* and *Journal of Politics*), *only* eleven articles dealt significantly with Central Asia and the Caucasus. The majority of these appeared in *Foreign Affairs,* most of which were written by area specialists and not international relations researchers.

31.   For instance, in the *Clash of Civilizations,* Samuel Huntington refers to the Nagorno-Karabagh conflict between Armenia and Azerbaijan as a "fault line war." Moreover, he makes policy prescriptions based on *Clash of Civilizations* that should guide U.S. policy toward the conflicts in the former Soviet Union. For instance, he recommended in an op-ed to the *New York Times* (December 16, 1999) that the United States support Moscow in its campaign against the Chechens, since as Muslims, the confrontation with Russia was inevitable; he described the Chechen conflict as an additional fault line war.

and explain their acts. In addition, the specter of the subsequent open displays of enthusiasm for the terrorist acts against the United States among many Muslims around the globe and the popularity of Osama bin Laden in many Muslim-populated states reinforced the view that religion is a potent force in the policies of Muslim-populated states. In the post–September 11 examination of the role of Islam in policy formation, however, it seemed that many analyses failed to separate between the actions of states and non-state actors.

CHALLENGE TO THE CULTURALIST ARGUMENT: ALLIANCES, CONFLICT CAMPS, AND DESIGNATIONS OF THREATS IN THE CASPIAN REGION

The major academic forces promoting the importance of culture in foreign policy emanated from different research camps, and many possessed different reasoning that led to the view that culture is an important variable in international relations.

As stated, the leading proponents in the last decade of the culturalist argument in international relations have come from the constructivist approach. Constructivism argues that all human activity, including politics, is understood by the meaning that people give to their world and that such meaning is intersubjectively constructed with the events and institutions in the world. Thus, culture and material interests are seen as a nexus that cannot be separated. Constructivists claim that culture shapes foreign policy decisions, because politics in general and the interests of a state are shaped by shared meanings held by people in a state.

Among the major deficiencies of the constructivist argument on culture and foreign policy is that it meshes the discussions and case work on global norms and culture with that of particular, local cultures—two quite distinct variables. Moreover, the constructivists have failed to provide an answer as to how states resolve the conflict between their cultural goals and survival threats to the existence of the regime and state. States and ruling regimes possess a wide spectrum of foreign policy interests, but all states share the goal of physical existence and control of territories, and it does not seem reasonable that state and regime survival can be "contextualized" or dependent on a certain cultural context or process of identity construction. Specific cultures may have an important impact on the articulation of interests in luxury spheres that are beyond regime and state survival, and the constructivists do not seem to have presented an answer as to how regimes and states tend to resolve the issues when vital material and cultural interests clash.

The Caspian states' behavior specifically challenges the constructivist argument that accounts of identity provide an important basis for a state's conceived threat perceptions and consequent alliance choices and foe designations.[32] The constructivist school claims that the previous behavior of states produces a picture of how this state behaves and that this serves as a structure for their relations, influencing designation of threat and view of friend. In the case of the Caspian region, however, history of interactions and shared cultural affinities had no impact on the trends in alliance formation or perception of threat during the new states' first post-independence decade. For instance, all of the former Soviet republics shared centuries of Russian colonialism and post-colonial public residue. Yet, each state in the South Caucasus adopted a very different strategy toward dealing with Russia—a most compelling example. All three are weak, small states that all shared long periods of Soviet domination and a post-colonial heritage. Armenia chose to forge a military alliance with Moscow—to fortify this powerful neighbor's military presence in the republic through long-term basing agreements and to integrate many aspects of their military, such as air defenses—in order to foster Moscow's interest in Armenia's viability. Georgia, in contrast, chose to entice the United States into a military presence in the new republic and adopted pro-U.S. positions on security and foreign policy issues in order to develop a U.S. interest in serving as a deterrent to Moscow. Azerbaijan, in contrast to both Armenia and Georgia, attempted to balance relations with Russia and the United States and create interest in both powers, especially in the economic sphere, for cooperative relations and stability in the Caspian region.

Following the Soviet collapse, the new states of the Caspian region were presented with options for military cooperation with a variety of eager external powers that courted them for strategic cooperation and partnerships. Each needed to develop a new army as part of its state-building and to determine who would become its major arms supplier. The chief external powers that offered significant strategic cooperation were Russia, Turkey, Iran, and the United States. In addition, the new states confronted a variety of actual and potential threats to their security and, in their early years of independence, defined their primary threats. Analysis of the Caspian region's new states' choices of their primary strategic backers and definitions of their major security threats does not indicate any special role for culture and, specifically, for history of relations in determining either cooperation patterns or perceptions of threat. In fact, for most of the Muslim-populated states of Central Asia and the Caucasus, fellow Muslim-populated states were indicated as primary security threats. (See Table 1.1.)

---

32. Hopf, p. 187.

Table 1.1. Caspian States' Major Strategic Backers and Threats

State	Strategic cooperation options	Main Strategic cooperation	Definition of primary security threat(s)
Armenia	Russia, United States, Iran	Russia, Iran	Azerbaijan, Turkey
Georgia	Russia, United States, Turkey, Iran	United States, Turkey	Russia, intertwined with internal
Azerbaijan	Russia, United States, Turkey, Iran	Turkey, United States	Armenia, Iran
Uzbekistan	Russia, Turkey, United States, Iran	United States	Afghanistan, Tajikistan, Kazakhstan, Turkmenistan, intertwined with internal in most cases
Kazakhstan	Russia, Turkey, United States, China	Russia, United States	Uzbekistan
Kyrgyz Republic	Russia, Turkey, United States, China	United States	Uzbekistan
Tajikistan	Russia, Iran, United States	Russia	Afghanistan, Uzbekistan
Turkmenistan	Russia, United States, Iran, Turkey	Iran	Azerbaijan, Uzbekistan, Kazakhstan, intertwined with internal

Seemingly, Armenia could be a case used to illustrate the relevance of common culture in fashioning alliances and determining threats: Yerevan forged its major military cooperation with Russia, with which it shares a common Orthodox Christian background. Armenia views Turkey and Azerbaijan as its primary threats based on historical conflicts with Turkey and, as emphasized in Yerevan's rhetoric, its threat perception of Baku is influenced by Azerbaijan's shared Turkic background with Turkey. Conversely, however, Yerevan conducts intensive security cooperation and trade with Shi'i Iran. In addition, Armenia trades and cooperates with Turkmenistan, which shares the same ethnic Turkic background as Turkey and Azerbaijan.

Common Orthodox background did not lead Georgia to pursue strategic cooperation with Russia—Tbilisi views Moscow as its primary security threat. Ethnic Turkic Azerbaijan did seek and forge intensive security cooperation with its co-ethnics in Turkey, but, at the same time, views its co-religionists in Iran as one of its primary security threats. Uzbekistan and Kazakhstan succeeded in forging stable relations with Russia and China, with which they share no cultural commonality, but they view

Table 1.2. External Powers: Primary Caspian Security Cooperation Partners and Primary Security Concern.

External Power	Primary Cooperation	Primary Security Concern
Russia	Armenia	Georgia
United States[a]	Armenia, Uzbekistan, Georgia	external to region
Iran	Armenia, Turkmenistan	Azerbaijan, Uzbekistan
Turkey	Georgia	Armenia

a. Represented by proportion of military aid and overall aid.

each other and other neighboring Central Asia co-religionists and co-ethnics as their primary security threats.

Analysis of the extent of security cooperation from the perspective of powers operating in the region particularly illuminates the lack of the role of culture in the formation of security cooperation. (See Table 1.2.)

Common culture played no discernable role in the determination of alliance and cooperation partners for the majority of the external powers active in the region, especially in the cases of the active Muslim-populated powers, Turkey and Iran. Iran's choice of primary security co-operation partners in the region and its primary security concerns run counter to its official designation as an Islamic Republic dedicated to the promotion of rights of Muslims and the spread of Islam. Tehran's positions on the region's conflicts contradict its official self-designation as the champion of Shi'i rights and causes (for more detail, see the Shaffer chapter on Iran in this volume). Tehran maintains its most problematic relations in the region with the Shi'i-majority state of Azerbaijan. At the same time, Iran maintains extensive trade and its most intensive security cooperation with Armenia, regardless of the fact that Yerevan is embroiled in a conflict with Shi'i Azerbaijan and currently occupies almost 20 percent of Azerbaijan's territory, making refugees of close to a million Azerbaijani Shi'a. When relating to its cooperation with both Azerbaijan and Armenia—two states at war—Tehran uses shared cultural heritage with Armenia to justify its cooperation and ties. In addition, Tehran enjoys especially cooperative relations with Turkmenistan, one of its most highly secularized Muslim-populated neighbors.[33]

In the case of the Islamic Republic of Iran, an interesting phenomenon is Tehran's discussion of its cultural solidarity with Shi'i-populated

33. The form of leadership cult institutionalized in Turkmenistan could easily be viewed as sacrilegious within the context of Islam.

Azerbaijan in order to endow these relations with legitimacy, despite its *de facto* intensive security cooperation with Armenia:

Irano-Azeri relations, despite the two countries' common historical and cultural traditions, are sensitive. We should not forget that the Republic of Azerbaijan is one of the few states whose leaders belong to the Shi'i School of Islam and the common culture of the Shi'i School of Islam is a significant factor in the relations of the two countries.[34]

At the same time, Tehran has often used the claim of common cultural ties to promote its relations with Christian-populated Armenia: "In view of the historical cultural ties between the two nations, the authorities in Tehran and Yerevan were in favour of political cooperation."[35]

Despite sharing a common ethnic and Muslim background with Azerbaijan and the states of Central Asia, Turkey conducts its most intensive cooperation in the Caspian region with the Republic of Georgia, especially in the military sphere. This is despite the fact that the Muslim and Turkic minorities in Georgia maintain a precarious relationship with Tbilisi, and some view the regime as being discriminatory toward these groups. Strong Turkic cultural identity among the states of Central Asia did not translate into an alliance with Turkey.

Russia maintains its most intensive military cooperation in the region with the Republic of Armenia, with which it shares an Orthodox Christian background. But, at the same time, Moscow has its most problematic relations in the region with its fellow Orthodox Christians in Georgia. Thus, it is difficult to see common religion as a factor in Moscow's security partnerships in the region.

The Caspian states' choice of sides with regard to regional conflicts did not run on cultural lines, and they certainly defied Huntington's paradigm. (See Table 1.3.) The analysis of the major conflicts (Nagorno-Karabagh, Chechnya, Tajikistan's civil war, and the Georgian-Abkhaz conflict) that afflicted the Caspian region clearly shows that common culture—especially in the form of religion and ethnicity—played no significant role in the formation of the positions of the various actors in the region. Moreover, the alliances and coalitions shifted from conflict to conflict, further reinforcing the image that overall cultural allegiances did not determine their formation. Even players that were in conflict in one arena were able to cooperate in another arena.

---

34. Iran News (Tehran, in English) March 4, 1996, p. 2.

35. Tehran Voice of the Islamic Republic of Iran Radio, March 4, 2002 (FBIS-NES-2002-0304).

Table 1.3. Coalitions in Conflicts in the Caspian Region.

Conflict	Side A	Side B	Shifting positions
Nagorno-Karabagh	Armenia, Iran, Russia	Azerbaijan, Georgia, Turkey	United States
Chechnya	Russia, Iran	Azerbaijan, Georgia	United States
Tajikistan's civil war	Russia, Uzbekistan	Tajik Islamic forces, Afghanistan militias	Iran
Georgia-Abkhaz	Russia, Chechens[a]	Georgia, Azerbaijan	

a. In terms of non-state actors, it is interesting to note that Chechen fighters fought alongside Russian forces in support of the Abkhaz insurgency.

In addition, the cases of the Caspian states show that common cultural identity does not necessarily lead to a higher propensity to form alliances. For example, all of the Muslim states of Central Asia and the Caucasus mark the Novruz (Iranian New Year Spring holiday) as their major holiday festival and identify with many other aspects of Iranian culture, such as Iranian literature. Yet, most view the modern state of Iran as a primary security threat. Likewise, most of the states and populations of Central Asia enthusiastically identify with their common Turkic identity and speak Turkic languages, but this did not lead to identification with the Republic of Turkey, and some of the states of the region, such as Uzbekistan, Turkmenistan, and Kazakhstan, maintain cautious relations with Ankara.

Organization of this Study

This volume includes the works of researchers working in different disciplines and living in a variety of states and cultures. The first section of *The Limits of Culture* focuses on the theoretical issues connected to the relationship between culture and foreign policy. In Chapter Two, Markus Fischer discusses the definition of culture and the difference between culture and ideology. While determining that culture and ideology are two separate items, Fischer concludes that in the analysis *vis-à-vis* material interests, culture and ideology should be grouped together, and this approach is reflected in this book. He presents the approaches of different paradigms within international relations theory to the topic of culture and foreign policy: liberalism, realism, Marxism, and constructivism. Fischer propounds that culture can be a means of foreign policy by serving as a pretext that aims at foreign or domestic support. It can impact foreign policy formation by biasing the perceptions of leaders and by promoting or retarding economic development. He postulates that culture can affect the ends of foreign policy by trapping leaders in their own cultural rhetoric at times and by genuinely inspiring them to make the resources of the state serve religious and ethnic concerns. Fischer asserts, however, that when cultural and material interests conflict, material interests will prevail in most cases. Fischer claims, however, that there will be instances, even in the contemporary world, where leaders risk security and prosperity for the sake of their religious and ethnic aspirations, especially in the cases of the "militant effort" by indigenous peoples to defend their cultural communities against dissolution by Westernization and globalization.

In Chapter Three, Douglas Blum employs a constructivist approach and presents culture and foreign policy as a nexus: interactively based cultural assumptions and identity constructs exert influence on foreign policy, primarily in a constitutive manner, rather than causal. He claims that interactively influenced versions of Self and Others in state-to-state relations, especially in the nation-building process, impact foreign policy actions. In his final analysis, however, Blum contends that local culture does not generally drive foreign policy choices, but once articulated as an official basis for policy, it can constrain policy options. In addition, Blum points out that there are often vast differences between the official culture designated by a state and the culture or cultures which influence the identities and attitudes of the residents of a state, and, consequently, proponents of the culturalist argument need to assess which culture influences the policies of a state, and its relationship to the other cultural factors within a state. In addition, in the discussions on the impact of culture on coalition and alliance building, Blum asserts that rather than culture determining coalition partner choices, at times, cultural practices are a result of coalition choices. To support this claim, he cites the example of Central Asian and other Caspian states that have held elections and conducted democratic rituals in order to forge an alliance with the United States, gain admission into the Council of Europe, and enter into other European and Western political and economic groupings.

In Chapter Four, Ronald Suny also approaches the question of culture and foreign policy from a constructivist perspective and states that culture plays a role in the articulation of a state's interests. Suny, however, presents the view that culture and versions of history are fungible and, accordingly, their impact on foreign policy varies depending on how local political forces choose to present their collective history. Suny argues that, in each state, elites can choose among the repertoire of available identities and discourses to promote inter-ethnic peace or exacerbate conflict. He writes, "While identity matters in foreign policy, it is not always clear which identity may prove more powerful." Thus, conflict and assessment of security is impacted by how political leaders choose to construct their nation's view of Self and Others and their nation's past. Suny presents the different views of the past and the decisions on which specific incidents in the nation's history and cultural values are accentuated by various leaders of the Caspian region in order to produce and make possible the new states' adoption of specific political policies and orientations.

In Chapter Five of this volume, Ido Oren and Robert Kauffman explore the question of the causal relationship between alliances and publicly held cultural images. In addressing this task, the authors examined how the U.S. public viewed Saudi Arabia, Azerbaijan, and Kazakhstan before and after September 11, 2001.[36] Their research indicates that, in these cases, changes in cultural views and in alliances took place almost hand in hand and that one change did not cause the other. In their analysis, this point is quite evident with regards to Saudi Arabia. Up until September 11, the U.S. public rarely appraised the domestic practices in Saudi Arabia, especially the state of human rights there, which could have led them to perceive Saudis as fundamentally different from Americans. Only after September 11, when signs began to emerge that the security alliance between the United States and Saudi Arabia was crumbling, did the image of Saudi Arabians as being fundamentally culturally different from Americans emerge.

The next section of this book explores the impact of domestic politics on the relationship between culture and foreign policy. In King and Pomper's chapter entitled "Culture, Congress, and the Caspian," the authors illustrate that in certain political systems, domestic interest groups (or "lobbies") can force a state to implement a cultural policy in defiance of the state's executive branch's material preferences. King and Pomper examined U.S. policy toward the Nagorno-Karabagh conflict between Armenia and Azerbaijan from the perspective of the impact of domestic U.S. lobbies on congressional policies toward the conflict. Armenian-Americans succeeded in compelling the United States to *de facto* alignment with "Christian" Armenia over Washington's material-driven preference to a balanced or even Azerbaijan-leaning policy. The domestic factor can render material policy choices of the regime as too domestically

---

36. Saudi Arabia is not a Caspian country, but is included in this study for methodological comparison.

costly to implement. This is evident in the case of canceling Section 907 of the Freedom Support Act sanctions against Azerbaijan.[37] Since enactment, each U.S. administration has supported canceling these congressional sanctions, but has not had the political will to pay the costs of angering the Armenian-American lobby.

In Chapter Seven, Roger Kangas explores the impact of domestic political culture on the foreign policy decisions of the Central Asian states and the political legitimacy of those regimes. He looks at the prevailing political culture in the societies of the states of Central Asia and concludes that the customary practice of Central Asian officials is to report to their superiors what they assume their superiors want to hear. Kangas claims that this cultural practice impacts foreign policy decisions, because high-level decision-makers in the region do not receive comprehensive information before formulating their policy decisions. Kangas also explores the question of leaders getting trapped in their own cultural rhetoric. He describes how almost all the leaders of the Central Asian states have used Islamic rituals in public ceremonies and public displays of themselves observing Islamic rituals in order to boost the legitimacy of their regimes. Neither these rituals nor the potential public desire that the ruling regimes be endowed with Islamic legitimacy has forced the ruling regimes in Central Asia to adopt more Islamic-leaning foreign policies, especially in regard to coalition partners. For example, the energy producers of the region have all decided to build their pipeline routes out to Western markets and declined options through Muslim-populated countries, such as Iran, which intensely campaigned to be so linked to the new states.

In Chapters Eight through Eleven, the book examines some of the presumably stronger cases for the culturalist argument: Iran, Pakistan, and Taliban Afghanistan. All three of these states declared themselves to be "Islamic Republics"; they have formally articulated that Islam serves as the guiding force of their state policies and that the state should serve

---

37. Section 907 was enacted by the U.S. Congress in 1992 and prohibits U.S. assistance (with the exception of humanitarian assistance and assistance for nonproliferation and disarmament programs) to the government of Azerbaijan under the Freedom for Russia and Emerging Eurasian Democracies and Open Markets Support Act of 1992 (also known as the Freedom Support Act) "until the President determines, and so reports to the Congress, that the Government of Azerbaijan is taking demonstrable steps to cease all blockades and other offensive uses of force against Armenia and Nagorno-Karabakh." The legislation imposes sanctions only on Azerbaijan, despite the fact that both Armenia and Azerbaijan fought a war over the territory of Nagorno-Karabagh, which the United States recognizes as legally being part of Azerbaijan.

as an instrument of Islam. Chapter Eight, "The Islamic Republic of Iran: Is It Really?" by Brenda Shaffer examines the foreign policy of Iran in the Caspian region in the ten years since the Soviet Union's dissolution. This chapter focuses on the various identities of the state. It claims that the officially articulated cultural identity of the state—in this case Islam— does not necessarily determine the foreign policy preferences of that state. The case of Iran reveals that common Islamic identity or solidarity played no significant role in Iran's choice of alliance partners in Central Asia and the Caucasus or the sides that it chose to support in regional conflicts. Additionally, Iran often used Islam instrumentally to pursue material state interests.

In Chapter Nine, in contrast, Ali Ansari presents a constructivist approach to Iran's foreign policy; he illustrates Iran's cultural and material interests as intertwined and zig-zagging in influence over Tehran's foreign policy choices. Moreover, Ansari argues that a variety of identities vie with material interests for influence over Iranian foreign policy, of which Islamic civilization is only one. Ansari makes the point that culture influences the foreign policy of states, because other states tend to judge them and interact with them on the basis of their rhetoric. He illustrates this point with the case of U.S.-Iranian relations. Ansari claims that the United States tends to view Iran in revolutionary and religiously fanatic terms and crafts its policies toward Tehran accordingly. Ansari purported that for the Islamic Republic of Iran, the viability of the state itself and the promotion of Islamic values are one and the same, and the leadership of the Islamic Republic advocates pursuit of both as inseparable goals. Ali Ansari points out that Washington's policies toward the Islamic Republic of Iran were highly influenced by the fact that it took Tehran's revolutionary rhetoric seriously. Washington was willing to accept at face value Iran's martyrdom rhetoric and thus perceive Tehran as willing to preclude material interests—and even survivability—in order to promote its cultural-ideological goals. Iranians have often been surprised by the extent to which the regime's rhetoric is taken seriously and how its domestic practices, such as the murder of dissidents and the threat to assassinate *The Satanic Verses* author Salman Rushdie, have impacted the way the United States, and to a certain extent Europe, view the potential for cooperation with Iran.

In Chapter Ten, Svante Cornell examines the role of culture in Taliban Afghanistan, especially in its existential decisions during the last two years before its demise. Cornell propounds that even some of the most seemingly Islamic-based policies of the Taliban, such as the refusal to hand over Osama bin Laden following the September 11 terrorist attacks and the decision to destroy the opium poppy crops in Afghanistan, also had material motivations. Moreover, a variety of cultural factors influenced the Taliban's decision-making, such as Pashtun tribal customs, and it was not clear in many of their decisions whether their officially declared policy of Islam was always the primary motivating factor. In fact, according to Cornell, it is difficult to distinguish between Pashtun culture and Islamic culture in the case of the Taliban. Hence, this chapter raises the point that even when a regime attempts to act in accordance with a professed culture or ideology, this does not necessarily endow analysts with the ability to predict their policies, because their interpretation of that culture or ideology can be quite unique.

In addition, Cornell claims that cultural influences had a high impact on the Taliban due to the nature of its decision-making process and the composition of its decision-makers. The Taliban was not always a monolithic movement, and it had wings that emphasized more material policies. With the progressive growth of the power of Mullah Omar over the movement, the impact of culture on the movement's decisions grew. Moreover, since the Taliban leadership was extremely uneducated and operated in an information vacuum, many of its decisions were made without an ability to calculate the material trade-offs of these decisions, illustrating the importance of decision-makers' access to information as a factor in the impact of culture on foreign policy.

In Chapter Eleven, Svante Cornell examines the case of Pakistan. In this chapter, Cornell claims that the main motivating factor for the Islamic component of Islamabad's foreign policy has been pragmatic and utile, and that support for Islamic causes has served the material national interests of Pakistan. Moreover, some Islamic policies share material interests. For instance, Islam has been a basis for a cohesive identity for the residents of Pakistan. Due to the multi-ethnic and multi-regional character of the society of Pakistan and the salience of these local identities for many residents of the state, especially outside the dominating Punjab, building a strong Islamic identity was necessary in order to create a unifying identity for the peoples of Pakistan. According to Cornell, while the declaration of Pakistan as an Islamic state may have had both material and cultural motivations, once established, it became politically risky for leaders of Pakistan to openly contradict the Islamic orientation of the state, and thus, the cultural factor serves as a constraint on its policy options. Consequently, in spheres where the costs are not very high, the regime in Pakistan seeks opportunity to prove its Islamic loyalty. Cornell claims that public opinion in Muslim-populated states, secular and religious alike, forces the ruling regimes to express support, at least rhetorically, to the Muslim actor in a variety of conflicts around the globe, such as the Palestinian-Israeli conflict and Chechnya.

This does not, however, necessarily lead to policy actions that com-
.promise the regimes' material interests in important areas. In forging its
alliance partners, Pakistan was willing to cooperate with almost any state
that would grant it support, regardless of the cultural background or
ideological orientation of the prospective partner. Moreover, Islamabad
often used Islamic groups in an instrumental fashion to promote its material interests *vis-à-vis* India and Afghanistan. Pakistan was, however,
willing to abandon its support for Islamic radical groups, such as the
Taliban, when it became materially costly—such as the anticipated damage to Pakistan's relationship with the United States if it continued to
support Islamic radicals in the aftermath of the September 11 terrorist
attacks.

Cornell also argues that the regime type strengthens the ability of Islam to influence Islamabad's policies. President Pervez Musharraf attempts to govern by wide consensus and not in a dictatorial manner.
Consequently, domestic Islamic constituencies often impact Musharraf's
policy choices to support Islamic causes. In addition, the regime restrains
itself from severely limiting the Islamic influences in state policies in order to keep the domestic Islamic elements engaged positively with the
regime.

The concluding chapter of this volume focuses on the level of significance of material costs to the pursuit of cultural interests and spheres
for future research. This chapter claims that while the contributing authors of this volume presented different approaches to the question of the
impact of culture on foreign policy, most stated that when cultural interests conflicted with material interests, cultural rarely trumped material.
The key to understanding when culture is most likely to impact upon foreign policy decisions is, in most cases, the anticipated degree of the material cost trade-off. When it is cost-free, or close to it, regimes will spew
rhetoric in support of and pursue policies that are culturally congruent to
their officially articulated culture and conceivably that of the state's polity—at least for the sake of strengthening the legitimacy of the regime.
The concluding chapter also underscores conditions under which culture
tends to have a greater impact on foreign policy choices, for example,
when decision-makers lack information on the material trade-offs of their
anticipated decisions or in democratic systems of government that allow
narrow-agenda lobbies, such as diaspora groups, to significantly influence foreign policy formation. This chapter emphasizes that—in the
Caspian region—culture has had little impact on how states forged their
alliances and selected cooperation partners. The concluding chapter also
discusses the policy implications of the research presented in *The Limits of*

Culture, recommending that the U.S. governmental policy community re-think the analyst training models which assign a prominent role to culture in forming the foreign policy choices of states. Furthermore, the "Islamic Republics" in the international system should be viewed as actors that often have material interests as guiding forces in their foreign policies, and are thus subject to deterrence and enticement just like other states in the system.

Chapter 2

Culture and Foreign Politics

Markus Fischer

The resurgence of ethnic violence after the end of the Cold War and the concomitant rise of militant Islamism have given culture a more visible role in foreign politics. This essay analyzes this role on philosophical, theoretical, and historical grounds. It begins by tracing the development of culture as an intellectual concept from its creation by the German philosopher Johann Gottfried von Herder to its reworking by the major figures of anthropology and eventual adoption by political science. It argues that culture, which was conceived in opposition to Enlightenment rationalism, ought to be distinguished from ideology, and finds culture's concrete content in religious practices and the traditional ways of ethnic communities.

Then, an inquiry into the major paradigms of international relations theory shows that their recognition of culture is inversely related to their acceptance of Enlightenment rationalism. Accordingly, liberalism rejects culture altogether as an impediment to progress; neorealism lets it "drop out" together with the "unit level"; traditional realism appreciates it as a source of foreign policy; Marxism accords it a legitimating role in the "superstructure"; and constructivism embraces culture as constitutive of international politics.

There are three motives that shape foreign policy—culture, ideology, and material interests—with the influence of culture and ideology being far more contingent, particular, and normative than that of interests in security, prosperity, and dominance. Culture can be a means of foreign policy by serving as a pretext that aims at foreign or domestic support. It can have a real impact on the means of foreign policy by biasing the perceptions of leaders and by promoting or retarding economic development. Culture can affect the ends of foreign policy by making leaders the prisoners of their own cultural rhetoric and by genuinely inspiring them to make the resources of the state serve religious and ethnic concerns. At times, such concerns will be in accord with material interests, as with wars of national liberation. When they conflict, material interests will prevail in most cases, but there will be instances, even in the contemporary world, where leaders risk security and prosperity for the sake of their religious and ethnic aspirations.

The essay concludes with a look at the future role of culture in foreign affairs. Should Muslims, Hindus, and other indigenous peoples succeed in their increasingly militant efforts to defend their cultural communities against dissolution by Westernization and globalization, culture will continue to affect foreign policy; on the other hand, should their resistance turn out to represent merely a temporary backlash against the coming of the global cosmopolitan society prophesied by philosopher Immanuel Kant, cultural particularity will become politically insignificant.

The Concept of Culture

Culture is a many-shaded word. In the original Latin, *cultura* referred to the tilling of the soil. Metaphorical extension of this root in early modernity led to the notion of a "culture of the mind"—the tilling of intellectual faculties. From the late-eighteenth century onward, German social thought endowed the word with the three principal meanings recognized today. First of all, culture signifies the development of the intellectual, moral, and aesthetic faculties of persons and societies toward some notion of perfection. Second, it stands for the products of these faculties, especially works of literature, painting, sculpture, film, etc. Third, and most relevant to our concern, culture refers to the particular meaning that a people gives to its shared life. This hermeneutic notion of culture goes back to the Romantic Movement in late eighteenth-century Germany, especially the thought of Johann Gottfried von Herder. Herder fundamentally opposed the Enlightenment belief in a rationality that stands outside history, promulgates universal laws, and imposes the modern state on traditional communities. Instead, he argued that every people had a particular tradition of thinking and acting that had to be understood in its own terms and cherished as an expression of its soul.

More precisely, Herder considered rational thought to be impossible without language.[1] Language, in turn, exists in a variety of forms that re-

---

1. Johann Gottfried Herder, *Against Pure Reason: Writings on Religion, Language, and History,* ed. and trans. Marcia Bunge (Minneapolis, Minn.: Fortress Press, 1993),

sult from very different circumstances and make its bearers perceive and understand the world in very different ways. Accordingly, the fact that human language has split into a host of mutually unintelligible tongues over the course of history implies that humankind has separated into peoples with different sets of ideas, sentiments, values, customs—the complex wholes called cultures. In Herder's words, "the best culture of a people . . . thrives only by means of the nation's inherited and inheritable dialect"; for "in [a people's] speech resides its whole thought-domain, its tradition, history, religion, and basis of life, all its heart and soul."[2]

Given its uniqueness, the merit of a particular culture cannot be judged against universal standards, such as the Enlightenment idea of progress, for "who," asks Herder, "can compare the differing modes of satisfaction of differing modes of happiness in differing worlds?"[3] Instead, one must understand a culture as a whole as much as possible from within—"transport [ourselves] into the age, into the region of the compass, into the entire history, feel [our] way into everything."[4]

Put differently, each people is endowed with a unique "soul that pervades all, that shapes all other inclinations and spiritual powers in its image, and colors the most indifferent of actions."[5] Each people affirms the assumptions, values, and norms of its particular culture as naturally given; they form its "horizon—not to look beyond; hardly to fathom what is beyond."[6] In other words, culture circumscribes how people understand the world and thus limits the actions of which they can possibly conceive. The core of this worldview, according to Herder, is formed by religious beliefs, for they are the natural way that people make sense of the world as a purposive whole, find their place within it, and define the ethical qualities that develop their humanity.[7]

This horizon endures over time because of the hold that tradition—"the teaching of previous times . . . the voice of their fathers, the saga over

---

pp. 58–59, 74–76; Johann Gottfried Herder, *On World History: An Anthology*, ed. Hans Adler and Ernest A. Menze, trans. Ernest A. Menze and Michael Palma (London: M.E. Sharpe, 1997), pp. 130, 132, 236.

2. Johann Gottfried Herder, "Materials for the Philosophy of the History of Mankind," in Paul Halsall, ed., *Internet Modern History Sourcebook*, <www.fordham.edu/halsall/mod/1784herder-mankind.html, accessed April 12, 2002>.

3. Herder, *World History*, p. 40.

4. Ibid., p. 36.

5. Ibid., p. 36.

6. Ibid., p. 40.

7. Ibid., pp. 83, 108, 273.

previous ages"[8]—has on people's minds. For, contrary to what Enlightenment philosophers may claim, "not one of us becomes a human being autonomously. An intellectual genesis, that is, education, connects the whole formation of an individual's humanity to that individual's parents, teachers, and friends, to all the circumstances in the course of that individual's life, consequently to that individual's people and their ancestors."[9] Indeed, Herder goes so far as to claim that the "genetic spirit and character of a people . . . is inexplicable and ineradicable, ancient as the nation, ancient as the country it inhabits"[10]

When the bearers of one culture encounter the meanings of another, they react with "insensitivity, coldness, and blindness," which readily turns into "contempt and repugnance."[11] Indeed, "when the distance between people and people has grown too far, behold how the Egyptian hates the shepherd, the nomad, how he despises the frivolous Greek!"[12] Two reasons seem to exist for this inherent tendency of cultural particularity to issue in rejection of the foreign. Arising from different languages, cultures perceive the world in different ways, making it difficult if not impossible for the bearers of one culture to understand what those of another take for granted. A few may be able to overcome this barrier by learning foreign languages and studying foreign cultures; however, this will rarely be possible for the majority. More important, human beings have an inherent need to affirm the assumptions, norms, and values that form the horizon of their own group as naturally good, and, consequently, suffer from the tendency to perceive the verities of other peoples as contrary to nature, truth, and morality.

Enlightenment rationalism may decry such a lack of cross-cultural understanding as "prejudice, rudeness, narrow nationalism," but it really is necessary for the kind of community of culture that human beings need in order to develop what Herder calls "humanity," that is, the capacity for ethical life.[13] Indeed, he thinks that "prejudice is good—in its time, for it causes happiness. It forces peoples to rest in their center, attaches them more firmly to their stems, to flourish in their own way, makes them more ardent and thus also more happy in their inclinations and

---

8. Ibid., p. 83; see also Herder, *Against Pure Reason*, p. 51.

9. Herder, *Against Pure Reason*, p. 50.

10. Herder, *World History*, p. 249.

11. Ibid., p. 41.

12. Ibid., p. 41.

13. Ibid., p. 41.

purposes."[14] In other words, it is natural for human beings to live in such a narrowly defined community because it alone can give them the substantive attachment that truly satisfies their need for belonging and provides them with the limiting horizon that enables their souls to remain whole. In contrast, estrangement sets in when "alien aspirations and wishful ventures abroad" become the order of the day and when "abstractions and scholarly concepts" displace the "sensuous, image-rich language" of living poetry.[15] Accordingly, the rise of rationalism in the West—from the Ionian Enchantment and Socrates' questioning to Enlightenment cosmopolitanism and the modern state—entails a gradual loss of culture, as reasoning in abstract universals, be they Platonic ideas, the laws of nature, or the rights of man, overtakes opining in concrete particulars derived from experience.

Hence, Herder's concept of culture implies what the contemporary philosopher Stanley Hauerwas calls a "community of character," that is, people who derive their identity from a historical narrative that prompts them to emulate the virtues displayed by its heroes.[16] More precisely, the virtues—e.g., courage, the capacity to form friendships, moderation, piety—are traits of character that enable people to function as members of a particular community, to carry its historical project forward, and to adapt it to new challenges. In other words, people form a community of character insofar as they are inspired by the same *epos,* such as the Greeks were by Homer's *Iliad,* the Norse by the *Sagas,* and the Hindus by the *Mahabharata;* for these tales give examples of an admirable way of life in the deeds of forebears, exhort contemporaries to continue the sacred tradition, and often give an account of the world as a whole—in short, provide them with the core beliefs of their culture.

At the same time, Hauerwas' notion of a cultural tradition serves as a salutary corrective to Herder's reification of culture into the "genetic" character of a people that in essence remains the same over time. For as people seek to remain faithful to their traditional virtues in order to meet contemporary challenges, they are bound to reinterpret them in light of their own experience, which cannot be but different from that of their forebears. Moreover, a community that fails to keep its tradition alive by giving the virtues of the past a fresh meaning in every generation will soon lose its capacity to cope with a human reality to which change is in-

---

14. Ibid., p. 41.

15. Ibid., pp. 41, 84.

16. Stanley Hauerwas, *A Community of Character: Toward a Constructive Christian Social Ethic* (Notre Dame, Ind.: University of Notre Dame Press, 1981).

herent. In other words, to function as a guide to the communal life in the long run, tradition must be a "living tradition."

Thus, a cultural community is twice removed from the metaphysically grounded community of classical Greek philosophy. Its virtues are relative to its particular cultural narrative, rather than taken to be universally true. Second, it develops their meaning over time by adapting them to current needs, rather than assuming them to be unchanging essences. In other words, no human community will be able to sustain a shared ethical life for long without cultivating the virtues of justice, courage, and temperance among its members; which kinds of character and action count as just, courageous, and temperate, however, will vary across cultures and periods. In the Roman republic, the prevailing sense of justice allowed for people who were unable to pay their debts to become the slaves of their creditors; in the Christian communities that sprang up in the later Roman Empire, the ideal was to forgive one's debtors. In Hauerwas' words, "the diversity of the meaning and kinds of virtues . . . reveals the historical nature of our human existence."[17] Since cultural communities are social constructs, they differ across time and space.

From the onset, this concept of culture was tied to the idea of the nation. Herder thus spoke of the "nation of which one [is] part, with its language, customs, and mentality," using the term interchangeably with "people."[18] In other words, to romantics like him, the scope of the term was limited to the cultural community. This changed with the rise of nationalism at the beginning of the nineteenth century as a political movement. Responding to the French occupation under Napoleon, German thinkers like Johann Gottlieb Fichte argued that their nation ought to acquire a political dimension as well—form a unified state that would safeguard its independence and recover its pride.[19] Ever since then, it has been the central claim of nationalism that every nation ought to have its own state, or, more precisely, that cultural units should be congruent with political units.[20] As a result, the meaning of "nation" has shifted to refer to a people that is not only a cultural entity but possesses or claims political sovereignty as well.[21]

---

17. Ibid, p. 123.

18. Herder, *World History*, p. 82, see also p. 236.

19. See Johann Gottlieb Fichte, *Addresses to the German Nation*, trans. Reginald F. Jones and George H. Turnbull (Chicago: University of Chicago Press, 1922).

20. Anthony D. Smith, *Nations and Nationalism in a Global Era* (Cambridge: Polity Press, 1995), p. 13.

21. In political science, there is no consensus as to the definition of nation.

From its inception, nationalism faced the problem of reconciling its romantic concern for a particular culture with the universal exigencies of a modern, rationally organized state. In other words, how could the state perform the functions—governing through laws and bureaucracies, taxing uniformly, maintaining a standing army, providing public education—that it shared with all others because they had proven so effective in the generation of power, without undermining the unique customs and traditional ways of life that the nation cherished? German nationalism answered this question by conceiving the state as the organic outgrowth of the nation. In the words of historian Heinrich von Treitschke, "the evolution of the state is, broadly speaking, nothing but the necessary outward form which the inner life of a people bestows upon itself."[22] In concrete terms, the rational institutions of the state, which are formally like those of others, ought to be animated by the nation's distinct culture. For instance, the army of a freedom-loving people may succeed by encouraging initiative in the ranks; the army of a nation that values the ways of the ancestors may be effective by requiring that orders be carried out unquestioningly.[23]

In the late-nineteenth century, the concept of culture became the central term of the emerging discipline of anthropology. In E. B. Tylor's classic definition from 1871, culture is the "complex whole which includes knowledge, belief, art, morals, law, custom and any other capabilities and habits acquired by man as a member of society."[24] In other words, culture

---

22. Heinrich von Treitschke, *Politics,* trans. Blanche Dugdale and Torben de Bille (New York: MacMillan Company, 1916), p. 12; cf. p. 10.

23. In contrast, French nationalism reduced the nation to a reflection of the state which created its shared culture by imposing norms, writing its history, supporting a civic religion, fostering the arts, schooling the young, etc. In 1789, the revolutionary Abbé Sieyès thus defined a nation as "a body of associates living under one common law and represented by the same legislature." Writing almost a century later, the French historian Ernest Renan found the essence of a nation in people's shared awareness "to have suffered, worked, hoped together" and to want to "realize the same program in the future"; "that is what one really understands despite differences of race and language," that is, cultural attributes. This political view of culture obviously reflects the fact that the common culture of the French had indeed been forged over the centuries by the subjection of quite distinct peoples—Normans, Bretons, Burgundians, Basques, Provençaux, Catalans, etc.—to the centralizing rule of the state, from its beginnings under the Capetians, its absolutist exaltation under the Bourbons, and its rationalization under the post-revolutionary republics. In theory as well as practice, French nationalism thus remained in the orbit of the Enlightenment. The quotations are from John Hutchinson and Anthony D. Smith, eds., *Nationalism* (Oxford: Oxford University Press, 1994), pp. 17, 249.

24. Edward Burnett Tylor, *Primitive Culture: Researches into the Development of Mythology, Philosophy, Religion, Art, and Custom* (London: J. Murray, 1871), p. 1.

stands for the integrated patterns of beliefs and behavior that human beings acquire by learning and hand down to subsequent generations, involving not only ideas, norms, and art, but all other human activity as well—from political authority to economic arrangements, productive technologies, and household items. Influenced by the sciences of geology and biology, Tylor assumed further that all cultures evolved from primitive to civilized states along a universal trajectory.

Franz Boas, writing around the turn of the twentieth century, restored historical particularism to the concept of culture when he argued that each culture resulted from a unique manifold of historical circumstances and thus had to be understood on its own terms. To explain how such manifolds came to be integrated into cultural wholes, Ruth Benedict postulated "patterns of culture" whereby the various cultural traits attained their coherence from an underlying set of core values that most people internalize.[25] According to Margaret Mead, this internalization took place mostly in childhood, as rearing practices shaped personalities that in turn give entire societies their distinct character.[26]

In contrast to these ideational and psychological approaches, Bronislaw Malinowski then defined culture as the complex ways in which social institutions function to meet human needs. For instance, it is the function of magic to give individuals a sense of control over objects that are otherwise beyond reach, such as the weather, plant growth, diseases, and powerful enemies.[27] Finally, arguing against the objectivity inherent in the functionalist approach, Clifford Geertz, writing in the 1970s, advocated the anthropological notion of culture—the hermeneutical bent culture has kept to this day. To Geertz, "culture is the fabric of meaning in terms of which human beings interpret their experience and guide their action," that is, the "framework of expressive symbols and values in terms of which individuals define their world, express their feelings, and make their judgments."[28] In short, culture is the web of significance that holds society together. The widely cited review of the anthropological notion of culture by Roger Keesing thus defines cultures as "systems of shared ideas, systems of concepts and rules and meanings

25. Ruth Benedict, *Patterns of Culture* (Boston, Mass.: Houghton Mifflin, 1934).

26. Margaret Mead, *Coming of Age in Samoa* (New York: William Morrow, 1928).

27. Bronislaw Malinowski, *Magic, Science and Religion, and other essays* (Boston, Mass.: Beacon Press, 1948).

28. Clifford Geertz, *The Interpretation of Cultures* (New York: Basic Books, 1973), pp. 144–145.

that underlie and are expressed in the ways that humans live," that is, their shared ideational codes or mind sets,[29] consisting in particular of their "beliefs, ritual practices, art forms, and ceremonies, as well as informal cultural practices such as language, gossip, stories, and rituals of daily life."[30]

Although this contemporary idea of culture as shared meaning has returned the concept to its anti-rationalist root in German Romanticism, it nonetheless differs from Herder's understanding in a crucial way. Herder considered the notion of culture so closely linked to the existence of a traditional, well-integrated community that he took its gradual dissolution by the forces of modernity to forecast the very loss of culture. Contemporary anthropology, in contrast, allows for culture even in the absence of traditional community because it understands culture as any kind of shared meaning that guides people's lives, including the self-serving pursuit of interest that the highly individualized members of modern society have in common. Thus, one speaks today of a "consumer culture" even though its values—self-indulgence and self-expression—are the very opposite of the virtues that hold communities of character together.

Political science—through the work of Gabriel Almond, Sidney Verba, and Lucian Pye—first adopted the concept in the 1950s and 1960s as "civic" or "political culture," defining it as "pattern of distribution of orientations members of a political community have toward politics," including perceptions, feelings, attitudes, values, and norms.[31] Contemporary political scientists largely follow anthropology's lead by understanding culture as any set of meanings that constrain behavior. In a widely cited article, culture is thus defined as a "mind set" which has the effect of limiting attention to less than the full range of alternative behaviors, problems, and solutions," based on such fundamental assumptions as to whether the world is morally ordered and causally determinate, what kind of events belong to the political context, whether war is inherent to

29. Roger M. Keesing, "Theories of Culture," *Annual Review of Anthropology,* Vol. 3 (1974), pp. 73–97, at p. 89; Roger M. Keesing, *Cultural Anthropology: A Contemporary Perspective* (New York: Holt, Rinehart and Winston, 1981), p. 68.

30. Ann Swidler, "Culture in Action: Symbols and Strategies," *American Sociological Review,* Vol. 51, No. 2 (April 1986), pp. 273–286, at p. 273.

31. Carole Pateman, "Political Culture, Political Structure and Political Change," *British Journal of Political Science,* Vol. 1, Part 3 (July 1971), pp. 291–305, at p. 293. For the classical statements, see: Gabriel A. Almond, "Comparative Political Systems," *Journal of Politics,* Vol. 18, No. 3 (August 1956), pp. 391–409; Gabriel A. Almond and Sidney Verba, *The Civic Culture: Political Attitudes and Democracy in Five Nations* (Boston, Mass.: Little, Brown, 1965).

the human condition, or to what extent other political actors should be trusted.[32]

Culture, Ideology, Religion, and Ethnicity

This contemporary understanding of culture as any kind of shared mindset puts the concept at odds with its original purpose of providing an alternative to the rationalist approach to politics. For to define culture as any kind of meaning that constructs society leads to the inclusion of systems of economic, social, and political thought that shape the minds of human beings on a large scale, such as liberalism, Marxism, Nazism, fascism, anarchism, pacifism, or environmentalism—ideologies, in short. Indeed, Ann Swidler defines ideology as the explicitly argued, self-conscious form of cultural meaning, which comes to the fore when lives are unsettled; in contrast, when lives are routine, cultural beliefs and practices are taken for granted and thus take the form of tradition.[33] For instance, as Geertz has argued, it was the loss of traditional certainty in the face of modern secularism that gave rise to "ideologized" Islam, whose followers are no longer "held" by their beliefs but "hold" them in the manner of political activists.[34]

This anthropological assimilation of ideology to culture, however, overlooks that ideology is a political phenomenon and thus fundamentally different from cultural and social ones. To sense this difference, consider how one may attribute the Cold War to the revolutionary tenets of Marxist-Leninist ideology, which motivated the leaders of the Soviet Union to seek the overthrow of the capitalist states of the West, or, alternatively, to the xenophobic traits of Russian culture, which considers the Motherland to be perennially surrounded by enemies; no one, however, has ever spoken of "Marxist-Leninist culture" in this context. Likewise, one may argue that many Germans supported their government from 1933 to 1945 because they believed in Nazi ideology or, alternatively, had been conditioned by German culture to obey whichever authority was

---

32. David J. Elkins and Richard E.B. Simeon, "A Cause in Search of Its Effect, Or What Does Political Culture Explain?" *Comparative Politics*, Vol. 11, No. 2 (January 1979), pp. 127–145, at p. 128. See also Richard W. Wilson, "The Many Voices of Political Culture: Assessing Different Approaches," *World Politics*, Vol. 52, No. 2 (January 2000), pp. 246–273.

33. Swidler, "Culture in Action," pp. 278–279. See also Clifford Geertz, "Ideology as a Cultural System," in *The Interpretation of Cultures* (New York: Basic Books, 1973), pp. 87–125.

34. Clifford Geertz, *Islam Observed: Religious Developments in Morocco and Indonesia* (New Haven, Conn.: Yale University Press, 1968), p. 61.

placed above them, but not because they had been shaped by "Nazi culture," which usually refers to a mere style in architecture, film making, and painting.

The deeper reason for this semantic difference is that cultures are made up of the concrete beliefs and practices of particular societies, whereas ideologies consist of abstract ideas that lay claim to universal validity, such as "classless society," "the purity of the Aryan race," and "the rights of man." In other words, the concept of ideology belongs to the rationalist approach to politics. Indeed, the etymology of "ideology" marks it as an offspring of the Enlightenment: in 1796, French revolutionary thinker Destutt de Tracy coined the term *idéologie* as a "science of ideas," which—drawing on the empiricist epistemology of philosopher John Locke—reduced thought to sensations and hoped to reform France's institutions, beginning with its schools.[35] This rationalist pedigree holds even for the peculiar sense that Marxism has given to ideology as a collective illusion or "false consciousness" that legitimates the existing and exploitative relations of production; for this definition denies only that ideologies can be rational in the sense of being true, but affirms that they are rationalizations—self-serving justifications by means of seemingly rational principles. On the most fundamental level, the rise of rationalism in the West, which goes back not just to the Enlightenment but to the natural and political philosophers of ancient Greece, has split our awareness of the world in two: the intuitive encounter with concrete particulars that are uncritically taken as given, and rational reflection that stands outside our immediate experience and generates abstract universals. Culture belongs to the former mode, ideology to the latter.

This distinction holds even in the case of nationalism, which is an ideology that exalts the merits of a particular culture, making those who engage in political action on ideological grounds at the same time agents on behalf of a cultural ideal. More precisely, there is an analytical difference between the abstract principle of nationalism, namely that every nation ought to have its own state, and the cultural particulars that define the nation in question. For instance, when the kingdoms of Piedmont and Sardinia fought wars against the Habsburg Empire in 1848 and 1860 in order to unify Italy, they did so both from the nationalist principle that each people ought to have its own state and from a cultural understanding of who belonged to the Italian people.

That culture is inherently particular may seem to separate it from religions that lay claim to universal truth as well, such as Christianity, Bud-

---

35. See David Braybrooke, "Ideology," in Paul Edwards, ed., *The Encyclopedia of Philosophy*, Vol. 3 (New York: Collier Macmillan, 1967), pp. 124–127.

dhism, and Islam. Religious truth is a matter of faith rather than reason, however, and thus tends to be experienced in a much more intuitive and felt way than ideological truth. In other words, the precepts, prayers, rituals, and ceremonies of religion tend to give meaning to people's lives on such a concrete level—in their daily observances, dress, mores, marriage customs, etc.—that they readily become part of their culture; for, as argued above, it is the sign of culture that people take its assumptions, values, and norms for granted, rather than subjecting them to reflection.

For instance, Muslims who harbor hostile sentiments toward the West are not so much disturbed by its disbelief in Islam, but by the fact that modernization and Westernization have undermined the traditional communities that they used to enjoy. Commenting on the growth of anti-Western sentiment in the Muslim world, British author Salman Rushdie put it this way:

Of course this is "about Islam." The question is, what exactly does that mean? After all, most religious belief isn't very theological. Most Muslims are not profound Koranic analysts. For a vast number of "believing" Muslim men, "Islam" stands, in a jumbled, half-examined way, not only for the fear of God—the fear more than the love, one suspects—but also for a cluster of customs, opinions and prejudices that include their dietary practices; the sequestration or near-sequestration of "their" women; the sermons delivered by their mullahs of choice; a loathing of modern society in general, riddled as it is with music, godlessness, and sex; and a more particularized loathing (and fear) of the prospect that their own immediate surroundings could be taken over—"Westoxicated"—by the liberal Western-style way of life.[36]

Thus, when Iran's Supreme Leader Ayatollah Khomeini denounced the United States as the "Great Satan," he referred to the well-known last verses of the Koran, which describe Satan as "the insidious tempter who whispers in the hearts of men"; as Middle East scholar Bernard Lewis explains; "Satan is not a conqueror, not an imperialist, not a capitalist, not an exploiter. He is a seducer. He comes with Barbie dolls and cocktails and provocative TV programs and movies and, worst of all, emancipated women."[37]

Apart from religious practices, culture often rests on ethnicity, which implies some distinct combination of idiom, physical appearance, genetic

36. Salman Rushdie, "Yes, This Is About Islam," *New York Times*, November 2, 2001, p. A21.

37. Bernard Lewis, "The West and the Middle East," *Foreign Affairs*, Vol. 76, No. 1 (January/February 1997), pp. 114–130, at p. 127 n. 2. See also Bernard Lewis, "The Revolt of Islam: When Did the Conflict with the West Begin, and How Could It End?" *The New Yorker*, November 19, 2001, pp. 50–63.

descent, customs, and mores. According to Anthony Smith, a contemporary scholar of nationalism, an *"ethnie"* or ethnic community is a "named human population with a myth of common ancestry, shared memories, and cultural elements; a link with a historic territory or homeland; and a measure of solidarity," with the cultural elements including "dress, food, music, crafts, and architecture, as well as laws, customs, and institutions."[38] Undoubtedly, there are some *ethnies* that have formed in a quasi-natural way through geographic, social, and political isolation, such as the Basques whose genetic distinctiveness seems to go back to the Stone Age, or the Japanese who had isolated themselves on their archipelago. But most ethnic groups are social constructs that formed in some fashion out of the many ways in which human beings are alike and different.

Above all, being subject to the laws of the same political authority for a long time tends to make people think of themselves as alike in their ways. Thus, the French became a nation through the coercive agency of the French state, which founded the *Académie Française* (1635) to standardize the French language, established public schools that taught in French (1830), required proficiency in French as a condition of state employment (1832), and imposed compulsory education and the prohibition to speak local idioms at school (1880s). The other major way in which ethnic groups have formed is by conscious promotion at the hands of intellectuals who collect folk songs, establish dictionaries, write monumental histories, compose literary works in the vernacular, and found cultural movements. Thus, it was that Czech, Slovak, Slovene, Serbo-Croatian, Finnish, and Ukrainian advanced from peasant dialects to *Kultursprachen* (languages of culture) during the nineteenth century, and that their speakers came to think of themselves as ethnic communities.[39]

In other words, ethnicity is ultimately a matter of shared awareness among people regarding the traits that they have come to consider significant enough to distinguish them as a group from others. This subjectivity, however, makes ethnicity only marginally less effective than if it were an inborn trait; for it satisfies one's natural need for a "we-feeling" more deeply than any other characteristic. Probably based on genetic urges that evolved over the millions of years that hominids lived in small,

---

38. Anthony D. Smith, "The Ethnic Sources of Nationalism," in Michael E. Brown, ed., *Ethnic Conflict and International Security* (Princeton, N.J.: Princeton University Press, 1993), pp. 27–41, at pp. 28–29.

39. See Benedict Anderson, *Imagined Communities: Reflections on the Origins and Spread of Nationalism* (London: Verso Books, 1983), pp. 67–79; John Plamenatz, "Two Types of Nationalism," in Eugene Kamenka, ed., *Nationalism: The Nature and Evolution of an Idea* (Canberra: Australian National University Press, 1971), pp. 23–36, at pp. 30–32.

tightly-knit bands, human beings have a deeply rooted urge to belong to groups of people who are like themselves.[40] To some extent, this likeness can consist of mutually accepted ideas, such as the beliefs that bind together the members of political parties or revolutionary movements. To be effective on the scale of peoples, however, it has to be something more concrete and immediately felt, such as facial features, hair and skin color, language and speech patterns, dress, manners and mores, customary forms of upbringing and work—in short, the markers of ethnicity.

Since human beings are not only social creatures that need to live in groups of likes, but also ethical beings that need to believe in the rightness of their actions, they tend to affirm the particular norms, ways, and assumptions of their group as inherently good. Indeed, lack of critical reflection and ignorance of alternatives makes most people think that the ways of their own society are naturally right and that the dimly perceived customs of other cultures are as wrong as they are strange. As sociologist William Graham Sumner observed long ago, "ethnocentrism" is thus a way of life with human beings: "each group thinks its own folkways the only right ones, and if it observes that other groups have other folkways, these excite its scorn."[41] In other words, cultural communities tend to be exclusive insofar as a culturally defined self implies the perception of a cultural "Other" or, indeed, "alien." Whether this perception allows for peaceful coexistence and economic exchange or leads to holy or ethnic war depends on a host of factors, such as the strength of civic engagement on the local level, the accessibility and effectiveness of political institutions, and the interpretation that charismatic leaders give to cultural norms.[42] Nonetheless, cultural community entails a significant potential for conflict on account of its particularity.

Culture and International Relations Theory

Given the fundamental opposition between Enlightenment rationalism and the concept of culture, its acceptance by the principal paradigms

---

40. On the evolutionary roots of kinship and ethnocentrism, see Peter L. van den Berghe, *The Ethnic Phenomenon* (New York: Elsevier, 1981); Gary R. Johnson, "Kin Selection, Socialization, and Patriotism: An Integrating Theory," *Politics and the Life Sciences*, Vol. 4, No. 2 (February 1986), pp. 127–140; Vernon Reynolds, Vincent Falger, and Ian Vine, eds., *The Sociobiology of Ethnocentrism: Evolutionary Dimensions of Xenophobia, Racism, and Nationalism* (London: Croom Helm, 1987).

41. William Graham Sumner, *Folkways: A Study of the Sociological Importance of Usages, Manners, Customs, Mores, and Morals* (New York: Dover Publications, 1906), p. 13.

42. See R. Scott Appleby, *The Ambivalence of the Sacred: Religion, Violence, and Reconciliation* (Lanham, Md.: Rowman & Littlefield, 2000); Ashutosh Varshney, *Ethnic Conflict*

of international relations theory—liberalism, realism, Marxism, and constructivism—increases with their critical distance from the Enlightenment. Liberalism, the true heir of the Enlightenment, rejects cultural motives altogether because they interfere with the universal rule of rationality, which is to be realized in two ways: by grasping the natural harmony of interests that underlies all human relations, be it among individuals or states, and by respecting the rights that individuals enjoy by nature and that states possess as a function of the rights of their citizens. The idea of a natural harmony of interests was conceived in the seventeenth century by such philosophers as Hugo Grotius, Thomas Hobbes, Samuel Pufendorf, and John Locke. Seeking to end the wars of religion that plagued Europe at the time, they sought to exclude salvation from the ends of the state and to limit them to what all human beings could be assumed to desire, namely peace, prosperity, liberty, and justice. In Hobbes' words, "all men agree on this, that peace is good; and therefore also [that] the way or means of peace (which . . . [are] . . . the laws of nature) are good"; a law of nature, in turn, is a "precept or general rule, found out by reason."[43]

Applying this framework to foreign affairs, contemporary liberals thus assume in general that states cooperate because they understand that conflictual behavior—although potentially rewarding in the short run—eventually makes all parties worse off, whereas sustained cooperation rebounds to everyone's long-term benefit.[44] In particular, the advocates of collective security expect states to come to the defense of any victim of aggression—even if their own security is not immediately threatened—in order to make the world a safer place for all.[45] The proponents of functional integration argue that states succeed at forming supranational entities, such as the European Union, by leaving the coordination of their technical and economic functions to experts, who are more likely to find rational solutions than politicians who are beholden to such

and Civic Life: Hindus and Muslims in India (New Haven, Conn.: Yale University Press, 2001).

43. Thomas Hobbes, *Leviathan, with Selected Variants From the Latin Edition of 1668* (Indianapolis, Ind.: Hackett, 1994), pp. 100, 79.

44. See Robert Axelrod, *The Evolution of Cooperation* (New York: Basic Books, 1984); Arthur A. Stein, *Why Nations Cooperate: Circumstance and Choice in International Relations* (Ithaca, N.Y.: Cornell University Press, 1990).

45. See Inis L. Claude, *Power and International Relations* (New York: Random House, 1966), chaps. 4–5; Charles A. Kupchan and Clifford A. Kupchan, "Concerts, Collective Security, and the Future of Europe," *International Security*, Vol. 16, No. 1 (Summer 1991), pp. 114–161; Richard K. Betts, "Systems for Peace or Causes of War? Collective Security, Arms Control, and the New Europe," *International Security*, Vol. 17, No. 1 (Summer 1992), pp. 5–43.

atavistic notions as *raison d'état*, national greatness, cultural identity, and ethnic solidarity.[46] Furthermore, the growing interdependence of states is thought to engender peace because going to war with one's suppliers and customers is costly; interdependence is also thought to lead to greater co-operation because it increases the number of problems that cannot be solved unilaterally.[47] States are also assumed to establish international in-stitutions—organizations such as the United Nations and regimes such as the Law of the Sea—in order to facilitate cooperation that is in everyone's interest but difficult to achieve *ad hoc*.[48] In short, interest-based liberalism understands cultural factors as mere obstacles to rational choice.

Regarding moral law and respect for rights, liberalism looks back again to the writings of Grotius, but, more important, to the thought of Immanuel Kant. For it was Grotius who first wrote of "right" as a faculty enjoyed by individuals and redefined natural law as the injunction to re-spect these rights, but it was Kant who argued persuasively that the rights of individuals do not derive from their interest in satisfying their desires, but from the assumption that their freely-willing rationality makes them deserving of being treated as ends in themselves.[49] Accord-ing to Kant, international law thus protects not only the rights of states but those of individuals as well, giving rise to the hope that progressive enlightenment will eventually turn the entire world into a cosmopolitan "kingdom of ends," that is, a fully rational condition where every human being is always treated as an end; to approximate this utopian goal, states

---

46. See David Mitrany, *A Working Peace System* (Chicago: Quadrangle Books, 1966); Ernst Haas, *Beyond the Nation-State: Functionalism and International Organization* (Stan-ford, Calif.: Stanford University Press, 1964); Philippe C. Schmitter, "Three Neo-Functionalist Hypotheses About International Integration," *International Organization*, Vol. 23, No. 1 (Winter 1969), pp. 161–166.

47. See Edward L. Morse, "The Politics of Interdependence," *International Organiza-tion*, Vol. 23, No. 2 (Spring 1969), pp. 311–326; Richard N. Cooper, "Economic Interde-pendence and Foreign Policy in the Seventies," *World Politics*, Vol. 24, No. 2 (January 1972), pp. 159–181; Robert Keohane and Joseph Nye, *Power and Interdependence: World Politics in Transition* (Boston, Mass.: Little, Brown, 1977).

48. See Karl W. Deutsch et al., *Political Community and the North Atlantic Area: Interna-tional Organization in the Light of Historical Experience* (Princeton, N.J.: Princeton Univer-sity Press, 1957); Inis L. Claude, *Swords into Plowshares: The Problems and Progress of In-ternational Organization* (New York: Random House, 1959); Robert Keohane, *After Hegemony: Cooperation and Discord in the World Political Economy* (Princeton, N.J.: Princeton University Press, 1984).

49. See Knud Haakonsen, "Hugo Grotius and the History of Political Thought," *Po-litical Theory*, Vol. 13, No. 2 (May 1985), pp. 239–265; Immanuel Kant, *Groundwork of the Metaphysics of Morals*, trans. H. J. Patton (New York: Harper, 1964), esp. pp. 61, 66–69, 73, 95–96, 100–102.

with liberal constitutions ought to form a pacific federation.[50] Applying these ideas to foreign policy, U.S. President Woodrow Wilson gave the U.S. intervention in World War I the goal of abolishing the workings of the balance of power in favor of an international system of democracies governed by the rule of law.[51] The League of Nations was to provide collective security against those states who had not yet realized the rationality of this new order.[52] The Kellogg-Briand Pact of 1928 outlawed war as a means of foreign policy.[53] The Nuremberg War Crimes Tribunals in 1945 punished individuals for violations of international law. The Universal Declaration of Human Rights of 1948 finally made the rights of individuals into the formal foundation of international law, to be applied "without distinction of any kind, such as race, colour, sex, language, religion, political or other opinion, national or social origin, property, birth or other status,"[54]—precisely those aspects of life that make up cultural particularity. This Kantian vision of foreign affairs has attained an astounding measure of reality in the pacific relations among the liberal democracies of the West, which has been celebrated by international relations students as the "liberal" or "democratic peace."[55]

Regarding the realist view of foreign affairs, one needs to make a distinction between traditional or classical realists, such as E. H. Carr, John Herz, and Hans Morgenthau, and neorealists, such as Kenneth Waltz.[56]

---

50. See Immanuel Kant, *Perpetual Peace; A Philosophical Sketch,* in Hans Reiss, ed., *Kant: Political Writings* (Cambridge: Cambridge University Press, 1991), pp. 93–130.

51. See Arthur Bernon Tourtellot, ed., *Woodrow Wilson: Selections for Today* (New York: Duell, Sloan, and Pearce, 1945), pp. 54, 131, 143–144; Joseph P. Tumulty, *Woodrow Wilson as I Know Him,* (Garden City, N.J.: Country Life, 1921), p. 274.

52. See Woodrow Wilson, "A League for Peace," in David L. Larsen, ed., *The Puritan Ethic in United States Foreign Policy,* (Princeton, N.J.: D. Van Nostrand, 1966), pp. 181–188.

53. See Salmon Levinson, *Outlawry of War* (Chicago: American Committee for the Outlawry of War, 1921).

54. United Nations, General Assembly, Resolution 217, *Universal Declaration of Human Rights,* December 10, 1948, A (iii), Art. 2.

55. See Michael W. Doyle, "Kant, Liberal Legacies and Foreign Affairs," *Philosophy and Public Affairs,* Vol. 12, No. 3 (Summer 1983), pp. 205–235; Michael W. Doyle, "Kant, Liberal Legacies and Foreign Affairs, Part 2," *Philosophy and Public Affairs,* Vol. 12, No. 4 (Autumn 1983), pp. 323–353; Bruce Russett, *Grasping the Democratic Peace: Principles For a Post-Cold War World* (Princeton, N.J.: Princeton University Press, 1993); Michael E. Brown, Sean M. Lynn-Jones, and Steven E. Miller, eds., *Debating the Democratic Peace* (Cambridge, Mass.: MIT Press, 1996); John M. Owen IV, *Liberal Peace, Liberal War: American Politics and International Security* (Ithaca, N.Y.: Cornell University Press, 1997).

56. See Hans J. Morgenthau, *Scientific Man vs. Power Politics* (Chicago: University of Chicago Press, 1946); John H. Herz, *Political Realism and Political Idealism* (Chicago:

Traditional realists appreciate the cohesiveness that culture provides as a means to the power of the state. In Hans Morgenthau's words, "national character" belongs to the "elements of national power."[57] More importantly, traditional realists accept that cultural particularity affects foreign policy in important ways. Morgenthau, for instance, traced the "scores of peace plans, logically perfect but impracticable, in which French statecraft excelled" to the "mechanistic rationality" of the French national character, and, less plausibly, linked the "traditional rudeness and clumsy deviousness of German diplomacy" to what "Tacitus said of the destructive political and military propensities of the Germanic tribes."[58] In George Kennan's more sophisticated judgment, the opportunistic expansiveness of Soviet foreign policy had much to do with Russian cultural traits of "caution, circumspection, flexibility, and deception," which, in turn, arose from the historical experience of a peasant society constantly threatened by unpredictable nomadic incursions.[59] Indeed, insofar as they are influenced by nineteenth-century German political thought, which sought to reconcile *raison d'état* and *Volksgeist,*[60] traditional realists hold that the interest of the state contains not only the objective ends of security, power, and wealth, but also the normative aspirations embedded in its culture. In Friedrich Meinecke's words, "between Kratos and Ethos . . . there exists at the summit of the state a bridge, namely *raison d'état.*"[61]

University of Chicago Press, 1951); E. H. Carr, *The Twenty Years' Crisis, 1919–1939: An Introduction to the Study of International Relations,* 2nd ed. (New York: Harper Torchbooks, 1964); Kenneth N. Waltz, *Theory of International Politics* (New York: Addison Wesley, 1979).

57. Hans J. Morgenthau, *Politics Among Nations: The Struggle for Power and Peace,* 6th ed. (New York: Alfred Knopf, 1985), pp. 151–153.

58. Morgenthau, *Politics Among Nations,* pp. 147–148.

59. X [George F. Kennan], "The Sources of Soviet Conduct," *Foreign Affairs,* Vol. 25, No. 4 (1947), pp. 566–582, at p. 575.

60. Friedrich Meinecke, *Machiavellism: The Doctrine of Raison d'Etat and its Place in Modern History,* trans. Douglas Scott (New York: Praeger, 1965), p. 372.

61. Meinecke, *Machiavellism,* p. 5, emphasis supplied. In the cited passage, Meinecke gives the meaning of the classical Greek terms *kratos* and *ethos* as "behaviour prompted by the power-impulse and behaviour prompted by moral responsibility." This is accurate as far as *kratos* is concerned, which the Greeks understood as strength, power, might, and force, as well as sway and dominion. It fails, however, to give the full meaning of *ethos*, which meant custom, usage, institute, and rite to the ancients and was broadened in the nineteenth century to the describe the distinguishing character, sentiment, moral nature, or guiding beliefs of a person, group, or institution. In other words, *ethos* is another word for culture.

However, and here traditionalist realists part company with true believers in culture: they maintain that the state will always choose *kratos* over *ethos* when the two ends come into serious conflict—which will happen sooner rather than later because the world is such that security, power, and wealth cannot be attained without breaching moral prohibitions and overriding cultural concerns. Ever since antiquity, but most paradigmatically in the thought of Niccolò Machiavelli, this proposition has been summarily expressed by the notion of "necessity"—the constraint to use unjust force and fraud to secure oneself and one's community. In other words, when the pursuit of cultural ends—virtue, honor, salvation, the maintenance of one's traditional way of life—undermines the security, power, and wealth of the community, it is rational to sacrifice the former to the latter. To quote Meinecke again, "*raison d'état* . . . takes on the profound and serious character of national necessity. The characteristic way of life of the individual state must therefore develop within an iron chain of cause and effect."[62] In the final analysis, traditional realism negates the cultural account of politics because of its commitment to the instrumental rationality that drives the doctrine of *raison d'état*.

Neorealism, created by Kenneth Waltz in 1979 as an effort to put realism on a social-scientific footing, transformed the traditional notion of necessity into the concept of "anarchic structure." More precisely, the fact that states exist under anarchy, that is, in the absence of central authority, constrains them to provide for their own security and leads to the recurrent formation of balances of power. Emulating their most successful rivals, states become alike in both their internal organization and external behavior. By implication, anarchic structure thus mitigates culture as a cause of foreign policy in two ways: first, laggard states are forced to impose the most rational forms of political, military, economic, and social organization on their peoples, suppressing and dissolving their traditional cultures; second, all states need to follow the same maxims of *raison d'état*—rather than cultural imperatives—in their dealings with each other.

This sounds similar enough to traditional realism, were it not for the additional neorealist tenet that the "unit-level," that is, the particular characteristics of states, "drops out" from anarchic structure.[63] Thus, culture is relegated by Waltz to the "theory of foreign policy," which explains at a lower level of generality how particularities in the internal

---

62. Ibid., p. 2.

63. Ibid., pp. 93–101.

composition of states lead to differences in their external behavior—insofar as the latter are not suppressed by anarchic constraint.[64] In principle, neorealism thus allows for the inclusion of culture in an overall account of the foreign realm. In practice, however, the sharp analytical separation between structural and unit-level causes, and, even more so, the adage that the latter drops out, have led neorealists to ignore culture as the domestic factor least amenable to a scientific explanation.[65] In so doing, they readily subsume ethnic and religious accounts to their standard rejection of "idealist" explanations of foreign politics, taking culture to consist of "collectively held ideas that do not vary in the face of environmental or structural changes."[66] In sum, whereas traditional realism's commitment to *raison d'état* frowns upon culture in the final analysis, neorealism's commitment to structuralism does so in the first.[67]

In the paradigm that takes its name from Karl Marx, culture belongs to the superstructure, that is, the "ideology" or "mental intercourse of men" as expressed in the "language of politics, laws, morality, religion, metaphysics, etc., of a people"; this superstructure, and therewith culture, is shaped in turn by the material base, that is, fundamental productive forces and the corresponding relations of production.[68] For instance, in a place where technology is limited to muscle power and simple mechanical devices and where the relations of production consist of small-scale farming on communal plots, society will take the form of a tribe held together by bonds of personal loyalty, the worship of legendary ancestors, specific rites and customs, etc. At the same time, the ideas that make up the superstructure serve to legitimate the existing relations of production, and thus express the interests of the ruling class, i.e., those who owns the means of production.[69] For instance, the liberal values of

---

64. Ibid., pp. 121–122.

65. While admitting to the usefulness of cultural accounts as supplements to realist explanations, the lone neorealist statement on the matter nonetheless dismisses them as epiphenomenal; see Michael Desch, "Culture Clash: Assessing the Importance of Ideas in Security Studies," *International Security*, Vol. 23, No. 1 (Summer 1998), pp. 141–170.

66. Ibid., p. 152.

67. See Yosef Lapid and Friedrich Kratochwil, "Revisiting the 'National': Toward an Identity Agenda in Neorealism?" in Yosef Lapid and Friedrich Kratochwil, eds., *The Return of Culture and Identity to IR Theory* (Boulder, Colo.: Lynne Rienner, 1996), pp. 105–126, esp. pp. 110–116.

68. Karl Marx, *The German Ideology: Part I*, in Robert C. Tucker, ed., *The Marx-Engels Reader*, 2nd ed. (New York: W.W. Norton, 1978), pp. 146–200, at p. 154; see also *Manifesto of the Communist Party*, in Tucker, *Marx-Engels Reader*, pp. 473–500, at p. 487.

69. Marx, *German Ideology*, pp. 172–173.

freedom, equality, and prosperity, together with the commercial practices in which they are embedded, legitimate capitalist relations of productions and serve the interests of the property-owning bourgeoisie. In other words, Marxism understands culture as ideology in the sense of rationalizations that reinforce the fetters of the oppressed.

While largely implicit in Marx's thought, this notion of culture attained a central place in the writings of Antonio Gramsci, who identified culture as the means by which the ruling class maintains its "hegemony,"—power that relies on consent and uses force only in marginal cases of deviancy. More precisely, shaping the consciousness of both ruling and subordinate classes, culture maintains cohesion and identity within the "historical bloc"—the complex whole of superstructure and material base, in which ideas and material conditions are always bound together and influence each other.[70]

In the foreign realm, Marxism first issued in the imperialism thesis by V. I. Lenin, who claimed that the bourgeois classes of the advanced capitalist states use their military power to acquire colonies in order to invest surplus capital, exploit local labor, and sell surplus goods.[71] With decolonization, this idea took the form of dependency theory, which argues that economies in the periphery of the international system are hamstrung in their development by the exploitative influence of the capitalists in the center, who control the flow of capital, own subsidiaries in the periphery, and pay off local politicians in exchange for repatriating profits.[72] Furthermore, the application of Gramsci's concept of hegemony to these ideas gave rise to the notion of "cultural imperialism," which holds that the spread of consumer culture—generated by capitalism and commodifying all cultural relations—turns the working classes of the periphery into the willing objects of exploitation by Western capitalists and their lo-

---

70. Robert W. Cox, "Gramsci, Hegemony and International Relations: An Essay in Method," *Millennium: Journal of International Studies*, Vol. 12, No. 2 (1983), pp. 162–175; Stephen Gill, ed., *Gramsci, Historical Materialism and International Relations* (Cambridge: Cambridge University Press, 1993).

71. See V. I. Lenin, *Imperialism, the Highest Stage of Capitalism* (Peking: Foreign Languages Press, 1975); Tom Kemp, "The Marxist Theory of Imperialism," in Roger Owen and Bob Sutcliffe, eds., *Studies in the Theory of Imperialism* (London: Longman, 1972), pp. 15–34.

72. See Theotonio Dos Santos, "The Structure of Dependence," *American Economic Review*, Vol. 60, No. 2 (May 1970), pp. 231–236; Raymond D. Duvall, "Dependence and Dependencia Theory: Notes Toward Precision of Concept and Argument," *International Organization*, Vol. 32, No. 1 (Winter 1978), pp. 51–78; Fernando Henrique Cardoso and Enzo Faletto, *Dependency and Development in Latin America* (Berkeley: University of California Press, 1979).

cal counterparts.[73] For instance, peasants who leave their village communities to become workers in industries owned by multinational corporations will be more willing to endure the attendant alienation if they internalize the consumerist promises on billboards and the screens of their newly acquired television sets. Urban professionals and civil servants come to accept the policy recommendations of the International Monetary Fund (IMF) and World Bank as their way of life becomes all but indistinguishable from that of their counterparts in New York and London. In other words, the spread of Western culture—produced and promoted by Western corporations—creates a "false consciousness" among people in the periphery, making them believe that development along capitalist lines and the related phenomenon of globalization are in their interest, when, in truth, they entail their exploitation and alienation.

In sum, the concept of culture in the sense of ideology holds an important place in Marxist analysis as one of the means by which the capitalist class dominates domestic and international society. As such, however, culture remains subservient to class interest and conditioned by the relations of production. Moreover, the claim that all hitherto existing cultures have propagated false consciousness implies that they ought to be abolished and replaced by the true consciousness of communist society. But since this consciousness will be universal, culture in the sense of norms and values specific to a ruling class will cease to exist. In the end, Marxism remains in the orbit of Enlightenment rationalism.

The only paradigm that embraces the cultural account as a fundamentally valid way of understanding international relations is constructivism.[74] At root, constructivism argues that all human activity, including politics, is best understood by the meaning that people give to their

---

73. See C. Flora and J. Flora, "The *Fotonovela* as a Tool for Class and Cultural Domination," *Latin American Perspectives,* Vol. 5, No. 2 (1978), pp. 134–150; Raquel Salinas and Leena Paldán, "Culture in the Process of Dependent Development: Theoretical Perspectives," in Kaarle Nordenstreng and Herbert I. Schiller, eds., *National Sovereignty and International Communication* (Norwood, N.J.: Ablex, 1979), pp. 82–98; Cees J. Hamelink, *Cultural Autonomy in Global Communications: Planning National Information Policy* (New York: Longman, 1983).

74. See Lapid and Kratochwil, eds., *Return of Culture and Identity;* R.B.J. Walker, ed., *Culture, Ideology, and World Order* (Boulder, Colo.: Westview, 1984); Jongsuk Chay, ed., *Culture and International Relations* (New York: Praeger, 1990); Peter J. Katzenstein, ed., *The Culture of National Security: Norms and Identity in World Politics* (New York: Columbia University Press, 1996); Valerie M. Hudson, *Culture and Foreign Policy* (Boulder, Colo.: Lynne Rienner, 1997); Dominique Jaquin-Berdal, Andrew Oros, and Marco Verweij, eds., *Culture in World Politics* (New York: St. Martin's, 1998).

world and that such meaning is intersubjectively constructed.[75] In consequence, constructivism rejects as "essentialist" the assumptions that realists and liberals make about human nature and state interests, for instance, that human beings naturally prefer survival to all other ends or take an ever-increasing material prosperity to define the good life. Furthermore, the constructs that make up world politics, e.g., the divine right monarchies of Europe, the protectionist world economy of the 1930s, the game of power politics among sovereign states, are seen as structures that constrain the practices of agents as long as most of them subscribe to their beliefs and norms. Should they cease to believe in them, however, these structures readily collapse and, given the human need for a meaningful world, are replaced by different ones, e.g., the republican order established by the French revolution, the free trade regime after World War II, and, perhaps, an international system based on collective security and peace.

The concept of culture is readily assimilated to this view because the meanings that make up a particular culture are shared on the basis of language, are inherently intersubjective, and because its horizon of taken-for-granted assumptions constructs a social world. Thus, the structure that shapes world politics has been described by constructivists as a "cultural structure" that finds embodiment in institutions and norms of cooperation, as well as threat complexes, ideological hegemony, and relations of enmity and fear such as the Cold War.[76]

Clearly, constructivism follows anthropology in elevating culture to an all-embracing concept by making it coextensive with social construction itself. Any set of meanings that intersubjectively shape social reality—be it the authoritarian culture of Wilhelmine Germany, the doctrine of raison d'état held by early modern statesmen, or the norms and values that make up liberalism—qualify as culture. For instance, the "international cultural environments in which national security policies are made" are said to consist of "formal institutions," such as the North Atlantic Treaty Organization (NATO) and the Non-Proliferation Treaty (NPT), "world political culture," which includes the norms of sover-

---

75. For the seminal articles, see Robert Cox, "Social Forces, States, and World Orders: Beyond International Relations Theory," *Millennium*, Vol. 10, No. 2 (1981), pp. 126–155; Richard K. Ashley, "The Geopolitics of Geopolitical Space: Toward a Critical Social Theory of International Politics," *Alternatives*, Vol. 12 (1987), pp. 403–434; Alexander Wendt, "Anarchy is What States Make of It," *International Organization*, Vol. 46, No. 2 (Spring 1992), pp. 391–426.

76. Alexander Wendt, "Identity and Structural Change in International Politics," in Lapid and Kratochwil, eds., *Return of Culture and Identity*, pp. 47–64, at p. 49.

eignty and international law, and "transnational political discourse," conducted by such movements as Amnesty International and Greenpeace.[77] Moreover, the phenomenon of globalization has led constructivists to lay claim to an emerging "global culture," thus denying that some kind of particularity is characteristic of cultural experience.[78] True to their postmodern orientation, constructivists thus reject the Herderian, community-bound notion of culture as a "'congruent cultural wholeness' superstition" that tends to elaborate culture in terms of "boundedness, homogeneity, and natural immutability."[79]

In addition to culture, constructivism views foreign politics through the lens of identity, that is, the specific and more or less stable set of meanings that agents attribute to themselves. Since such meanings derive in large part from one's surroundings, identity can also be defined as "a social category that an individual member either takes a special pride in or views as a more-or-less unchangeable and socially consequentially attribute."[80] Given the complexity of human consciousness, people tend to have multiple, partially overlapping, and not necessarily consistent identities. When applied to the state, the concept of identity refers to the collective understanding that shapes the assumptions and goals that underlie its policies—what realists and liberals would call the national interest. According to constructivists, different identities construct different international systems. "If states identify only with themselves, so to speak, the system will be anarchic. If they identify with a world state it will be hierarchical. . . . And if they identify with each other, such as that they have a collective identity in which each is bound to cooperate with the other, they would constitute a decentralized authority system."[81]

How does identity relate to culture? Whereas culture is by definition an intersubjective phenomenon, identity is more a subjective one, since it pertains to agents rather than structure. More precisely, culture and iden-

77.   Ronald L. Jepperson, Alexander Wendt, and Peter J. Katzenstein, "Norms, Identity, and Culture in National Security," in Katzenstein, ed., *Culture of National Security*, pp. 33–75, at p. 34.

78.   Mary C. Bateson, "Beyond Sovereignty: An Emerging Global Civilization," in R.B.J. Walker and Saul H. Mendlovitz, eds., *Contending Sovereignties: Redefining Political Community* (Boulder, Colo.: Lynne Rienner, 1990), pp. 145–158.

79.   Yosef Lapid, "Culture's Ship: Returns and Departures in International Relations Theory," in Lapid and Kratochwil, eds, *Return of Culture and Identity*, pp. 47–64, at p. 7.

80.   James D. Fearon and David D. Laitin, "Violence and the Social Construction of Ethnic Identity," *International Organization*, Vol. 54, No. 4 (Autumn 2000), pp. 845–877, at p. 848.

81.   Wendt, "Identity and Structural Change," pp. 47–48.

tity partake of the hermeneutic circle that connects social wholes and their parts in a mutually constitutive relationship: by assuming certain identities rather than others, communicating agents construct a corresponding kind of culture; at the same time, a given culture shapes the identities of these agents by rewarding certain attributes and punishing others, and, more fundamentally, by providing a finite number of meanings—roles, virtues, values, norms, etc.—which the agents use to construct their self-understandings. In other words, culture is the "'frame' in which people derive a sense of who they are, how they should act" and identity is the "action unit of culture," that is, "the problem-solving tool for coping in particular environments."[82]

Overall, international relations scholars are united in defining culture as any kind of mind set that constructs socio-political reality. Following the lead of anthropology, they thus assimilate ideologies to the concept of culture. They are, however, divided over the role of culture in foreign politics. Liberals and realists generally deny that cultural motives are of primary importance because they are committed to explaining international relations as rational choice in pursuit of given interests. Constructivists claim that all foreign politics should be understood in cultural terms because they assume in general that politics is constituted by shared meanings and argue in particular that the interests of states are shaped by their cultures. Marxists stand in the middle of this debate, accepting culture as a rationalization that intervenes between class interest and political action.

The Three Motives of Foreign Policy

Based on this differentiation of culture and ideology, it seems that foreign policy can be motivated by three kinds of concern: cultural goals, ideological aims, and material interests. For example, the foreign policy of the Islamic Republic of Iran has a cultural motive in its contribution to the Arab struggle against Israel, insofar as it acts from the religious belief that infidels must not rule in the realm of Islam. When West Germany sought a special relationship with East Germany in the 1970s, seeking, among other things, a lifting of travel restrictions, improvements in family reunification, and an end to the jamming of West German television broadcasts, it was clearly motivated by a concern for its ethnic brethren across the Elbe River. In contrast, Soviet foreign policy practice was driven at times by ideology insofar as it sought to bring about the world

82. Thomas K. Fitzgerald, *Metaphors of Identity* (Albany: State University of New York Press, 1993), p. 186.

proletarian revolution predicted by Marx, especially in far away places with little strategic value, such as Indonesia and Angola. Likewise, U.S. foreign policy has an ideological bent to the extent that it claims to promote human rights and democracy.

Material interests are ends of foreign policy that realists—and, to a lesser degree, liberals—take to be rooted in human nature and thus assume to be of overriding concern to all states. In particular, the interest in security rests on the human instinct to survive, the interest in prosperity arises from the need to live comfortably and the desire to improve materially, and the interest in dominance stems from the fact that power is a means to security and prosperity and that human beings enjoy the ability to lord it over others. Because these affects are shared by all human beings and because the goals of states ultimately reflect the desires of the people who make them up, the corresponding motives are assumed to constitute the "national interest" of any state. Moreover, since states are assumed to pursue their goals by rational means, they can be expected to behave in like ways under comparable circumstances. For example, when India signed a friendship treaty with the Soviet Union in 1971 in order to deter China, it acted from the same rationale as France did in 1892, when it formed an alliance with Russia to keep Germany at bay. Likewise, both the Soviet Union and China abandoned communism as an economic system around 1990, because their interests in prosperity and dominance proved stronger than their ideological commitment to the ideas of Marx, Lenin, and Mao.

Obviously, the policies suggested by these three motives in particular cases may conflict or combine. Cultural and ideological concerns will tend to be at odds with each other when a state's ideological commitment to a universal principle negates its attachment to cultural particulars. For instance, when West Germany gave up its claim to its former territories east of the Oder and Neisse Rivers in treaties with the Soviet Union and Poland in 1970, it gave precedence to its ideological commitment to a liberal vision of peace over the cultural attachment to ancestral lands felt by millions of its citizens.

Thus, as this case suggests as well, cultural concerns are weakened over time by the ongoing rationalization of Western society. Indeed, since the growth of ideology springs from this rationalization, it follows that ideology tends to replace culture as the primary source of what gives meaning to people's lives. More precisely, the immediately felt and concrete meaning that culture provides is replaced by the reflected and abstract meaning that ideology offers.

Accordingly, the more significant contrast lies between cultural and ideological concerns on one side and material interests on the other. Indeed, history is replete with cases in which states abandoned their religious and ideological commitments for the sake of security, prosperity, and dominance. Having lost his bid for the crown of the Holy Roman Empire to the Habsburg ruler Charles V in 1525, the Catholic king of France, Francis I, formed an alliance with the Muslim Turks in order to weaken the House of Habsburg, notwithstanding the fact that the Turks had subjugated major portions of Christendom and were threatening to advance into the heartlands of the Holy Roman Empire. Two hundred years later, Catholic France allied itself with the Protestant princes during the Thirty Years War (1618–1648), again, to undermine the power of the Catholic House of Habsburg. While committed on ideological grounds to liberal democracy and human rights, the United States has regularly backed authoritarian and dictatorial regimes for the sake of its economic and political interests: Shah Reza Pahlevi's Iran, Saddam Hussein's Iraq during the 1980s, the Pinochet regime in Chile, and the Somoza regime in Nicaragua, among others. To offset the growing power of the Soviet Union, the United States established relations with the People's Republic of China in 1972 and allowed it to become the sole representative of China in the United Nations. In short, the cleavage between the seemingly permanent interest of states in security, prosperity, and dominance and their far more diverse and contingent concerns for cultural and ideological ends has been an enduring aspect of foreign affairs.

The deeper reason for this endurance lies with the hierarchy of human needs (See Figure 2.1). The human affects that underlie the interests of states—the instinct to survive, the urge for sustenance and comfort, the appetite for delectations, the lust of feeling superior—are rooted in the lower and more primitive parts of the psyche, and thus can be taken to be relatively less shaped by one's consciousness. In contrast, cultural concerns rest on the relatively more developed need to belong to a community of people who are like oneself and thus to attain an assured sense of what one ought to be, which varies with the meanings that make up one's particular culture. Ideological concerns arise from the highest level of needs, namely our urge to consciously reflect on the world in order to make sense of it, which includes a coherent idea of how society ought to be constructed. In other words, the needs that underlie cultural and ideological concerns are much more mediated by consciousness than the needs that give rise to material interests. Thus, people experience their needs for meaning and truth in relatively more subjective ways than their needs for security, comfort, prosperity, and power.

This relative difference in the hierarchy of human needs engenders a corresponding difference in the motives of foreign policy, making the cultural and ideological concerns of states much more contingent and partic-

**Figure 2.1. The Hierarchy of Human Needs and the Cleavage Between
Material Interests and Cultural/Ideological Concerns.**

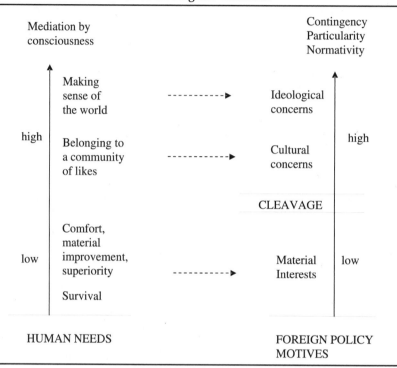

ular than their material interests. Cultural concerns change as traditions
evolve and people find new ways of giving concrete meaning to their
shared lives; ideological concerns change as they find different rational
principles by which to order their societies. In contrast, the fundamental
meaning of security, prosperity, and dominance is much more stable over
time and across different contexts. For instance, the fact that a strong wall
makes one's community more secure and that the possession of arable
land, livestock, and well-built houses improves one's material condition
is readily understood by people from as far apart as ancient Sumer, medieval Europe, Papua New Guinea, and the United States.

Moreover, cultural and ideological concerns are far more normative
than material interests. Culture affirms the way of life of the community
as good and celebrates the attributes of its heroes as virtues to be emu-
lated. Ideology postulates a moral principle, such as the rights of individuals, that guides its followers in the construction of a better political, social, or economic order. In contrast, when states pursue material interests
they care far less about what is right than about what serves their advan-

tage in terms of security, power, and wealth. For instance, whereas the United States and the Islamic Republic of Iran differ sharply over whether the propagation of religion by violent means constitutes legitimate conduct in foreign affairs, they agree that security includes not having to fear armed invasion or being compelled by nuclear threat and that having your own nuclear weapons is a highly efficient means to this end.

Constructivists are bound to reject these distinctions on the ground that the material interests of states cannot be understood apart from the cultural or ideological discourse that endows them with concrete meaning in the minds of the agents. Undoubtedly, this epistemological claim contains a significant amount of truth and may serve as a salutary warning against turning the merely relative differences between ideology, culture, and material interests into absolute ones. In other words, one should not "reify" the notion of material interests by assuming that people from very different historical periods and cultural backgrounds understand their security, prosperity, and dominance in precisely the same way or that they are not at all shaped by collectively held ideas, meanings, and norms. However to take this caution to the point of denying that most states strive for security and material well-being, enjoy domination of the weak, and pursue these ends in enduringly similar ways is to lapse into the opposite error.

In sum, there is a cleavage between cultural and ideological concerns and material interests because there are significant, albeit relative, differences in their contingency, particularity, and normativity, which in turn arise from the corresponding difference in the extent to which their underlying needs are mediated by consciousness.

The Effects of Culture on Foreign Policy

What can be said in general about the ways in which cultural motives affect foreign policy? On analytical grounds, cultural motives can either shape the ends of foreign policy or merely concern its means (See Figure 2.2). Regarding means, one can make the further distinction between culture having a real impact—for instance, when cultural bias limits the options that decision-makers can perceive—and culture being merely used as a pretext.

With regard to pretext, there can be no doubt that foreign policies with ostensibly religious and ethnic ends have often had interests at heart. In the nineteenth century, Russia appealed to the "Panslavic" sentiments of Poles, Czechs, Slovaks, Croats, Serbs, and Ukrainians to expand its sway over Central Europe and the Balkans at the expense of Austria-Hungary and the Ottoman Empire. Overseas, the European powers

Figure 2.2. The Effects of Culture on the Means and Ends of Foreign Policy.

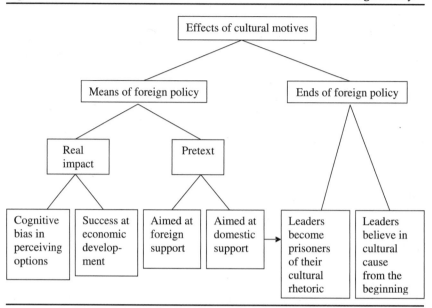

cloaked their self-serving acquisition of colonies in the cultural rhetoric of converting heathens to Christianity and carrying out a "civilizing mission." Such cultural pretense aims first of all at other states, insofar as the court of world opinion grants a greater measure of legitimacy to cultural goals than naked self-interest. Thus, Hitler got away with annexing Austria and the Sudetenland in part because his claim that Germany's territorial ambitions were limited to bringing fellow Germans home into the *Reich* aroused a measure of sympathy in the West. Today, Russia justifies its meddling in the affairs of the states that became independent after the Soviet Union's demise on the grounds of having to protect their ethnically Russian citizens, rather than admitting its desire to regain its former empire.

Second, cultural pretense is often used to gain domestic support for interest-driven foreign policies. Straining to survive the German onslaught during World War II, the Soviet government abandoned its ideological opposition to nationalism and religion, appealed to the people's love of Mother Russia, and revived the Russian Orthodox Church to keep them fighting. On the eve of the Gulf War, secular Ba'athist Saddam Hussein put *bismallah,* the Islamic profession of faith, on the Iraqi flag and made a show of praying in mosques, in order to mobilize support both in Iraq and neighboring Islamic countries.

Culture has a real impact on the means of foreign policy to the extent that culture-specific assumptions and values lead to cognitive bias in the way decision-makers perceive their options. For instance, Arab hostility to Israel and the West is nourished in part by a cultural tendency to believe in conspiracy theories that represent one's own disadvantages as the result of wrongdoing by others, and thus lead to a search for enemies rather than partners for peace.[83] Misunderstandings are the natural outcome of cultural bias. When Japanese leaders state to their Western counterparts that they will "do their best," the latter assume that their demand has a good chance of being met, whereas Japanese people understand that they it was denied in a face-saving way.[84] Obviously, the greater the cultural difference, the greater is the chance that cognitive dissonance will distort international communication.[85]

Further, cultural dispositions clearly influence the success that states have in developing their economies,[86] which affects the power at their disposal in making foreign policy. For instance, the economic success of Japan, Taiwan, South Korea, and Singapore surely had much to do with their Confucian values of thrift, hard work, and obedience to authority.[87] In contrast, the enduring political instability in Latin America has been attributed to its elite culture—the corruption of its politicians, the military's lack of respect for civilian institutions, the absence of entrepreneurship among the wealthy, and the anti-capitalism of the intellectuals—secular as well as clerical.[88] In addition, Sub-Saharan Africa's economic

83. Daniel Pipes, *The Hidden Hand: Middle East Fears of Conspiracy* (London: Palgrave, 1998).

84. Ole Elgstrom, "National Culture and International Negotiations," *Cooperation and Conflict*, Vol. 29, No. 3 (1994), pp. 289–301, at pp. 296–297.

85. R. Cohen, "International Communication: An Intercultural Approach," *Cooperation and Conflict*, Vol. 22, No. 1 (1987), pp. 63–80.

86. See Lucian Pye and Sindey Verba, eds., *Political Culture and Political Development* (Princeton, N.J.: Princeton University Press, 1965); Lawrence E. Harrison, *Who Prospers? How Cultural Values Shape Economic and Political Success* (New York: Basic Books, 1992); Robert Putnam, *Making Democracy Work: Civic Traditions in Modern Italy* (Princeton, N.J.: Princeton University Press, 1993); Thomas Sowell, *Race and Culture: A World View* (New York: Basic Books, 1994); Lawrence E. Harrison and Samuel P. Huntington, eds., *Culture Matters: How Values Shape Human Progress* (New York: Basic Books, 2000).

87. Peter Berger and H. H. Hsiao, eds., *In Search of an East Asian Developmental Model* (New Brunswick, N.J.: Transaction Publishers, 1987).

88. Lawrence Harrison, *Underdevelopment Is a State of Mind: The Latin American Case* (Lanham, Md.: University Press of America, 1988); Carlos Alberto Montaner, "Culture and the Behavior of Elites in Latin America," in Harrison and Huntington, eds., *Culture Matters*, pp. 56–64.

plight has been linked to such attitudes as living in the present rather than worrying about the future, lacking faith in the human ability to control the world, fearing the magical powers of persons in authority, and preferring conspicuous consumption over savings and investment.[89] As a result, Japan was capable of launching its imperial aggression during the 1930s and Taiwan and South Korea have charted an increasingly independent course since the end of the Cold War, whereas the nations of Latin America and Africa have remained weak and mired in debt.

How do cultural motives affect the ends of foreign policy? First, manipulation of the masses with the help of cultural rhetoric can generate so much support for the corresponding foreign policy that the leaders become constrained to do for real what they intended to be for show. For instance, Communist Serb leader Slobodan Milosevic began to talk about Serb victimization at the hands of Croats in order to preempt nationalist rivals. Having thus legitimated nationalism and helped raise nationalist passion, he was then constrained to prove his nationalist credentials by stirring up violent conflict in Croatia, Bosnia, and Kosovo. Since the days of Zia ul-Haq, the generals ruling Pakistan have used militant Islamism to maintain the conflict with India over Kashmir, which, by creating a permanent sense of threat, legitimates their hold over the country. This support for the Islamic insurgents in Kashmir, the radically Islamist Taliban regime of Afghanistan, and the religious schools in Pakistan that breed holy warriors came, however, at a high price: when the United States pressured Pakistan to cooperate in the war on al-Qaeda, Osama bin Laden's Islamist terror network, which had been sheltered by the Taliban, and then to hunt down the remaining al-Qaeda operatives in Pakistan, its military ruler, Pervez Musharraf, had to risk his overthrow at the hands of the militants in order to comply.[90] In short, leaders can become the prisoners of their own cultural rhetoric.

In other words, there are two inherent weaknesses to any purely instrumental account of culture-centered foreign policies. First, the very success of mass manipulation implies that cultural concern can rouse thousands if not millions of people to political action. To be useful as a means to the leaders, religious and ethnic concerns must be perceived as ends by the followers. True, some of those who fight for God and Fatherland are motivated by the personal advantages to be had in despoiling the enemy. Significant numbers who give their support because they per-

---

89. Daniel Etounga-Manguelle, "Does Africa Need a Cultural Adjustment Program?" in Harrison and Huntington, eds., *Culture Matters*, pp. 65–77.

90. For more on the Taliban and Pakistan, see Chapters Ten and Eleven in this volume.

ceive a threat to the cultural community that endows their lives with deeply felt meaning or ardently believe in an idea that promises to improve the world will, however, always exist. Second, leaders can lose control of the cultural manipulation of the masses and become constrained to turn into ends of foreign policy what they intended to be only means. Third, this constraint can become more than just another self-serving calculation for the leaders; for they are not just rational decision-makers, but flesh-and-blood beings who equally feel the need to be in tune with the predominant sentiment of their people. As more and more people take their cultural propaganda to be the truth, the leaders become less and less sure that it was only propaganda to begin with. Fundamentally put, insofar as people form a community that intersubjectively constructs their ideological and cultural reality, the themes that dominate its public discourse become its reality, regardless of their origin. In short, leaders can become prisoners of their cultural rhetoric also in the sense of believing it themselves.

Second, there are cases where the leaders believe in religious and ethnic motives from the beginning. At times, such motives will be in agreement with the course of action suggested by material interests and ideology, as, for instance, in the wars of national liberation that indigenous communities of Asia and Africa led during the twentieth century against the colonial powers of Europe.[91] Invariably, these communities had strong cultural motives for not wanting to be ruled by alien races that imposed strange norms, values, and customs, believed in a different god, and whose advanced forms of political, economic, and social organization undermined their traditional ways of life. Indeed, since these advanced forms sprang from a modern Western rationalism that is inimical to cultural community, the anti-colonial movements may well be understood as so many efforts to defend indigenous cultures against their dissolution by the bureaucratic efficiency of the modern state. In addition to these cultural motives, indigenous people obviously had a material interest in ending colonial rule: being no longer subject to the colonial police

91. Although usually taking place on territory that formally belongs to a colonial power, such wars are foreign policy events insofar as the indigenous population acts collectively to drive out the colonial rulers; for then there are really two distinct political communities, whose members consider each other as foreigners. Seen from this perspective, the relations between colonial power and indigenous community qualify as foreign affairs in the beginning, when the former conquers the latter by force of arms, turn into domestic affairs when the natives give up on resisting their occupiers, and become foreign affairs again when a new indigenous leadership—typically comprised of young intellectuals educated in the imperial metropoles—London, Paris, etc.—raises the consciousness of their people to the point where they act collectively to shake off the foreign yoke.

and army would make them more secure and ending colonial taxation and nationalizing colonial enterprises would make them more prosperous. They knew that the principle of nationalism, coupled with the Marxist rhetoric of anti-colonial liberation, legitimated their struggle on the level of ideas.

In other cases, however, the courses of actions suggested by culture, material interests, and ideology are not so readily reconciled. Given the historical tendency of ideology to displace culture, the ensuing motivational struggle is likely to occur between culture and material interests or between ideology and material interests, that is, across the cleavage identified above.

The foreign policy of the Islamic Republic of Iran provides an instructive example of how leaders with a strong religious motivation will constrain their zeal when the security and well-being of the regime is at stake.[92] Having come to power in the revolution of 1979, the Khomeini regime at first lived up to its religiously inspired anti-Westernism by allowing youthful militants to storm the U.S. embassy and take U.S. diplomats hostage. This act of war against a state of vastly superior power had all the makings of cultural motive trumping security interests, notwithstanding the widely shared perception in the developing world that the United States had lost its will to fight after its defeat in Vietnam and the election of President Jimmy Carter. When it became clear that the newly elected Reagan administration would respond militarily in a major way, the Khomeini regime released the hostages, not wanting to risk an escalation that might have led to its downfall. Having blinked in its contest with the United States, the Great Satan, the Iranian regime subsequently found a safer outlet for its religious zeal in fighting Israel, the Little Satan, by establishing Hizbollah as its terrorist proxy in Lebanon in the early 1980s; for, although Israel had the capability to conduct small-scale air attacks against Iran, it could not launch a conventional operation that would bring down the Khomeini regime and could be trusted not to use its nuclear weapons in response to mere terrorism.

This kind of expedient behavior is, of course, what interest-centered paradigms would expect when states have to make a choice between pursuing cultural imperatives and providing for their security and prosperity. To put it in the language of neorealism, when the constraint posed by the anarchic structure of international politics is relatively loose due to the absence of imminent threat, states have the freedom to indulge their cultural as well as ideological ends; but when the constraint tightens

92. For an extended discussion of Iran, see Chapters Eight and Nine in this volume.

through confrontation with a powerful adversary willing to use force, states will do what it takes to preserve their independent existence.

The Uncertain Future of Culture in Foreign Affairs

The continuing spread of the ideas and practices of modern rationalism—variously described as modernization, state building, globalization, and Westernization—may well put an end to culture as a significant factor in foreign affairs. In particular, the general acceptance of liberal and capitalist norms could give the world what it has so far created in the West, namely a zone of peace, democracy, free markets, and human rights, where religious and ethnic motives have been thoroughly excised from the purposes of foreign policy. In other words, Immanuel Kant's prophetic statement that the rational and "free exercise of the human will on a large scale" gives "hope that, after many revolutions, with all their transforming effects, the highest purpose of nature, a universal cosmopolitan existence, will at last be realized" may indeed come true.[93] For cultural particularity has been waning among the urban elites of the developing world, creating a "new breed of men and women for whom religion, culture, and ethnic nationality are marginal elements in a working identity."[94] The implication of such a global modern society for foreign politics is not difficult to infer: as habits of thought and action increasingly obey the liberal and consumerist modes laid down by Western rationalism and cultural identity is diminished to a matter of holiday foods and costumes, culture ceases to affect both the ends and the means of foreign policy in any significant way.[95]

On the other hand, it has become clear since the end of the Cold War

---

93. Immanuel Kant, *Idea for a Universal History with a Cosmopolitan Purpose*, in *Kant's Political Writings*, ed. Hans Reiss, trans. H.B. Nisbet (Cambridge: Cambridge University Press, 1970), pp. 41–53, at 41, 51.

94. Benjamin R. Barber, *Jihad vs. McWorld: How Globalism and Tribalism Are Reshaping the World* (New York: Ballantine Books, 1995), p. 16.

95. This inference obviously rests on my definition of culture as the integrated, affectively-rooted meaning that shapes a Herderian community of character. For if one followed the postmodern idea of culture as any kind of meaning, one may arrive at the idea that globalization has given rise to a "global culture," based on the shared experience of working in modern factories and offices, wearing blue jeans, driving cars, listening to rock music, and watching American sitcoms—as suggested by Mary C. Bateson, "Beyond Sovereignty: An Emerging Global Civilization," in R.B.J. Walker and S. Mendlovitz, eds., *Contending Sovereignties: Redefining Political Community* (Boulder, Colo.: Lynne Rienner, 1990). Then, however, one would have trouble understanding why culture continues to engender violent conflict on account of its particularity.

that the global spread of modern ways has generated considerable resistance in the non-Western world. In the terms coined by contemporary philosopher Benjamin Barber, the "globalism" of "McWorld" has been challenged by the "tribalism" of "Jihad."[96] The Islamic world has been shaken by a radicalism that seeks to eliminate Western influences from society and return to the days of the Prophet Mohammad. In India, leadership has passed from the secular Congress Party to Hindu nationalists. To make up for the collapse of communism, the rulers of China have created a nationalist sentiment that yearns to recover the country's ancient supremacy. More significantly, East Asian nations have defended their authoritarian policies on the grounds that human rights are Western conventions rather than universal truths and, moreover, conflict with their "Asian values," that is, their tradition of communal authority. In Eastern Europe and Central Asia, the collapse of Soviet communism has left a void of meaning that nationalism is rushing to fill. In Africa, the widespread failure to turn administrative areas carved out by colonial cartographers into functioning nation-states has led to an upsurge of violence along ethnic lines.

Is this resurgence of religious and ethnic motives in foreign affairs merely a traditionalist reaction that will be overcome in due course by the onward march of rationalism, as it happened in the West itself? Or is it a sign that this march is nearing a limit, as traditional and indigenous peoples rise to the defense of their cultural communities in order to keep at bay the alienation that liberalism and capitalism bring?

For it can at least be doubted whether it is natural for people at all times and in all places to worship individuality, presuppose equality, celebrate diversity, and maximize profit. After all, being an autonomous individual also undermines community, assuming equality in all matters mitigates the aspiration for what is higher, and rejoicing in diversity deprives us of a rooted sense of how one ought to live. Profit maximization leads not only to prosperity but also to a highly competitive society with ever-rising requirements for success, the cancerous growth of shopping malls, industrial zones, and housing developments, and the mere simulation of cultural and natural experience in theme parks, such as Disneyland and SeaWorld. In addition and perhaps most significantly, Western rationalism leads to a loss of respect for the sacred, as science and technology demystify the world and enable us to manipulate nature and life.

Hasan al-Banna, founder of the Muslim Brotherhood and thus grandfather of today's militant Islamist movements, railed already in 1920

96. Barber, *Jihad vs. McWorld*.

against "the wave of atheism and lewdness" that led to the "devastation of religion and morality on the pretext of individual and intellectual freedom."[97] An official of the Iranian Ministry of Culture and Islamic Guidance expressed the same idea in 1994 in reference to Western satellite television: "these programs, prepared by international imperialism, are part of an extensive plot to wipe out our religious and sacred values."[98] Similarly, Hindu nationalism can be traced to the founding of *Arya Samaj* (Society of Arians) in 1875 by Dayandad Saraswati, who vowed to fight British rule, end the Islamic and Western corruption of Hindu values, and return Hindu society to the Vedic Golden Age (A.D. fourth–fifth centuries, when India was ruled by the god Ram). Although Hindu nationalism's visceral impetus has been directed mostly against Muslims, it is also hostile to the Western cosmopolitan ideal, hoping to make India into an assertive nation-state based on the cultural ideal of *hinduttva* (Hinduness). Thus, the leaders of the Bharatyia Janata Party, the parliamentary face of contemporary Hindu nationalism, not only exploded two thermonuclear warheads in 1998 to intimidate the Muslim state of Pakistan (which posed no existential threat to India), encouraged the massacre of Muslims by Hindu mobs in Gujarat in 2002, and politicized conversions to Christianity, but also made the rejection of Western-style secularism their guiding principle.

True, these traditionalists are constrained by the anarchic structure of international politics to build or, at a minimum, buy the weaponry that Western science and technology have invented. To this end, they also need to generate a sufficiently large economic surplus, which in turn implies a capitalist mode of production. Thus, as Middle East scholar Bernard Lewis has observed, "the argument is increasingly heard in the Middle East that what the region's countries need is modernization without westernization—that is, to say, accepting, or rather, acquiring the products of Western material culture, perhaps also the science and technology that produced them, but without the cultural baggage and false values and depraved way of life attached to them."[99] Thus far, a number of countries, such as Saudi Arabia, the Gulf emirates, Singapore, and China, seem to have succeeded at this task rather well, having introduced modern forms of production, communication, and administration, while

---

97. John O. Voll, "Fundamentalism in the Sunni Arab World," in Martin E. Marty and R. Scott Appleby, eds., *Fundamentalisms Observed* (Chicago: University of Chicago Press), p. 360.

98. Chris Hedges, "Teheran Journal," *New York Times*, August 16, 1994, p. A2.

99. Bernard Lewis, "The West and the Middle East," *Foreign Affairs,* Vol. 76, No. 1 (January/February 1997): pp. 114–130, at 116.

keeping at bay such influences as individualism, pluralism, constitution-alism, and democracy.

Whether they can do so over the long run, however, remains an open question, for modern means of resource utilization may be so closely tied to rationalist modes of thought and social organization that people who use the former will eventually adopt the latter. For instance, the fact that industrialization requires people to become laborers that freely enter into employment contracts and to move to cities where they live as individu-als ought to make them realize their potential to be free. Alternatively, the need to think analytically and critically about technological and scientific matters ought to lead them to apply these skills to religious and political matters. Indeed, it is effects like these that modernization theory has taken to explain the correlation between economic development and po-litical liberalization.[100] The most important contemporary evidence for this argument comes from East Asia, where Japan, South Korea, and Tai-wan established democratic and partially liberal institutions in roughly the same order in which they developed economically.

To explore this question further is beyond the scope of this essay. Suffice it thus to end with the observation that the future of culture as a significant factor in foreign politics will depend on the willingness and ability of the least Westernized peoples to maintain their cultural particu-larity, while being constrained to adopt modern and increasingly univer-sal forms of resource utilization. Should they fail in this difficult en-deavor, the notion that religious and ethnic motives ought to be taken seriously would eventually become as quaint to them as it is to most Westerners today.

---

100. See David Lerner, *The Passing of Traditional Society* (Glencoe, Ill.: Free Press, 1958); Seymour Martin Lipset, "Some Social Requisites of Democracy: Economic De-velopment and Political Legitimacy," *American Political Science Review*, Vol. 53, No. 1 (March 1959), pp. 69–105; Lucian Pye, *Communications and Political Development* (Princeton, N.J.: Princeton University Press, 1963); Walt W. Rostow, *The Stages of Eco-nomic Growth: A Non-Communist Manifesto* (Cambridge: Cambridge University Press, 1967).

Chapter 3

Beyond Blood and Belief: Culture and Foreign Policy Conduct

Douglas W. Blum

The point of departure for this essay is the interrelationship between foreign policy conduct and culture in the former Soviet Caspian states. As argued below, the two affect one another, although in different ways. Formal, highly symbolic traditional culture generally does not drive foreign policymaking, although once articulated as a basis of policy, it can subsequently exert constraining effects. However informal, interactively based cultural assumptions and identity constructs do exert effects on policy, even though these tend to be constitutive rather than directly causal. Often, interactively shaped changes in images of Self and Other give rise to new understandings of appropriate conduct, leading to consolidated, deepened, or changed textures of relations among states. The development of foreign policy is therefore contingent: strongly influenced by prevailing *Realpolitik* views but filtered through specifically national culture and identity discourse.[1]

A veritable ocean of scholarly ink has been spilled on the topic of "culture"; no effort will be made to review this vast literature here. Instead, as a mercifully brief statement of definitions, culture will be treated as a set of meanings, values, and symbolic representations characteristic of a particular group; in this case, the focus will be on official state culture. A key related concept is identity, understood here as being implicated in culture in the sense that such meanings, values, and symbols constitute the proximate framework within which conceptions of Self

---

1. For an additional view of culture and foreign policy as a nexus, see Ido Oren, "Is Culture Independent of National Security? How America's National Security Concerns Shaped 'Political Culture' Research," *European Journal of International Relations,* Vol. 6, No. 4 (December 2000), pp. 543–573.

emerge to play their "problem-solving" role.[2] The focus here, then, will be the influence of such ideas on foreign policy conduct, as well as the reciprocal influence of foreign policy conduct on such ideas.

So far, however, culture and culturally bounded identities have been described in relatively passive terms as something that happens within society and across social boundaries, rather than something actively created through conscious agency. This is far from being the case. On the contrary, "nation-building" is a *political* project undertaken in order to constitute a social and institutional framework for the realization of elite values and interests.[3] As such, nation-building occurs through a variety of official and non-official cultural channels: the mobilization of historical myths, social values, symbols of nationhood, and political norms, the crystallization of which imparts a construct of national identity. Identities, finally, confer interests that in turn imply basic tendencies for international conduct. While national identities are often multiple and contingent instead of singular and fixed, nevertheless the set of possible Other- and Self-understandings is limited. The result is that in constructing national identity, the state also constitutes a range of meaningful and legitimate actions, which both facilitates and, inevitably, constrains its policymaking flexibility.[4] From this perspective, foreign policy is largely a matter of attempting to arrange Self-Other relations in such a way as to be consistent with and reproductive of national identity.

Yet foreign policy interests do not arise only from and in response to social discourse at home. As one will also see, external conditions at times powerfully impinge on state interests, constraining action in pre-

---

2. T.K. Fitzgerald, *Metaphors of Identity* (Albany: SUNY Press, 1993), pp. 186–194. In his own work, the author has treated culture and identity as constituent parts of larger political belief systems incorporating relevant ontological, normative, and concrete "factual," as well as causal beliefs. Douglas Blum, "The Soviet Foreign Policy Belief System: Beliefs, Politics, and Foreign Policy Outcomes," *International Studies Quarterly*, Vol. 37, No. 4 (December 1993), pp. 373–394.

3. It is important to bear in mind that culture is fluid and constantly evolving, or being reinscribed in social awareness through reflexive behavior and reinterpretation. The same is of course true of identities, which are still more directly open to challenge and adaptation. As Yosef Lapid has observed, "cultures and identities are emergent and constructed (rather than fixed and natural), contested and polymorphic (rather than unitary and singular), and interactive and process-like (rather than static and essence-like). . . ." See Yosef Lapid, "Culture's Ship: Returns and Departures in International Relations Theory," in Yosef Lapid and Friedrich Krachtowil, eds., *The Return of Culture and Identity in IR Theory* (London: Lynne Rienner, 1996), pp. 3–20.

4. A good introduction to the main strands and concepts of the constructivist literature is ibid.

dictable ways. To some extent, this is a function of material conditions (and the often predictable ways in which these are construed) as well as the basic need to survive. In addition, neoliberal notions of modernity and power influence policymaking in the Caspian region just as elsewhere in the world. Here the essay returns to culture, but not simply in the sense of an independent national culture constructed by agents free from external constraints. Instead, because the ideas and identity constructs associated with neoliberalism are hegemonic in nature, they must be analyzed at the global level rather than at the national level alone. Just as culture and identity arise from domestic processes connected with state building and thereby affect foreign policy, so too foreign policy interests—themselves partly exogenously and even hegemonically influenced—affect official articulations of culture and identity.

The following sections begin with an overview of native-traditional[5] imagery, which is explored as a medium of discourse within which state actors attempt to construct national identities consistent with state-building and the consolidation of sovereignty. As one will see, some elements of this discourse have been more consequential for foreign policy behavior than others. Next, the role of pragmatic considerations (themselves rooted in a systemic culture of international relations) are explored for their effect on policy outcomes. The result is to differentiate areas of relative sensitivity to national culture versus other areas of externally constrained identity and foreign policy practice.

Culture, Nation-building, and State-building

Since gaining their independence at the end of 1991, the Caspian states have undertaken nation-building for two main reasons: as a way of consolidating the leadership's power and as a means of fostering social cohesion and political stability amid the wreckage of the Soviet system. Along the way, the state seeks legitimacy by presenting itself as the guardian of supposedly quintessential national ideas and characteristics. Portraying largely reinvented constructions as deeply embedded traditions requires considerable artifice. The entire process rests on making explicit cultural claims, some of which are accepted more or less unproblematically while others must be sedulously promoted. Additionally, as mentioned above, in pursuing these goals, the state both empowers and constrains its own ability to develop policies consistent with its preferred cultural narrative.

---

5. In other chapters in this book, authors have used the term local, indigenous culture, instead of "native-traditional culture."

The question, then, is what influence nation-building has on the determination of foreign policy interests through the mobilization of culture and national identity.

Before continuing, one important caveat must be made. Unfortunately, the ability to link national culture and identity to Caspian states' foreign policy in any definitive way remains limited. In Azerbaijan and Armenia, which are caught up in the turmoil of military conflict, the leaderships appear to enjoy very high levels of elite agreement on strategic issues as well as public support for official foreign policy goals. Elsewhere throughout the Caspian basin, however, it is difficult to gauge the extent to which political culture is united or fragmented as well as relevant to foreign policy matters. This is largely a function of repression and the inability of marginal groups to publicize their views widely, especially in Kazakhstan and still more so in Turkmenistan. Nevertheless, it is possible to gauge prevailing (and often well institutionalized) social constructions relevant to national identity. Therefore, without pretending to provide a definitive answer, the following sections offer a tentative and illustrative sketch of the various interrelationships between culture and foreign policy in the post-Soviet Caspian states.

Native-Traditional Culture and Foreign Policy

Indigenous (or pseudo-indigenous) culture and identity constructs quickly emerged in the social discourse of the post-Soviet states. As developed in elite formulations, these ideas were intended to contribute to the consolidation of state institutions as well as a new national identity, themselves constitutive of each state's newfound sovereignty.

Perhaps the most obvious and ultimately the most consequential form of national identity construction involves the narrative of intrinsic uniqueness. All of the former Soviet states have engaged in such "invention of tradition" as a means of consolidating society around new institutions, and as the basis for conducting independent foreign relations. For example, in Kazakhstan, the process of inculcating nationhood has been explicitly linked to the establishment of sovereignty, even while the country's allegedly historic "Eurasian" character has been officially presented as a solid basis for seeking institutional accommodation with Russia.[6] Similarly, scholars and cultural elites elsewhere have dutifully (and

---

6. Martha Brill Olcott, *Kazakhstan: Unfulfilled Promise* (Washington, D.C.: Carnegie Endowment for International Peace, 2002), pp. 58–67.

often, eagerly) labored to produce "homeland myths," as well as myths of ancient origin, glorious descent, and intrinsic national character.[7]

Among the many cultural claims articulated as part of these state- and nation-building projects, the idea of Turkic roots stands out as a common theme for Azerbaijan and the Central Asian countries. In the aftermath of the Soviet collapse (and to a significant extent even before, among the elite), notions of Turkism quickly spread throughout most of Central Asia. Not surprisingly, this notion was especially actively promoted in Turkey itself, where state elites clearly hoped to use such myth-making in order to expand Turkish cultural, economic, and geopolitical influence.[8] The idea of a shared Turkic heritage has also consistently been espoused by cultural figures in the new states, however, including leading political figures as well as academics and political analysts, and has featured prominently in official historiography as part of the effort to establish central myths of origin and descent.[9]

On the other hand, the particular construction of Turkism shared among the post-Soviet states is extremely broad and inclusive, allowing national ideologists to assert ancestral linkages or cultural resonances among seemingly disparate tribes and thereby legitimating the drive for continued political integration and centralization.[10] The official promulgation of Turkic cultural identity on the part of the post-Soviet states was also quite clearly strategic in helping to substantiate historically the assertion of political distance from the Soviet Union. In these ways, the early rhetoric and symbolism of Turkism was neither superficial nor cynical. Instead, it represented a serious attempt to ground an autonomous national identity in plausible, culturally meaningful, and historically respectable terms. For these reasons, it did not imply any particular affinity for Turkey, either in domestic institutional or international politics.[11]

---

7. For example, see Graham Smith, *The Post-Soviet States: Mapping the Politics of Transition* (New York: Oxford University Press, 1999).

8. Shireen Hunter, *The Transcaucasus in Transition: Nation-building and Conflict* (Washington, D.C.: Center for Strategic and International Studies, 1994), pp. 161–170.

9. Viktor Shnirelman, "National Identity and Myths of Ethnogenesis in Transcaucasia," in Graham Smith, Edward Allworth, and Vivien Law, eds., *Nation-Building in the Post-Soviet Borderlands: The Politics of National Identities* (Cambridge: Cambridge University Press, 1998), pp. 48–66; Edward Allworth, "History and Group Identity in Central Asia," in *Nation-Building in the Post-Soviet Borderlands,* pp. 67–90.

10. For comparison, see the literature on use of Arab nationalism to unite various tribal identities. Philip S. Khoury and Joseph Kostiner, eds., *Tribes and State Formation in the Middle East* (New York: I.B. Tauris, 1991).

11. R. Craig Nation, "The Turkic and Other Muslim Peoples of Central Asia, the Cau-

Even in Azerbaijan, which bears by far the closest cultural and linguistic resemblance, the turn toward an explicitly Turkic identity did not emerge overnight and was ultimately the subject of intense political dispute under the ultranationalist Abulfaz Elchibey regime.[12] Since coming to power, the Heydar Aliev regime and its official cultural apparatus followed a more balanced, independent path resting on a unique national identity blending elements of Eastern and Western heritage. Also, certainly none of the other states have gravitated toward a Turkish sphere of influence. From Ankara's perspective, then, the practical results of this cultural advance have been meager.

Similar observations may be made about Islam in the same countries: despite the prominent emphasis on religious themes as part of the narrative of independence, the specific uses of such ideas have been overwhelmingly secular.[13] That is, Islam provides a cultural vehicle for the state in its claim to represent an indigenous national identity. The role played by Islam in this process is largely symbolic, limited to evocative representations on state flags, currencies, and the like, as well as marking seasonal changes and social rituals. The ruling regimes hope that, along the way, those truly religious groups in society are co-opted or at least deflected in their political goals. All states of the region share a deep concern over the prospect of militant Islamism sparking unrest, which could undermine the dominant identity discourse and the state's social foundation. For all of these reasons, the practical effect of Islam on foreign policymaking is marginal at best. Perhaps its most significant influence lies in facilitating membership in various non-Western Muslim intergovernmental organizations (IGOs), especially the Economic Cooperation Organization and the Organization of the Islamic Conference, as well as eliciting these organizations' support on various policy issues, such as the Nagorno-Karabagh conflict.

Despite the limited effect of stereotypical cultural factors on foreign

casus, and the Balkans," in Vojtech Mastny and R. Craig Nation, eds., *Turkey Between East and West: New Challenges for a Rising Regional Power* (Boulder, Colo.: Westview Press, 1996), pp. 97–130.

12. Shireen Hunter, "Azerbaijan: Search for Identity," in Ian Bremmer and Ray Taras, eds., *Nations and Politics in the Soviet Successor States* (Cambridge: Cambridge University Press, 1997), pp. 225–260; Tadeusz Swietochowski, "Azerbaijan: Perspectives from the Crossroads," *Central Asian Survey*, Vol. 18, Issue 4 (December 1999), pp. 419–435.

13. On Islam's political uses for the state, see Graham Smith, *The Post-Soviet States: Mapping the Politics of Transition* (New York: Oxford University Press, 1999), especially Chapter 4.

policy decision-making, culture—and identity—nevertheless play an important role in shaping perceptions as well as understandings of appropriate and meaningful responses to external developments.

For example, consider the shift in 2000–2001 by Azerbaijan away from balancing against Russia and toward seeking some sort of lasting accommodation. This included convergence of positions on Caspian Sea delimitation as well as limited security cooperation.[14] Following "geopolitics," it may be argued that lower expectations of U.S. assistance, especially military aid, led to Baku's sober readjustment of seeking to mend fences with Moscow. Yet on an empirical level, Azerbaijan's policy betrayed an emotionality and almost spiteful prickliness at odds with the rational strategic calculations ascribed to *Realpolitik*. Indeed, the shift in Baku's diplomacy was marked by expressions of irritation at Western pressure over Nagorno-Karabagh, especially U.S. Section 907 of the Freedom Support Act (which remained in full force until January 2002), as well as U.S. and European rebukes over domestic political repression.[15] At the same time, changes in Russia's Caspian policy were taking place under President Vladimir Putin, associated with a new understanding of Russia's place in the world. This led Russian diplomacy to become more assertively pragmatic in seeking to divide subsoil energy resources among the littoral states.[16]

Certainly there is no evidence to suggest that prevailing images of Russia within the Azerbaijani elite changed diametrically; indeed, elements of suspicion remain. Clearly U.S. willingness to project a modicum of military force after September 11, 2001, led to a renewed warming of

---

14. "Protokol o sotrudnichestve mezhdu sovetami bezopastnosti Azerbaidzhana i Rossii podpisan v Baku" [Protocol on Cooperation Between Security Councils of Azerbaijan and Russia Signed in Baku], *Ezhednevnye novosti* (Baku), June 16, 2000; "Russian Official Hopes for 'New Impetus' in Relations with Azerbaijan," *BBC Monitoring Service*, July 3, 2000, from Turan news agency, Baku, in Russian, June 29, 2000; "Pozitsii Rossii i Azerbaidzhana po Kaspiiu sblizhaiutsia" [Positions of Russia and Azerbaijan On Caspian Come Closer], *Ezhednevnye novosti* (Baku), October 17, 2000.

15. Personal interviews, Azerbaijan Foreign Ministry, June 2000. In addition, in the words of then First Vice-President of the State Oil Company of the Azerbaijan Republic (SOCAR) and son of the president, Ilham Aliev, the West is attempting to "thrust a humiliating peace on Azerbaijan" in order to "destabilize the situation in Azerbaijan and bring to power weak and insignificant forces obedient to the West." See "Karabagh: Azeri President's Son Quoted on 'Military' Option, Slams West," *BBC Monitoring*, March 3, 2001, from Interfax news agency, Moscow, March 3, 2001.

16. Douglas Blum, "Russia's New Caspian Policy," PONARS Memo 162 (October 2000), online at: <http://www.csis.org/ruseura/ponars/>.

relations between Washington and Baku.[17] In understanding the consolidation of stable relations between Russia and Azerbaijan, however, identity would seem to be implicated. Intriguing indications of this can be glimpsed in published accounts of meetings between Heydar Aliev and Vladimir Putin, for example, Aliev's observation that "cooperation with Russia progresses intensively in all directions: in the sphere of science, culture, and education."[18] Such public expressions both reflect and significantly reproduce identity change. The partially disconfirmed images of benevolent Others (the United States and Europe) and of an unalterably hostile Other (Russia), therefore, necessarily affected future Azerbaijani concepts of national identity and appropriate foreign policy action.[19] In this case, the resulting reconfiguration of identities has opened up a number of newly viable options, leading to a lasting shift in alignment. Although this insight does not provide a causal explanation for Azerbaijan's initial change in foreign policy, it does shed light on how and why that change took the particular form that it did.

Simple material or geographical explanations alone cannot account for the sustained and apparently deepening rapprochement in Russian-Azerbaijani relations, which obviously stands in contrast to relations between Russia and some other former Soviet states. Thus, the foreign policies of Belarus, Moldova, and Georgia have differed markedly (Belarus "bandwagoning" with Russia, and Moldova and Georgia "balancing" against Russia instead) depending on internal politics and associated identity platforms, despite essentially similar structural positions *vis-à-vis* their powerful neighbor. Indeed, as numerous analysts have observed, the revised neorealist argument that states balance against perceived threats smuggles in a cultural or identity-based factor, inasmuch as it begs the question of what constitutes threat perception.[20] Here the expla-

---

17. See "Remarks by Deputy Secretary of State Richard Armitage at a United States–Azerbaijan Chamber of Commerce Conference," Renaissance Hotel, Washington, D.C., March 8, 2002, available from Azerbaijan Internet Links, online at: <http://resources.net.az/d/us0302.htm#05>.

18. "Vladimir Putin udovletvoren intensivnym razvitiem sotrudnichestva Rossii i Azerbaidzhana v razlichnykh oblastiakh" [Vladimir Putin is satisfied with the intensive development of cooperation between Russia and Azerbaijan in various areas], *Trend* (Baku), September 23, 2002.

19. The observations of prominent Azerbaijani analyst Eldar Namazov are revealing on this point. "Vremia sobirat miny" [Time to Gather Up Mines], *Obschaya Gazeta*, January 24, 2002.

20. See Michael Barnett, "Identity and Alliances in the Middle East," in Peter J. Katzenstein, ed., *The Culture of National Security: Norms and Identity in World Politics* (New York: Columbia University Press, 1996), pp. 400–447.

nation for the changed tenor of Russian-Azerbaijani relations must be sought at the level of identity and associated perceptions. The increasingly well-institutionalized nature of their relationship suggests—although it is still too early to say with certainty—that it is beginning to undergo a fundamental change in terms of mutual trust.

Another example of the subtle effects of culture and identity may be found in Turkmenistan's foreign policy. On the one hand, its virtually unchanged, bunker-like policy is hard to gauge due to the surrounding veil of secrecy. Nevertheless, the broad contours of official policy are clear enough: despite an erratic tendency to align with Iran on various specific questions of Caspian Sea delimitation, Ashghabad's international posture has remained fastidiously neutral, thus providing a fine example of "hiding" behavior (as opposed to balancing or bandwagoning).[21] This diplomatic stance is mirrored by a general closedness to the outside world, including media, foreign travel, investment, and so on. Given the dictatorial structure of decision-making, this stance presumably reflects the personal preferences of Turkmenistan's supreme leader himself, Saparmurad Niyazov, who has offered his own cultural explanation, suggesting that Turkmenistan requires a separate route to democratization and development in view of its unique and historically backward national character.

Yet even Niyazov's preferences require explanation. In this instance, beneath the declarative policy appears to be a fervent wish to avoid Russian dominance coupled with a deep distrust of Western political institutions. For such reasons, from 1997–2001 the Turkmen regime refused to transport natural gas through the Russian-controlled pipeline system at advantageous prices, regardless of the ruinous effect this had on the already disastrous Turkmen economy. Not only has the associated image of Russia not been disconfirmed by any dramatic overture from Moscow (despite a more conciliatory approach by Gazprom under Chief Executive Alexei Miller's leadership), but lack of involvement with the West prevents the emergence of any potentially offsetting source of national identification. On the contrary, Russia remains the essential Other in opposition to which Ashghabad's foreign policy interests are defined. This perspective was formally institutionalized almost immediately after independence, in January 1992, when Niyazov announced plans to rebuild the Gok-Tepe fortress. The site of a major Turkmen victory over Tsar Alexander III's troops in 1879, the rebuilding of the fortress made symbolic resistance to Russian encroachment a fundamental component of

---

21. On this term and its broader theoretical relevance, see Paul Schroeder, "Historical Reality vs. Neo-realist Theory," *International Security*, Vol. 19, No. 1 (Summer 1994), pp. 108–148.

national political culture.[22] This symbol and its explicit geopolitical significance remain central to official constructions of Self and Other.[23] In this way, regardless of the clearly entrepreneurial uses of culture, the fact remains that the presence of such cultural and identity constructs and their discursive salience appear to affect the availability and even the appropriateness of various policymaking options.[24]

Before concluding this assessment, it should be noted that native-traditional political culture may not be distributed uniformly and evenly throughout society—or even within the ruling elite. Thus, the very existence of a "prevailing" political culture or set of identity formations is itself an empirical question. A case in point is Russia, where political culture appears essentially fragmented rather than whole, except perhaps at the highest level of generality. Indeed, the constellation of foreign policy orientations currently represented in Moscow includes such a multiplicity of cultural ideas and identity attachments that even such opposed parties or movements as Vladimir Zhirinovskii's ultranationalists, Gennadi Ziuganov's anti-Western communists, and Andrei Kozyrev's westernized liberals have, at various times, garnered considerable support since the fall of the Soviet Union. The overt emphasis on cultural arguments has not diminished under Vladimir Putin, according to whom "Russia was and will remain a great power. It is preconditioned by the inseparable characteristics of its geopolitical, economic, and cultural existence. They determined the mentality of Russians and the policy of the government throughout our history and they cannot help but do so now."[25]

While Putin acknowledges that this quality is not based primarily on military strength, his conceptualization of Russian greatness is nevertheless linked here to its geopolitical power and imperial past. Thus, even while the officially articulated national self-image may be rather restrained, a deeper tendency remains to perceive developments around

22. Shahram Akbarzedeh, "National Identity and Political Legitimacy in Turkmenistan," *Nationalities Papers*, Vol. 27, No. 2 (June 1999), pp. 271–290, at p. 273.

23. "V edinstve–nasha sila" [In Unity is Our Strength], *Novosti Turkmenistana*, January 10, 2002.

24. Ahmet Kuru, "Between the State and Cultural Zones: Nation Building in Turkmenistan," *Central Asian Survey*, Vol. 21, No. 1 (March 2002), pp. 71–90.

25. Putin's statement of the "Russian Idea" was first published on the Russian government website and is available in Vladimir Putin, with Nataliya Gevorkyan, Natalya Timakova, and Andrei Kolesnikov, *First Person: An Astonishingly Frank Self-Portrait by Russia's President;* translated by Catherine Fitzpatrick (New York: PublicAffairs, 2000), Appendix, "Russia at the Turn of the Millennium."

the country's borders in terms of potentially zero-sum changes in Russia's geopolitical influence.[26]

Yet national identity is not singular but multiple, and domestic as well as international developments affect the salience of particular constructs. Thus, Putin has also been able to draw on other cultural values and identities in order to negotiate a major shift in foreign policy orientation following the terrorist attacks of September 11, 2001, moving closer to the United States and emphasizing the similar aspects of the two countries' respective cultural endowments. To some extent, this is related to the increasingly pro-European orientation in Russia's identity discourse and international conduct.[27] It remains to be seen whether the new rapprochement will become consolidated in a lasting way, including acceptance of further expansion of the North Atlantic Treaty Organization (NATO) and an abiding U.S. role in Eurasian security matters. Even if it does, a distinct cluster of values and practices derived from Soviet and pre-Soviet experience will long remain and, with them, an alternative Russian identity tied up with empire and the exertion of power.[28] For the purposes of this essay, however, more important than foretelling the future is understanding the profound role of cultural and identity factors in shaping whatever outcomes occur. In this context, the above observations reaffirm the point that "national" culture is not necessarily reduceable to a single uniform or static cluster of beliefs and norms but may instead be dynamic and varied, including numerous overlapping layers of partly shared symbols and intertwined meanings—some of which at any given moment are accepted more widely than others.

---

26. For example, Aleksandr Dugin, despite his hardline expansionist predilections, remains influential as an "expert" on geopolitical matters. For a discussion, see Ilan Berman, "Slouching Toward Eurasia?" *Perspective*, Volume 12, No. 1 (September–October 2001), online at: <http://www.bu.edu/iscip/>. Another prominent example is Aleksandr Neklessa, who asserts that Russia is inherently opposed to the spread of "Western European civilization" and carries within itself an alternative, Orthodox basis for reestablishing global community. Aleksandr Neklessa, "Konets tsivilizatsii, ili zigzag istorii," *Znamia*, No. 1 (1998): pp. 165–179. A good overview is Timo Piirainen, "The Fall of an Empire, the Birth of a Nation: Perceptions of the New Russian National Identity," in Chris Chulos and Timo Piirainen, eds., *The Fall of an Empire, the Birth of a Nation: National Identities in Russia* (Burlington, Vt: Ashgate, 2000), pp. 161–196.

27. Alla Kassianova, "Russia: Still Open to the West? Evolution of the State Identity in the Foreign Policy and Security Discourse," *Europe-Asia Studies*, Vol. 53, No. 6 (September 2001), pp. 821–839.

28. Igor Zevelev, "The Russian Quest for a National Identity: Implications for Security in Eurasia," in Sharyl Cross et al., eds., *Global Security Beyond the Millennium: American and Russian Perspectives* (New York: St. Martin's Press, 1999), pp. 110–130.

Foreign Policy Conduct and the Strategic Appropriation of Culture

It is possible to discern numerous instances in which prevailing culture and identity tend to foster national interests and general foreign policy orientations. Yet in keeping with the artificial, state-led character of national culture in the Caspian region, it is also the case that culture—at least officially promulgated culture—*follows* foreign policy.[29] In this scenario, governing elites seek institutional affiliations and display normative ideas for pragmatic reasons related to international affairs, in spite of their weak historical roots. In such cases, instrumentalism is involved, as external pressures (themselves partly normative and institutional) influence the development of national identity constructs and foreign policy conduct.

Before proceeding further, a clarification is needed. As already discussed, the theoretical orientation of this chapter is that culture and related identity constructs play a critical role in shaping foreign policy by providing a delimited frame of reference and problem-solving capacity, as well as a logic of meaningfulness to guide action. Such cultural and identity constructs are not exclusively indigenous, however; this is all the more true under conditions of globalization. In the former Soviet Union, new ideas have made extensive inroads into elite (and to a lesser extent, popular) culture, with an often-telling effect on foreign policymaking. An example is the widespread conclusion among post-Soviet leaderships that market institutions and foreign investments are conducive to national growth, and therefore that international integration (including membership in the World Trade Organization) would promote national welfare in the long run.

The critical point here is that such ideas represent a truly hegemonic international discourse of neoliberalism.[30] While culture and identity are inextricably bound up in their appropriation at the national level, it is not the case that pre-existing constructs are affecting foreign policy choices. The advent of what may be termed "global-modern" culture imparts new values and practical understandings of international politics, as well as a new identity with which to pursue national goals.[31] In this respect, it

---

29. The sequence of the influence of culture and foreign policy is also discussed in Chapter Four in this volume.

30. Robert W. Cox, *Production, Power, and World Order: Social Forces in the Making of History* (New York: Columbia University Press, 1987), pp. 211–253.

31. Nadezhda Lebedeva, "Rol kulturnoi distantsii v formirovanii novykh identichnostei" [The Role of Cultural Distance in the Formation of New Identities] in Martha

seems more accurate to speak of exogenously imposed foreign policy interests influencing domestic uses of culture than of culture (in the native-traditional sense) influencing foreign policy interests. For example, in an interview, Azerbaijan Minister of Education Misir Mardanov called for introducing a new system focused on middle school and based on international experience. When asked which model was preferable, Soviet or Western, he responded, "Without a doubt, Western!" In Mardanov's view, the Soviet system did away with illiteracy but was too centralized and "closed to the outside world."[32] In sum, systematic state programs are designed to promote changes in culture and identity in ways calculated to foster desired foreign policy outcomes.

An example is the formal endorsement of democratic elections, as in the case of municipal government reform in Azerbaijan. After being denied entry into the Council of Europe in 1998 due in part to its lack of local self-government, the state hastily arranged public meetings to advertise the European approach and mandate its formal adoption.[33] Not surprisingly, despite superficial appearances, such lip service to liberal precepts soon ran afoul of other, more deeply rooted practices, and reports of transgressions against democratic rules and procedures soon abounded. The same is true in other Caspian states, especially Armenia and Kazakhstan.[34] This is generally not a matter of local authorities refusing to implement national policy guidelines. Instead, in many cases, it appears that the federal authorities themselves are behind the obstruction of election laws, inasmuch as the introduction of democracy threatens the upper echelons of political power in these highly centralized, authoritarian states.[35] This pattern of conduct reveals the purely symbolic and legitimating significance of engaging in ostensible democratization.

Olcott, Valery Tishkov, and Alexei Malashenko, eds., *Identichnost i konflikty v post-sovetskikh gosudarstvakh* [Identity and Conflict in the Post-Soviet States] (Moscow: Carnegie Center, 1997), pp. 64–82, especially pp. 71–74.

32. "Ministerstvo obrazobaniia nachinaet reformu" [Ministry of Education Begins Reform], *Zerkalo*, July 1, 2000.

33. "Models of Local Administration and Municipal Government in Europe," *AzadInform* 49, March 2, 1999, in *Habarlar-L Digest*, March 2, 1999; "CCS Held a Workshop on the Theme 'Municipal Elections'," *AzadInform* 74, April 5, 1999, in *Habarlar-L Digest*, April 6, 1999; "Azerbaijan Holds Local Elections," RFE/RL *Newsline*, Vol. 3, No. 240, Part I (December 13, 1999).

34. For OHDIR reports on irregularities in elections in these states, see the official Organization for Security and Co-operation in Europe (OSCE) website, <www.osce.org>.

35. Indeed, the official acceptance of democratic norms may also be used against authorities who comply only in form, not substance. See "Lenkoran Is Being 'Privatized'," *Azadlyq*, December 1, 1998, in *Habarlar Digest*, December 19, 1998.

Another example concerns the ambivalence of the Caspian region's elites regarding the establishment of civic versus ethnic national identities. Without exception, each state has officially institutionalized an inclusive definition of national citizenship, while at the same time privileging narrower ethnically-based criteria in actual practice. Several factors appear to account for this pattern. First, although civic identity may be desirable in the abstract as a means of integrating highly diverse ethnic populations, it tends to lack a solid political foundation in the Caspian region. Instead, most of the countries are predominantly populated by the titular ethnic group, and mobilization efforts on the part of centralizing elites have therefore been highly effective as the titular ethnicity has successfully mobilized to capture the lion's share of plum political appointments and bureaucratic positions. Such mobilization has depended to a significant extent on the orchestrated assertion of a common ethnic identity.[36] No alternative cultural or ethnic connection exists which could serve to unite the remaining groups into a viable countercoalition. Furthermore, there appears to be no shared idea of the past capable of connecting society as a whole. On the contrary, recollections of the Soviet period tend to fragment diverse social groups (especially Russians and non-Russians) rather than bring them together.[37]

For these reasons, the nation-building project—as undertaken by the post-Soviet states—has jarringly collided with the normative evolution of the international system as a whole, including the emerging civic ideal of equal citizenship. The result has been a rather contradictory pattern of compliance and resistance, as illustrated by the case of Armenia. President Robert Kocharian's regime has been mindful of international pressures to avoid exclusivist ethnic national rhetoric and religious intolerance, pledging to eschew any such practices, while in reality it has prohibited proselytizing by any group other than the Armenian Orthodox Church and has granted citizenship rights to ethnic Armenians from the diaspora.[38] A similar general pattern may be observed in Kazakhstan,

---

36. The obvious exception to this rule is Kazakhstan, where Kazakhs make up only about 53 percent of the population as compared to roughly 30 percent ethnic Russians, and where, not surprisingly, a relatively greater emphasis has been placed on constructing a unifying civic-national identity. Even here, however, the Russian population has expressed resentment over its rapid marginalization within the political and adminstrative elite. Olcott, *Kazakhstan: Unfulfilled Promise*, pp. 174–183.

37. Pal Kolsto makes this point in "Bipolar Societies?" in Pal Kolsto, ed., *National Building and Ethnic Integration in Post-Soviet Societies: An Investigation of Latvia and Kazakstan* (Boulder, Colo.: Westview, 1999), pp. 15–43, at pp. 39–41.

38. *Human Rights Watch*, 1999, 2000, 2001. E.g., although Armenia signed the Convention for the Protection of Human Rights and Fundamental Freedoms in its bid for

where despite constitutional safeguards of equal treatment, in practice Kazakhification has taken place in the spheres of government employment and culture, including language policy.[39] Kazakhstani President Nursultan Nazarbaev has attempted to manage the ongoing polarization of identities between Russians and Kazakhs in a context of perceived vulnerability, especially regarding the Russian diaspora and the possibility of intervention by Moscow.[40] This external constraint has resulted in a noticeably less assertive form of ethnic national identification in Kazakhstan as compared with, say, Uzbekistan.[41]

Another instance of symbolic maneuvering concerns the use of "European" self-imagery. Elites in all of the states of Western Eurasia have sought to cultivate a European identity in the broadest sense. Doing so serves to legitimate domestic goals by helping regimes distance themselves from the Soviet past, and has also been useful for gaining acceptance as members of the fraternity of "advanced" states.[42] This is most consistently true of Georgia, although propounding a European self-

membership in the Council of Europe, harassment of Jehovah's Witnesses continued. "The Impact of Council of Europe Membership on Armenia," *Eurasia Insight*, June 27, 2000, online at: <http://www.eurasianet.org/departments/insight/articles/eav062700.shtml>.

39. Azamat Sarsembayev, "Imagined Communities: Kazak Nationalism and Kazakification in the 1990s," *Central Asian Survey*, Vol. 18, No. 3 (September 1999): pp. 319–346.

40. Martha Brill Olcott, "Nursultan Nazarbaev and the Balancing Act of State-building in Kazakhstan," in Timothy Colton and Robert Tucker, eds., *Patterns in Post-Soviet Leadership* (Boulder, Colo.: Westview Press, 1995): pp. 169–190.

41. The 1995 Constitution, which enshrines Kazakh as the official state language, also designates Russian as an "official language." John Glenn, *The Soviet Legacy in Central Asia* (New York: St. Martin's, 1999), p. 6. See also Annette Bohr, "The Central Asian States as Nationalising Regimes," in Graham Smith, Edward Allworth, and Vivien Law, eds., *Nation-Building in the Post-Soviet Borderlands: The Politics of National Identities* (Cambridge: Cambridge University Press, 1998), pp. 139–164; Victoria Koroteyeva and Ekaterina Makarova, "The Assertion of Uzbek National Identity: Nativization or State-Building Process?" in Touraj Atabaki and John O'Kane, *Post-Soviet Central Asia* (New York: Tauris, 1998), pp. 137–143.

42. On legitimation, see Andrew Cortell and James Davis, "How Do International Institutions Matter? The Domestic Impact of International Rules and Norms," *International Studies Quarterly*, Vol. 40, No. 4 (December 1996), pp. 451–478. All the Eurasian successor states immediately turned for help and guidance to the West and to the major Western-dominated international organizations. All joined the World Bank and International Monetary Fund (IMF), while Georgia and Moldova have joined the World Trade Organization (WTO) and all others except Turkmenistan have observer status. Furthermore all joined the OSCE, and all but Kazakhstan and Turkmenistan, which are geographically ineligible, joined the Council of Europe.

image is a prominent (but highly contested) tendency in Russia as well. Even Azerbaijan has officially echoed this claim to "Europeanness," although the state here and in Kazakhstan also tends to embrace "Eurasianism" and to present both nation and state as an historical bridge between Europe and Asia.[43]

Once more, such self-representations often appear to be essentially strategic. First, attaining European status is calculated to help attract development assistance and foreign investment, smooth the way to closer political ties with the West, and so on. The practical importance of such goals is, however, perhaps less important than what they represent at home and abroad. In particular, such public policy ploys constitute an effort to simulate a desired public identity for international audiences in hopes of gaining legitimacy and inclusion, yet without actually internalizing that identity's principle features or seriously attempting to reconstruct ambient national culture in similar terms. In one sense, the official embrace of such values serves a pragmatic domestic purpose in facilitating the introduction of other functional neoliberal norms, which are themselves conducive to the establishment of neoliberal economic institutions. Here again, it also plays a useful foreign policy role. Enunciating such values provides a way of authenticating claims of "Europeanness" or of demonstrating behavior requisite for membership in symbolically important organizations like the Council of Europe.[44] Such calculations tend to win out despite considerable resentment of U.S. and European "meddling" in domestic affairs with regard to human rights violations and nondemocratic practices.[45]

One may adduce many other instances of prevailing international and Western models being used to show Caspian officials how to conduct themselves in virtually all matters: how to relate to the media; what labor legislation must be enacted for accession to the World Trade Organization (WTO); how the police should be organized and supervised; how the agricultural sector should be reorganized; how pension, tax, and other public sector reforms should be conducted.[46] Eager to achieve strategic as-

43. Elin Suleymanov, "Azerbaijan, Azerbaijanis and the Search for Identity," *Analysis of Current Events*, Vol. 13, No. 1 (February 2001).

44. See Jeffrey Checkel, "Norms, Institutions, and National Identity in Contemporary Europe," *International Studies Quarterly*, Vol. 43, No. 1 (March 1999), pp. 83–114.

45. For example, Kazakhstan parliamentarian Jabaikhan Abdildin, head of a presidential commission on human rights, denounced "the fabrications of overseas defenders of democracy and so-called human rights." Abdrey Sviridov, "Astana Rails Against US Rights Report," IWPR, *Reporting Central Asia*, No. 47 (April 10, 2001).

46. A few representative examples are "International Seminar on Relations with

similation, most states have tended to adopt the prescribed practices with little or no overt protest. Thus, tolerance toward homosexuals was professed in Azerbaijan, the death penalty was renounced in Russia, and so on. In sum, one observes numerous foreign and domestic policy adjustments among the post-Soviet Caspian states driven by globalization and the requirements of political integration. Along the way, it remains an important empirical question whether the cultural accompaniments of such policy adjustments are internalized or merely mimicked for political show. As one has seen, tactically motivated and superficially constructed national identities may prove unsustainable when they contradict other, more fundamental identity constructs and social practices.

Conclusion

As an integral part of the post-Soviet process of nation- and state-building, elites have (re)invented traditions and animated culturally specific practices. At home, these symbols and narratives are manipulated by the state in order to facilitate basic institutional changes, even where, at times, these rest only on a dimly recalled native tradition. The process of mobilizing such symbols and identities is a highly political one, in the sense that distinct domestic and foreign policy preferences are implicated in various constructs. Not surprisingly, where an open polity exists, as in Russia, the assertion of national cultural themes evokes vigorous opposition and value contestation. In analyzing the discourse of state-building, nation-building, and foreign policymaking, one glimpses the workings of entrepreneurs operating within different cultural systems, which not only confer a particular interpretation of state interests but also bound the consideration of policy options.

Culture and identity formation also bestow interests on nation-building elites, which through practice constitute more or stable self-understandings and foreign policy leanings. In the Caspian region, intertwined state-building and nation-building projects have largely succeeded in constructing self-representations of states as culturally distinct and historically dominated by outside forces, especially Russia.[47] This

Mass Media Being Held in Kazakh Parliament," *Kazakh News*, March 2, 1999; National Trilateral Workshop Starts its Work," *AzadInform* 71, March 30, 1999, in *Habarlar Digest* 746, March 30, 1999; "A. Kerimov: 'We Will Ascertain Which Proposals of the European Council's Experts Do Not Conform to National Mentality'," *AzadInform* 38, February 17, 1999, in *Habarlar Digest*, February 17, 1999; "Astrakhanskoe selo propubaiet okno v Evropu" [Astrakhan Village Opens Up a Window to Europe], *Astrakhanskie vedomosti*, September 30, 1999.

47. Similar observations are made in Paul Kubicek, "Regionalism, Nationalism and

has exacerbated tensions and influenced the prospects for collective security among the former Soviet states. Indeed, even for Russia such themes of subjugation and resistance are central, although here they tend to turn on one or another variant of Russia's own imperial legacy and destiny.

Identity is reproduced through practice and is therefore subject to change when interaction disconfirms established images of Others. The shift in Azerbaijan's relations with Russia under Putin is a clear case in point. Similarly, U.S. intervention into the Caspian region in the aftermath of September 11, 2001, constitutes a key opportunity for the consolidation or evolution of shared understandings of Self and Other on the part of all states in the region. The process is, however, neither linear nor unidirectional. Interests may remain tentatively segmented from identities, at least in the fully realized sense of self-representations associated with richly articulated narratives and expressed consistently across a range of venues. The claim to "Europeanness," with its attendant material and reputational benefits, provides an example of such an officially manipulated identity functioning as a thin veneer for interests, where the latter appear to have been derived essentially from pragmatic concerns. This is not to suggest that other, perhaps more subtle or less manifestly representational identities are not implicated in such pretensions. Images of modernity and the new global standard of civilization constitute elements of such an underlying identity construct, which may, however, remain tacit at the level of official foreign policy discourse.

Finally, one has to be struck by the immense momentum of cultural globalization as it sweeps across post-Soviet Eurasia. Despite its particular hybridized outcomes as articulated by nation-building elites, globalization at a deeper level tends to produce an attachment to international constitutive norms and associated self-understandings. It is this massive force of neoliberalism, and of the world polity, which most directly challenges the narratives and identities constructed through elite discourse until now. For this reason alone, the future evolution of globalization and the extent to which states will be able to mediate the process for their own ends will have profound consequences for the development of national identities and foreign policies throughout Central Asia and the Caspian basin.

Realpolitik in Central Asia," *Europe-Asia Studies*, Vol. 49, No. 4 (June 1997), pp. 637–655.

Chapter 4

History and Foreign Policy: From Constructed Identities to "Ancient Hatreds" East of the Caspian

Ronald Grigor Suny

Even wishing won't make it so. Culture may matter, and civilizations may appear to clash, but the world is far more complicated than the simple mental maps that paint one people red and another green. Complexity and ambiguity are particularly rife in the lands that surround the landlocked Caspian Sea. From Chechnya and Dagestan in the North Caucasus, through Armenia, Azerbaijan, and Georgia, to Kazakhstan and Central Asia, religious and secular, cultural and civilizational, regional and local identities overlap, reinforce, and undermine each other in ways that can only be unraveled by close historical and ethnographic investigations. In lands where history is taken so seriously, however, it is too important to be left to historians. Where culture underlies state legitimacy, ethnographers cannot be left on their own. Ironically, the search for stability leads to insecurity, not only within and between states, but in the very construction of identities and ideas of culture. If the world were as simple as parsimonious social scientists would have it, the questions asked in this volume would have long ago been answered. Just as one seems to get closer to "culture" and intimate with "identity," however, those elusive concepts slip away.

This chapter suggests that nations and nationalisms, identities and interests, ought to be seen as less hardwired and fixed than they are often

This chapter is an elaboration of an ongoing investigation of identities, cultures, and state policies. Parts of this paper were published as: "Southern Tears: Dangerous Opportunities in the Caucasus and Central Asia," in Rajan Menon, Yuri E. Fedorov, and Ghia Nodia, eds., *Russia, the Caucasus, and Central Asia: The 21st Century Security Environment* (Armonk, N.Y.: M. E. Sharpe, 1999), pp. 147–176; "Provisional Stabilities: The Politics of Identities in Post-Soviet Eurasia," *International Security*, Vol. 24, No. 3 (Winter 1999–2000), pp. 139–178; and "Constructing Primordialism: Old Histories for New Nations," *Journal of Modern History*, Vol. 73, No. 4 (December 2001), pp. 862–896.

thought of by analysts and policymakers. In order to understand the evolving national interests of the states of Central Asia and the Caucasus, it is necessary to evaluate the national identities and conceptualizations of interest in the region and appreciate that identities and interests can change rapidly in politically fluid moments. The ways in which these peoples and states think of themselves are historically produced and are subject to change—they are constructed and fluid, even as they are thought to be fixed, eternal, and even products of nature rather than history. Since identities are to some degree fluid, multiple, and overlapping, predicting from identities is extremely difficult, if not impossible. Yet sensitivity to identity gives the analyst a handle on how state actors conceive of their interests. Identities are a "congealed reputation," i.e., the closest one can get in social life to being able to expect confidently the same actions from another agent time after time.[1] In this view, known as constructivism, one is presented with an international arena of ordered contingency, understandable only through contextualized, historicized investigation of identities.

For constructivists, states potentially have multiple identities, just as do individuals or social collectives. Within existing discourses, they have a repertoire of identities and, therefore, choices that elites are able to make. Whether an elite views its state as a democracy, a great power, an empire, the victim of others, or a carrier of civilization is key to its understanding of its state's interests. The states that emerged from the Soviet Union are involved in a desperate ongoing process of identity construction, deliberately and often reactively reconceptualizing their identities and interests. Instead of thinking of nations as primordial, with their continuous existence stretching back to the time when the first humans emerged from the primeval ooze, they may be seen as narrations that shift over time and can potentially be reshaped in the future as they have been in the past. Rather than pre-existing, objective differences between people leading to violence, it is often the indistinctness of differences and contests over what the ethnicity or nation should include or exclude that produces conflict.

As scholars have moved from a more naturalistic understanding of nations to a constructivist view that nations are modern "imagined communities," the possibility has opened up to see how certain constructions of nations, certain national narratives, and certain styles of discourse are more productive of conflict than others. "National histories" must be in-

---

1. The phrase is from an earlier version of Hopf's essay, "The Promise of Constructivism in International Relations Theory," *International Security*, Vol. 23, No. 1 (Summer 1998), pp. 171–200.

vestigated, not so much to discover the "real" story behind the Serb-Albanian conflict in Kosovo or the Armenian-Azerbaijani hostility over Nagorno-Karabagh, as if one side's claims could convincingly outweigh the others, but rather how particular conceptualizations of nationhood, threats to national security, and opportunities for improved national welfare are constructed. Once nations and nationalisms are seen as less hardwired and fixed, policymakers can evaluate which kinds of national discourses may alleviate problems and which may perpetuate violence. Finally, rather than seeing conflict arising from power imbalances, such as exist between Russia and the other post-Soviet states, or making an automatic assumption that "another group's sense of identity and the cohesion it produces, is a danger," that will lead to conflict, this approach suggests that threat perception is linked closely to identities of Self and Other, that identities and images of the Other can be changed, and that, therefore, the security dilemma can be avoided.[2]

Theory and Practice

Much of security studies and international relations theory has been based on an epistemological picture of a real world in which bounded, coherent territorialized sovereign states exist in conditions of international anarchy and aim to increase their security and independence of action. In a simple version of such a picture, states have but one identity—that of self-interested security seekers. That essential identity comes with being a state—it is eternal, unchanging through history or across the globe. Presumably, it would be the same for states on other planets, in other universes. Although changing balance-of-power conditions may affect interests, competition and conflict are highlighted in this model; cooperation recedes as a long-term possibility. For neorealists, anarchy is the real condition of international life, and states are caught in a "security dilemma": as they take actions to increase their security, they tend to decrease the senses of security of other states. As a theory, neorealism is elegant and parsimonious, but in analyzing actual historical conflicts, it almost inevitably must concede some of its simplicity and bring in factors of domestic variables, existing political discourses, and cultural norms.[3]

The end of the Cold War, along with the decline of inter-state warfare

---

2. The language quoted here is from Barry Posen, "The Security Dilemma and Ethnic Conflict," *Survival*, Vol. 35, No. 1 (Spring 1993), pp. 27–28, 31.

3. On this point, see Rajan Menon and Hendrik Spruyt, "The Limits of Neorealism: Understanding Security in Central Asia," *Review of International Studies*, Vol. 25, No. 1 (January 1999), pp. 87–105.

and the rise of ethnic conflict, has encouraged analysts to extend this hardened image of states to more fluid social categories such as ethnicities and nation and to use international relations theory to explain nationalism. This image has been challenged by constructivists who propose a more historicized, contextualized, relativized picture of states and nations. For constructivists, like Alexander Wendt or Ted Hopf, identity and interest can neither be taken for granted nor simply deduced from an abstract model of international relations—they become dependent variables to be explained.[4] Unlike neorealism, constructivism "assumes that the selves, or identities, of states are a variable; they likely depend on historical, cultural, political, and social context."[5] The identities of actors and agents are the product of the social practices among agents and between agents and structures. Neither actors nor structures are assumed to be fully formed and unchanging, but mutually constituting one another in actual social practices. For constructivists, power is both material and discursive—it is also about the generation of meanings that are shared subjectively between different actors.

Like cultures, identities remain fragile and openly contested. They are embedded in the stories that people tell about themselves individually and collectively, implied in the way individuals and groups talk and give meaning to their being, their selves, and their roles. Identities, whether gender, ethnic, religious, or national or state identity, are constrained by experiences and available possibilities and may be thought of as part of a search for a useable past and an acceptable modernity to stave off anxiety about the present and future. One may think of identity as a provisional stabilization of a sense of self or group that is formed in actual historical time and space, in evolving economies, polities, and cultures, as a continuous search for some solidity in a constantly shifting world—but without closure, without forever naturalizing or essentializing the arrived-at provisional identities.

Ordinary identity-talk, however, is almost always about unity and internal harmony and tends to naturalize wholeness. It defaults to an earlier understanding of identity as the stable core. Almost unavoidably, particularly when one is unselfconscious about identity, identity-seeking

---

4. For an appreciative statement of the constructivist approach, see Hopf, "The Promise of Constructivism in International Relations Theory."

5. Ibid, p. 176. Similarly, Wendt points out, "Identities are the basis of interests. Actors do not have a 'portfolio' of interests that they carry around independent of social context; instead, they define their interests in the process of defining situations." See Alexander Wendt, "Anarchy is What States Make of It: The Social Construction of Power Politics," *International Organization*, Vol. 46, No. 2 (Spring 1992), p. 398.

is an essentializing practice with all the limitations and dangers that such a way of viewing the world entails. It tends to ascribe behaviors to given identities in a simple, unmediated transference. One does *this* because one is *that*. Thus, the analyst in theory takes a "postmodern" position, standing aside from ordinary usage and insistently claiming that as difficult as it is to accept, the apparent and desired wholeness and unity is made up—imagined—in order to create a source of provisional stability in a changing world, while in practice that same analyst may take a "modernist" position and appreciate the importance of essentialism in creating a point of stability from which to act. In the words of sociologist Zygmunt Bauman, "If the *modern* 'problem of identity' was how to construct an identity and keep it solid and stable, the *postmodern* 'problem of identity' is primarily how to avoid fixation and keep the options open."[6]

National identity is a particular form of political identification. As universal as it tends to be in modern times (roughly from the late-eighteenth century), it neither encompasses all peoples and communities, nor does it exist exclusively or in isolation from other competing identities. As scholars have attempted to demonstrate in the last few decades, nation is not natural or given but must be worked for, taught, and instilled, largely through the effort of intellectuals, politicians, and activists who make the identification with the "imagined political community" of the nation a palpable and potent source of emotional and intellectual commitment.[7] Yet in much of the world, supranational religious or imperial affiliations coexist comfortably with subnational ethnic, local, regional, tribal, clan, and other affiliations and may work to undermine as much as to support national identities.

Whatever language and ideas were used by ancient and medieval people to understand the societies in which they lived, they were different from the current discourse in which one speaks of nations. Modern nations are those political communities made up of people who believe they share characteristics, perhaps perceived origins, values, historical

---

6. Zygmunt Bauman, "From Pilgrim to Tourist—or a Short History of Identity," in Stuart Hall and Paul du Gay, eds., *Questions of Cultural Identity* (London: Sage Publications, 1996), p. 18.

7. Ernest Gellner, *Nations and Nationalism* (Oxford: Basil Blackwell, 1983); Benedict Anderson, *Imagined Communities: Reflections on the Origin and Spread of Nationalism* (London: Verso Press, 1991); Anthony D. Smith, *The Ethnic Origins of Nations* (Oxford: Basil Blackwell, 1986); and E. J. Hobsbawm, *Nations and Nationalism Since 1780: Programme, Myth, Reality* (Cambridge: Cambridge University Press, 1990) have been recognized as among the key texts in this discussion. See also the essays collected in Geoff Eley and Ronald Grigor Suny, eds., *Becoming National, A Reader* (Oxford: Oxford University Press, 1996).

experiences, language, territory, or any of many other elements, that give them the right to self-determination, perhaps control of a piece of the earth's real estate (their homeland), and even statehood and the benefits that follow from that. Like other identifications, nations are articulated within the stories that people tell about themselves and can be thought of as arenas in which people dispute who they are, argue about boundaries, who is in or out of the group, where the "homeland" begins and ends, what the "true" history of the nation is, what is "authentic" about being national, and what is to be rejected. The narrative is most often a tale of origins and continuity, often of sacrifice and martyrdom, but also of glory and heroism.

Most important, modern nations exist within a universe of meaning that holds that the only source of legitimacy for state authorities is that they somehow represent that nation and rule with some kind of assent. The particularly modern form of "imagining a nation" contains within it a notion of popular sovereignty—the people have the right to rule themselves, and they impart legitimacy to those who govern them. In many of the actual instances of nationalism, it is argued that each nation, however constituted, should have its own state, and that in all but anomalous cases, each state should have within it a single nation. This powerful but ultimately utopian idea is the basis of much of modern politics, and much of the conflict in the twentieth century was precisely about the ill fit between self-described nations and existing states.

Within many nationalisms, there is a premium placed on longevity, antiquity, and continuity in the calculus of the nation. Yet since all human beings have been on the earth since roughly the same time, it is apparently the availability of a written or archaeological tradition that empowers the claims of some peoples over others to nationhood and territory. Those with written language, a textual record, and clearly-recognized state forms are privileged over those who might have roamed the steppes in nomadic bands or lived in smaller non-literate communities. Even so, quite long-lived "nations," such as Armenians, Georgians, or Jews, who have written traditions that go back millennia, have in modern times reconstructed and made consistent the varied and changing identities and ways of conceiving of themselves that existed in the past. The discursive particularities of earlier identities have been reinterpreted in the frame of later templates, particularly that of the nation, so that a discontinuous and varied history has been simplified into the story of a relatively fixed "nation" moving continuously through time, struggling to realize itself in full nationhood and eventually independent statehood.[8] Since the times

8. On the reconstructions of Armenian history, see Ronald Grigor Suny, *Looking*

when people were more polyglot and polytheistic than people are today, relatively "soft boundaries" between ethnic or religious communities have been "hardened" into artificially clearer differences between peoples.[9] The move to nationhood was also an effort at shoring up distinctions between those in and out of the nation and state policing of the boundaries between members and foreigners.

Once nations are seen as historical constructions based on ideas of culture, difference, and commonality, one can then discern what perceived "interests" follow from particular national identifications. No need exists, theoretically, to pose an either-or dichotomy between "culture" and "identity," on the one hand, and "security interests," on the other. Because, arguably, interests are tied to identities—what people think they need is connected to who they think they are—the whole question of self-understandings, goals and aspirations, and fears and anxieties must be investigated as a prerequisite to analyzing the security requirements of states. If it is understood that identity formation is intimately connected to the generation of threat perception and allows possible ways out of such perceptions, the ways in which groups define themselves and others lies at the base of how secure they and other nations and states feel. States want to survive, but survival is most often thought of as including a way of life, or what many anthropologists call a culture.

As many cases have shown, national identities and conceptualizations of interest can change rapidly in politically fluid moments. In Georgia, for example, within a few years (1989–1993), exclusivist nationalism gave way to a more pragmatic, inclusive idea of the nation (at least on the part of state actors) that opened discussion of the possible restructuring of the state along federalist lines. It took defeat and state collapse, however, for this shift to occur. Georgia's experience differed from that of Armenia, where victory in war and opposition from the international community resulted in a turn toward a more exclusivist nationalism, an increasingly self-reliant foreign policy, and a more uncompromising position on the Nagorno-Karabagh question. In neighboring Azerbaijan, successive failures of national mobilizations and a nationalist government gave way to a pragmatic tactician who played down nationalism and em-

---

Toward Ararat: Armenia in Modern History (Bloomington: Indiana University Press, 1993); on Georgia, Ronald Grigor Suny, *The Making of the Georgian Nation* (Bloomington: Indiana University Press, 1994); on the Jews, Maxime Rodinson, *Cult, Ghetto, and State: The Persistence of the Jewish Question* (Thetford, Norfolk: Al Saqi Books, 1983).

9. Prasenjit Duara, *Rescuing History from the Nation: Questioning Narratives of Modern China* (Chicago: University of Chicago Press, 1995); Duara, "Historicizing National Identity, or Who Imagines What and When," in Eley and Suny, eds., *Becoming National*, pp. 151–177.

phasized his own competence and an oil-rich future. Most ominously, in Russia, the problem has been less one of changing national identity than of a chronic failure to construct an identity effectively. Prediction of Russia's future intentions, even what it may consider its interests, thus, is rendered particularly difficult.

Central Asia's Overlapping Identities

It was in the study of the traditionally Islamic peoples of Central Asia that Western scholars writing in the years of the Cold War erred most egregiously in deducing behavior from essential religious and cultural characteristics. A number of historians predicted that all Soviet Muslims would gravitate toward an all-Islamic identity, that religious identification would prove stronger than ethnic, that Muslims would be by nature anti-Soviet, and that post-Soviet Muslims would gravitate toward closer relations with Turkey, Iran, and the Arab world. Most of these expectations have proven to be false. Based as they were on official Soviet anti-Islamic materials and in the absence of fieldwork, which was difficult if not impossible to do before the regime of Soviet President Mikhail Gorbachev, several Western authors exaggerated the religiosity of Soviet Central Asians.[10] Some analysts apocalyptically predicted the rise of Islamic fundamentalism as a threat to European civilization, and they were joined by fearful Russians who imagined dangers from the "green crescent" that extended from the Caucasus through Central Asia and up the Volga River.[11] The post-Soviet Islamic unity has, however, proven to be illusory, and supranational civilizational identities based on religion have been far weaker than national and subnational identifications. Perhaps most surprising of all is the remarkable attraction of post-Soviet peoples

---

10. See, for example, Alexandre A. Bennigsen and Marie Bennigsen Broxup, *The Islamic Threat to the Soviet State* (New York: St. Martin's, 1983); and Alexandre A. Bennigsen and S. Enders Wimbush, *Muslims of the Soviet Empire: A Guide* (Bloomington: Indiana University Press, 1985); Hélène Carrère d'Encausse, *Decline of an Empire: The Soviet Socialist Republics in Revolt,* trans. Martin Sokolinsky and Henry A. la Farge (New York: Harper & Row, 1981), pp. 244–265. For critical and sensitive discussions of these issues, see Elizabeth E. Bacon, *Central Asians under Russian Rule: A Study in Culture Change* (Ithaca, N.Y.: Cornell University Press, 1966); Michael Rywkin, *Moscow's Muslim Challenge: Soviet Central Asia* (Armonk, N.Y.: M. E. Sharpe, 1982); and Jo-Ann Gross, *Muslims in Central Asia: Expressions of Identity and Change* (Durham, N.C.: Duke University Press, 1992).

11. Alexei Malashenko, "Does Islamic Fundamentalism Exist in Russia?" in Yaacov Ro'i, ed., *Muslim Eurasia: Conflicting Legacies* (London: Frank Cass, 1995), pp. 41–51; Hélène Carrère d'Encausse, *The End of the Soviet Empire: The Triumph of the Nations,* trans. Franklin Philip (New York: Basic Books, 1993), pp. 268–270.

to other post-Soviet peoples, even Russians, rather than to non-Soviet foreign powers, and the fear that anti-Russian pogroms would follow the end of Soviet colonialism proved to be misplaced. Even though great wariness exists about the reimposition of colonial authority among Central Asians, this has not been reflected in intensely anti-Russian feeling. While identity matters in foreign policy, it is not always clear which identity may prove to be more powerful. As it happened, identification with Islam proved to be far less important in the foreign policy of states that had experienced seventy years of Soviet rule than it was in Muslim-populated states like Saudi Arabia and Pakistan. Nation-building in Central Asia has been a top-down, state-generated project, rather than a "natural" evolution up from language or culture. Language does not match up easily with nation in Central Asia, for the various Turkic languages of the region are closely related. "Classifying Central Asian Turkic languages/dialects," writes one specialist, "is rather like cutting soup."[12] Those Western analysts who believed that the linguistic ties among the Turkic-speaking peoples might have unified them or created an affinity with the Turks of Anatolia or a foreign policy orientation toward Turkey failed to note that the languages of Central Asia are quite different from Anatolian Turkish. The fact that Azerbaijan and Turkey have close ties, on the other hand, may be primarily related to their mutual conflict with Armenia, and only secondarily to their identity as "Turks." Even after seventy years of an Uzbek republic, the linguistic homogenization of an Uzbek people remains incomplete. Uzbeks in the west speak a dialect close to that of Turkmen, while those in the east are easily understood by Kazakhs or Kyrgyz. One Central Asian people blends into another, sharing much in common—religion, language, culture, and sense of place. What distinguishes them most clearly from one another are the Soviet-constructed identities listed in their passports and the Soviet-created republics in which they now live. When it comes to foreign policy, identity with state and nation, rather than with religion or Central Asia, appears to be most important.

In pre-Soviet times, the most prevalent identification for Central Asian native peoples was Muslim—an identity that remains salient today. "Muslim" in Central Asia is not a narrowly religious but a more inclusive cultural and even spatial identity—something akin to "European" for many Westerners. "Being Muslim" involves some attachment to customary practices and distinction from being Russian. Armenians, Jews,

---

12.   John Schoeberlein-Engel, "Identity in Central Asia: Construction and Contention in the Conceptions of 'Özbek,' 'Tâjik,' 'Muslim,' Samarqandi,' and Other Groups" (Ph.D. dissertation, Harvard University, 1994), p. 58.

Ukrainians, and Russians are generally lumped into a general category of European or Russian. Yet being Muslim in Central Asia is not so much an identification with all Muslims. In the self-conception of Central Asian Muslims, family and community—the one related closely to the other—are central in their lives, and they recognize paradoxically both differences among Central Asian Muslims and a basic cultural unity.[13] They have a shared sense that "Russians" have encroached upon the Muslim peoples.[14] Some Kazakhs and Turkmen to whom the author has spoken feel even more strongly that Russians or Soviets have obliterated their distinct culture, leaving them not only without voice but without tongue.

The identity "Muslim," then, must be understood broadly, as a vaguely and loosely formed identity, one with less religion and oppositional politics than many Western analysts had thought. It was not generally counterposed to "Soviet" identity, as the work of Mark Saroyan shows.[15] While the Soviet state tried in many ways to eliminate Muslim identifications and replace them with national (Uzbek, Kazakh) and Soviet ones, their own practices reinforced national and Muslim identities and exaggerated differences between Central Asians and Russians.[16] In the end, like the use of Uzbek or Tajik, which may not distinguish one Muslim from another, the term Muslim was most often used to distinguish Muslim from non-Muslim, from Russian or European.[17]

---

13. Ibid., p. 225.

14. Ibid., p. 230.

15. The Muslim clergy in the Soviet Union, Saroyan argues, had its own agenda and was "engaged in a creative process of constructing new forms of identity and religious organization in order to situate and establish itself and its community in a complex set of constantly changing power relations. The repressive means by which the Muslim clergy constitutes itself and its image of the Muslim community are much more relevant to its aspirations for hegemony in Muslim society than to its relations with state authorities." Mark Saroyan, *Minorities, Mullahs, and Modernity: Reshaping Community in the Former Soviet Union*, ed. Edward W. Walker (Berkeley: University of California, Berkeley, International and Area Studies, 1997), pp. 25–26.

16. Recent work by anthropologists and visitors to the region indicates that commitment to Islam varied greatly over the span of Central Asia, and Soviet policies effectively eroded popular devotion, although a lingering identification with the Muslim world and Islam as a culture remains and is being actively promoted. In Uzbekistan, it is not the cities that exhibit devotion to Islam, and certainly not the urban intelligentsia (which is the most Russified and secular part of the population), but certain distinct regions like the Ferghana Valley and the mountain villagers in the Hisar-Zarafshan ranges.

17. Schoeberlein sums up the connection between nationality and religion by noting, "All that can really be said is that 'Özbeks,' with few exceptions, are 'Muslims,' and that this has three broad meanings for 'Özbeks' as for other Central Asians: 1) They be-

Besides national, regional, and religious identities, yet another supranational identification retains power in Central Asia—"Soviet" identity, not so much in the sense of an identification with the Soviet Union as a system or political project, but rather as a shared identity with a cosmopolitan Russian and Soviet multi-ethnic culture. This much-neglected topic has fallen victim to the apparent success of national identities that, combined with the progressive weakening of the central Soviet state, led to the collapse of the Soviet Union and the creation of independent national states. The argument usually made is that the generalized Soviet identity promoted by Soviet authorities was artificial and imposed and proved far weaker than the more "natural," primordial identities of nationality. Yet Central Asians imbibed much of Soviet culture and thinking, and were notable in not participating in massive nationalist or separatist movements in the late Soviet period. Moreover, a sense of shared values stemming from a common Soviet experience persists more than a decade after the disintegration of the Soviet Union. The frequently proclaimed *druzhba narodov* had a positive residue, but perhaps one can also find here one of the most insidious effects of empire. By subscribing to the Soviet discourse of civilization, progress, socialism, and development, Central Asians acquiesced to the idea that Muslim peoples were "backward," that they received "civilization" from Russia, and that (in perhaps an unacknowledged way) the imperial or colonial aspects of Soviet policy were justified for developmentalist reasons.[18] Rather than complete or passive acceptance, however, colonialized people may buy into the given hierarchies and dominant values while experiencing the burden and pain of an enforced inferiority. The most successful intellectuals and politicians were successful precisely because they knew Russian well and were otherwise competent in the Sovietized culture. No matter how Russified Central Asians might have been, however, they often experienced discrimination, particularly when they left the region to continue their education or serve in the Soviet army. With inadequate knowledge of their own histories, Central Asians experienced a sense of disconnection and subjugation, yet many did not feel particularly hostile to Soviet culture.[19] Indeed, by the late Soviet period, it was nearly impos-

---

lieve in the basic tenets of Islamic religion, such as that 'there is no God but Allah and Muhammad is his prophet'; 2) They adhere to traditional practices and beliefs associated with Islam; and 3) they are 'native' to this fundamentally 'Muslim' part of the world, in contrast to the Russians and others who are viewed in Central Asia as outsiders." Schoeberlein-Engel, "Identity in Central Asia," p. 50.

18. Ibid., p. 248.

19. Ibid., p. 250.

sible to sever actually experienced Central Asian culture from many aspects of Soviet culture. A sense that they have been shaped by the Soviet experience (particularly for males who served in the army), with all the ambivalences attached, links Central Asians to Russia in complex ways and keeps them distant from Muslims outside the former Soviet Union who have had quite different social and political experiences.

To illustrate the variety of potential identities and their effects in post-Soviet Central Asia, the discussion now turns to three cases of identity formation: Uzbekistan, Tajikistan, and Kazakhstan. In Uzbekistan, the legacy of Soviet territorial nationhood has proven to be more powerful than older supranational identities, like those of Turkistan or Islam, which cut across the boundaries created in 1924, perhaps because the national has been institutionalized in administration and resource distribution. In Tajikistan, in contrast, identity with an inclusive nation proved to be weak, and regional allegiances proved to be more powerful. The collapse of the Soviet order did not so much defrost old identities chilled by a repressive old regime, but rather opened up new opportunities for reconstructed regional and political identities around which conflict flared. Finally, in Kazakhstan, a binational state, the government has been able to create a supra-ethnic identity that unites, at least rhetorically, ethnic Kazakhs and non-Kazakhs in a common civic national identity.

Uzbekistan: Inclusive Identity in an Authoritarian State

The peoples of Central Asia were among the last of the Soviet peoples to adopt clearly differentiated "national" identities. Though Soviet Uzbek scholars sometimes claimed that the Uzbek "nation" reached back to the first millennium B.C. and perhaps even earlier, most analysts contend that Uzbek is a quintessentially modern identity and should properly be associated only with the twentieth-century Soviet and post-Soviet republics. In a careful study of Uzbek identities, anthropologist John Schoeberlein demonstrates that "the name 'Uzbek' entered Central Asia with the Shaybanid conquest in the 16th century" and was thereafter "associated with the several dynasties descended from the Shaybanids which ruled the Khanates until they lost their independence to Russia."[20] Uzbek came to mean those related to the ruling elites, soldiers of the conquering armies, and even the subjects of the Uzbek dynasties. They may speak Turkic or Tajik, be nomadic or settled, have strong tribal affiliations

20. John Schoeberlein-Engel, "The Prospects for Uzbek National Identity," *Central Asia Monitor,* No. 2 (1996), p. 13.

or not, and this sense of identification with Uzbek was relatively attenuated, had no sense of national identity, and was less firmly held than tribal, other lineage, or local regional identities. Peoples were distinguished less by language and more by whether they were sedentary or nomadic. Settled peoples were known as Sarts, while nomads were often called "Kazakhs."[21]

With the establishment of the Soviet republic of Uzbekistan in 1924, the identities of the population shifted dramatically. The category "Sart" was abolished; Turkic-speaking Sarts became Uzbeks, and Iranian-speaking Sarts became Tajiks. The linguistic identification cut across social lines, uniting some townspeople with nomads and villagers, while dividing the settled population into distinct "nationalities."[22] A host of identities with smaller Turkic groups—the Lakays, Karluks, Kipchaks, Chaghatays—and "Turk" itself were eliminated (and those people integrated into the Uzbeks), while Kazakh, Turkmen, and Karakalpak were retained.[23]

In independent Uzbekistan, Uzbek can have the double meaning that the word "nationality" holds in English—ethnicity on the one hand, citizenship on the other. Many visitors to Uzbekistan have noted that in cities like Samarqand, the majority of people appear to be Tajik speakers, even though official Soviet census figures claimed that the majority just a decade ago was Uzbek. Many Tajik speakers are listed as Uzbek on their passports and may, indeed, see themselves as Uzbek, in the sense of a member of the republic and the nation that inhabits its territory.[24] A number of "Tajiks" in Samarqand attempted to create a Tajik revival move-

---

21. Martha Brill Olcott, *The Kazakhs*, 2nd ed. (Stanford, Calif.: Hoover Institution Press, 1995); and Edward A. Allworth, *The Modern Uzbeks, from the Fourteenth Century to the Present: A Cultural History* (Stanford, Calif.: Hoover Institution Press, 1990).

22. Schoeberlein-Engel, "The Prospects for Uzbek National Identity," p. 14.

23. In his own field work, Schoeberlein found that some of the identities that had been officially abolished seventy years earlier had survived the Soviet period. Kipchaks in the Ferghana Valley continue to see themselves as a separate people, closer to the Kyrgyz and Kazakhs than to the non-Kipchak Uzbeks, to whom they still refer as "Sarts." Vertical identities with ethnic connotations also continue to exist. Khojas are people who see themselves as descendants of important religious figures and marry within the group of Khojas, even though they may speak different languages.

24. Schoeberlein's field work indicates that "the great majority of Tajik speakers in Samarqand are apparently quite accepting of their position in Uzbekistan and have even come to adopt a kind of superficial Uzbek identity. The notion that Tajik identity in Samarqand is inherently destabilizing for Uzbekistan is an assumption which is not borne out by experience." Ibid., p. 19.

ment in 1989–1990 and found themselves up against general indifference to the problem of official nationality even before the Uzbekistan government repressed their efforts.[25] "Neither the 'nation,' officially promoted "Özbek' [Uzbek] identity, nor the 'national minority,' 'Tâjik', identity have been particularly compelling for Samarqand Tâjik-speakers."[26] Though one should not exaggerate the cohesion and ubiquity of Uzbek national consciousness, what is most striking in Uzbekistan is that subnational and regional identities and the traditional attachment to supranational Islam have coexisted with identification with the Uzbek nation and the Uzbek republic. But even as post-Soviet authorities work to construct new national identities, they must recognize that an overlapping series of identities from neighborhoods to cities to tribes and ethnicities, on to nation, republic, and religion cohabitate quite effectively in independent Uzbekistan—and, one may say, elsewhere in the southern tier of the former Soviet Union.

Uzbekistan, then, is a relatively recent nation with ethnic, religious, regional, and even Soviet layers of identity. Like most of the other Muslim-populated republics, it had little popular nationalist mobilization against the Soviet regime, and Uzbeks voted nearly unanimously to remain within the Soviet Union in the all-union referendum of March 1991. Ethnic violence in 1989 and 1990 was not directed at Russians or the Soviet state, but at fellow Muslims—Meskhetian Turks who had been exiled by Stalin from Georgia and Kyrgyz in the Osh region of Kyrgyzstan—and was largely the result of economic competition. The state authorities turned toward independence only after the abortive coup against Gorbachev in August 1991, and the old party elite essentially maintained its control of the republic through the 1990s, now free of Moscow's control. No revolution took place in Uzbekistan—and not much reform either. The Communist bosses who became leaders of the state systematically repressed or co-opted any opposition. President Islam Karimov promoted Uzbek national culture but restrained more chauvinistic efforts that might have encouraged badly needed skilled Russian workers to leave the republic. A huge statue of Timur, the conqueror of Central Asia, stands in a central park in Tashkent where Lenin's statue once stood. Though a Mongol, Timur, who is buried in Samarqand, has been appropriated into the Uzbek national tradition.

Yet as the Uzbek leadership develops a national Uzbek identity, it does so without great emphasis on ethnicity. Uzbek citizenship is open to

---

25. Ibid., p. 218.

26. Ibid., p. 219.

all long-term residents of the republic, while at the same time proficiency in the Uzbek language is being encouraged. The official Uzbek literary language, based on the dialect of the Ferghana Valley in the east, is not easily understood by all Uzbeks, and Russian, Tajik, and other Turkic languages are used by many citizens with little inconvenience.[27] Uzbek identity is broad and inclusive, reflecting the variety of peoples that became the Uzbek nationality in Soviet times. The combination of political authoritarianism and inclusive national identity has contributed, at least for the time being, to an enviable level of social stability. The authoritarian regime has been pragmatic and cautious and skillfully used the post–September 11 "war against global terrorism" to end its international isolation and vulnerability to Russia. By drawing closer to the United States and opening its territory to U.S. bases, the Uzbek government won its own war against Islamic rebels with U.S. troops and their Afghan allies doing the hard fighting. Civilizational, religious, or cultural allegiances had little to do with the imperatives of the battlefield or the new strategic positioning of Uzbekistan. For its own pragmatic reasons, the government has been cautious about including Islam into the identity repertoire of the new republic. Instead, Uzbekistan acts as a secular nation-state, even as it continues to define and consolidate its national identity.

Tajikistan: Overwhelming the National Identity

Tajikistan is ethnically heterogeneous. In the last Soviet census of 1989, 3.1 million were listed as Tajiks, 1.2 million as Uzbeks, and about 400,000 "Europeans."[28] The republic was cobbled together from contiguous areas in which Persian speakers were numerically dominant, but the two principal Persian-speaking cities, Bukhara and Samarqand, were left in Uzbekistan, thus depriving the new state (only separated from Uzbekistan in 1929) from much of its intelligentsia. Tajiks are conventionally understood to be the Persian speakers of Central Asia—distinct and distant from the Turkic speakers like the Uzbeks or Turkmen. This usage of the ethnonym is, however, a relatively recent one. Before the nineteenth century, "Tajik" referred to people who lived in oases, not to a par-

27. Gregory Gleason, "Uzbekistan: The Politics of National Independence," in Ian Bremmer and Ray Taras, eds., *New States, New Politics: Building the Post-Soviet Nations* (Cambridge: Cambridge University Press, 1997), pp. 583–584.

28. Although not listed separately, it is estimated that Pamiris numbered approximately 200,000. Olivier Roy, *The Civil War in Tajikistan: Causes and Implications: A Report of the Study Group on the Prospects for Conflict and Opportunities for Peacemaking in the Southern Tier of Former Soviet Republics* (Washington, D.C.: United States Institute of Peace, 1993), p. 9.

ticular linguistic group. Later it referred to city dwellers or to particular peoples in the mountains.[29] Over the years of Soviet rule, Tajiks in Uzbekistan were formally, statistically assimilated into the dominant Uzbek nationality, while in Tajikistan, peoples who had had separate identities noted by ethnographers or census-takers were integrated over time into the Tajik nationality. Most dramatically, the Pamiri peoples (Shughnis, Yazulemis, Rushanis, Ishkashimis, Wakhis, and others), many of whom had lived in the Gorno-Badakhshan Autonomous Region, which had been founded in 1925, were eliminated as categories in the 1959 Soviet census. Despite the state's policy of assimilation, however, many of these Pamiris, who are Shi'a unlike the Sunni Tajiks, insisted on "speaking Russian rather than Tâjik (which they often speak very badly) as an expression of their distinctness from the 'Tâjik,' whom they sometimes view with condescension."[30] In the late 1980s and early 1990s, Tajikistan fell apart in civil and ethnic wars. Here the fragility of national identity and the reinvigoration of alternative political and regional identities were fundamental to the social breakdown.[31] People divided along lines of "ethnicity" (Uzbek versus Tajik versus Pamiri), along regional lines (Khojand and Kulab on one side, Karategin, Jurgan Teppe, and Pamir region on the other), as well as sociological lines (old Communist elite versus emerging intelligentsia). Tajikistan's descent into civil war originated as a contest between Communist conservatives and a "democratic" opposition based in rival regions. One side in the political struggle was made up of the traditional Communist leaders with their complex networks of patrons and clients embedded in extended families, clans, and local relations, along with their Uzbek allies.[32] The Communists were prepared to promote and proclaim regional loyalties in any effort to gain support in the absence of any broader, more appealing program. The "socialist" system in Tajikistan had only a superficial relationship with anything resembling Marxism but rather was what the political scientist Olivier Roy calls a "retraditionalization" of the Soviet economy. "The *kolkhoz* became the modern tribe, and the secretary of the Party the mod-

---

29. Schoeberlein-Engel, "Identity in Central Asia," pp. 118; 123–153.

30. Ibid., p. 133.

31. Roy, *The Civil War in Tajikistan*, p. 15.

32. Although the civil war is also fueled by ideological and strategic objectives, the main domestic factor seems to be a lack of common Tajik identity and a common will to build a unified Tajik state, in contrast to an increasing Uzbek ethnic assertiveness." [Ibid., p. 11] See also Muriel Atkin, "Tajikistan: Reform, Reaction, and Civil War," in Bremmer and Taras, eds., *New States, New Politics*, pp. 602–627.

ern tribal leader. In fact, the communists were better adapted to this neotraditional society than the mullahs or the 'democrats.'"[33]

The opposition was a broad political coalition of cultural revivalist intellectuals (the *Rastokhez* movement), the Pamiris, the Democratic Party of Tajikistan, and the Islamic Renaissance Party. The "common thread of this alliance was that it represented those who had long been excluded from the Communist party system of clientelism based on region."[34] The Tajik intelligentsia generally identified more with their regions than with Tajikistan as a whole, and the "democrats and nationalists recruited mainly from among the small university-educated intelligentsia who did not originate from the ruling districts of Kulab and Khojand."[35] Their hopes lay in capturing the presidency in the elections of fall 1991, but when that effort failed and an old Communist boss received a Soviet-style majority, the impossibility of working through the electoral process opened the way to renewed street demonstrations that began in earnest in March 1992 and continued into spring. Even more conservative Communists organized a military effort, manned by Kulabi militants, to bring down the government. In the ensuing fighting, it is estimated that 50,000 people perished and another 10 percent of the population became refugees. The turn from a democratic struggle into a war employing regional and ethnic identities shattered what was left of the weak Tajik national identification that the Soviets had attempted to build up. The fragility of the state (and national identification) allowed Russia to intervene in Tajikistan's civil war and maintain a presence in the country in the name of regional stability.

Kazakhstan: Civic Nation-Building in a Binational State

Kazakhstan provides an example of a state with potentially serious challenges of national and political identity that might have led to conflict, but whose leadership was able to avoid violence and to negotiate provisional solutions.

The Kazakhs have never been a majority in their own republic. In the northern parts of the republic bordering on Russia, some 80 percent of the population is non-Kazakh, and many Russians hold that the northern

---

33. The Communist elite had strong local bases in Leninabad Province (the capital of which is Khojand) and Kulab Province, as well as an ethnic coloration, because Leninabad is an area that is either Uzbek or "Uzbekicized" and somewhat "Russian" in culture. Pamiris were generally excluded from high party positions.

34. Roy, *The Civil War in Tajikistan*, p. 22.

35. Ibid.

Kazakh steppe and eastern Kazakhstan are rightly parts of Russia.[36] Nursultan Nazarbaev, the last Soviet Communist Party chief in Kazakhstan, was a confirmed Gorbachevite dedicated to the preservation of the Soviet Union and a gradual transition to a more liberal society. Independence was thrust upon him and Kazakhstan when the three Slavic republics trilaterally left the Soviet Union on December 8, 1991. As president of the new state, he cautiously and skillfully maneuvered between Kazakhs—some of whom were becoming more nationalistic—and Russians who were fearful about their future in the newly independent state.

In 1992, political scientist Bhavna Dave asked her Kazakh informants about the "plight" of the Kazakhs, how they, their language and culture had "become marginalized" in their own homeland, and she heard consistent responses: "it was the Soviet system, its unmitigated policy of Russification and colonization, the 'genocide' [the loss of about two million Kazakhs during the forced sedentarization of the nomadic Kazakhs in the early Stalin period], the influx of settlers to till the so-called Virgin Lands [in the late 1950s] that resulted in this unfortunate state of affairs."[37] In this late Soviet and post-Soviet construction of the recent past, all agency passed from the Kazakhs to the "Soviet system," and Kazakhs were rendered victims of a brutal and alien state. The moment of independence just a year earlier had essentially jumpstarted a new era in Kazakh history that was starkly contrasted to the dark experience of the Soviet period. With statehood would come the revival of the national culture and the reversal of the Russification that had been imposed by the Soviet regime. Yet the experience of ordinary Kazakhs included more than memories of oppression and Russification. The modernizing project of the Soviet government had had profoundly transformative effects on the republic, many of which were judged positively by ordinary Kazakhs.

In contrast to other southern Soviet republics, where the national languages dominated over Russian, the Russian language was overwhelmingly the language of urban Kazakhs—not to mention that more than 50 percent of Kazakhstan's population was not Kazakh. Although the government and party apparatus had been populated with ethnic Kazakhs since the 1960s, that elite and most of the educated population preferred speaking Russian rather than Kazakh in both their official and daily lives. Since the urban centers of Kazakhstan had largely been Russian, Kazakhs

---

36. Martha Brill Olcott, "Kazakhstan: Pushing for Eurasia," in Bremmer and Taras, eds., *New States, New Politics*, pp. 554–555.

37. Bhavna Dave, "Politics of Language Revival: National Identity and State Building in Kazakhstan (Ph.D. dissertation, Syracuse University, 1996), p. 3.

Strand Book Store
828 Broadway
New York, New York 10003
212.473.1452
strandbooks.com
strand@strandbooks.com

Date: 04-11-2015
Sale: 3712872   Time: 03:16 PM

Limits of Culture: Islam and Foreign Policy
0262693216   Item Price: $12.50 $12.50
Phenomenology of Perception
0415834333   Item Price: $26.95 $26.95

2 Items   Subtotal: $39.45
                       Sales Tax (8.875 %): $3.50
                                    Total: $42.95

              Credit (Visa) Payment: $42.95
Card Number ************1978 XX/XX
                            LOPEZ/LEAH M
Approval # 240324788

              Amount Tendered: $42.95
                 Change Due: $0.00

Cust Sign: _____

Manager Sign: _____

Printed by: peterm   Register: Reg3-Shift2

        April 11, 2015 03:16 PM

   Hardcovers/Merchandise are returnable
        within 3 days for a full refund.

All other books, excluding clearance items, may be
   returned for store credit only within 14 days.

  Receipts must accompany all returns and exchanges.

          Follow @strandbookstore
        Show us your #STRANDHAUL
           Happy Reading!

: dominant language. About 40 themselves in their "mother n Kazakhs used Russian rather azakh had a low status among he language, whereas Russian dium for social advancement. -action policies of the Soviet tions of influence, gave them gher education (which was al- them from nomads into urban party chief Dinmukhammed became the dominant national- ccess required cultural compe- icantly knowledge of Russian. ssimilation did not occur. The understandings of ethnicity between nationalities, both as- se that ethnicity was deeply common sense in everyday one of Dave's informants re- never think of myself as any- Pushkin, even though I have dial idea of Kazakhness con- otion of those Kazakh nation- " ("no language, no nation"). oly rooted coexisted with the fforts were not made, particu- national culture. ctive identity had been based Kazakh" meant nomad, and stinguished themselves from ary life.[39] The nomads most inkages, either the tribal con- ipa), rather than with any no-

tion of "nation." A Kazakh intelligentsia promoted literacy in Kazakh be-

---

38. Ibid., p. 227.

39. Martha Brill Olcott, *The Kazakhs* (Stanford, Calif.: Hoover Institution Press, 1995), p. 18; Dave, "Politics of Language Revival," p. 125. For an account of earlier uses of the word "Kazak," see Zeki Velidi Togan, "The Origins of the Kazaks and the Özbeks," in H. B. Paksoy, *Central Asia Reader: The Rediscovery of History* (Armonk, N.Y.: M. E. Sharpe, 1994), pp. 32–36.

fore the Russian revolution, published a newspaper, *Qazaq*, that reached 8,000 subscribers, and in 1906, formed a patriotic organization, *Alash*, which came to prominence in the revolutionary years. Nationalism among the literati, however, should not be equated with mass allegiance to an idea of the nation. The Soviet state's "nativization" programs of the 1920s and 1930s assisted the development of a standardized literary language that was employed in official institutions. Ethnic Kazakh membership in the Kazakhstan Communist party grew from 8 to 38 percent in four years (1924–1928), but these developments pale before the disaster of the late 1920s and early 1930s. Led by the non-Kazakh F. I. Goloshchekin, the party carried out a "small October" to transform the Kazakh way of life and eliminate traditional social relations. The state authorities ordered the collectivization of Kazakh herds and compelled the nomads to settle on the land. The herdsmen resisted by slaughtering their livestock. Hundreds of thousands fled to China, and in the chaos of collectivization, over 40 percent of the Kazakh population was lost. The demographic catastrophe was later compounded by Kazakh losses in World War II and the influx of Slavic and other settlers in the late 1950s during the Virgin Lands campaign. Kazakhs became a minority in their own republic.

At the same time, Soviet-mandated modernization created a new Kazakh society: party and state officials, intellectuals with privileged access to state-subsidized institutions, and a working class tied to state industry. Upwardly mobile Kazakhs imbibed many of the values of Soviet modernization, even as they complained about the excesses of Stalinism and the failure of the system to meet its own standards of justice, equality, and material well-being. In the view of nationalists, modern Soviet Kazakhs resembled the *mankurts* of Chingiz Aitmatov's novel, *The Day Lasts a Hundred Years,* who were deracinated, denationalized amnesiacs without a sense of the past. Like other Central Asians, Kazakhs did not participate in dissident or nationalist movements before 1989—the sole exception being the street protests of December 1986 against the installation of a Russian as head of the Communist Party of Kazakhstan. By the time *glasnost* and *perestroika* were opening up the "blank spots" of Kazakh history, the removal of Kunaev and his replacement by a Russian from outside the republic violated the deep feeling that Kazakhstan ought to be governed by the titular nationality.

Independence in 1991 abruptly changed the political salience of nationality and nationalism. Overnight a radical status reversal turned the ethnic Kazakhs from a subordinate people in a multinational empire into the "state-bearing" nation in a new state, while the former "elder brother," the "Russians" (actually Russian-speaking peoples) of

Kazakhstan found themselves no longer living in their Soviet homeland but living as beached diaspora in a new, potentially foreign state. The Communist Party chief, Nazarbaev, easily converted to national leader, even as he resisted the call of independent nationalists for a more vigorous nationalizing program. He argued that Kazakhstan now required energetic state intervention in the cultural sphere, particularly in the development of the language of the titular nationality, to foster the consolidation of nationhood. In a major policy statement in the fall of 1993, he asked, ". . . to what can we turn if the previous [socialist] tenets have proven bankrupt?" And he answered, to cultural traditions, to one's historical cultural roots, which "enable a person to 'keep his bearings' and adapt his way of life to the impetuous changes of the modern world."[40] Kazakhness and Kazakh language and traditions now took on a new value—one that contrasted markedly with the marginalization of Kazakh culture in late Soviet times.

At first, it appeared that ethnicity and ethnonationalism would be the easy fallback position of state builders in the post-Soviet republics. Yet to maintain internal stability and to avoid confrontation with their Russian neighbor to the north, Kazakhstan, like a number of other post-Soviet states, experimented with an ethnically-inflected variant of civic nationhood. The Kazakh government maneuvered between the legacy of Soviet internationalism and an emerging ethnonationalism. As Edward Schatz notes, "If internationalism had a Russian face in the Soviet period, given the privileged position accorded Russians throughout the republics, the weak post-Soviet state in Kazakhstan turned Soviet-style internationalism on its head by offering a normatively appealing discourse to its nontitular population and a diffuse and ill-defined set of privileges to titular Kazakhs."[41] Employing a kind of retreaded Soviet internationalism, former party boss Nazarbaev proposed a Eurasian identity for Kazakhstan, linking Russians and Kazakhs into a single category. Kazakhstan was seen as a crossroads of civilizations, with legal protection for all peoples in a non-ethnic state. "But, just as Soviet-era internationalism ultimately had a Russian face (holding a privileged position for ethnic Russians

40. Nursultan Nazarbaev, *Ideological Consolidation of Society as an Essential Prerequisite to Kazakstan's Progress* (Almati, Kazakhstan: Daewir, 1994), p. 40, cited in R. Stuart DeLorme, "Mother Tongue, Mother's Touch: Kazakhstan Government and School Construction of Identity and Language Planning Metaphors," (Ph.D. dissertation, University of Pennsylvania, 1999), p. 100.

41. Edward Schatz, "The Politics of Multiple Identities: Lineage and Ethnicity in Kazakhstan," *Europe-Asia Studies*, Vol. 52, No. 3 (2000), p. 491.

in the evolutionary march toward the 'bright future'), post-Soviet Kazakhstani state ideology had a Kazakh face, singling out Kazakhs for linguistic, demographic, political and cultural redress."[42]

In the discourse of the nation, culture is the source of political power. The right to rule belongs to the people or nation that is imagined as coherent, bounded, and conscious of its position as the foundation of the state's legitimacy. Specific territories are understood to "belong" to particular nations that either currently occupy those territories or have prior historical claims. Soviet state practices spent much time and energy connecting specific peoples to specific territories, primordializing the nationalities of the Soviet Union by employing anthropologists and historians to establish the original moment of ethnogenesis. Appearance of the ethnonym in travelers' accounts or other sources was often enough to conclude that a nation existed. For Soviet Kazakhs, it was eventually settled that the "nation" was formed in the mid-fifteenth century.[43] But when they were freed from the restraints imposed by the imperial metropole, post-Soviet Kazakh scholars extended Kazakh continuity even deeper into the past. "According to several informants in the Institute of History and Ethnography," writes Schatz, "the institute's director, a powerful ally of the president, issued an instruction (*instruktazh*) to researchers to find the roots of Kazakh statehood in the Sak period (the first millennium B.C.). This was a clear departure from established historiography that located such statehood in the mid-15th century."[44] One scholar attempted to incorporate Chingis Khan and his empire into the Kazakh past in order to show that the Kazakh were "a more ancient and historically well-known people than the Mongols."[45] The efforts of historians, as well as ethnographic expeditions sponsored by the state, aimed at ethnicizing the past of Kazakhstan, erasing its more multi-ethnic features, and establishing an ethnic Kazakh claim to territory. The experiences of pre-Kazakh Turkic tribes were assimilated into a Kazakh narrative.[46] The cultural activists found ancient heroes, called for preservation of monuments, and organized excavations.

In a rerun of the original *korenizatsiia* program of the 1920s, the inde-

---

42. Ibid., p. 492.

43. The consensus is that the Kazakh people or Kazakh nation was formed in the mid-fifteenth century when Janibek (Dzhanibek) and Kirai (Girei), sons of Barak Khan of the White horde of the Mongol empire, broke away from Abul'l Khayr (Abulkair), khan of the Uzbeks." (Olcott, *The Kazakhs*, p. 3)

44. Schatz, "The Politics of Multiple Identities," p. 496.

45. Ibid.

46. Ibid., pp. 496–498.

pendent state promoted Kazakh media, higher education in Kazakh, greater Kazakhization of the state apparatus, and repatriation of diaspora Kazakhs. Kazakh would be the state language, and Kazakh-language education would be stressed. The Kazakh state was imagined as a caring, kind mother; Kazakhs were envisioned as a generous, hospitable people who opened their arms to other peoples. Kazakhstan, then, where Kazakhs were the first among equals, was a place where many nationalities could coexist. While the Kazakh national anthem proclaimed how the Kazakhs had suffered "on the anvil of fate, from hell itself," and the state emblem emphasized the antiquity and indigenousness of the ethnic Kazakhs, the successive drafts of the constitution (1993, 1995) moved in an internationalist direction. The preamble to the second constitution was boldly inclusive of all peoples of the republic. Its first sentence reads, "We, the people of Kazakhstan, united by a common historical fate . . . " A later article stated even more clearly: "No part of the people . . . can appropriate to themselves the sole right to exercise state power."[47] The winning design for the state flag was certainly symbolic of Kazakh ethnic dominance—a sky blue background, a golden sun, and a woven Kazakh design. The sun, however, could be understood as inclusive in a way that the Islamic crescents of the Azerbaijani, Turkmen, and Uzbek flags could not.[48]

For Nazarbaev, Kazakhstan is both the homeland of the Kazakhs, where the Kazakh language and a more national version of Kazakh history must be promoted, and a multinational state in which all "Kazakhstanis" would have equal civil rights and opportunities. He suppressed virulent nationalists, punished Islamists (the so-called Wahhabis), and agreed to slow down the shift to Kazakh language. Russian was recognized as an official language in the constitution of 1995, an apparent reversal of the 1989 law that established Kazakh as the official state language. The law on language of July 1997 seemed to confirm the status of both languages—on the one hand promoting the spread of Kazakh while on the other allowing Russian to be used in official capacities.

As Nazarbaev set out on the road of nation-building, he was faced not only by Kazakh nationalists dedicated to Kazakh cultural dominance in the new state and the threat of massive Russian out-migration with the

47. DeLorme, "Mother Tongue, Mother's Touch," pp. 87–89, 94–95.

48. Ibid., pp. 83–84. One scholar argues that an official document, "Concept for the Forming of a State identity of the Republic of Kazakhstan," (May 1996) signaled "a retreat from the studious ethnic neutrality of the 1995 constitution." See Pål Kolstø, "Anticipating Demographic Superiority: Kazakh Thinking on Integration and Nation Building," *Europe-Asia Studies*, Vol. 50, No.1 (1998), p. 58.

consequent loss of skilled labor, but also by a general indifference to the project of nationalizing the country. Dave found that in the early 1990s, "most Kazakhs remain as apathetic to the nationalizing state as they were indifferent to the communist ideology. Soviet-style internationalism is in fact closer to their life experience than is the ongoing ethnicization of personal identities and the public sphere by a nationalizing state."[49]

While Nazarbaev's nationality policy, pulled as it was between ethnic and civic conceptions of the nation, allowed for stable and tolerant relations within the bicultural population of Kazakhstan, priority was to be given to reviving Kazakh ethnic culture "because it cannot be sufficiently developed in a true sense in any other place than Kazakhstan."[50] Colonial victimization was to be redressed.[51] These strategic choices by moderate state officials to promote an inclusive civic identity that best guarantees peaceful relations among its multi-ethnic population has clear foreign policy implications. Prudence and balance, presumably to foster a sense of commitment to a new, just, and caring nation, are not only aimed at keeping radical nationalists at bay and Russian-speakers from leaving the country, but also at maintaining good relations with Russia.[52] Russian nationalists, like author Alexander Solzhenitsyn, have long expressed interest in the Russian-populated regions of northern Kazakhstan. Nazarbaev's measured policies inhibit the kinds of discontent and disorder among Kazakhstan's Russians that may encourage irredentist claims from the other side of the border. In a bold move to cement northern and southern Kazakhstan under a single authority, Nazarbaev moved the capital from Almati in the southeast to the forbidding town of Akhmola (later called Astana) in the northwest.[53] By transferring the capital 745 miles to the northwest, the president sought to preempt potential Russian separatism and encourage Kazakh migration to the north. In his vision, the Kazakh president sees Kazakhstan as a multinational state, neither

49. Dave, "Politics of Language Revival," p. 229.

50. From the pamphlet issued by the Kazakhstan Republic President's Office, *Kazakstan Respublikasy aelewmettik-maedenij damuwynyng tuzhyrymdasy/Kontseptsiia sotsiokulturnogo razvitiia respubliki Kazakhstana* [*Concept of Sociocultural Development in the Republic of Kazakhstan*] (Almati: Kazakstan, 1993), pp. 8–9; cited in DeLorme, 'Mother Tongue, Mother's Touch," p. 107.

51. Schatz, "The Politics of Multiple Identities," pp. 498–502.

52. For a pessimistic assessment of the possibility of maintaining the civic national balance in Kazakhstan, see David D. Laitin, *Identity in Formation: The Russian-Speaking Populations in the Near Abroad* (Ithaca, N.Y. and London: Cornell University Press, 1998), pp. 359–360.

53. David Hoffman, "The Long Road to Akmola: Is Nazarbayev Tilting at Windmills?" *CERA Decision Brief*, June 1997, pp. 1–7.

eastern nor western, neither Islamic nor Christian, but a bridge between Europe and Asia.[54]

Conclusions

As should be evident in the above discussion of Central Asia, current identities and antagonisms should not be seen as simply the reemergence from slumber of atavistic, repressed, or primordial identities and conflicts. Rather, in the late Soviet and post-Soviet period, older selectively revived or reconstituted cultural, religious, and regional identities compete with national identities of relatively recent origin. Within limits, elites can choose among the repertoire of available identities and discourses to promote inter-ethnic peace or exacerbate conflict. But when constrained by popular understandings, they challenge discursive boundaries at their own peril. Occasionally a leader like Kazakhstan's Nazarbaev pushes against the grain and successfully reconstructs identities. This may be called statesmanship.

State leaders in new states with evolving national identities face a serious dilemma at the beginning of the new millennium. The absence of an effective, unifying national identity in a political world in which nations are the source of legitimacy for states generally contributes to state weakness and the greater possibility for instability and violence. In a discursive universe of normative nationalism and an international system in which nation and state are welded together, political communities that identify as nations can be more easily mobilized around issues of "national" defense, "national" honor or pride, "national" survival, as if the victory or defeat of the state would mean the life or death of the cultural community. The experiences of Russia, the Caucasus, and Central Asia demonstrate that with all the dangers that certain national identities and national discourses may present, coherent national identity is indispensable for state builders in the present political environment.

Why and at which moments discourses and identities may shift or be changed are questions that can best be answered with reference to particular cases from which more general propositions may be drawn. In conditions of uncertainty and instability, leaders have unprecedented opportunities to choose among available identities. The easy choice of ethnonationalism is not a foregone conclusion, for in several cases, like

---

54. Olcott, "Kazakhstan: Pushing for Eurasia," p. 557. It is estimated that in September 1996 just over 40 percent of Kazakhs were sending their children to Russian schools. Pål Kolstø and Irina Malkova, "Is Kazakhstan Being Kazakhified?" *Analysis of Current Events*, Vol. 9, No. 11 (November 1997), p. 4.

Karimov's Uzbekistan or Nazarbaev's Kazakhstan, leaders may calculate that greater chances for stability lie in policies of inclusion and tolerance. Although the demands of state building require some conception of the national community and an ethnic criterion for membership may at first glance appear to be the easy road to political cohesion and mobilization, in fact recognition of the ethnic diversity of the polity and calculation of the costs of enforcing ethnic homogenization may encourage some politicians to choose a broader definition of citizenship—as in Uzbekistan and Kazakhstan. Ethnonationalism is an option that, like revolution, is highly unpredictable and can lead to debilitating social violence, as evidenced by Georgia and certainly by the former Yugoslavia. A sober politician may choose a cool pragmatism rather than risk stirring the pot of ethnic emotions. On the other hand, creating a civic nation, which lacks the emotional and affective association with a historically-constituted cultural community, may be much harder to sell to a population already steeped in ethnic politics.

Identities formed in Soviet and post-Soviet Central Asia have also influenced the foreign policies of the new states. Much as it had been exaggerated by analysts in the past, however, Islam has proven to be a weak identity in the region, less of a religious affiliation with the non-Soviet Muslim world than a local distinction between the indigenous peoples and the "Europeans" who live among them. In contrast, the most potent identification has been with the nation, engendered and cultivated during the Soviet years, though national identity has proven to be stronger in Uzbekistan and Kazakhstan than in regionally divided Tajikistan. Soviet primordialism and the policy of tying a specific ethnicity to a particular territory has both solidified the claims of the titular nations to their states and restrained Russia from pretensions to lands in other republics. Inclusive civic ideas of the nation have proven to have pragmatic value both in keeping domestic peace and preventing conflicts that could provoke conflict with the great neighbor to the north. And finally (though this is a more speculative point) identification of the Central Asian elites and nationalities with the transnational concepts of Central Asia, Eurasia, and Islam has probably played a role in lowering the sense of threat from immediate neighbors and heightening a notion of common destiny. The ways in which policymakers and opinion shapers see the world have profound effects on the constitution of that world. Choices of the elite are key to determining political identifications, but such choices can be made only within certain discursive limits. In contrast to some neorealist theories, the constructivist approach presented here proposes that recognition of the centrality of identities, representations, and discourses is key to evaluating the conditions for conflict or cooperation. Mere proximity of a mammoth state to much smaller ones does not necessarily lead to imperialism or even hegemony, for the actual relations between states depend on the forms of national identity and discourse, the perceived threats that follow from the way the world is imagined on all sides, and distributions of power and resources. Analysts must be wary of the "creeping essentialism" that invades much of the writing on post–Cold War conflict. Not only are nations and cultural communities arenas of contestation and debate, with internal divisions and differences, and shared commonalities with those they distinguish themselves against, but even more so are such hybrid conglomerates as "civilizations." A world as clear, crisply delineated, and differentiated by bright colors as a Rand McNally map, with nations and civilizations homogenized and coherent within and radically different at the points where they bump up against one another, may be nothing more than a figment of the imagination.

Chapter 5

Culture and Alliances: U.S. Portrayals of Saudi Arabia, Azerbaijan, and Kazakhstan Before and After September 11, 2001

Ido Oren with Robert Kauffman

The notion that cultural affinity between nations significantly affects their political-diplomatic relations has a long pedigree. More than two hundred years ago, philosopher Edmund Burke wrote that "nothing is so strong a tie of amity between nation and nation as correspondence in laws, customs, manners, and habits of life." Though British statesman Lord Palmerston famously declared that England had permanent interests, not permanent friends, in practice he often sought, as he put it in the 1830s, "to form a Western confederacy of free states as a counterpoise to the Eastern League of arbitrary governments." Additionally, in the 1950s, political scientist Karl Deutsch argued that the "compatibility of major values" held by West European and North American elites was essential to the successful formation of a "pluralistic security community" in the North Atlantic area.[1]

The idea that patterns of cultural similarity (or dissimilarity) shape international relations survived repeated attacks by realist scholars during the Cold War,[2] and its popularity surged markedly in the 1990s. Thomas Risse-Kappen, echoing Deutsch's argument, attributed the en-

---

1. Edmond Burke, "Three Letters to a Member of Parliament on Proposals for Peace with the Regicide Directory of France," quoted in Arnold Wolfers and Laurence W. Martin, eds., *The Anglo-American Tradition in Foreign Affairs: Readings from Thomas More to Woodrow Wilson* (New Haven, Conn.: Yale University Press, 1956), pp. 111–112; Palmerston is quoted in Stephen Walt, *The Origins of Alliances* (Ithaca, N.Y.: Cornell University Press, 1987), pp. 33–34; Karl Deutsch et al., *Political Community and the North Atlantic Area* (Princeton, N.J.: Princeton University Press, 1957), p. 66.

2. See Hans Morgenthau, *Politics Among Nations*, 6th ed. (New York: McGraw-Hill, 1985), pp. 201–206; Edwin Fedder, "The Concept of Alliance," *International Studies Quarterly*, Vol. 12, No.1 (1968): p. 86; Walt, *Origins of Alliances*.

durance of the North Atlantic Treaty Organization (NATO) to the liberal values shared by its member states. Michael Barnett similarly explained alliance patterns in the Middle East in terms of shared cultural identities, which produced common definitions of external threats.[3] Bruce Russett claimed that liberal democracies lived in peace with each other partly because *"the culture, perceptions, and practices* that permit compromise and the peaceful resolution of conflicts without the threat of violence within countries come to apply across national boundaries toward other democratic countries." If people in a democracy, Russett added, "perceive themselves as autonomous, self-governing people who share norms of live-and-let-live, they will respect the rights of others to self-determination if those others are also perceived as self-governing."[4] *Clash of Civilizations* author Samuel Huntington famously argued that "in the post–Cold War world, states increasingly define their interests in civilizational terms. They cooperate with and ally themselves with states with similar or common culture and are more often in conflict with countries of different culture."[5]

Huntington, much like Russett, recognized the importance of states' perceptions and "understandings" of each other's cultural traits. He wrote that "states define threats in terms of the intentions of other states, and those intentions and how they are perceived are powerfully shaped by cultural considerations. Publics and statesmen are less likely to see threats emerging from people they feel they understand and can trust because of shared language, religion, values, institutions, and culture. They are much more likely to see threats coming from states whose societies have different cultures and hence which they do not understand."[6]

Different though they may be from each other in substance and method, the cultural arguments of Huntington, Russett, and other international relations scholars all posit, explicitly or implicitly, an explanatory model in which the cultural characteristics of states serve as causes of these states' political relations with each other. They all imply that the

3. Thomas Risse-Kappen, "Collective Identity in a Democratic Community: The Case of NATO," and Michael Barnett, "Identity and Alliances in the Middle East," both in Peter Katzenstein, ed., *The Culture of National Security: Norms and Identity in World Politics* (New York: Columbia University Press, 1996), pp. 357–399 and 400–447 respectively.

4. Bruce Russett, *Grasping the Democratic Peace: Principles for a Post–Cold War World* (Princeton, N.J.: Princeton University Press, 1993), p. 31; emphasis in original.

5. Samuel P. Huntington, *The Clash of Civilizations and the Remaking of World Order* (New York: Touchstone Books, 1997), p. 34.

6. Ibid., p. 34; emphasis added.

norms, practices, or institutions of foreign states are perceived, understood, and characterized independently of (and prior to) the politics of
these states' relations with our own state. These cultural arguments do
not allow for the possibility that a state's perceptions and characterizations of another state are in fact intertwined with and colored by the politics of their bilateral relations.

In this essay, the authors intend to demonstrate how—*contra* conventional culturalist arguments—perceptions of cultural similarity (dissimilarity) between states change *jointly with* (rather than prior to) changes in
these states' bilateral diplomatic relations. The strategy is to compare
how the U.S. print media has characterized three Muslim-majority, energy-rich nations—Saudi Arabia, Azerbaijan, and Kazakhstan—before
and after the terrorist attacks of September 11, 2001. In the aftermath of
these attacks, of which Saudi citizens comprised the majority of the perpetrators, diplomatic relations between the United States and Saudi Arabia have chilled considerably as influential figures in Washington openly
questioned Saudi Arabia's commitment to combatting terrorism and as
the Saudis refused to openly support the U.S. invasion of Iraq. On the
other hand, U.S.-Azerbaijani relations have improved as Azerbaijan
openly and unambiguously supported both the war on terrorism, which
had been launched in response to the September 11 attacks, and the war
on Iraq. U.S.-Kazakh relations have initially been strengthened by
Kazakhstan's decision to assist the U.S. war effort in Afghanistan, but the
bilateral relationship later cooled off somewhat when Kazakhstan, unlike
Azerbaijan, declined to join the U.S.-led coalition against Iraq. In sum,
after September 11, 2001, the "temperatures" of U.S. diplomatic relations have decreased markedly with Saudi Arabia and increased with
Azerbaijan. The temperature of U.S.-Kazakh relations experienced some
fluctuations; on balance, it can be said to have increased moderately.

The results show that the U.S. news media's characterizations of the
domestic institutions, customs, and practices of the three states after September 11, 2001, shifted in ways that tracked and reflected the changes in
the quality of U.S. strategic-diplomatic relations with these states (which
were being simultaneously reported by the same media). The Saudi dynasty had always professed allegiance to the fundamentalist Wahhabi
form of Islam, yet the U.S. press had almost never mentioned the terms
"Wahhabi" or "Wahhabism" prior to September 2001, preferring to characterize Saudi Arabia predominantly as "oil-rich." Since the September 11
attacks, the image of Saudi Arabia that has been reflected by the U.S.
press has been transformed from that of a wealthy and modernizing, if
not quite democratic, major oil exporter which happened to be the birthplace of some Islamic terrorists, into a Wahhabist, fundamentalist Islamic

kingdom whose principal export is terrorism and who is not a reliable ally of the United States. In contrast to this darkening image of Saudi Arabia, the depictions of Azerbaijan and Kazakhstan in the U.S. press (to the extent that the U.S. press covered these countries at all) remained as dominated by the image of promising oil deposits after September 2001 as they had been prior to the terrorist attacks. Azerbaijan's image evolved from that of a promising oil frontier that was still burdened by the legacies of military defeat (to Armenia), poverty, and Soviet misrule into a promising oil frontier that is friendly to the West. Kazakhstan also evolved from a promising, if corrupt and repressive, oil frontier to a promising oil frontier that, though hardly democratic, was becoming a friend of the United States.

The changes in the U.S. media's portrayals of the domestic features of Saudi Arabia, Azerbaijan, and Kazakhstan thus coincided with rather than preceded changes in the quality of U.S. diplomatic relations with these nations. No neat line separated characterizations of these states' domestic institutions and practices from characterizations of the status of their political partnership with the United States—the two were intertwined. This belies the conventional view that perceptions of cultural similarity or difference constitute an independent cause of political friendship or enmity between states. The findings suggest that perceptions of other states' institutions, norms, and practices are mutually constituted with perceptions of political friendship or enmity. Perceived cultural dissimilarity may be an effect of political tension between states as much as its cause.

Research Design and Method

Saudi Arabia, Azerbaijan, and Kazakhstan are appropriate cases for comparison because they resemble each other on two salient dimensions. First, Islam constitutes the largest religious grouping in all three countries. Saudi Arabia's population is nearly 100 percent Muslim, while in Azerbaijan and Kazakhstan Muslims comprise over 90 and about 50 percent of the population respectively.[7] Second, the economies of all three countries depend heavily on the exploitation of energy resources. Saudi Arabia is the world's largest oil producer, and it possesses one-fourth of the world's proven oil reserves. Kazakhstan has benefited from massive Western investment in its energy sector since it gained independence in

7. CIA World Factbook, 2002, accessed at <www.cia.gov/cia/publications/factbook> on June 2, 2003.

1991. According to the U.S. Department of Energy, Kazakhstan's substantial proven oil reserves are dwarfed by its vast "possible" reserves, estimated to range between thirty and fifty billion barrels of oil.[8] The recently discovered Kashagan field, located off the Kazakh shore of the Caspian Sea, has been hailed as the largest oil discovery in the world in the past thirty years. Contingent upon continuing development of export pipelines, Kazakhstan could become one of the world's largest oil exporters in the next decade. Azerbaijan, too, has attracted enormous foreign investment in its bountiful oil and natural gas sectors since gaining its independence. The country's oil production is predicted to exceed one million barrels per day by 2010, which is comparable to the current production level of Oman. Azerbaijan is also poised to become a major exporter of natural gas; the Shah Deniz field, discovered in 1999, is thought to be the world's largest natural gas discovery since 1978.[9]

Although these three countries exhibit significant, if imperfect, similarities in terms of both the professed religion of the majority of their populaces and their dominant economic sector,[10] their strategic-diplomatic experiences *vis-à-vis* the United States, as noted above, have differed substantially after September 11, 2001. This state of affairs allows the authors to conduct a doubly comparative analysis of the characterization of Saudi Arabia, Azerbaijan, and Kazakhstan in the U.S. press. On one level, the authors compare the characterizations of these states with each other, in cross-sectional fashion. Have these characterizations been equally dominated by the image of oil wealth (or promise thereof)? If not, does variation in the salience of oil across the characterizations of the three states correspond to the variation in their strategic relations with the United States?

The second comparative dimension of the analysis is longitudinal. For each state, the authors compare its characterization by the U.S. media in the eighteen months preceding September 11, 2001 (namely the period beginning on March 11, 2000) with its characterization in the subsequent eighteen months (through March 11, 2003). How did the image of, say, Saudi Arabia, as reflected in the U.S. press during the post–September 11

---

8. U.S. Department of Energy, Energy Information Administration, "Country Analysis Brief: Kazakhstan," July 2002, p. 2, accessed at <www.eia.doe.gov> in May 2003.

9. See U.S. Department of Energy, Energy Information Administration, "Country Analysis Briefs" for Saudi Arabia, Kazakhstan and Azerbaijan, at <www.eia.doe.gov>, accessed in May 2003.

10. The religious similarity among the three countries is imperfect inasmuch as one of the three (Saudi Arabia) is a monarchy governed by Islamic law while the other two are officially secular republics.

period, differ from Saudi Arabia's image prior to September 11, 2001? Also, to the extent that the country's image has changed, has the change corresponded to the change in its bilateral relations with the United States?

To represent the "U.S. press," the authors selected four well-known publications: the *New York Times*, the *Wall Street Journal*, *USA Today*, and *Newsweek*. *Newsweek* is one of the country's two top-selling weekly magazines; its circulation in the United States is more than 3.1 million copies. The other three publications are top-selling U.S. daily newspapers, with paid circulation of 2.6 million (*USA Today*), 1.8 million (the *Wall Street Journal*), and 1.7 million copies (the *New York Times*). These newspapers are distributed nationally, and their readers tend to be better educated and more affluent than the average American.[11] Analyzing these four publications would thus yield a fair, if not comprehensive, idea of the images of Saudi Arabia, Azerbaijan, and Kazakhstan harbored by the proverbial "American mind," or at least the minds of U.S. elites. Smaller national and regional newspapers provide far less foreign news coverage than the top-circulation publications chosen for analysis (and even some of the analyzed newspapers did not significantly cover the Caspian Sea region). Moreover, much of the foreign news or commentary reprinted in smaller news publications originates in newspapers such as the *New York Times*.[12]

The analysis proceeded in the following stages. First, computerized search engines combed all issues of the *New York Times*, the *Wall Street*

---

11. Audit Bureau of Circulations, "Top 100 Newspapers by Largest Reported Circulation," <www.accessabc.com/reader/top100.htm<, accessed on May 25, 2003; "History of Newsweek: Synopsis," at <www.msnbc.com/modules/newsweek/info>, accessed on May 25, 2003; *Wall Street Journal* "circulation/audience" at <http://advertising.wsj.com/circaud>, accessed on May 25, 2003; *New York Times*, "Circulation" at <http://nytadvertising.nyt.com/adonis>, accessed on May 25, 2003; *USA Today*, "Audience," at <www.usatoday.com/media_kit/usatoday>, accessed on May 25, 2003. The circulation figure for the *New York Times* refers to the Sunday edition; weekday circulation is over 1.1 million.

12. For many Americans, television may be a more significant source of news than the print media. But throughout the 1990s, the television networks and cable news channels have increased their focus on entertainment, personalities, and other "soft news" at the expense of foreign news. The three major networks closed many of their overseas news bureaus and reduced the scope of their foreign coverage by two-thirds between 1989 and 2000. In light of this state of affairs, it is highly unlikely that Americans whose main source of news is television would get a significant idea about the politics, societies, or economies of Saudi Arabia, let alone Azerbaijan and Kazakhstan. See Jim Ruttenberg, "A Nation Challenged: The Coverage," *The New York Times*, September 24, 2001.

Journal, USA Today, and *Newsweek* published between March 11, 2000, and March 11, 2003.[13] The search engines selected all articles (including news reports, op-eds, editorials, and letters to the editor—"article" referring below to a generic category aggregating all these types of content) whose headline or lead paragraph contained the term(s) "Saudi Arabia," "Azerbaijan," or "Kazakhstan."[14] Second, the authors read carefully all the articles that matched the terms of the search; but many of these articles mentioned the country only in passing, often without even an adjective attached to its name and without giving any meaningful context or texture. Examples of such insignificant, "in passing" references include reports on the Olympic medal tally from the Sydney 2000 games in which either Kazakhstan or Azerbaijan was listed among many other states, or a *Newsweek* interview with the American basketball coach of the Iranian national team, who happened to have "spent the last 14 years teaching basketball teams in countries ranging from Bahrain to Saudi Arabia to Mongolia"—in this article, neither any subsequent mention of Saudi Arabia nor the name Saudi Arabia was accompanied by an adjective.[15] All such insignificant mentions of Saudi Arabia, Azerbaijan, or Kazakhstan were excluded from the sample. This cut eliminated approximately half of the articles that had matched the search terms "Saudi Arabia" or "Kazakhstan" and a quarter of the articles that matched the search term "Azerbaijan."[16]

The third step in the analysis was the construction of categories based on themes that recurred in the sample's articles. The authors did not impose their own *a priori* categories upon the articles but rather in-

---

13. To search the contents of the *New York Times, Newsweek,* and *USA Today* the authors used LexisNexis; to search the *Wall Street Journal,* the authors used Factiva.com, a service owned by the Dow Jones Corporation, which also owns the *Wall Street Journal* (the content of the *Wall Street Journal* is not available on LexisNexis, but the authors employed the same search parameters).

14. The authors have not analyzed articles in which the names Azerbaijan, Kazakhstan, or Saudi Arabia appeared beyond the lead paragraph because in such articles the relevant country was usually mentioned in passing only. The authors have no reason to believe that including these articles in the sample would have influenced the results in a systematic way.

15. Maziar Bahari, "An American in Tehran," *Newsweek,* August 13, 2001.

16. The search for articles containing "Saudi Arabia" in the headline or lead paragraph between March 11, 2000, and March 11, 2003, yielded 1824 articles (in all four publications combined), of which the authors excluded 981 (54 percent) that were judged as insignificant. Of the 289 articles containing "Kazakhstan" published during the same time period the authors excluded 152 (53 percent), and of the 146 articles mentioning Azerbaijan, 37 (25 percent) were excluded.

ferred these thematic categories from the articles themselves. A few of the
identified themes were common across all three cases. Most notably, oil
was a recurrent theme in the U.S. press's characterization of each one of
the three states. Because the recurrent themes depend in large part on history, geography, and other contextual factors unique to each state, however, many of the constructed thematic categories do not overlap across
the three cases. For example, some news reports on Azerbaijan and
Kazakhstan dealt with the issue of protecting the Caspian Sea's dwin-
dling sturgeon population—a theme that was unsurprisingly absent from
reports on Saudi Arabia. On the other hand, articles about Saudi Arabia
often referred to the kingdom as the birthplace of terrorist Osama bin
Laden—a theme that was obviously absent from articles about the Caspian states. Overall the authors identified thirteen, sixteen, and thirteen
recurrent themes in the U.S. press's coverage of Saudi Arabia, Azerbaijan,
and Kazakhstan respectively. The following discussion of the findings offers specific descriptions and examples of these thematic categories.

The fourth stage of the analysis involved coding each article in the
sample in terms of the theme, or themes, evident in it. Many articles featured two or more themes, and in such cases, the authors counted all of
these themes. For example, in December 2001, the *New York Times* published a news report datelined Almati, Kazakhstan, that discussed a corruption scandal at some length, contained several references to
"Kazakhstan's vast oil reserves" and depicted Kazakhstan as "a country
that Western observers regard as insular and authoritarian." The authors
thus coded this article under three thematic categories: corruption, oil
frontier, and political repression. Another example of multiple coding is
a *Newsweek* news analysis published shortly after the September 11
attacks, which depicted Saudi Arabia as a "real source of modern Islamic
terrorism" and as a "Wahhabi" kingdom; the authors counted this
article under two categories: supporter of terrorism and Wahhabism/
fundamentalism.[17]

Finally, the authors tallied and tabulated the results by thematic categories. For every one of the four analyzed publications, the authors
counted the number of times that each theme appeared in articles published in the eighteen months prior to September 11, 2001, and the number of times that it appeared in the eighteen months following that date.
The authors then totaled the counts for the four publications combined.

17. David Johnston, "Kazakh Mastermind, or New Ugly American?" *New York Times*,
December 17, 2000; Fareed Zakaria, "The Allies Who Made Our Foes," *Newsweek*,
October 1, 2001.

In addition to counting the absolute frequency of the appearance of each theme, the authors calculated each theme's frequency relative to other themes (relative frequency) by dividing its absolute frequency by the total number of articles in the relevant sample. For example, during the pre–September 11 period, the *New York Times* published twenty-four articles characterizing Saudi Arabia as an oil exporter, while in the post–September 11 period, it published twenty-six such articles. Because the overall number of *New York Times* articles mentioning Saudi Arabia had jumped from 99 before September 11, 2001, to 413 in its aftermath, however, the relative frequency of the oil theme declined precipitously from 0.24 to 0.06: in other words, if in the earlier time period, 24 percent of *New York Times* articles about Saudi Arabia associated the kingdom with oil, after September 11, 2001, only 6 percent of the articles had done so. The relative frequency measure thus describes the salience of each theme as part of the overall, composite image of the foreign country as portrayed by the U.S. press.

Some of the changes in the U.S. press's characterizations of Saudi Arabia, Azerbaijan, and Kazakhstan over time may have actually reflected objective developments in the politics, societies, or economies of these states rather than shifts in their relations with the United States. Reports on oil may increase in frequency because of the actual discovery of a new oil field; increased reporting about harassment of opposition leaders may reflect an actual intensification of political repression, and so forth. Nevertheless, this study does not attempt to "control" systematically for such objective changes because such an attempt would have been tantamount to constructing yet another image of these states— the authors' own—rather than a pristine, objective "truth." This study does not focus on the unadulterated true reality of these states, but rather on the U.S. press's representation of this reality. Still, it is extremely unlikely that the objective realities of Azerbaijan, Kazakhstan, and Saudi Arabia—especially the latter—had changed as fundamentally and as abruptly as the characterizations of these states by the U.S. press had changed in the aftermath of September 11, 2001. The precipitous decline in the salience of the oil theme and the concomitant rise in the salience of Islamic fundamentalism in the U.S. print media's portrayals of Saudi Arabia could not have been mere reflections of a sudden objective decline in Saudi Arabia's oil reserves or an instant conversion of the kingdom to Wahhabism. What appears to have changed after September 11, 2001, was not Saudi Arabia itself, but the U.S. print media's *interpretation* of the Saudi state (a change that was colored by the growing strains in U.S.-Saudi relations).

Saudi Arabia

Saudi Arabia was the first area outside the Western hemisphere where U.S. strategic influence replaced that of the United Kingdom. The strategic relationship between the United States and Saudi Arabia originated with the discovery of oil in the kingdom by U.S. companies in the 1930s, and it was cemented by a historic 1945 meeting between the kingdom's founder, King Ibn Saud, and President Franklin D. Roosevelt. Shortly after the meeting, *New York Times* foreign affairs correspondent C. L. Sulzberger observed that "the immense oil deposits in Saudi Arabia alone make that country more important to American diplomacy than almost any other smaller nation." The intimate strategic relationship survived the Saudi oil embargo of the early 1970s, and it reached a new level in 1990 when King Fahd applied for U.S. protection immediately after the Iraqi occupation of Kuwait. Washington shipped more than 500,000 troops to Saudi Arabia, and several thousands troops continued to be stationed on Saudi soil long after the U.S.-led coalition dislodged the Iraqi army from Kuwait in 1991.[18]

In the aftermath of the September 11 terrorist attacks, most of whose perpetrators were Saudi citizens, many Washington policymakers and governmental officials have come to question the U.S.-Saudi partnership and even portray Saudi Arabia as a foe. The reluctance of the Saudi government to support the U.S.-led war on Iraq further strained bilateral relations. As *USA Today* reported on August 9, 2002, although "in public the Bush administration insists that Saudi Arabia is a trusted ally in the war against terrorism . . . in private the administration is hearing from critics who support radical changes in U.S. policy, including 'liberating' the Saudi province that contains the oil fields." The critics were gaining a hearing, the report added, partly because of "the Saudi government's refusal to back a U.S. invasion of Iraq." The *New York Times* similarly reported a few days later that "growing talk of the Bush administration's plans for war with Iraq has once again thrown into sharp relief Washington's delicate relationship with Saudi Arabia . . . some of the most vocal advocates of military action against Iraq are also among those pressing hardest in Bush administration circles for a tough new American posture

---

18. See Madawi Al-Rashid, *A History of Saudi-Arabia* (New York: Cambridge University Press, 2002), pp. 91–104, 163–164; Nadav Safran, *Saudi Arabia: The Ceaseless Quest for Security* (Cambridge, Mass.: Belknap Press, 1985); Sulzberger is quoted in Daniel Yergin, *The Prize: The Epic Quest for Oil, Money and Power* (New York: Touchstone Books, 1992), pp. 404–405.

toward the Saudis in the aftermath of the Sept. 11 attacks."[19] One of the most prominent expressions of the anti-Saudi sentiment that these reports alluded to was a July 2002 briefing before the Department of Defense's Defense Policy Board, in which the speaker, a RAND Corporation analyst, depicted Saudi Arabia as a "kernel of evil" and the "most dangerous opponent" of the United States in the Middle East.[20] Although Secretary of Defense Donald Rumsfeld insisted that the briefing did not reflect "dominant opinion" within the George W. Bush administration, it was hard to escape the impression that, as a foreign observer put it, "the upper reaches of U.S. policymaking are rethinking the relationship with the Saudis."[21]

The U.S.-Saudi partnership has come under sharp criticism not only in the hallways of the Bush administration and its allied think-tanks, but also from leading congressional Democrats. Senator Carl Levin of Michigan declared that the Saudis "have not been a consistent ally of ours," while New York Senator Charles Schumer "sharply criticized [Saudi-financed] militant Islamic *madrasas* that preach anti-Americanism."[22] The sharp rise in the incidence and tone of anti-Saudi rhetoric in Washington prompted one news analyst in December 2002 to characterize the relations between Washington and Riyadh as "dangerously precarious."[23] Even if this characterization of the state of U.S.-Saudi bilateral relations is somewhat exaggerated, it is clear that these relations became significantly more strained after September 11, 2001. The growth of this diplomatic tension was coincident and intertwined with a significant darkening of Saudi Arabia's portrayal in the U.S. press.

The results of the analysis of Saudi Arabia's characterization by the U.S. press are presented in Table 5.1, which shows clearly that the amount of attention that the *New York Times,* the *Wall Street Journal, Newsweek,* and *USA Today* devoted to Saudi Arabia rose dramatically after September 11, 2001. Overall, the number of articles which mentioned Saudi Arabia in

---

19. Barbara Slavin, "Anti-Saudi Arguments Get Heard," *USA Today,* August 9, 2002; Todd Purdum, "Bush Team Is Divided Over Getting Tougher With Saudis," *New York Times,* August 12, 2002.

20. Quoted in Jacob Heilbrunn, "The Right Should Let Up on Saudis," *Los Angeles Times,* December 8, 2003.

21. Purdum, "Bush Team Is Divided"; "Peter Hartcher, "A Slick Alliance Threatens to Spill Over," *Australian Financial Review,* November 29, 2002.

22. Purdum, "Bush Team Is Divided"; James Dao, "Washington Asks: How Firm Are Saudis on Extremists," *New York Times,* May 14, 2003.

23. Heilbrunn, "The Right Should Let Up on Saudis."

Table 5.1. Recurrent Themes in Media Coverage of Saudi Arabia Before and After September 11, 2001.

Theme	New York Times Before		After		Wall Street Journal Before		After		Newsweek Before		After		USA Today Before		After		Total Before		After	
Oil Exporter	24	0.24	26	0.06	22	0.73	21	0.16	0	0.00	6	0.10	8	0.38	4	0.05	54	0.34	57	0.08
Saudi-born terrorists	19	0.19	151	0.37	2	0.07	46	0.35	6	0.55	8	0.13	5	0.24	40	0.52	32	0.20	245	0.36
Supporter of Terrorism	0	0.00	53	0.13	0	0.00	12	0.09	0	0.00	17	0.28	0	0.00	12	0.16	0	0.00	94	0.14
Wahhabism/fund'm	2	0.02	55	0.13	0	0.00	37	0.28	0	0.00	9	0.15	1	0.05	8	0.10	3	0.02	109	0.16
Political Repression	8	0.08	36	0.09	1	0.03	16	0.12	2	0.18	8	0.13	4	0.19	5	0.06	15	0.09	65	0.10
Women	5	0.05	21	0.05	0	0.00	10	0.08	1	0.09	3	0.05	4	0.19	5	0.06	10	0.06	39	0.06
Modernization	10	0.10	13	0.04	6	0.20	7	0.05	1	0.09	0	0.00	5	0.24	2	0.03	22	0.14	22	0.03
Reliable U.S. Ally	9	0.09	22	0.05	1	0.02	4	0.03	0	0.00	10	0.16	1	0.05	3	0.04	11	0.07	39	0.06
Tension with U.S.	4	0.04	32	0.08	4	0.13	12	0.09	0	0.00	12	0.20	0	0.00	8	0.10	8	0.05	64	0.09
Diplomatic Broker	2	0.02	17	0.04	2	0.07	6	0.05	0	0.00	8	0.13	0	0.00	4	0.05	4	0.02	35	0.05
Wealth	11	0.11	26	0.06	3	0.10	10	0.08	0	0.00	8	0.13	3	0.14	2	0.03	17	0.11	46	0.07
Corruption	2	0.02	18	0.04	1	0.03	8	0.06	0	0.00	4	0.07	0	0.00	1	0.01	3	0.02	31	0.05
Islamic Intolerance	4	0.04	8	0.02	1	0.03	10	0.08	2	0.18	7	0.11	1	0.05	5	0.06	8	0.05	30	0.04
Total Items Coded	99		413		30		131		11		61		21		77		161		682	

NOTES: "Before" denotes the frequency of the theme in the newspaper's coverage of Saudi Arabia between March 11, 2000, and September 11, 2001. "After" denotes the frequency of the theme in the newspaper's coverage of Saudi Arabia between September 12, 2001, and March 11, 2003. The integers denote absolute frequency, namely the number of articles in which the theme was evident. The decimals denote relative frequency, namely the absolute frequency divided by the total number of articles coded. The sum of the relative frequencies exceeds 1.0 because some articles contained more than one theme. The sum of the absolute frequencies exceeds the total number of articles for the same reason.

significant fashion rose from 161 in the pre–September 11 period to 682 thereafter, an increase of 324 percent. Table 5.1 also shows that the *New York Times* covered Saudi Arabia far more extensively than the other publications; significantly more than half of the analyzed articles were published in the *New York Times*. The *Wall Street Journal* was a distant second with roughly 17 percent of the total coverage.

Although the four publications differed somewhat in terms of the relative salience (or the trend over time) of their coverage of various themes—for example, the *Wall Street Journal*, a financial newspaper, had been more focused on Saudi Arabia's oil sector than the *New York Times* had been both before and after September 11, 2001—these differences were by and large rather nuanced. The authors therefore chose not to differentiate among the newspapers in the following discussion of the results and to focus on the aggregate numbers. The data in Table 5.1 are broken down by individual publications.

The thematic category "oil exporter" denotes articles dealing with the business of oil exploration, production, and export or articles that referred to Saudi Arabia as a major oil producer or exporter. As noted above, Saudi Arabia's putative strategic significance for the United States stems largely from its possession of the world's largest oil reserves. Indeed, as Table 5.1 shows, in the eighteen months preceding September 11, 2001, "oil exporter" was by far the most frequent characterization of Saudi Arabia in the U.S. press. In the four analyzed publications, 34 percent of the articles that significantly mentioned Saudi Arabia characterized it as an oil-rich country. News reports commonly referred to the Saudi kingdom as "the world's largest producer and the most powerful OPEC [Organization of Oil Producing Countries] member,"[24] as OPEC's "kingpin,"[25] or as the country that controls the bulk of the world's spare production capacity.[26]

In the eighteen months following September 11, 2001, the U.S. press continued to devote roughly as much attention to Saudi Arabia's oil riches as it had devoted in the preceding eighteen months. For example, in November 2002, the *New York Times* reported that "what gives Saudi Arabia its considerable political strength is its role as the only producer

24. Edmund L. Andrews, "OPEC Divided on Increase in Production," *New York Times,* March 25, 2000.

25. Bhushan Bahree, "OPEC Leans Toward Another Oil-Supply Cut—Consuming Nations Caution Against Further Trims Amid High Crude Prices," *Wall Street Journal,* February 20, 2001.

26. Thaddeus Herrick, "Oil Prices Spike Amid Shrinking Supply—Promised Increase by Saudis Has Yet to Materialize," *Wall Street Journal,* August 16, 2000.

with the spare capacity to replace millions of barrels a day of lost oil."[27] A
few months later, when oil prices were rising before the U.S.-led war on
Iraq, the *Wall Street Journal* reported that "Saudi Arabia is the only oil-
producing country with significant spare capacity at a time when the
world faces a potential supply crunch."[28]

But relative to other components of the U.S. media's characterization
of Saudi Arabia, oil declined greatly in salience after September 11, 2001.
Far more extensive media coverage of Saudi Arabia after that date resulted in the oil connection being present in only 8 percent of the articles,
about a quarter of its relative frequency prior to the terrorist attacks. The
tenor of the post–September 11 coverage changed as well. A number of
articles critical of Saudi Arabia lamented U.S. reliance on Saudi oil and
suggested that the United States meet its energy needs in other ways.
One *New York Times* op-ed sarcastically proposed replacing the destroyed
World Trade Center towers with "electrical energy-generating wind tur-
bines . . . [that] would show that we do not have to turn a blind eye to the
Saudis' financing of terrorists to meet our energy needs."[29]

Another prevalent theme in the U.S. media coverage of Saudi Arabia
before September 11, 2001, was "modernization": characterizing Saudi
society as undergoing either economic and social modernization or liberalization or both (namely, a society in the process of becoming more like
United States). In June 2000, *USA Today* reported that "in recent months,
economic liberalization has gathered force. The goal: a bold shift from an
economy shaped by government-drafted five-year plans to heavier reliance on the private sector."[30] Crown Prince Abdullah bin Abdul Aziz al-
Saud, *de facto* ruler of the country, was often portrayed favorably as an
advocate of modernization. "In the four years since King Fahd suffered a
stroke and relinquished day-to-day management to Abdullah," the *Wall
Street Journal* reported in December 2000, "barricades have slowly begun
to crumble."[31] Just under a month before September 11, 2001, the *New
York Times* reported that the Ericcson Corporation had won a contract

27. Jeff Gerth, "U.S. Fails to Curb Its Saudi Oil Habit, Experts Say," *New York Times*,
November 26, 2002.

28. Bhushan Bahree and Thaddeus Herrick, "Saudis to Ensure Supply of Oil If War
Begins—OPEC Declines to Endorse Proposal to Suspend Limits On Output if U.S. Attacks," *Wall Street Journal*, March 11, 2003.

29. Gary J. Ferdman, "To Signal the Saudis," *New York Times*, June 8, 2002.

30. David J. Lynch, "Saudis Shed Veils, Offer New Face to Investors," *USA Today*,
June 5, 2000.

31. Susan Sachs, "Saudi Heir Urges Reform, and Turn From U.S.," *New York Times*,
December 4, 2000.

worth upward of $800 million U.S. to make Saudi Arabia's cellular telephone system the largest in the Middle East.[32] The "historic reopening of Saudi Arabia's energy industry" received much discussion before September 11, 2001, as did Saudi Arabia's attempt to open itself up to limited tourism.[33] A July 2000 travel column in *Newsweek* urged readers to reconsider stereotypes of the Middle East as a land of despotism and "Islamic severity"; Saudi Arabia, the writer pointed out, "just appointed a popular prince-astronaut as the new tourism minister."[34] Additionally, in April 2001, *USA Today* reported that "despite all the limitations, Saudi women are finding ways to promote their own liberation movement within the confines of their system, and trying to drag this conservative society into the modern world" (a discussion of the U.S. press's coverage of the status of Saudi women will follow at greater length).[35]

In the eighteen months after September 11, 2001, twenty-two articles contained significant characterizations of Saudi Arabia as a modernizing country, exactly equal to the number of such articles published over the eighteen months prior to that date. Modernization was the only theme of the characterization of Saudi Arabia whose absolute frequency did not increase even slightly after September 11, 2001. Thus, modernization fell from being the third most frequent theme prior to that date, found in 14 percent of analyzed articles, to being the second *least* frequent characterization after this date, found in only 3 percent of articles. This decline is very significant because articles that depicted Saudi Arabia as modernizing were almost always positive in tone, and they tended to imply a growing similarity between Saudi Arabia and the United States, thus naturalizing the identity of the two countries as "friends." The decline of this characterization of Saudi Arabia after September 11, 2001, on the other hand, was conducive to representing the two countries as enemies.

The category "Saudi-born terrorists" refers to articles that mentioned Saudi Arabia as the birthplace of terrorists, most notably Osama bin Laden, or the country that had exiled bin Laden, without in any way implicating the Saudi royal family, the Saudi government, or Saudi elites in supporting terrorism themselves.

As Table 5.1 indicates, even before September 11, 2001, Saudi Arabia

---

32. "Contract for Ericsson," *New York Times* Business Desk, August 13, 2001.

33. Bhushan Bahree, "Exxon, Shell Poised to Win Saudi Deals—They Appear Favored To Lead Key Projects In Coveted Gas Sector," *Wall Street Journal,* June 1, 2001.

34. Carla Power, "Rules of the Road for Visits to Islamic Countries," *Newsweek,* July 10, 2000.

35. Barbara Slavin, "Women Find Ways to Promote Their Liberation; Saudi Men May Accept New Roles," *USA Today,* April 18, 2001.

was mentioned rather often as the birthplace of Islamic terrorists. While Osama bin Laden was not yet a household name in the United States, the media mentioned him rather frequently in the wake of the October 2000 attack on the *USS Cole* in the port of Aden, often in conjunction with references to al-Qaeda and to previous terrorist activities. Shortly after the Cole bombing, *USA Today* reported that "speculation continued to mount that Osama bin Laden, a Saudi exile accused by the United States in earlier attacks, was involved,"[36] while the *New York Times* reported that "administration officials said they see enough similarities between the Cole attack in the port of Aden and the bombing of two American embassies in East Africa in 1998, which have been blamed on Al Qaeda, the group headed by the Saudi financier Osama bin Laden, to warrant taking this precaution against a second or third attack."[37]

If the characterization of Saudi Arabia as the birthplace of terrorists was common prior to September 11, 2001, it became practically dominant afterward. Not only did the absolute frequency of this theme increase dramatically, but its relative frequency increased from 20 to 36 percent of all articles. Thus, after that date "Saudi-born terrorists" became the leading characterization of Saudi Arabia.

Many of these articles contained mentions of Osama bin Laden in the same context as before. Three days after the attacks on the World Trade Center and the Pentagon, the *New York Times* reported that "while they [U.S. intelligence officials] once debated Mr. bin Laden's specific connection to the terrorism his networks have spawned, they now acknowledge that this frail, squeaky-voiced Saudi has mobilized hundreds of Muslims in far-flung countries to fight and die for his embittered vision of Islam, if not for him."[38] Over a year later, after U.S. newsreaders had become very familiar with Osama bin Laden and the September 11 hijackers, an article about terrorism mentioned that "Osama bin Laden, the leader of Al Qaeda, is a Saudi of Yemeni descent, as were many of the Sept. 11 hijackers"; the article did not connect the Saudi regime to terrorism, though.[39] The fact that fifteen of the nineteen hijackers were Saudi citizens has been mentioned even more frequently than Osama bin Laden. *New York Times*

36. Steven Komarow and Dave Moniz, "Yemeni Port Was Navy's Best Option," *USA Today*, October 20, 2000.

37. Elizabeth Becker, "U.S. Military Placed on Highest Alert in Several Hot Spots," *New York Times*, October 24, 2000.

38. Judith Miller, "Bin Laden: Child of Privilege Who Champions Holy War," *New York Times*, September 14, 2001.

39. Eric Schmitt and Thom Shanker, "U.S. Moves Commandos to Base in East Africa," *New York Times*, September 18, 2002.

columnist William Safire, for example, opened his September 12, 2002, column with the statement that "fifteen of the 19 suicide bombers who killed 3,000 Americans a year ago yesterday were Saudi citizens."[40]

As long as depictions of Saudi Arabia as the birthplace or home country of individual terrorists did not imply that the Saudi regime was in any way associated with Islamic terrorism, however, the damage to Saudi Arabia's overall image was rather limited. Far more damaging to Saudi Arabia's image in the United States was the extremely sharp rise in the frequency of articles that either drew a connection between the Saudi state and Islamic terrorism ("supporter of terrorism") or that associated Saudi Arabia (or its regime) with Islamic fundamentalism, usually of the Wahhabi hue ("Wahhabism/fundamentalism"), or both. In the above-cited column William Safire wrote that

one conclusion cannot be escaped: The murderous fanatics were the product of an oil-besotted monarchy that has long been the prime sponsor of the radical Islamic spewing of hatred at all "infidels"—Christians and Jews, as well as the majority of Muslims who refuse to accept medieval Saudi Wahhabism. In light of that monarchy's production of terrorists, and considering the refusal of Saudi intelligence to let the U.S. interrogate Al Qaeda prisoners it holds, we are entitled to ask the John Gunther question: "Who runs this place?"

This statement nicely illustrates a dramatic shift in the U.S. media's association of Saudi Arabia with Islam. It is not that the U.S. media did not associate the two prior to September 11, 2001, but that it tended to do so indirectly, without characterizing Saudi Islam as being either Wahhabist or fundamentalist. For example, a *New York Times* report on a Saudi Arabian initiative to attract Western tourists mentioned that "the religious types, who constitute a sizable group . . . are . . . convinced that opening the country to tourists will produce the kind of Sodom and Gomorrah conditions prevalent in other travel destinations in everything from clothing to the use of food banned by Islam to the spread of AIDS."[41]

The Saudi family adopted the Wahhabist movement in the eighteenth century. The founder of the movement, Muhammad ibn Abd al-Wahhab (1703–1792) "was concerned with purifying Islam from what he described as innovations and applying a strict interpretation of the *shari'a*."

---

40. William Safire, "The Split in the Saudi Royal Family," *New York Times*, September 12, 2002.

41. Neil McFarquhar, "Saudis Offer Veiled Welcome to Tourists of a Certain Age," *New York Times*, July 9, 2001.

The Saudi royal family continued to embrace Wahhabism after it had consolidated its control over modern Saudi Arabia in 1932, and Saudi school textbooks had always emphasized Wahhabist teachings.[42] One could hardly learn these facts about Saudi Arabia, however, by reading major U.S. print publications before September 11, 2001. In the eighteen months preceding the attacks, only three of the 161 articles about Saudi Arabia published in the four analyzed publications associated Saudi Arabia with Wahhabism or Islamic fundamentalism. After the terrorist attacks, however, that number increased exponentially to 109 articles, or 16 percent of all significant articles about Saudi Arabia.

These terms were never used by the media in a positive context, and they were usually presented in either an overtly negative context or in association with other characterizations that most Westerners would consider negative. Shortly after the September 11 terrorist attacks, senior *Newsweek* editor Fareed Zakaria explained that "embracing Wahhabism, a puritanical version of Islam, the Saudi regime has tried to bolster its faltering legitimacy in the past two decades by fueling a religious revival in the Arab world. It funds mosques, trains preachers and builds schools across the globe that teach its fiery interpretation of Islam."[43] The *Wall Street Journal* reported that "while Saudi Arabia is already one of the most fundamentalist Islamic societies in the world—alcohol is forbidden and women are not permitted to drive—its government is under increasing public pressure to make the country even more fundamentalist, experts say."[44] A few months later another *Wall Street Journal* article, this time on the repression of the Shi'i Muslim minority in Saudi Arabia (an article that also falls under the category "political repression") stated that "Saudi Arabia's Sunni Muslim leaders practice a severe form of Islam called Wahabbism [sic], which demands strict adherence to the traditions of the Prophet Muhammed. The country's religious authorities say Ismailis [a Shiite sect] are infidels who fail to live in accordance with those traditions."[45]

As these reports indicate, the term "Wahhabism" (or Wahhabi) had become a media buzzword after September 11, 2001. Between these two terms, Wahhabism is the one most frequently mentioned. Yet another

42. Al-Rashid, *A History of Modern Saudi Arabia*, pp. 16, 188–217.

43. Fareed Zakaria, "The Allies Who Made Our Foes," *Newsweek,* October 1, 2001.

44. Yaroslav Trofimov, "Hijackers' Saudi Identities, Real and Fake, Raise Uncomfortable Questions," *Wall Street Journal,* September 25, 2001.

45. James Dorsey, "Saudi Tribe Sees the War as a Chance to Win Some Rights—Aggrieved Shiites Hope Scrutiny of Monarchy Will Help Their Struggle," *Wall Street Journal,* January 9, 2002.

Wall Street Journal article, whose long title read "Captive Audience: How a Chaplain Spread Extremism to an Inmate Flock—Radical New York Imam Chose Clerics for State Prisons; Praise for 9/11 'Martyrs'—Saudi Arabia's Helping Hand," discussed Mr. Warith Deen Umar's promotion of the "fundamentalist offshoot of Sunni Islam known as Wahhabism. Rooted in Saudi Arabia, it stresses a literal reading of the *Quran* and intolerance for people and sects that don't follow its absolutist teaching." The report stated that "with help from the Saudi government, [Umar] traveled to Saudi Arabia and brought that country's harsh form of Islam to New York's expanding ranks of Muslim prisoners."[46]

Several books published after September 11, 2001, have expressed strong anti-Saudi sentiments, and their arguments have been recapitulated by book reviews published in the *New York Times*. In November 2002, book critic Richard Bernstein favorably reviewed Stephen Schwartz's *The Two Faces of Islam: The House of Saud from Tradition to Terror*, whose central argument, according to Bernstein, was that:

Wahhabism has over the centuries waged a bitter struggle against all other variants of Islam, most particularly the tolerant, peaceful, poetically mystical schools of thought that, in Mr. Schwartz's view, are the true and admirable historic Islam. Moreover, he maintains that Wahhabism, which gave rise to Osama bin Laden and the Afghan Taliban among others, is the most dread menace faced in the world today by the forces of tolerance and pluralism, whether Muslim or otherwise. "Wahhabism exalts and promotes death in every element of its existence, the suicide of its adherents, mass murder as a weapon against civilization, and above all the suffocation of the mercy embodied in Islam," Mr. Schwartz writes. "The war against Wahhabism is therefore a war to the death, as the Second World War was a war to the death against fascism. But triumph over death is the victory of life."[47]

While not all portrayals of Wahhabism were so thoroughly negative, Wahhabism and its negative associations clearly became an important part of the broader image of Saudi Arabia following September 11, 2001. In a letter to the editor of the *New York Times* from November 2002, a reader asked, "how can 'Saudi officials take offense at suggestions that the kingdom bears any responsibility for anti-American terrorism,' as you say in your editorial? Their dominant educational curriculum is designed by extremist Wahhabi Muslims who teach Saudi children to hate

46. Paul M. Barrett, "Captive Audience: How a Chaplain Spread Extremism To an Inmate Flock," *Wall Street Journal*, February 5, 2003.

47. Richard Bernstein, "The Saudis' Brand of Islam and Its Place in History," *New York Times*, November 8, 2002.

Americans."[48] This was but one of several letters to the editor that employed the term "Wahhabi" in response to an article that did not use the term, and it thus nicely shows the penetration of this characterization of Saudi Arabia into the proverbial "American mind."

The above-quoted letter drew a connection between Saudi Arabia and terrorism and expressed concern about Saudi schooling. This is another facet of Saudi Arabia's image that underwent a fundamental change after the September 11 terrorist attacks. As discussed earlier, the only link between Saudi Arabia and terrorism discussed by the U.S. press prior to September 11, 2001, was the identification of individual Saudi citizens as terrorists. No single article implied that the Saudi government, Saudi royal family, Saudi elites, or Saudi Arabia as a whole was directly or indirectly involved in supporting terrorism ("supporter of terrorism"). After that date, however, this theme was present in no fewer than ninety-four articles. The two most prominent linkages discussed in these articles were Saudi financing of Islamic charities that allegedly sponsored terrorist organizations and Saudi promotion of militant (often labeled "Wahhabi") Islam in Saudi schools as well as overseas.

Of the reports on Saudi financing of Islamic charities, arguably the most damaging to the Saudi image were those reports which linked Haifa al Faisal, daughter of King Faisal and wife of the Saudi ambassador to the United States, to two of the September 11 hijackers. In November 2002, the *Wall Street Journal*, for example, stated that "reports that charitable contributions from the Saudi embassy inadvertently may have aided two Sept. 11, 2001, terrorists could both intensify criticism of the Federal Bureau of Investigation and exacerbate strains between the U.S. and Saudi Arabia."[49]

The theme of Saudi financing of terrorist organizations appeared frequently in post–September 11 articles. An October 2001 report in the *New York Times* was emblematic of such media coverage:

They are the elite of Saudi society—wealthy, respected men with investments that span the globe and reputations for generosity. Yasin al-Qadi is among the prominent Saudis who those in need of charity or shrewd business advice could turn to. But the United States government now says that Mr. Qadi and many other well-connected Saudi citizens have transferred millions of dollars to Osama bin Laden through charities and trusts like the Muwafaq Foundation supposedly established to feed the hungry, house the poor and alleviate

48. Mark S. Nadel, "Time for Saudis to Look Inward," *New York Times*, November 28, 2002.

49. Robert S. Greenberger and Glenn Simpson, "Princess's Gift Strains Saudi-U.S.," *Wall Street Journal*, November 25, 2002.

suffering. A statement accompanying the list yesterday said this about the foundation: "Muwafaq is an al-Qaeda front that receives funding from wealthy Saudi businessmen. Blessed Relief is the English translation. Saudi businessmen have been transferring millions of dollars to bin Laden through Blessed Relief."[50]

The fact that this characterization of Saudi Arabia had penetrated the proverbial "American mind" was illustrated by the following report, published in *USA Today* in October 2002: "A barstool poll is certainly not statistically valid. But the comments from half a dozen patrons of the watering hole they call 'The I.D.' suggest both a reservoir of trust in the president and lingering concerns about military action. When Bush declared, 'We know that Iraq is continuing to finance terror,' Republican attorney Todd Becker murmured, 'So is Saudi Arabia.'"[51]

The second major thread of the characterization of Saudi Arabia as "supporter of terrorism" has to do with Saudi state sponsorship and exportation of Wahhabi Islam, particularly its teaching in Saudi schools. An April 2002 report on U.S. Secretary of State Colin Powell's trip to the Middle East mentioned that, in a meeting with King Mohammed VI of Morocco and Crown Prince Abdullah of Saudi Arabia, "both American and Saudi officials said that none of the various other tensions in Saudi-American relations, including Saudi government support for schools that preach extremism, were addressed at the dinner and meeting tonight, but that Secretary Powell had focused solely on the prospects for peace in the Middle East."[52] A few months earlier, a lengthy article in the *New York Times* discussed how, to quote its title, "Anti-Western and Extremist Views Pervade Saudi Schools." Although "senior members of the ruling family reject the idea that they somehow allowed the education system to help shape extremists," the report read, "other Saudis suggest the [extremist] environment does exist within the kingdom because of the constant barrage of messages that Wahhabi teachings are the purest form of Islam. The [September 11] attack has left the government looking for options. 'Embracing the Islamist forces was a way to channel fervor and to distract criticism,' one Western official said."[53]

50. Jeff Gerth and Judith Miller, "Philanthropist, or Fount Of Funds for Terrorists?" *New York Times*, October 13, 2001.

51. Walter Shapiro, "War Cry Seems to Be, 'If We Must . . . ,'" *USA Today*, October 9, 2002.

52. Todd Purdum, "In Morocco, Powell Pleads for Arab Help in Mideast," *New York Times*, April 9, 2002.

53. Neil MacFarquhar, "Anti-Western and Extremist Views Pervade Saudi Schools," *New York Times*, October 19, 2001.

Again, the impact of such characterization of Saudi Arabia on the U.S. public's mind can be seen in the "letters to the editors" section. Many post–September 11 letters discussed Saudi schools and Saudi support for terrorism. In November 2001, for example, a *New York Times* reader wrote that "Prince Alwaleed bin Talal bin Abdul Aziz Al-Saud's suggestion that Saudi Arabia is a loyal ally of the United States (op-ed, Oct. 31) is belied by the fact that public school textbooks in Saudi Arabia tell their students to regard non-Muslims as the enemy."[54] A year later another reader wrote:

You report that a Saudi official "lashed out at the kingdom's critics, arguing that Americans had been consumed by anti-Saudi sentiments that bordered on hate" (front page, Dec. 4). It is telling that the Saudi government fails to see the irony in this. Its representative is accusing the American people because we dare to question a system that produced the majority of the Sept. 11 attackers and that fosters and finances the strain of Islamic fundamentalism that is the primary face of global terror today. Perhaps some introspection would be more fitting for a country where the educational and religious systems do not even bother to disguise their hate of the West and their anti-Semitism.[55]

Another strong indication of the post–September 11 association of Saudi Arabia with Islamic terrorism can be found in the writings of *New York Times* foreign affairs columnist Thomas Friedman. From 1995, when he became a regular columnist, through September 11, 2001, Friedman composed over a dozen columns that contained significant references to Saudi Arabia. In these columns, he expressed concern about the lack of democracy in Saudi Arabia and the economic difficulties facing the kingdom. In summer 1996, Friedman wrote that "there are internal problems in Saudi Arabia. Something is boiling there beneath the sands, and it's more than a few fringe fanatics," but he did not give specific details about these "internal problems."[56] None of the columns discussed Wahhabism, the Saudi school system, or Saudi financing of Wahhabi schools abroad.

After September 11, however, Friedman had become preoccupied with the Saudi school system and its training of Islamic militants. In a mock letter from President George W. Bush to the Saudi Minister of Islamic Affairs, Friedman wrote: "You have a problem with the American

---

54. Jay Diamond, "To a Saudi Prince Bearing Gifts," *New York Times,* November 1, 2001.

55. Josh Trevers, "The War on Terror: Advice for Saudis," *New York Times,* December 6, 2002.

56. Thomas L. Friedman, "Will the Center Hold?" *New York Times,* June 30, 1996.

people, who, since Sept. 11, have come to fear that your schools, and the thousands of Islamic schools your government and charities are financing around the world, are teaching that non-Muslims are inferior to Muslims and must be converted or confronted."[57] In another column he wrote:

On Sept. 11 we learned all the things about Saudi Arabia that we didn't know: that Saudi Arabia was the primary funder of the Taliban, that 15 of the hijackers were disgruntled young Saudis and that Saudi Arabia was allowing fund-raising for Osama bin Laden—as long as he didn't use the money to attack the Saudi regime. And most of all, we've learned about Saudi schools. As this newspaper recently reported from Riyadh, the 10th-grade textbook for one of the five required religion classes taught in all Saudi public schools states: "It is compulsory for the Muslims to be loyal to each other and to consider the infidels their enemy." This hostile view of non-Muslims, which is particularly pronounced in the strict Saudi Wahhabi brand of Islam, is reinforced through Saudi sermons, TV shows and the Internet.[58]

Friedman basically acknowledged here that Saudi schools taught Wahhabi Islam long before the September 11 attacks, but he neglected to acknowledge that the reason "we didn't know" about the Saudi curricula was that U.S. journalists, such as himself, did not inquire about it.

Several months later Friedman wrote that "Saudi Arabia financed the Taliban, has hundreds of its citizens in Al Qaeda, has private charities that support Hamas and Islamic Jihad, funds Islamic fundamentalist schools all over the world, was home to 15 of the 19 hijackers of 9/11, has no democracy, and its leader, Crown Prince Abdullah, was invited to President Bush's ranch."[59] The tone of this column contrasted with a 1996 column, following a terrorist bombing of U.S. targets in Saudi Arabia, in which Friedman urged his readers to "make no mistake, Saudi Arabia has been a loyal and important ally of the United States. We should not abandon it now just because a few fringe groups try to drive the U.S. out."[60]

Under the category "political repression," the authors classified articles that depicted Saudi Arabia as being either autocratic or authoritarian; which highlighted Saudi violations of human rights; or both (with the exception of discrimination against women, a theme sufficiently recurrent to merit a separate category). Whenever articles explicitly attrib-

---

57. Thomas L. Friedman, "Dear Saudi Arabia," *New York Times*, December 12, 2001.

58. Thomas L. Friedman, "Drilling for Tolerance," *New York Times*, October 30, 2001.

59. Thomas L. Friedman, "The View From Tehran," *New York Times*, June 26, 2002.

60. Thomas L. Friedman, "The Oil Factor," *New York Times*, July 3, 1996.

uted repressive practices to Islam, or Islamic clerics, the authors also classified them under the category "Islamic intolerance."

The number of articles associating Saudi Arabia with political repression rose by more than 300 percent after September 11, 2001, but the relative frequency of this theme rose only slightly. Still, a careful reading of these articles suggests that a significant change of tone and emphasis had taken place. Consider, for example, a *USA Today* report from October 2000 on the friction caused by the presence of U.S. troops in Saudi Arabia. "As defenders of Islam's most sacred sites at Mecca and Medina, oil-rich Saudi Arabia has viewed non-Muslims warily. Although a key U.S. ally in the Persian Gulf, Saudi Arabia has state-run media and restricts freedom of speech and religion, bedrock American values."[61] That was the only mention of human rights violations throughout the article. Another *USA Today* item from August 2000 reported that Saudi Arabia had blocked access to the Yahoo! Web site due to pornographic and other offensive content.[62] This article neither associated Islam with this ban nor put it in a broader context of the state of human rights in Saudi Arabia, however. In March 2001, the *New York Times* mentioned Saudi Arabia as one of the countries that received the lowest score on UN Watch's "freedom index." This report merely listed Saudi Arabia along with other states, without providing any specific details about the lack of freedom in the kingdom.[63] The other three publications did not report Saudi Arabia's poor freedom ranking at all.

These examples show that, although prior to September 11, 2001, Saudi human rights violations were reported in the U.S. media, they were neither elaborated upon nor were they embedded in overly negative representations of Saudi Arabia. This changed in the post–September 11 period. Multiple articles harshly criticized the lack of religious freedom in Saudi Arabia. An October 2002 article in the *Wall Street Journal* called on readers to "behold the bracing clarity of a simple declarative sentence. 'Freedom of religion does not exist.' The reference is to Saudi Arabia, and the sentence comes from the State Department's just-released index of religious freedom." The article proceeded to raise the question: "If Saudi Arabia has no freedom of religion, and if punishment for those outside

61. David Moniz, "Middle East Duty Presents Volatile Set of Risks for U.S. Military," *USA Today*, October 25, 2000.

62. Janet Kornblum, "Ancestry.com Senses Census-Record Need," *USA Today*, August 15, 2000.

63. Barbara Crossette, "U.N. Paradox: Some on Rights Panel Are Accused of Wrongs," *New York Times*, March 13, 2001.

the Wahhabi fold includes arrest and credible reports of torture, why has the State Department not designated Saudi Arabia one of its 'countries of particular concern'?"[64] An op-ed titled "The Saudi Threat," published by the *Wall Street Journal* several months earlier, expressed concern that

Instead of an instability that opens the door to freedom, the Saudis foment instability that leads to still-greater oppression, backwardness and bigotry. By funding religious extremists from Michigan to Mindanao, the Saudis have done their best to destroy democracies, turn back the clock on human rights and deny religious freedom to Islamic and other populations—while the United States guarantees Saudi security. It is the most preposterous and wrongheaded policy in American history since the defense of slavery.[65]

Thus, even though the relative frequency of reports on political repression in Saudi Arabia rose only slightly after September 11, 2001, these examples suggest that the tone with which the issue had been described had become far more negative and critical in the aftermath of the attacks.

Articles on the treatment of women in Saudi Arabia, as previously noted, constituted a sufficiently large portion of reports on political repression to justify a separate thematic category. The pattern of U.S. press coverage of this issue was similar to the pattern of its coverage of political repression. The number of articles that contained this theme rose from ten before September 11 to thirty-nine after the attacks, but their relative frequency remained constant at 6 percent. Yet both the tone of the coverage and its context had changed markedly. In April 2001, *USA Today* reported that "under the Saudis' restrictive interpretation of Islam, women here are not allowed in cemeteries on grounds that their mourning might distract men. Nor can they drive, travel without male permission, serve on the country's 90-member consultative council, appear in public without a flowing black cloak or, in all but a few cases, study or work alongside men."[66] Still, the overall tenor of the report was optimistic, and its focus was on the modernization of Saudi society, especially the progress that Saudi women were making in the workplace. A June 2001 report in the *New York Times* characterized women's rights in Saudi Arabia as "severely limited," but ended with the words of a progressive Saudi woman: "in Saudi Arabia, the Wahabis really are the puritans, yet one of the great-

64. "Taste—Review & Outlook: A State of Denial," *Wall Street Journal*, October 11, 2002.

65. Ralph Peters, "The Saudi Threat," *Wall Street Journal*, January 4, 2002.

66. Barbara Slavin, "Women Find Ways to Promote their Liberation Saudi Men May Accept New Roles," *USA Today*, April 28, 2001.

est advances there has been in girls' education. It's one of our main success stories."[67] Yet another *New York Times* article focused on shopping
malls and described the discrimination against women mostly as a way
of making a point about the cultural clash, evident in Saudi malls, between conservative Saudi Arabia and Western consumer culture.[68]

After September 11, 2001, articles that mentioned the treatment of
Saudi women became, on balance, more critical and sometimes sarcastic
in tone. For example, in August 2002, *New York Times* columnist Maureen
Dowd asked:

If America is going to have a policy of justified pre-emption, in Henry
Kissinger's clinical phrase, why not start by chasing out those sorry Saudi
royals? If we're willing to knock over Saddam for gassing the Kurds, we
should be willing to knock over the Saudis for letting the state-supported religious police burn 15 girls to death last March in a Mecca school, forcing
them back inside a fiery building because they tried to flee without their
scarves. And shouldn't we pre-empt them before they teach more boys to
hate American infidels and before they can stunt the lives of more women?[69]

Many of the post–September 11 articles that criticized the treatment of
women in Saudi Arabia were concerned with "kidnapping" cases such as
the case of Alia and Aisha Gheshayan, two sisters spirited out of the
United States by their Saudi father. The Saudis claimed that the sisters
simply had no desire to return to the United States, but the *Wall Street
Journal* was skeptical of this claim. "As Congressman Burton put it in his
letter," the *Wall Street Journal*'s chief editorial writer stated, "we're asked
to believe that a 'Saudi government, which refuses to respect the wishes
of women when it comes to travel, appearing in court, dress or even driving a car, respects the purported wishes of the [Gheshayan] sisters to refuse to travel to the United States or meet with their mother.'" The article
went further:

Or what about Amjad Radwan, a 19-year-old American who did finally get
permission to leave—but not until personal intervention from the president
of the United States? No sooner did she get her exit visa, than it turned out
she'd been recently married off by her Saudi father. The Saudis say that she is
free to go, but Miss Radwan's mother says the pressure on her daughter has

---

67. Barbara Crossette, "Woman With a New View of Culture," *New York Times*, June
20, 2001.

68. Susan Sachs, "Saudi Mall-Crawlers Shop Till Their Veils Drop," *New York Times*,
December 5, 2000.

69. Maureen Dowd, "I'm With Dick! Let's Make War!" *New York Times*, August 28,
2002.

been intense, with the Saudis telling the frightened 19-year-old that if she got on that plane her father would be punished, and that she could never return, etc.[70]

The accusations became so intense that Bandar bin Sultan, the Saudi Ambassador to the United States, felt compelled to rebut them. In a letter to the editor of the *Wall Street Journal*, he wrote that "watching the news media and reading the editorials, one would be led to believe that cases of child abduction exist only in Saudi Arabia. This is hardly the case."[71] The Ambassador may have had a point. The majority of these cases, including the Gheshayan case, date back to the 1990s or even earlier. It is interesting, if not surprising, that they came to receive far greater attention in the U.S. press following September 11, 2001.

The re-characterization of Saudi society and politics after September 11, was concurrent and went hand in hand with the growing tension in diplomatic relations between the two states (previously discussed in this chapter). Thus, in the analyzed publications, the relative frequency with which Saudi Arabia was portrayed as a longtime, reliable, or trustworthy ally of the United States ("reliable U.S. ally") declined in the aftermath of September 11 attacks, whereas the frequency with which the press reported on strains in U.S.-Saudi relations, sometimes even referring to Saudi Arabia as an enemy ("tension with U.S."), increased markedly. Prior to September 11, 2001, the few references to tensions in U.S.-Saudi relations mainly concerned previous terrorist activities that had been linked to Saudi individuals, such as the attack on the *USS Cole*. For example, in June 2001, the *Wall Street Journal* reported that "federal prosecutors charged 13 Saudi men and a Lebanese man with a truck bombing in Saudi Arabia that killed 19 American airmen, and alleged the conspirators were linked to Iranian government officials. The charges . . . , are the first lodged after a difficult investigation that strained relations between the U.S. and Saudi Arabia."[72]

In post–September 11 articles, the terrorist attacks on New York and Washington, D.C., were usually described as the source of strain in bilateral relations (often along with mentions of the Saudi hijackers), but other sources included Saudi displeasure with U.S. handling of the

70. William McGurn, "Truth, Lies and Videotape," *Wall Street Journal*, October 1, 2002.

71. Bandar bin Sultan bin Abdulaziz, "We Are Not Holding Americans Captive," *Wall Street Journal*, September 12, 2002.

72. David S. Cloud, "U.S. Brings Charges Against 14 Men For 1996 Bombing in Saudi Arabia," *Wall Street Journal*, June 22, 2001.

Israeli-Palestinian conflict, U.S. displeasure at lack of Saudi action to curb the financing of terrorist organizations, and the tension surrounding the presence of U.S. military forces in Saudi Arabia. A December 2001 *New York Times* article stated that "the White House has continued to praise Saudi Arabia publicly for its efforts to fight terrorism, but in private there has been strain between the two nations, particularly over financial matters."[73] An August 2002 report in the same newspaper nicely captured the multiple layers of the growing U.S.-Saudi tension when it explained that

since Sept. 11, there has been an additional, intangible element corroding Saudi-American relations—something between uncertainty and mistrust over the heavy Saudi representation among Osama bin Laden's martyrs and the Saudi tolerance for the culture of jihad. The Saudis, for their part, resent the loss of American initiative to secure a Palestinian homeland, so evident under the first President Bush and during most of the Clinton years. Today, America and Saudi Arabia drink tea laced with the hemlock of unstated recriminations. "The psychological factor is there," an adviser to the royal family conceded.[74]

After September 11, 2001, a growing number of news reports dealt with Saudi economic corruption or senseless flaunting of wealth ("corruption"). Although this category was not a major part of the composite image of Saudi Arabia before or after that date, the fact that the number of reports of corruption jumped from three before the terrorist attacks to thirty-one afterward is significant nonetheless.

Most articles in which the theme of corruption was present focused on members of the Saudi royal family. In response to an interview with billionaire Saudi Prince Walid bin Talal, a reader wrote to the editor of the *New York Times* that "it is simple for Prince Walid bin Talal to call for elections in Saudi Arabia ("A Saudi Prince With an Unconventional Idea: Elections," news article, Nov. 28); after all, he has already earned his billions under the old corrupt system. A representative Saudi government will never peacefully come into existence so long as there is a Saudi monarchy with vested interests in the existing system."[75] Another wealthy member of the royal family who was associated with corruption in a

---

73. Elisabeth Bumiller, "U.S. and Saudis to Meet on Guidelines for Blocking Terrorist Funds," *New York Times,* December 7, 2001.

74. Patrick E. Tyler, "When Energy Comes From Russia, It's Also Power," *New York Times,* August 4, 2002.

75. Ahmed Al-Zaboot, "The Saudi Monarchy," *New York Times,* December 3, 2001.

handful of articles was Prince Sultan bin Abdul Aziz.[76] Former Crown Prince Abdullah, on the other hand, was often portrayed as a crusader against corruption, but such favorable portrayals of him inevitably implicated the Saudi elite as a whole in widespread corruption. Abdullah, a September 2001 report in the *Wall Street Journal* stated, "advocates battling the country's notorious corruption by making the monarchy more transparent and professional, and he has moved closer to the U.S. since the Sept. 11 terrorist attacks strained relations between Washington and Riyadh."[77]

Prior to September 11, 2001, Saudi "wealth" was the fourth most frequent theme in U.S. news coverage of Saudi Arabia. This thematic category applies to reports that portray Saudi Arabia or individual Saudis as being either very wealthy or as major players in global markets or both. Nearly half of the reports that associated Saudis with great wealth prior to that date focused on the aforementioned billionaire Prince Walid bin Talal. For example, in May 2000, the *New York Times* reported that "Prince Walid bin Talal of Saudi Arabia said today that he had spent $1 billion buying shares in 15 American companies, including Amazon.com, WorldCom, Coca-Cola, PepsiCo and AT&T." The report went on to describe Prince Walid as a "a nephew of King Fahd and one of the wealthiest people in the world, [who] regularly makes investments in companies with strong brand names and lagging share prices."[78]

After September 11, 2001, Prince Walid continued to be depicted by the media as a wealthy man, but his reputation was tarnished when New York City mayor Rudy Giuliani turned down his offer to donate $10 million U.S. to assist the victims of the terrorist attacks. [79] Furthermore, after that date, some of the U.S. media's characterizations of Saudis as rich were embedded in reports that also implicated wealthy Saudis in the financing of terrorism. For example, in December 2002, the *New York Times* reported that "while both countries say that progress has been made, American officials are finding it hard to stop the longtime flow of money from wealthy Saudis and Saudi-financed charities to people and

---

76. See, for example, Aram Roston, "Who's Who in the House of Saud," *New York Times*, December 22, 2002.

77. Yaroslav Trofimov, "After King Fahd, a Saudi Feud?—Succession Could Take Kingdom Down Sharply Divergent Paths," *Wall Street Journal*, September 25, 2002.

78. "Saudi Reports $1 Billion of Investments," *New York Times*, May 17, 2000.

79. Jennifer Steinhaur, "Citing Comments on Attack, Giuliani Rejects Saudi's Gift," *New York Times*, October 12, 2001.

groups deemed by the United States to be supporting terrorist attacks around the world."[80]

The only thematic category which portrays the Saudis in positive, or at least neutral, terms, and whose frequency increased in the aftermath of September 11 terrorist attacks was that of "diplomatic broker"—a category applied to articles that depicted Saudi Arabia as a significant player or diplomatic broker in Middle Eastern politics. The increase in this theme's frequency was almost entirely attributable to the Saudi plan for Israeli-Palestinian peace, which was unveiled in a February 2002 op-ed by columnist Thomas Friedman in the *New York Times*.[81] The Saudi peace plan gained some momentum in subsequent months, and it received substantial U.S. press coverage.

Arguably the best way to grasp the *composite* image of Saudi Arabia and see how radically it had changed over time is to compare the five themes that appeared most frequently in the U.S. press coverage of Saudi Arabia during the eighteen months preceding September 11, 2001, with the dominant five themes during the subsequent eighteen months. The top five themes for each period, in descending order of frequency, are presented in Table 5.2, and it takes but a glance at the table to recognize that the overall image of Saudi Arabia in the U.S. media had darkened greatly in the aftermath of the terrorist attacks. Prior to September 11, 2001, the four print media outlets whose content was analyzed basically portrayed Saudi Arabia as a wealthy and modernizing, if authoritarian, leading oil producer that happened to be the birthplace of Islamic terrorists, but was not itself implicated in terrorism. After the September 11 terrorist attacks, Saudi Arabia was radically transformed in the U.S. press into a Wahhabi, repressive Islamic kingdom that was not only a major source of terrorists but also a fountain of terrorism that could no longer be trusted by the United States. It is extremely unlikely that Saudi Arabia itself had changed so dramatically within such a short period of time. After all, Saudi school children and Pakistani students in Saudi-financed *madrasas* were being taught Wahhabi principles long before 2001, as many of the post–September 11 articles implicitly acknowledged. As Thomas Friedman put it, however, "we didn't know" this yet—or the U.S. public didn't care.

---

80. Jeff Gerth and Judith Miller, "Threats and Responses: The Money Trail," *New York Times,* December 1, 2002.

81. Thomas L. Friedman, "An Intriguing Signal From the Saudi Crown Prince," *New York Times,* February 17, 2002.

Table 5.2. Top Themes in U.S. Press Coverage of Saudi Arabia.

Before Sept. 11	Frequency	
Theme	Absolute	Relative
1) Oil Exporter	54	0.34
2) Saudi-born terrorists	32	0.20
3) Modernization	22	0.14
4) Wealth	17	0.11
5) Political Repression	15	0.09
After Sept. 11	Frequency	
Theme	Absolute	Relative
1) Saudi-born terrorists	245	0.36
2) Wahhabi/fundamentalist	109	0.16
3) Supporter of terrorism	94	0.14
4) Political Repression	65	0.10
5) Tension with U.S.	64	0.09

Azerbaijan

The first forays by Americans into Azerbaijan after the country had declared its independence in 1991 were by U.S. oil company executives—
even before Washington extended formal recognition to the new republic.
In 1994, U.S. oil companies signed a major deal with the Azerbaijani government and proceeded to lobby the U.S. government to extend its diplomatic and military influence in the region. By the mid-1990s, the Clinton
administration indeed began to pay growing attention to Azerbaijan. In
April 1997, the State Department reported to Congress that it has become
U.S. policy "to promote rapid development of Caspian energy resources"
in order to "reinforce Western energy security." The government of
Azerbaijan, for its part, was pursuing closer ties with the United States as
a counterbalance to Russian pressure. President Heydar Aliev visited
Washington in summer 1997, where President Bill Clinton assured him
that the United States would work closely with Azerbaijan to tap the Caspian region's energy resources and that the United States supported
Aliev's plan to export Caspian oil to the West. The Clinton administration
assiduously promoted the plan to build a 1,094-mile pipeline from Baku
to Ceyhan, on Turkey's Mediterranean coast (the plan was later endorsed
by the George W. Bush administration and construction began in 2002).
In 1999, U.S. and Azerbaijani officials even discussed the possibility of

establishing a permanent U.S. military base in Azerbaijan.[82] In September 2000, Azerbaijani troops joined U.S. paratroopers in peacekeeping exercises conducted in Kazakhstan.[83]

It can thus be said that diplomatic-strategic relations between the United States and Azerbaijan were rather warm before September 11, 2001. Since the launching of U.S. military operations in Afghanistan in response to the September 11 attacks, U.S.-Azerbaijani relations have grown even closer. In October 2001, the *Wall Street Journal* reported that "Azerbaijan has emerged as increasingly important partner for Washington" because it "could become a useful center for U.S. intelligence and a coveted landing base along flight paths to Afghanistan."[84] Azerbaijan indeed granted the United States overflight rights and was rewarded with a visit to Baku by Secretary of Defense Donald Rumsfeld and with a lifting of restrictions on U.S. aid imposed by Congress in 1992 at the urging of the powerful Armenian-American lobby.[85] In early 2003, Baku granted the United States overflight rights again in the context of the war on Iraq; Azerbaijan was among forty-nine nations (only a handful of which were Muslim-majority populated) listed by the White House as publicly participating in the U.S.-led "Coalition of the Willing" against Iraq. Recently Baku had committed a small military contingent to peacekeeping operations in Iraq.[86]

In sum, U.S. strategic relations with Azerbaijan were already rather good in September 2001, and they have grown stronger since then. Has the U.S. press's portrayal of Azerbaijan improved in concert with the improvement in the bilateral strategic relations?

The results of the analysis of Azerbaijan's characterization by the U.S. press are presented in Table 5.3. Arguably the most striking characteristic of the U.S. press's coverage of Azerbaijan is the dearth thereof. *Newsweek* and *USA Today* printed almost nothing on Azerbaijan between March 2000 and March 2003, and even reports about Azerbaijan in the *New York Times* (which, as in the case of Saudi Arabia, provided the most extensive

82. Michael T. Klare, *Resource Wars: The New Landscape of Global Conflict* (New York: Metropolitan Books, 2001), pp. 3–5.

83. "A Drill in Central Asia," *New York Times*, September 11, 2000.

84. David Rogers, "Campaign Against Terrorism," *Wall Street Journal*, October 31, 2001.

85. Thom Shanker, "A Nation Challenged: The Allies," *New York Times*, December 16, 2001; "A Nation Challenged: U.S. Lifts Sanctions," *New York Times*, March 30, 2002.

86. "Coalition Then and Now," *St. Petersburg Times*, March 30, 2003; "War on Iraq—Coalition of the Willing," *Weekend Australian*, April 5, 2003; "Pledges by U.S. Allies," *USA Today*, May 30, 2003.

Table 5.3. Recurrent Themes in Media Coverage of Azerbaijan Before and After September 11, 2001.

Theme	New York Times				Wall Street Journal				Newsweek				USA Today				Total			
	Before		After		Before		After		Before		After		Before		After		Before		After	
Oil Frontier	24	0.49	18	0.06	14	0.87	8	0.89			2	1.0	1	1.0	1	1.0	39	0.58	29	0.69
Friend of the West	4	0.08	5	0.17	1	0.06	6	0.67									5	0.07	11	0.26
Conflict w/Armenia	15	0.31	5	0.17	3	0.19	2	0.22	1	1.0							19	0.28	7	0.17
Russian Influence	6	0.12	2	0.07	1	0.06					1	0.5					7	0.10	3	0.07
Poverty/Social Ills	8	0.16	1	0.03													8	0.12	1	0.02
Modernization	3	0.06			1	0.06	1	0.11									4	0.06	1	0.02
Soviet Legacy	6	0.12	2	0.07	2	0.12											8	0.12	2	0.05
Political Repression	4	0.08	1	0.03	1	0.06	2	0.22									5	0.07	3	0.07
Secular State	1	0.02	1	0.03			4	0.44									1	0.01	5	0.12
Islamic Threat	3	0.06	2	0.07													3	0.04	2	0.05
Democratic Process	2	0.04					1	0.11									2	0.03	1	0.02
Arts and Culture	3	0.06	3	0.10													3	0.04	3	0.07
Crime	2	0.04	2	0.07													2	0.03	2	0.05
Tension w/Iran	4	0.08	1	0.03	1	0.06	1	0.11									5	0.07	2	0.05
Corruption	2	0.04			3	0.19	1	0.11									5	0.07	1	0.02
Caviar	3	0.06	3	0.10													3	0.04	3	0.07
Total Items Coded	49		30		16		9		1		2		1		1		67		42	

NOTES: "Before" denotes the frequency of the theme in the newspaper's coverage of Azerbaijan between March 11, 2000, and September 11, 2001. "After" denotes the frequency of the theme in the newspaper's coverage of Azerbaijan between September 12, 2001, and March 11, 2003. The integers denote absolute frequency, namely the number of articles in which the theme was evident. The decimals denote relative frequency, namely the absolute frequency divided by the total number of articles coded. The sum of the relative frequencies exceeds 1.0 because some articles contained more than one theme. The sum of the absolute frequencies exceeds the total number of articles for the same reason.

coverage) were relatively few and far between. Also striking is the contrast between the sharp increase in the attention of the U.S. press to Saudi Arabia after September 11, 2001, and the concomitant decrease in its attention to Azerbaijan (down from sixty-seven articles that mentioned Azerbaijan in significant fashion before September 11, 2001, to forty-two thereafter). In fact, the two trends may be indirectly related. It appears that the decline in the frequency of the coverage of Azerbaijan was precipitated, in part at least, by the shifting priorities of *New York Times* Istanbul correspondent Douglas Frantz (or those of his editors). Frantz used to travel regularly to Baku and dispatch detailed reports on Azerbaijani politics and society, but after September 11, 2001, he appears to have been reassigned to report from locations more immediately relevant to the war on terrorism such as Hamburg and Tel Aviv.

In light of the scarcity of U.S. press coverage, the case may well be that the proverbial "American mind" harbors no image whatsoever of Azerbaijan. Certainly those Americans who obtain their international news exclusively from *Newsweek* or *USA Today* could hardly have formed an image of that country. Still, Americans who read the *New York Times* and *Wall Street Journal* regularly and carefully may have developed an image of Azerbaijan, faint though it may be, as a land of oil rigs and energy pipelines. Oil had been by far the predominant theme in these newspapers' coverage of Azerbaijan, both before and after September 11, 2001 (the authors have labeled this thematic category "oil frontier" rather than "oil exporter" to denote the fact that, unlike the case of Saudi Arabia, the Caspian region's oil riches, during the examined periods, were a future promise more than the present reality). In the *New York Times*, the theme of oil was present in 49 percent of all articles which mentioned Azerbaijan significantly between March 11, 2000, and September 11, 2001; in the subsequent eighteen months, the relative frequency of this theme rose to 60 percent even as the absolute number of references to oil declined slightly (along with the number of articles on Azerbaijan in general). In the *Wall Street Journal*, a financial newspaper, the predominance of oil was even higher; nearly 90 percent of this newspaper's articles that mentioned Azerbaijan associated it with petroleum both before and after September 11, 2001. The increased salience of oil as the predominant characterization of Azerbaijan in the aftermath of the September 11 terrorist attacks contrasts sharply with the sharp concomitant decline in its salience in U.S. press coverage of Saudi Arabia.

The *New York Times* and *Wall Street Journal*, to the extent that they covered Azerbaijan at all, repeatedly referred to it as an "oil-rich" nation, or placed it in the context of the "resource-rich" Caspian Sea basin. Such references to Azerbaijan often appeared in articles whose focus was on subjects other than oil. For example, an April 2001 report about peace talks between Azerbaijan and Armenia stated that U.S. Secretary of State Colin "Powell's direct involvement in talks between the two former Soviet entities was a sign that the United States would like to see a resolution of the dispute to encourage stability in the oil-rich region of the Caucasus."[87] A July 2001 report on an allegedly corrupt Czech financier indicated that he was accused of "defrauding investors in the Czech Republic and the oil-rich Caspian nation of Azerbaijan."[88] An August 2001 article on relations between Azerbaijan and Iran depicted Azerbaijan's president, Heydar Aliev, as sitting "atop many billions of barrels of oil and large natural gas reserves."[89] In addition, a January 2002 report on the diplomatic dispute over delimiting the Caspian Sea called it a "resource-rich sea."[90]

Azerbaijan's promising energy reserves were not only alluded to repeatedly in the context of other issues; the *New York Times* and the *Wall Street Journal* published a substantial number of news stories whose exclusive focus was on the Caspian oil business. For example, in June 2000, the *Wall Street Journal* reported from Baku that "executives of a consortium led by BP Amoco Corp. yesterday presented ambitious plans to export natural gas to Turkey from Azerbaijan's huge new Shah Deniz field in the Caspian Sea." Two weeks later, the *Wall Street Journal* carried a lengthy news story, datelined Baku, which explained that despite some recent disappointments, "new signs of progress in exploration and production show that the oil community isn't ready to give up on this Caspian gamble. . . . One large offshore consortium . . . has tapped a significant flow of oil . . . . The group said it would draft engineering plans in the summer to begin its next phase of development that would triple production by 2004."[91]

A number of news stories on Caspian oil focused on the Baku-Tbilisi-Ceyhan (BTC) export pipeline. In February 2001, the *New York Times* carried a detailed report about the prospects of the pipeline, which were given a boost by Chevron's decision "to take part in the pipeline as a po-

87. Jane Perlez, "Powell Begins New Talks With Leaders of Caucasus," *New York Times*, April 3, 2001.

88. Peter S. Green, "Private Sector: Pirate of Prague, or Comeback Kid," *New York Times*, July 15, 2001.

89. Douglas Frantz, "Iran and Azerbaijan Argue Over Caspian Riches," *New York Times*, August 30, 2001.

90. "Progress Made in Dispute Over Caspian," *New York Times*, January 27, 2002.

91. Jeanne Whalen, "BP Amoco Lays Out Plan for Turkey," *Wall Street Journal*, June 8, 2000; Jeanne Whalen, "Oil-Drilling Efforts in Azerbaijan Intensify, Fuel Caspian Comeback," *Wall Street Journal*, June 20, 2000.

tential means of moving oil from a new field it was exploring in Azerbaijan."[92] A few months later, the *New York Times* again reported optimistically about the prospects of the pipeline, noting that BP firmly decided to back the plan and that "the much debated pipeline was backed by the Clinton administration and adopted by the Bush administration as a way to diversify the transportation routes for the vast amounts of oil that have been discovered in the Caspian Sea region."[93] In September 2002, a *New York Times* correspondent was present at the groundbreaking ceremony for the BTC pipeline in Baku, in which U.S. Secretary of Energy Spencer Abraham declared that "the pipeline would give Western nations 'greater energy security with a diversified supply' of oil that depends less on the Middle East."[94]

As Secretary Abraham's statement hints, in the aftermath of September 11, 2001, articles about the promise of the Caspian oil industry commonly put it in the context of concerns about Middle Eastern oil supplies. An October 2001 *New York Times* report from Moscow began with the statement that "the developed world [was] nervously eyeing the security of oil supplies in the Middle East" and proceeded to discuss the booming oil industry in the former Soviet Union, including the development of the Caspian Sea basin's "immense reserves."[95] A January 2002 op-ed written by Richard Butler, former chief weapons inspector in Iraq, stated that "the war had led many Americans to feel that Saudi Arabia is not the best of allies," and that the newly-independent states of the Caspian region, including Azerbaijan, "have oil and gas deposits that, taken together, are thought to be equal to the remaining reserves of Saudi Arabia and Iraq." In sum, not only had oil reserves become a more salient attribute of Azerbaijan in the U.S. press after September 11, 2001, its importance came to be increasingly associated with the diminishing reliability of Saudi Arabia as a U.S. ally.

The second most frequent theme present in the U.S. press coverage of Azerbaijan before the September 11 attacks was the Nagorno-Karabagh conflict between Azerbaijan and Armenia—close to one third of the articles which significantly mentioned Azerbaijan between March 11, 2000,

---

92. Douglas Frantz, "Chevron Talks to Azerbaijanis About Pipeline," *New York Times*, February 10, 2001.

93. Douglas Frantz, "Oil Pipeline to Turkey Backed by Chief of BP," *New York Times*, June 21, 2000.

94. Richard Allen Greene, "Work Begins on Oil Pipeline Bypassing Russia and Iran," *New York Times*, September 19, 2002.

95. Sabrina Tavernise with Birgit Brauer, "Russia Becoming an Oil Ally," *New York Times*, October 19, 2001.

and September 11, 2001, contained significant references to this conflict or its legacy ("conflict w/Armenia"). In July 2000, the *New York Times* carried a lengthy front page report about the plight of the hundreds of thousands of Azerbaijani refugees who were driven by Armenian forces out of the predominantly Armenian-populated enclave of Nagorno-Karabagh in 1992–1993. Many of the refugees, *New York Times* correspondent Douglas Frantz observed, were "insufficiently cared for by their government and on the verge of abandonment by international aid organizations. They live without running water, electricity or medical care in railroad cars, tents, temporary prefabricated houses and holes in the ground, surviving on a few dollars a month."[96] A UN official familiar with Azerbaijan responded to Frantz's story in a letter to the editor acknowledging the refugees' "destitution, which the government has been inclined to maintain as stark evidence of the urgency of return," but also asserting that "the situation is not without hope."[97] In May 2001, the *New York Times* printed another lengthy story which explained that "Azerbaijan staggers under the weight of hundreds of thousands of refugees from Armenian-occupied territory" and discussed the miserable living conditions in the refugee camps.[98] Several other news stories mentioned the refugee issue more briefly. For example, an obituary for Abulfaz Elchibey, Azerbaijan's "first democratically elected president," stated that "his brief term was also marred by economic upheaval and military losses in the breakaway region of Nagorno-Karabagh, where Armenian-backed forces claimed 20 percent of Azerbaijan and turned about a million Azerbaijanis into refugees."[99]

In early 2001, a number of news reports focused on international efforts to mediate the dispute between Armenia and Azerbaijan, including U.S.-sponsored peace talks held in April in Key West, Florida. The *Wall Street Journal* later observed that President George W. Bush's efforts to promote the talks and his subsequent hosting of the leaders of Armenia and Azerbaijan at the White House was a "rare exception to his arms' length approach to foreign disputes," while the *New York Times* editorialized that although President Bush's "involvement in negotiations over Nagorno-Karabagh . . . is undoubtedly in part due to the extensive oil

96. Douglas Frantz, "Hope Erodes for Azerbaijan's Sea of Refugees," *New York Times*, July 21, 2001.

97. Francis M. Deng, "Displaced in Azerbaijan," *New York Times*, July 28, 2000.

98. Michael Wines, "Trying to Tell a Truce From a War," *New York Times*, May 27, 2001.

99. Douglas Frantz, "Abulfaz Elchibey, Who Led Free Azerbaijan, Dies at 62," *New York Times*, August 23, 2000.

and gas reserves in the Caspian region . . . it is a welcome move, which we hope signals that Washington will remain engaged with troubled regions of the globe. . . . Mr. Bush no doubt hopes to increase American influence. It is welcome that he is doing so by furthering the possibility of peace."[100]

In the eighteen months following September 11, 2001, the frequency of U.S. press coverage of Azerbaijan's conflict with Armenia declined not only in absolute but also in relative terms, down to 17 percent of all articles. Moreover, the tone and content of the articles had changed significantly. After that date, the *New York Times* (and the other publications) did not publish even a single report on the plight of the conflict's refugees comparable to Douglas Frantz's grim story that the paper had earlier carried on its front page. Both Frantz's report and the letter to the editor responding to it criticized the government of Azerbaijan for its insufficient attention to the refugees' plight; thus, the absence of continued reporting on this problem had the indirect effect of putting the government in a less negative light. Furthermore, most of the post–September 11 news stories that mentioned Azerbaijan's conflict with Armenia did not discuss the conflict in itself but considered the conflict's detrimental effects on U.S. efforts to combat terrorism. Thus, in October 2001, the *Wall Street Journal* lamented the fact that although Azerbaijan "could become a useful center for U.S. intelligence collection and a coveted landing base along flight paths to Afghanistan," U.S.-Azerbaijani strategic cooperation is hampered by "Azerbaijan's bitter conflicts with neighboring Armenia [which] have hurt the Baku government in Congress, where the powerful Armenian-American lobby has kept a tight lid on all but humanitarian assistance."[101] A few weeks later, the *Wall Street Journal* published an op-ed whose author called upon the United States to "diminish dependence on Saudi Arabia [by] focus[ing] on oil from the Caspian Sea," and to remove the "glitch" impeding U.S.-Azerbaijani relations, namely the sanctions imposed on Baku in retaliation for the Nagorno-Karabagh conflict.[102]

At the same time that the U.S. press's attention to the Nagorno-Karabagh conflict had diminished and that the U.S. press had begun to view that conflict through the prism of the U.S. war on terrorism, the fre-

---

100. Steve LeVine, "Peace Talks Boost Hopes for an Accord Between Foes in Oil-Rich Caspian Region," *Wall Street Journal*, May 17, 2001; "Mr. Bush's Caspian Diplomacy," *New York Times*, April 16, 2001.

101. David Rogers, "Campaign Against Terrorism."

102. Brenda Shaffer, "A Caspian Alternative to OPEC," *Wall Street Journal*, November 7, 2001; the sanctions were indeed lifted several months later. See "A Nation Challenged: U.S. Lifts Sanctions."

quency with which the press depicted Azerbaijan as a "friend of the west" (including the United States) has increased in both absolute and relative terms. It is not that prior to September 11, 2001, Azerbaijan was never portrayed as being either pro-Western or as leaning toward the West. For example, in August 2001, the *New York Times* remarked that "from his seat atop many billions of barrels of oil and large natural gas reserves, Mr. Aliyev [sic] leans to the West."[103] Still, whereas before September 11, 2001, only 7 percent of all articles contained such characterizations, in the following eighteen months their relative frequency rose to 26 percent. Thus, several post–September 11 articles in the *Wall Street Journal* depicted Azerbaijan as "an increasingly important partner of the United States," a "pro-American state," "pals not only with the United States but also with Turkey and Israel," and an "enthusiastic" supporter of the U.S. war on terrorism.[104] The *New York Times*, though it did not explicitly use such strong words to describe Azerbaijan's stance, nevertheless published a number of news stories that gave texture and meaning to the growing partnership between Azerbaijan and the United States: Donald Rumsfeld's visit to Baku, which was hailed as the first visit to Azerbaijan by a U.S. Secretary of Defense; U.S. Secretary of Energy Spencer Abraham's trip to Baku to attend the BTC pipeline's groundbreaking ceremony; and the establishment of a regional antiterrorism law enforcement center in Baku , which is supported by the United States.[105]

The third most frequent theme in the U.S. press coverage of Azerbaijan before September 11, 2001, was "poverty/social ills," under which the authors classified reports that either depicted Azerbaijan as an impoverished country or described social problems there or both. In June 2000, a report from International Red Cross headquarters in Geneva noted the rapid spread of malaria in Azerbaijan.[106] A July 2000 profile of President Aliev gave him credit for "bringing a measure of economic stability . . . particularly by forging joint ventures with Western oil compa-

---

103.   Frantz, "Iran and Azerbaijan Argue Over Caspian Riches," *New York Times*, August 30, 2001.

104.   Rogers, "Campaign Against Terrorism"; Shaffer, "A Caspian Alternative to OPEC"; Claudia Rossett, "Potentate Jr.," *Wall Street Journal*, November 6, 2002; Brenda Shaffer, "Letter to the Editor: Young Leader or an Affront to Democracy?" November 12, 2002.

105.   Thom Shanker, "A Nation Challenged: The Allies, Rumsfeld to Visit Troops Stationed in Afghanistan, *New York Times*, December 16, 2001; Greene, "Work Begins on Oil Pipeline"; David Binder, "U.S. Supports Anticrime Groups in the Caucasus and Central Asia," *New York Times*, January 26, 2003.

106.   Elizabeth Olson, "Red Cross Says Three Diseases Kill Many More Than Disasters," *New York Times*, June 29, 2000.

nies," but also noted that "critics complain that little of the promised oil wealth has trickled down to the general population, which includes a million impoverished refugees."[107] Frantz's above-mentioned exposé of the refugee problem suggested that in Azerbaijan "promised oil riches have yet to materialize and per capita income is less than $2,000 a year." Additionally, a later report by the same correspondent contrasted Baku's wealth during its first oil boom a century ago to the present, "with the country's post-Soviet economy fraying and a restive population facing energy shortages."[108]

In the aftermath of September 11, 2001, however, only one of the forty-two articles which had significantly mentioned Azerbaijan made a reference—a rather casual one—to the country's poverty. A report on Pope John Paul II's visit to Baku noted that "Azerbaijan is often described as oil-rich, but energy profits are not very apparent in much of downtown Baku, where potholed streets are lined by shabby Soviet-era high-rises."[109] The almost complete disappearance of references to Azerbaijan's poverty, combined with the diminished attention to the plight of the refugees, served to turn Azerbaijan into a more prosperous place after the September 11 attacks, in perception if not reality.

Another theme that figured rather prominently in pre–September 11 coverage of Azerbaijan but subsequently diminished greatly in importance is "Soviet legacy," referring to articles that discussed various ways in which the legacy of the Soviet Union was constraining Azerbaijan. An October 2000 article in the *Wall Street Journal* explored the "nine years of alphabetic fits and starts" experienced by Azerbaijanis since "they announc[ed] they would junk the Cyrillic alphabet that had been imposed by Soviet rule for 50 years."[110] In January 2001, the *New York Times* reported that "since the collapse of the Soviet Union a decade ago, its former republics in the Caucasus and Central Asia have struggled to make a transition to democracy and to wean themselves from the centralized economy that dominated the region from Moscow for 70 years."[111] A

107. Douglas Frantz, "In Azerbaijan's New World, An Old Fox Clings to Power," *New York Times*, July 23, 2003.

108. Frantz, "Hope Erodes for Azerbaijan's Sea of Refugees"; Douglas Frantz, "Baku Journal: How the Nobels Made a Prize of Baku," *New York Times*, February,3, 2001.

109. Alessandra Stanley, "Frail Pope Takes His Message of Peace to the Azerbaijanis," *New York Times*, May 23, 2002.

110. Hugh Pope, "Freed of Russian Yoke, Turkic Nations Find They Miss the Alphabet," *Wall Street Journal*, October 24, 2000.

111. Douglas Frantz, "Russia's Firm Hand on Heating Gas Worries Its Neighbors," *New York Times*, January 8, 2001.

month later the *New York Times* reported from Baku about President Aliev's desire to install his son, Ilham, as his successor. "This model of monarchy," the reporter commented, "seems increasingly to take hold in the former Soviet lands, republics that have often become the personal fiefs of the rulers who mostly were part of the Soviet system. In many ways the autocracies are an outgrowth of the Soviet era, when regional leaders were chosen in Moscow and few people took an active role in politics."[112] Even the dispute over delimiting the Caspian seabed (and thus, its riches) was laid by the *Wall Street Journal* at the door of the Soviet Union: "the border disarray shows how the Soviet Union's collapse still reverberates through this corner of the defunct communist empire, even as these new nations gain importance to the West."[113]

References to Russian meddling in Azerbaijani affairs or Russian economic or political pressure on Azerbaijan ("Russian influence") appeared in one-tenth of the pre–September 11 articles about Azerbaijan. For example, Douglas Frantz's profile of President Aliev from July 2000 stated that "Moscow's recent push to regain control of far-flung Russian regions and to recapture lost influence in former Soviet republics presents a new challenge for Mr. Aliyev [sic]."[114] Frantz's above-cited report on Azerbaijan's "monarchic" model warned that "the prospect of instability or violence when one of the current leaders leaves office also raises the prospect of intervention by Russia, which is already reasserting its influence."[115] After September 11, 2001, such references to Russian pressures, or potential pressures, on Azerbaijan have diminished in both absolute and relative terms. Moreover, post–September 11 reports on Russia's role in the region tended to depict Russian pressures in past tense. *Newsweek,* for example (in one of its very rare articles dealing with Azerbaijan), reported in December 2001 that Russian Federation President Vladimir Putin's stance on Azerbaijan "has shifted dramatically in recent weeks. Moscow has long opposed Azerbaijan's Baku-Ceyhan pipeline project . . . But two weeks ago Russian Deputy Premier Viktor Khristenko effectively gave the project his blessing."[116]

Two thematic categories' relative frequency more than doubled after

---

112. Douglas Frantz, "Fresh Dynasties Sprout in Post-Soviet Lands as Democratic Succession Withers," *New York Times,* February 20, 2001.

113. Steve LeVine, "Sea or Lake?" *Wall Street Journal,* August 3, 2001.

114. Frantz, "In Azerbaijan's New World, An Old Fox Clings to Power," *New York Times,* July 23, 2003.

115. Frantz, "Fresh Dynasties Sprout in Post-Soviet Lands."

116. "Former Glory," *Newsweek,* December 3, 2001.

September 11, 2001: friend of the West (discussed earlier) and "secular state," denoting articles which, though they may have acknowledged Islam as the predominant religion of Azerbaijan's populace, specifically mentioned the secular nature of Azerbaijan's regime or portrayed Azerbaijani Islam as being relatively lax and tolerant. This theme was evident in five post–September 11 articles (four of them in the *Wall Street Journal*), up from only one during the preceding eighteen months. The *New York Times* contrasted the suspicion with which the Pope was received in Orthodox Bulgaria to the warmer welcome he subsequently received in Muslim Azerbaijan. The report noted that many "Muslim guests" attended the papal mass in Baku and quoted an Azerbaijani Muslim who "said she was moved. 'To me the pope looks like a very old, sick man who has a lot of love in his heart.'" The aforementioned *Wall Street Journal* op-ed, written by Brenda Shaffer of Harvard University, suggested that "the U.S. should deal with Azerbaijan and Kazakhstan because, although they are predominantly Muslim states, they maintain complete separation of religion and state. The overwhelming majority of the populations of these states are secular and their foreign policies, especially in Azerbaijan, are staunchly pro-American."[117] A year later Shaffer, in a letter to the editor of the *Wall Street Journal*, again depicted Azerbaijan as a "secular, moderate Muslim-majority country."[118] Even an article that was otherwise critical of the authoritarianism of the Azerbaijani regime acknowledged that "Azerbaijan has a secular government, huge oil reserves and a helpful stance toward the war on terror."[119]

Several other themes present in the U.S. press coverage of Azerbaijan were relatively marginal both before and after September 11, 2001,—for example, news stories on the endangered sturgeon population of the Caspian Sea ("caviar") or stories centering on economic corruption. The study does not consider these marginal themes.

As Table 5.4 clearly shows, the promise of vast energy resources was the predominant theme in the U.S. press (the *New York Times* and *Wall Street Journal*, to be more precise) portrayal of Azerbaijan both before and after the attacks of September 11, 2001. If anything, its predominance had risen in the later period. This pattern contrasts sharply with the marginalization of oil relative to other themes in the composite image of Saudi Arabia, as reflected by the U.S. press.

Overall, the table suggests that prior to September 11, 2001,

117. Shaffer, "A Caspian Alternative to OPEC."

118. Shaffer, "Letter to the Editor."

119. Claudia Rossett, "Potentate Jr.," *Wall Street Journal*, November 6, 2002.

Table 5.4. Top Themes in U.S. Press Coverage of Azerbaijan.

Before Sept. 11	Frequency	
Theme	Absolute	Relative
1) Oil Frontier	39	0.58
2) Conflict w/Armenia	19	0.28
3) Poverty	8	0.12
4) Soviet Legacy	8	0.12
5) Russian Influence	7	0.10
After Sept. 11	Frequency	
Theme	Absolute	Relative
1) Oil frontier	29	0.69
2) Friend of the West	11	0.26
3) Conflict w/Armenia	7	0.18
4) Secular State	5	0.12

NOTE: For the post–September 11 period, four thematic categories were tied for fifth place, with only three articles each.

Azerbaijan was represented by the *New York Times* and *Wall Street Journal* as a state that would become wealthy in the future—once it fully realized its potential as an energy exporter—yet that for the time being remained heavily burdened by poverty, military weakness, a massive refugee problem, Russian pressure, and the legacy of seventy years of totalitarian rule. As for Azerbaijan's post–September 11 composite image, it has undoubtedly improved markedly and concurrently with the strengthening of Azerbaijan's military and diplomatic ties with the United States. This composite image is almost perfectly captured by a *Wall Street Journal* op-ed (previously quoted), whose author described Azerbaijan as a "secular" and "pro-American state, awash with oil, non-coordinated with OPEC, and begging to have [its] oil flow westward. Does this sound too good to be true? One glitch is the continuing Nagorno-Karabagh conflict."[120]

Kazakhstan

Kazakhstan had attracted U.S. oil executives even before the final collapse of the Soviet Union. In 1992, shortly after Kazakhstan became independent, its government signed a major deal with the Chevron Corpora-

120. Shaffer, "A Caspian Alternative to OPEC."

tion to develop the Tengiz oil field, one of the world's largest. The Clinton administration recognized the importance of Kazakhstan earlier than it had "discovered" Azerbaijan because a part of the Soviet Union's nuclear arsenal had been deployed on Kazakhstan's soil. Kazakhstan agreed to surrender its nuclear weapons in exchange for U.S. aid. In early 1994, President Nursultan Nazarbaev of Kazakhstan visited the White House and obtained a commitment to increase U.S. aid to his country from $91 million U.S. to $311 million U.S. for 1994.[121] In 1999, U.S. Ambassador to Kazakhstan Richard Jones described U.S.-Kazakh relations as "very important." Kazakhstan's strategic importance to the United States was underscored by the participation of forces from the U.S. Army's 82nd Airborne Division in military exercises on Kazakh soil in 1997 and 2000.[122]

But unlike Azerbaijan, which clearly chose to lean toward the United States in order to counterbalance Russian influence, Kazakhstan preferred to embed its budding strategic relationship with the United States in a broader, "multidimensional" framework. In other words, Kazakhstan attempted to maintain good strategic relations with Russia, China, and the United States at the same time.[123] Such a balance was relatively easy to strike after the September 11 attacks, when both Russia and China expressed strong support for the U.S.-led war on terrorism. As the *Wall Street Journal* reported, Kazakh President Nazarbaev "has wholeheartedly supported the war on terrorism and permitted the U.S. to use Kazakhstan airfields for emergency landings."[124] Later, however, when Russia broke ranks with the United States over the war on Iraq, Kazakhstan, in contrast to Azerbaijan, opted out (publicly, at least) of the U.S.-led "Coalition of the Willing." After the end of the war, though (and beyond the period covered by this study) Kazakhstan tried to mend fences with the United States by committing a group of military medics to assist the "stabilization" of Iraq.[125] In sum, U.S. strategic relations with Kazakhstan can be said to have been fairly good before September 11,

121.   Nozar Alaolmolki, *Life After the Soviet Union: the Newly Independent Republics of the Transcaucasus and Central Asia* (Albany: SUNY Press, 2001), pp. 29–30, 68.

122.   Ibid., p. 69; Klare, *Resource Wars*, pp. 1–5.

123.   "We Cannot Renounce Multidimensional Foreign Policy; Interview with Kazakhstan's Secretary of State K. Tokaev," *Kazakhstan News Bulletin*, Vol. 2, No. 8 (May 20, 2003), at <www.kazakhembus.com>.

124.   Steve LeVine, "Caspian Intrigue: Odd Family Drama in Kazakhstan Dims Democratic Hopes," *Wall Street Journal*, September 12, 2002.

125.   "Kazakhstan to Send Medical Troops to Iraq: President Bush Praises Move," *Kazakhstan News Bulletin*, Vol. 2, No. 5 (April 29, 2003), at <www.kazakhembus.com>.

2001, if not as warm as U.S.-Azerbaijani relations, and to have improved at best moderately in the aftermath of the attacks on New York and Washington, D.C. Kazakhstan's image as reflected by the U.S. press would be expected then to have exhibited a relatively moderate change, perhaps a slight improvement, within the same time frame.

The results of the analysis of Kazakhstan's characterization by the U.S. press are presented in Table 5.5. Kazakhstan, like Azerbaijan, had not received much U.S. media attention overall. Again, *Newsweek* and *USA Today* printed very few articles about Kazakhstan, and even the *Wall Street Journal* coverage was rather thin, especially prior to September 11, 2001. Almost 85 percent of the analyzed articles were printed in the *New York Times,* and the reader should keep this in mind even as the authors continue, for convenience, to refer to "the U.S. press" below. In general, after September 11, 2001, the frequency with which the U.S. press covered Kazakhstan increased moderately—an increase that is at least partly attributable to Kazakhstan's proximity to Afghanistan, the war on terrorism's primary theater of action.

The promise of oil riches has been the predominant theme of the U.S. press coverage of Kazakhstan—just over half the articles dealing with Kazakhstan, both before and after the September 11 terrorist attacks, discussed this subject or at least made significant references to Kazakhstan's oil potential. Kazakhstan's oil reserves turned out to be larger than those of Azerbaijan, and the greater use of terms such as "huge" or "vast," as opposed to merely "rich," to describe Kazakhstan's oil fields reflects this fact. For example, in May 2000, the *Wall Street Journal* reported that Chevron agreed to acquire an additional stake in "the vast Tengiz oil field in Kazakhstan," while a November 2002 report in the *Wall Street Journal* described the same field as "huge."[126] In November 2002, the *Wall Street Journal,* in a report datelined Almati, Kazakhstan, also characterized the region's energy supplies as "enormous."[127] The *New York Times,* too, described Tengiz as a "huge find of six billion to nine billion barrels of oil."[128] The more recently-discovered Kashagan oil field was described by the *New York Times* as being, "by some estimates . . . the largest oil deposits found in decades" and as a "huge" field that "many in the industry be-

---

126. "Chevron is Set to Buy Additional 5% Stake in Kazakhstan Project," *Wall Street Journal,* May 18, 2000; Thadeus Herrick and Steve Levine, "ChevronTexaco Copes With Halt of Big Oil Project in Kazakhstan," *Wall Street Journal,* November 15, 2002.

127. Steve Levine, "Turkmen President Escapes Attempt at Assassination," *Wall Street Journal,* November 26, 2002.

128. Neela Banerjee and Mary W. Walsh, "1 New Oil Company, 2 Corporate Cultures," *New York Times,* October 17, 2000.

Table 5.5. Recurrent Themes in Media Coverage of Kazakhstan Before and After September 11, 2001.

Theme	New York Times Before		After		Wall Street Journal Before		After		Newsweek Before		After		USA Today Before		After		Total Before		After	
Oil Frontier	25	0.48	28	0.43	3	1.00	9	0.90	3	0.75	2	0.66			2	1.00	31	0.53	41	0.52
Corruption	11	0.21	6	0.09	2	0.66	2	0.20	1	0.25	1	0.33					14	0.24	8	0.10
Political Repression	5	0.10	11	0.17	1	0.33	4	0.40	1	0.25	1	0.33					7	0.12	16	0.20
Corruption & Repression	16	0.31	17	0.27	3	1.00	6	0.60	2	0.66	1	0.33					21	0.36	24	0.30
U.S. Partner	2	0.04	13	0.20			5	0.50							1	0.50	2	0.03	20	0.25
Regional Diplomacy	6	0.11	12	0.19			1	0.10									6	0.10	13	0.16
Modernization	2	0.04	7	0.11			1	0.10									2	0.03	8	0.10
Soviet Legacy	3	0.06	9	0.14			1	0.10			1	0.33					3	0.05	11	0.14
Poverty/Social Ills	3	0.06	3	0.05													3	0.05	3	0.04
Caviar	3	0.06	3	0.05													3	0.05	3	0.04
Islamic Threat	3	0.06	6	0.09											1	0.50	3	0.05	7	0.09
Environment, nature	1	0.02	2	0.03													1	0.02	2	0.02
Grassroot particip'n	1	0.02	2	0.03													1	0.02	2	0.02
Drug Trafficking	2	0.04	1	0.02													2	0.03	1	0.01
Total Items Coded	52		64		3		10		3		3		0		2		58		79	

NOTES: "Before" denotes the frequency of the theme in the newspaper's coverage of Kazakhstan between March 11, 2000, and September 11, 2001. "After" denotes the frequency of the theme in the newspaper's coverage of Kazakhstan between September 12, 2001, and March 11, 2003. The integers denote absolute frequency, namely the number of articles in which the theme was evident. The decimals denote relative frequency, namely the absolute frequency divided by the total number of articles coded. The sum of the relative frequencies exceeds 1.0 because some articles contained more than one theme. The sum of the absolute frequencies exceeds the total number of articles for the same reason.

lieve will prove to be the world's largest oil development project."[129] Indeed, the Kashagan field was so "huge," according to another *New York Times* news story, that its discovery prompted President Nazarbaev to predict that it "would help Kazakhstan export as much oil as Saudi Arabia by 2015."[130] The *New York Times* also made numerous references to the "vast," "huge," or "immense" oil reserves of the country as a whole.[131]

The second most frequent theme that recurred in U.S. media coverage of Kazakhstan during the eighteen months prior to September 11, 2001, was economic corruption; every fourth article that contained a significant mention of Kazakhstan discussed, or significantly alluded to, allegations of corruption. The corruption scandal that attracted the U.S. press's greatest attention involved allegations of major bribes funneled by U.S. oil companies into Swiss bank accounts that were controlled by Kazakh leaders. Thus, most of the articles that discussed corruption also depicted Kazakhstan as a promising oil producer.

The *New York Times* first covered the story in a brief news item in its business section in early July 2000. Federal prosecutors, the report read, "are investigating whether an American trade consultant funneled millions of dollars in payments from major oil companies like Philips Petroleum and Mobil to Kazakhstan officials who are his clients . . . Last month, the Justice Department asked Swiss authorities for help in investigating the financial activities of James H. Giffen, a prominent consultant for trade deals in Russia and former Soviet republics."[132] A few weeks later *Newsweek* picked up the story, reporting at some length that the Justice Department was investigating Giffen, "a long time adviser to Kazakh President Nursultan Nazarbaev," for violating "the Foreign Corrupt Practices Act by transferring money to senior Kazakh officials from oil companies that, in return, received oil concessions in Kazakhstan." The State Department and the White House, *Newsweek* added, were not enthusiastic about the Department of Justice's investigation because "U.S. diplo-

---

129. "Exxon Venture May Delay Caspian Sea Project," *New York Times*, November 29, 2000; Christopher Pala, "BP Amoco Will Sell Stake in Caspian Sea Oil Field," *New York Times*, February 3, 2001.

130. Eric Schmitt, "U.S. Oil Consultants Face Inquiry on Kazakh Deals," *New York Times*, August 3, 2000.

131. See, for example, Birgit Brauer, "A Breakthrough for Kazakhstan's Oil," *New York Times*, October 2, 2001; Sabrina Tavernise with Birgit Brauer, "Russia Becoming an Oil Ally," *New York Times*, October 19, 2001; Patrick E. Tyler, "Kazakh Leader Urges Iran Pipeline Route," *New York Times*, December 10, 2001.

132. "U.S. Investigating Conduct of Adviser to Kazakhstan," *New York Times*, July 3, 2000; see also Sabrina Tavernise, "No Kazakhstan Inquiry on Consultant," *New York Times*, July 11, 2000.

macy in the Caspian region actively encouraged American energy companies to seek contracts" in Kazakhstan.[133] The *New York Times* followed with a lengthy story dispatched from Switzerland, which indicated that "Swiss and American authorities have blocked Kazakhstan's government from access to bank accounts holding roughly $100 million that they suspect Western oil companies may have used to bribe senior Kazakh officials . . . Some of the accounts were available for the benefit of the Kazakh president, Nursultan A. Nazarbayev [sic], as well as other officials and their families, officials said."[134]

In December 2000, the *New York Times* carried an unflattering profile of Nazarbaev's U.S. adviser James Giffen, which discussed the above mentioned allegations in great detail.[135] Several months later the *Wall Street Journal* added a new wrinkle to the story when it reported that Giffen may have also played a role "in a deal in which oil from Kazakhstan was shipped to Northern Iran in return for Iranian oil delivered in the Persian Gulf." The federal government, the report added, was investigating whether the Mobil Corporation was involved in such swaps, banned under the U.S. trade embargo against Iran.[136]

A May 2001 *New York Times* report on the business environment in Kazakhstan noted that "Central Asian nations fare poorly on the annual ranking of corrupt countries by Transparency International," and quoted a U.S. business executive who said that "bribery is as big a problem as it ever was."[137] The precipitous decline in the frequency of U.S. press reporting on Kazakh corruption after September 11, 2001, suggests, however, that either this executive had been wrong or, more likely, that the press had shifted its attention elsewhere.

At the same time that the frequency of the U.S. press's association of Kazakhstan with corruption had declined (from 24 percent of all stories before September 11 to 10 percent thereafter), the frequency with which the press depicted Kazakhstan as being politically repressive had in-

---

133. Steve LeVine and Bill Powell, "New Clues on the Trail of Cash, Oil and Politics," *Newsweek*, July 24, 2000.

134. John Tagliabue, "Kazakhstan is Suspected of Oil Bribes in the Millions," *New York Times*, July 28, 2000.

135. David Johnston, "Kazakh Mastermind, or New Ugly American?" *New York Times*, December 17, 2000.

136. David S. Cloud and Steve LeVine, "Feds Widen Probe of Exxon Mobil in Iran-Oil Deal, *Wall Street Journal*, April 9, 2001.

137. Douglas Frantz, "Generating Much Heat But No Kazakh Profits," *New York Times*, May 13, 2001.

creased (under "political repression," the authors classified articles that either labelled the regime "autocratic/authoritarian" or dealt with abuse of power, harassment of opposition leaders, human rights violations, and electoral fraud or both). It is not that characterizations of the Kazakh regime as repressive were absent from the pre–September 11 media. For example, a September 2000 *New York Times* story about Islamic guerrilla attacks in Central Asia indicated fears that "the threats will be used by the governments as a cover for getting tougher on internal dissent in Kazakhstan, Kyrgyzstan and Uzbekistan, where human rights groups already complain that political freedom is suppressed."[138] A December 2000 report lamented the "mounting pressure on any news outlets that veer from the government line" in Kazakhstan and other Central Asian republics, and described Central Asia's leaders as "authoritarian." [139] Another *New York Times* story noted that "many Western observers" regard Kazakhstan as "insular and authoritarian," while a brief item in *Newsweek,* titled "Busting Hobbits," reported that "the police in Kazakhstan have reportedly harassed, arrested and tortured" fans of novelist J.R.R. Tolkien's work.[140]

In the aftermath of September 11, 2001, political repression remained the third most frequent theme in the U.S. press's depiction of Kazakhstan, but its incidence actually increased both in absolute and relative terms. This increase probably reflected an actual intensification of repressive practices by the Kazakh regime as it was exploiting U.S. reluctance to criticize an ally whose assistance was needed to prosecute the war in Afghanistan. As *Newsweek* reported in June 2002, the United States "turn[ed] a blind eye" to human rights violations in Central Asia during the war in Afghanistan. "Emboldened by promises of uncritical U.S. support, the leaders of Uzbekistan, Tajikistan, Turkmenistan, and especially Kyrgyzstan and Kazakhstan have unleashed a new wave of oppression." President Nazarbaev, *Newsweek* further reported, "has responded to the founding of a moderate democratic opposition movement by pressing criminal charges against its leaders and slamming the independent media."[141]

138. Douglas Frantz, "Guerrilla Attacks Raise Worries in Central Asia," *New York Times,* September 6, 2000.

139. Douglas Frantz, "Free Press Is Battered in Post-Soviet Central Asia," *New York Times,* December 7, 2000

140. Johnston, "Kazakh Mastermind, or New Ugly American?"; "Busting Hobbits," *Newsweek,* August 27, 2001.

141. Christian Caryl, "Turning a Blind Eye," *Newsweek,* June 3, 2002.

Most, if not all, of the other post–September 11 articles which discussed repression in Kazakhstan also placed the issue in the context of U.S.-Kazakh cooperation in the war on terrorism. A *New York Times* story printed a few days after the United States began bombing Afghanistan reported that the Central Asian republics, including Kazakhstan, "are now being urgently courted as the United States seeks to destroy terror bases in nearby Afghanistan." The article went on to explain that "for centuries the region was the domain of colorful emirs and khans" and that it remains "dominated by rulers whose ruthlessness in crushing dissent has, according to some specialists, fed the very extremism they seek to suppress."[142] In April 2002, the *New York Times* reported that President Nazarbayev [sic] "imprisoned two of his leading political rivals," and that the "authoritarian turn" in Central Asia's republics "is problematic for Washington, which is relying on their support for the military operation in Afghanistan. The Bush administration has criticized the human rights record of several of the governments but has been careful not to undermine them."[143] In late 2002, the *Wall Street Journal* carried two reports on the harassment of a well-known Kazakh opposition journalist which interpreted the incident as emblematic of "an abrupt deterioration in human rights in Central Asia, an oil-rich region bordering Afghanistan that is key in the U.S. war against terrorism."[144]

As these reports suggest, the characterization of Kazakhstan as an important partner of the United States ("U.S. partner") became commonplace in the U.S. press after September 11, 2001, even as some of these characterizations appeared in the context of otherwise less favorable characterizations. The number of articles characterizing Kazakhstan as a friend, partner, or ally of Washington rose tenfold in the aftermath of the September 11 attacks, making it the second most frequent theme evident in post–September 11 media coverage of Kazakhstan. Two weeks after the terrorist attacks, *USA Today* commented favorably on the rallying of the Central Asian "stans" behind the U.S. war effort. It added that "Washington could also see fringe benefits from this new level of cooper-

142. Stephen Kinzer, "5 Ex-Soviet Asian Republics Are Now Courted by the U.S.," *New York Times*, October 10, 2001.

143. Edmund L. Andrews, "Spotlight on Central Asia Is Finding Repression, Too," *New York Times*, April 11, 2002.

144. Quotation from Steve LeVine, "Central Asia Cases Bring Charge of Diminishing Human Rights," *Wall Street Journal*, December 27, 2002. See also Steve LeVine, "Central Asia Resist Pressure From West to Improve Human Rights," *Wall Street Journal*, November 11, 2002.

ation—including greater access for U.S. companies to Kazakhstan's oil reserves."[145] In December 2001, the *New York Times* printed two stories that discussed Secretary of State Colin Powell's visit to Kazakhstan and President Nazarbayev's [sic] upcoming visit to Washington. Both stories quoted Powell's statement, in a breakfast with U.S. oil executives in Kazakhstan, that he was "particularly impressed" with the vast investments made by U.S. energy companies in the country.[146] A year later the *Wall Street Journal* reported that "the U.S. maintained relatively strong relations with the five Central Asian States . . . Much of the relationship has been based on the region's enormous energy supplies. However, after the terrorist attacks the U.S. . . . strengthened military relations with Kazakhstan . . . Financial assistance to the republics as a whole more than doubled."[147]

Some U.S. press coverage also included reports of U.S.-Kazakh cooperation in weapons of mass destruction nonproliferation. In October 2001, the *New York Times* reported that "under the Pentagon's Cooperative Threat Reduction Program, Kazakhstan . . . has worked closely with Washington to dismantle its own former Soviet biological weapons facilities and prevent potentially lethal germs and weapons expertise from spreading to rogue states and terrorist groups." Kazakh officials were also reported to have assisted U.S. scientists in investigating a Soviet-era accident in a biological weapons facility.[148] Also, interestingly, in an op-ed published in the *New York Times* in January 2003, then-National Security Advisor Condoleezza Rice rested her case for war against Iraq partly on the example of Kazakhstan. "The World knows from examples set by South Africa, Ukraine and Kazakhstan," she wrote, "what it looks like when a government decides that it will cooperatively give up its weapons of mass destruction." She added that "in one instance, Kazakhstan revealed the existence of a ton of highly enriched uranium and asked the United States to remove it, lest it fall into the wrong hands." Deputy Sec-

---

145. Bill Nichols, "Russian Rallies 'Stans' in Support of U.S. Fight," *USA Today*, September 26, 2001.

146. Patrick E. Tyler, "Kazakh Leader Urges Iran Pipeline Route," *New York Times*, December 10, 2001; Neela Banerjee with Sabrina Tavernise, "As the War Shifts, Alliances, Oil Deals, Follow," *New York Times*, December 15, 2001.

147. Steve LeVine, "Turkmen President Escapes Attempt at Assassination," *Wall Street Journal*, November 26, 2002.

148. Judith Miller, "U.S. Agrees to Clean Up Anthrax Site in Uzbekistan," *New York Times*, October 23, 2001; William Broad and Judith Miller, "Traces of Terror: The Bioterror Threat," *New York Times*, June 15, 2002.

retary of Defense Paul Wolfowitz, too, was reported to have cited Kazakhstan as a "significant example" of full cooperation in dismantling weapons of mass destruction.[149]

As noted earlier, Kazakhstan pursued a foreign policy of "multi-dimensionality," attempting to balance its partnership with the United States with good relations with China and Russia. Indeed, a significant number of news reports about Kazakhstan either dealt with its relations with Russia and China or depicted it as a significant participant in regional diplomatic meetings or initiatives ("regional diplomacy") or did both. The frequency of this theme increased after September 11, 2001, but it remained ranked fourth relative to other themes, just as before. Examples of articles that depicted Kazakhstan as a participant in regional diplomacy included a May 2000 report on an antiterrorism and anti-smuggling pact between Russia and five other former Soviet nations, a June 2000 report on a summit of Russian, Chinese, and Central Asian leaders, several reports on regional negotiations on resolving the dispute over delimiting the resource-rich Caspian Sea, and reports on the Shanghai Cooperation Organization, described by the *New York Times* as a "loose economic and security alliance" whose members include China, Russia, and four Central Asian countries.[150]

The constraints imposed on Kazakhstan by the legacy of the Soviet Union constituted another significant theme in U.S. press coverage of the country, especially after September 11, 2001. The Soviet legacies covered by the U.S. press included Kazakhstan's poor transportation infrastructure, the decaying laboratories in which the Soviets conducted biological weapon research, the "devastating" effects of the numerous nuclear tests conducted by the Soviets on the Kazakh steppe, and the environmental crisis caused by the Soviet-era massive irrigation projects in Central Asia.[151]

---

149. Condoleezza Rice, "Why We Know Iraq Is Lying," *New York Times,* January 23, 2003; "In Wolfowitz's Words: It's Up to Hussein," *New York Times,* January 24, 2003.

150. "Russia: 6 Nation Pact," *New York Times,* May 25, 2000; "Putin and Jiang in Central Asia Accord," *New York Times,* July 6, 2002; "Turkmenistan: Caspian Summit Meeting," *New York Times,* April 23, 2002; "Russia, Kazakhstan: Caspian Pact," *New York Times,* May 14, 2002; Elisabeth Rosenthal, "China, Russia and 4 Neighbors Seek Common Front on Terror," *New York Times,* January 8, 2002.

151. Douglas Frantz, "600 miles in 18 Hours," *New York Times,* September 16, 2001; Fred Guteri and Eve Conant, "In the Germ Labs," *New York Times,* February 25, 2002; Judith Miller, "U.S. Agrees to Clean Up Anthrax Site in Uzbekistan;" Sabrina, Tavernise, "Cold War Legacy," *New York Times,* May 19, 2002; Michael Wines, "Grand Soviet Scheme for Sharing Water in Central Asia Is Foundering," *New York Times,* December 9, 2002; Steve LeVine, "Caspian Intrigue."

Table 5.6. Top Themes in U.S. Press Coverage of Kazakhstan.

Before Sept. 11	Frequency	
Theme	Absolute	Relative
1) Oil Frontier	31	0.53
2) Corruption	14	0.24
3) Political Repression	7	0.12
4) Regional Diplomacy	6	0.10

After Sept. 11	Frequency	
Theme	Absolute	Relative
1) Oil frontier	41	0.52
2) U.S. Partner	20	0.25
3) Political Repression	16	0.20
4) Regional Diplomacy	13	0.16
5) Soviet Legacy	11	0.14

NOTE: For the pre–September 11 period, four thematic categories were tied for fifth place, with only three articles each.

Several other themes whose presence in U.S. press reports about Kazakhstan was relatively thin before as well as after September 11, 2001, are excluded from the discussion and delineation of Kazakhstan's composite image as reflected by the U.S. press during those periods.

Table 5.6 presents the most salient themes in the U.S. press's characterization of Kazakhstan. The findings here are consistent with the findings on the U.S. press's characterization of Azerbaijan inasmuch as the media portrayed Kazakhstan primarily as a promising oil frontier both before and after September 11, 2001. Again, this result contrasts sharply with the marginalization of oil as a chief theme in the media's concomitant portrayal of Saudi Arabia.

Of the three analyzed cases, in the case of Kazakhstan, the post–September 11 change in the country's composite image appears to have been the smallest. Not only did oil remain the predominant theme, but the third and fourth themes, political repression and regional diplomacy respectively, also remained stable (in ranking though not exactly in value) across the two time periods. The most significant change involved the precipitous decline in the salience of corruption as an attribute of Kazakhstan and its replacement by "U.S. partner" as Kazakhstan's second most salient attribute. On balance, Kazakhstan's composite image can be said to have improved somewhat, corresponding to the moderate improvement in U.S.-Kazakh relations. From a potentially very wealthy

but corrupt and somewhat authoritarian land whose main strategic partners were Russia and China, Kazakhstan evolved into a potentially very
wealthy land that, though quite authoritarian, had become a trustworthy,
but not exclusive, partner of the United States.

Conclusion

In this study, the authors analyzed the ways in which the U.S. press, as a
surrogate for the proverbial "American mind," portrayed three energy-
rich, Muslim-majority states before the terrorist attacks of September 11,
2001, and in their aftermath. The findings show that prior to September
11, 2001, Saudi Arabia, Azerbaijan, and Kazakhstan were all portrayed
predominantly as oil-rich (or potentially rich) states, and that none of
them, not even Saudi Arabia, was prominently associated with Islam. In
the aftermath of the terrorist attacks, however, the images of these countries that were reflected by the U.S. press diverged to such a great extent
that it can hardly be attributable to objective changes in their values,
practices, political regimes, or social conditions. Whereas the image of
Saudi Arabia has come to be associated prominently with Islam—an extremist, threatening Islam, supportive of terrorism—the images of
Azerbaijan and Kazakhstan continued to be dominated by the prospect of
oil riches; to the extent that Islam had become a secondary component of
their respective images at all, the "Islam" component was portrayed as
decidedly secular and hence rather unthreatening.

In all three cases, the shift in the country's image harbored by the
proverbial "American mind" corresponded to, and was concurrent with,
changes in the quality of that country's diplomatic relationship with the
United States. Saudi Arabia's transformation from a modernizing (that is,
becoming more like the United States) if repressive oil exporter to an extremist, Wahhabist exporter of terrorism (that is, radically different from
the United States) was intimately intertwined with the crisis in the bilateral relations triggered by the attacks on New York and Washington,
D.C., and exacerbated by the Saudi reluctance to support the war on Iraq.
No neat sequence of shifting perceptions of the religion, politics, or eco-
nomics of Saudi Arabia followed by a worsening of its bilateral political
relationship with the United States occurred. The two changes occurred
in lockstep with one another, and if one of them preceded the other, it
was the politics that changed first.

The cases of Azerbaijan and Kazakhstan also evinced a significant, if
less striking, pattern of correspondence between the portrayal of these
countries by the U.S. press and their political relations with Washington.
Azerbaijan's image improved markedly and concomitantly with the

strengthening of its strategic relationship with the United States in the context of the war on terrorism and the war on Iraq. Finally, Kazakhstan's image improved moderately in conjunction with its support of U.S. military operations in Afghanistan, which did not extend to the U.S.-led war on Iraq.

The findings thus call into question the conventional view of the role of culture in international politics, which implicitly posits cultural differences, or perceptions thereof, as existing independently of the causes of political conflict among states, or prior to its emergence. This critique should not be construed, however, as a wholesale dismissal of the utility of cultural analysis. Ways of thinking about culture and politics exist other than those which are framed in terms of cause and effect, most notably French philosopher Michel Foucault's notion of a "nexus" of power/culture. The authors' argument bears an affinity to Foucault's position even though they did not present it in his terms.

Chapter 6

Congress, Constituencies, and U.S. Foreign Policy in the Caspian

David King and
Miles Pomper

With neighborhood talk focusing on schools, transportation, taxes, Social Security, welfare, and patriotism, former U.S. House Speaker Thomas P. (Tip) O'Neill, Jr. told anyone who would listen, "All politics is local."[1] Members of Congress quickly learn that "if you don't pay attention to the voters, you soon will find yourself right back there with them."[2] U.S. foreign policy is sometimes best viewed through the lens of local politics, even if that lens occasionally distorts a more detached and rational analysis of U.S. national interests. Consider congressional involvement in Armenia, Azerbaijan, and the disputed enclave of Nagorno-Karabagh.

Uncommon Grounds, a breakfast spot in Watertown, Massachusetts, is the kind of haunt that attracts members of Congress who want to hear what people are talking about "back home." U.S. foreign policy is rarely raised in most cafes and coffeehouses, so there is little incentive for members of Congress to pay close attention to international affairs. With frequent references to faraway politics in Yerevan and Baku, however, the crowd at Uncommon Grounds is different. Armenian-Americans densely populate Watertown, and Father Dajad Davidian holds court over cof-

The authors would like to thank Eileen O'Connor, who helped gather materials for this chapter, and Elizabeth Balcom of Project Save, who provided background on Armenians in Watertown, Massachusetts. David King thanks Marc Mamigonian for interesting him in this subject. The authors also thank Doug Blum, Pepper Culpepper, Tom Huddleston, Hamlet Isaxanli, Roger Kangas, Gerard Libaridian, Brenda Shaffer, Richard Sobel, Ronald Suny, and Steve Teles for their input.

1. Tip O'Neill with Gary Hymel, *All Politics Is Local* (Holbrook, Mass.: Bob Adams, 1994), p. xvi.

2. Ibid.

fee. Talk turns to politics, to the merits of State Representative Rachel Kaprielian, to the Armenian economy, and to the long-simmering conflict between Armenia and Azerbaijan.

Immigrant and ethnic political groups in the U.S. legislature have posed a serious dilemma for scholars who found, in *e pluribus unum*, that the dissimilarity between America's ethnic groups makes unity in politics especially difficult. Pluralists have worried that immigrant communities may view themselves as alien participants in the U.S. democratic process, with allegiances maintained abroad.[3] This is an old concern that recurs with each new wave of immigrants.[4] Recalling the U.S. civil rights movement, observers noted the role that ethnic interest groups play in domestic politics.[5] Few believed, however, that such a tendency existed in U.S. foreign politics, especially when the U.S. national interest seemed fairly easy to divine during the Cold War.

With the end of the Cold War, pluralists purported increasing the influence of diaspora interest groups. The breakup of the Soviet Union overturned the U.S. role in the international system and also created fledgling states whose relationship to the United States was historically groundless.[6] While some research has been done on the effects of diasporas—especially with respect to policy toward Israel and Cuba—the growing number of states, combined with political pressures inherent in globalization, should awaken interest in how local diaspora communities can influence U.S. foreign policy.[7]

When U.S. national interest in a particular foreign region is not immediately apparent, diaspora communities may (but often do not) be-

3. Tony Smith, *Foreign Attachments: The Power of Ethnic Groups in the Making of American Foreign Policy* (Cambridge, Mass.: Harvard University Press, 2000); Steven M. Teles, "Public Opinion and Interest Groups in the Making of U.S.–China Policy," in Robert S. Ross, ed., *After the Cold War: Domestic Factors and U.S.–China Relations* (Armonk, N.Y.: M.E. Sharpe, 1998).

4. Alexander DeConde, *Ethnicity, Race, and American Foreign Policy: A History* (Boston, Mass.: Northeastern University Press, 1992).

5. Mark Schneider, *Ethnicity and Politics* (Chapel Hill, N.C.: Institute for Research in Social Science (IRSS) Research Reports, 1979).

6. Eric Alterman, *Who Speaks for America?* (Ithaca, N.Y.: Cornell University Press, 1998); James Schlesinger, "Fragmentation and Hubris," *National Interest*, Vol. 49, No. 3, (Fall 1997).

7. Tony Smith, *Foreign Attachments*; Yossi Shain, *Marketing the American Creed Abroad: Diasporas in the U.S. and their Homelands* (Cambridge: Cambridge University Press, 1999); and Yossi Shain, "Ethnic Diasporas and U.S. Foreign Policy," *Political Science Quarterly*, Vol. 109, No. 4, (Winter 1994–95), pp. 811–841.

come important in shaping U.S. foreign policy. Influential diaspora communities are typically well organized at the local level where political activists learn the arts of local politics, geographically concentrated, active in voting for local and national political offices, and well funded. Dozens of diaspora communities are present in the United States, and they tend to be geographically concentrated, sometimes in unexpected places such as the large Hmong population in Appleton, Wisconsin, or the growing Mongolian community in Boulder, Colorado. Yet few of these geographically concentrated communities have much influence in Washington, D.C.—let alone in Madison and Denver. Why has the Armenian diaspora been so influential?

Since Armenia and Azerbaijan broke from the Soviet Union in 1991, Armenian-Americans have successfully lobbied for policies punishing Azerbaijan.[8] Lobbies for both countries have been very active in Washington since the early 1990s, though the Azerbaijani lobby was for most of that time a shell working on behalf of U.S. petroleum companies. Until January 2002, U.S. foreign policy had been tilted against Azerbaijan—not simply because of Armenia's diplomatic presence in Washington, but because Armenian-Americans are successfully integrated into local political organizations in places like Watertown, Massachusetts, and Glendale, California.

In this chapter, the authors explore the history and contingent political power of the Armenia diaspora in the United States. This geographically concentrated diaspora has had disproportionate influence over U.S. foreign policy with respect to Armenia and Azerbaijan, culminating in the passage of Section 907 of the 1992 Foreign Assistance Act. This essay describes how members of Congress react to diaspora communities generally—and Armenian lobbying groups specifically. In the wake of Azerbaijan's assistance to the United States in the war in Afghanistan, and much to the delight of U.S. petroleum companies that had been lobbying against Section 907 for nearly a decade, President George W. Bush officially waived Section 907 in January 2002. The essay presents an engaging case study of the link between local politics, diaspora interests, and U.S. foreign policy. The authors show that local culturally-based interests can determine U.S. national foreign policy choices, at times in defiance of the executive's branch definition of policy preferences for promoting U.S. national interest. These cases are limited, however, to issues which do not attract widespread national interest.

---

8. Edmund Herzig, *The New Caucasus: Armenia, Azerbaijan and Georgia* (New York: Chatham House, 1999), chap. 4.

U.S. Foreign Policy as "Local Politics"

Foreign policy is not very important for most members of Congress, and legislators seldom compete for seats on the House or Senate committees that oversee foreign affairs. Political careers are more likely to be made on committees that handle important regulatory issues (such as House Commerce or Senate Finance), and the odds of reelection are enhanced by serving on committees that distribute money for special projects (such as appropriations, transportation, and infrastructure committees). Usually, investing one's time in foreign policy brings a bad return back home because the constituents sitting around neighborhood haunts like Uncommon Grounds are more likely to be talking about education, roads, jobs, and clean water. Except in communities with a politically active diaspora, focusing on foreign policy can be a political liability for members of Congress.

Several diaspora communities have had a marked influence on U.S. foreign policy in a variety of congressional districts. Congressional support for the Marshall plan was strongest in districts populated by Polish, Hungarian, and Czechoslovakian expatriates.[9] Outside of Poland, the largest pro-Solidarity rallies in the world were held in North Chicago, Illinois, in Representative Daniel Rostenkowski's heavily Polish-American congressional district. At the time of those rallies in the late 1980s, Rostenkowski's district had the fourth highest density of Polish-Americans in the country, and Rostenkowski chaired the powerful House Ways and Means Committee which oversaw U.S. trade policy. Rostenkowski had the institutional power to spearhead a change in U.S. policy toward Poland, but change did not originate from his intrinsic interest in foreign policy theories. Rather, his constituents cared about the issue, and he wisely responded. Similarly, Armenians chanced upon a congressional district—the Massachusetts Eighth—that produced legislators even more powerful than the legendary Rostenkowski: John F. Kennedy and Tip O'Neill.

Armenian-Americans and the Massachusetts Eighth Congressional District

Within the Armenian-American community, a strong commitment to a democratic culture particular to their experience as political refugees fleeing despotic regimes has continued to exist. Many Armenian families came to the United States in the early 1900s and after World War I, first

9. Tony Smith, *Foreign Attachments*, p. 28.

fleeing massacres at the hands of Ottoman Turks and later escaping the dominance and suppression of the Soviet regime. While estimates vary, it is likely that as many as 1.5 million Armenians were either killed or starved to death between 1915 and 1923.[10] A brief uprising against the Bolsheviks by the Dashnak party in February 1921 sent pro-democracy and nationalist movements either deep underground or into the embrace of a growing Armenian diaspora in Syria, Lebanon, France, and, especially, the United States. Beginning with the Woodrow Wilson administration, Armenian-Americans became vocal supporters of de-Sovietization of the Caspian Sea region and ardent practitioners of democratic politics in their new communities. No similar culture of political activism took root and persisted within the tiny gatherings of immigrants from Kazakhstan, Uzbekistan, Azerbaijan, or Turkmenistan.

Throughout the U.S. Congress, the interest that legislators show in foreign policy often springs from local wells of support within politically active diaspora communities. Liberal intellectuals working at Harvard University, the Massachusetts Institute of Technology, Tufts University's Fletcher School of Diplomacy, and other Boston-area institutions populate the Massachusetts Eighth Congressional District, which is, as of this writing, represented by Democrat Michael Capuano. Membership in groups such as Greenpeace and Amnesty International is especially high in the area as well. Yet Congressman Capuano primarily hears about just one foreign policy issue: Armenia.

The local Armenian-American lobby is very well organized. Uncommon Ground's patriarch, Father Dajad Davidian, a retired senior pastor at Saint James Church, is well known to Jon Lenicheck, Congressman Capuano's liaison to Watertown. Lenicheck identifies Father Davidian as "a statesman for Armenians in the United States," and while neither Capuano nor Lenicheck are Armenian, both know and care about the diaspora community.[11] Approximately 5,000 of the 33,000 people living in Watertown identify themselves as Armenian-American, and politicians would ignore them at their own political peril.[12] Congressman Capuano

---

10. Joseph R. Masih and Robert O. Krikorian, *Armenia at the Crossroads* (Amsterdam: Harwood Academic Publishers, 1999), p. xxv.

11. Telephone interview with Jon Lenicheck, January 8, 2002.

12. According to the 2000 U.S. Census, 28,395 Massachusetts citizens reported "Armenian" as their "first ancestry." Populations in the congressional districts (CD) were as follows. 1st CD: 539, 2nd CD: 1,949, 3rd CD: 3,182, 4th CD: 203, 5th CD: 1,782, 6th CD: 4,803, 7th CD: 6,601, 8th CD: 6,951, 9th CD: 615, 10th CD: 1,770. So even within Massachusetts, the Armenian diaspora was geographically concentrated in just three districts.

was sworn into office in January 1999. His first trip overseas as a member of Congress came in August of that year: he went to Armenia.

Upon returning from Armenia, freshman Congressman Capuano co-sponsored House Resolution 398, commemorating the victims of the Armenian Genocide. On the House floor, he admonished Turkey, which he said continues to "deny the crimes committed against the Armenian people [and to] block the flow of humanitarian aid and commerce to Armenia."[13] As a former mayor of Somerville, Massachusetts, who was elected on the pledge to improve local schools, Capuano's newfound interest in U.S. foreign policy toward Armenia may have surprised some observers in Yerevan. It was, however, entirely expected in Watertown, Massachusetts.

Almost a half-century earlier, during the Cold War, Tip O'Neill—also serving his first term in Congress and also representing Watertown—took to the floor of the House of Representatives praising Armenians, who had thrived despite what "ruthless Communists" had done "to eradicate the spirit of independence and freedom among the Armenians."[14]

The Massachusetts Eighth Congressional District has an impressive lineage of famous politicians who got their political start in the kitchens and coffee houses of Boston's ethnic neighborhoods. Fresh from his tour in the Navy, a young John F. Kennedy represented Watertown in the House of Representatives after World War II. He later proved attentive to Armenian issues throughout his years in the U.S. Senate and the White House. Tip O'Neill succeeded Kennedy, rose through the Democratic Party leadership, and served ten years as the Speaker of the House. For O'Neill, Armenian issues—and especially recognition of the Armenian Genocide—were quintessentially "local" concerns. Fiercely anti-Soviet, Armenian political activists in the district sometimes toyed with supporting the Republican Party, so the Armenian community received special attention to keep them in O'Neill's camp. O'Neill took on a national role, even appearing at large annual Armenian rallies in New York City.

On May 3, 1975, O'Neill became the first recipient of the Armenian Church of America's "Friend of the Armenian People" award given on behalf of 200,000 Eastern Diocese parishioners and handed to O'Neill by, naturally, Watertown's Father Dajad Davidian. Before and after becoming the House Speaker, O'Neill routinely introduced legislation marking April 24 as a day of remembrance for victims of the Armenian genocide. When O'Neill retired, John F. Kennedy's nephew, Joseph P. Kennedy II,

13. *Congressional Record.* April 12, 2000, H2177.

14. *Congressional Record,* March 5, 1954, H2769.

was elected to Congress from the Massachusetts Eighth District, showing the same zeal for Armenia as those who had been elected before him.

Immigrant communities like Polish-Americans in North Chicago and Armenian-Americans in Watertown are, in a sense, lucky to have been represented by people who went on to hold powerful institutional positions. U.S. policy toward Armenia may not have been as favorable had Armenians settled someplace else in the early 1900s. It is not the total number of expatriates in the United States that matters as much as the concentration within a handful of key districts. This is as true for Armenian-Americans in Glendale and Fresno, California, and Watertown, Massachusetts, as it is for Ukrainian-Americans in Toledo, Ohio, and Cuban-Americans in Miami, Florida.

Armenian-American Lobbies in Congress

While it is clear that the Armenian-American community of Watertown is a dynamic force in its own congressional district, why has the Armenian-American lobby been so effective in shaping U.S. foreign policy in Congress? Some point to a large political action committee (PAC) run by the Armenian National Committee. Indeed, that PAC has been very active at the national and—especially—the state and local levels. Others note that Armenian-Americans have gained prominence in business; they are entrepreneurial, and along with Indian-Americans and Jewish-Americans, Armenian-Americans are far more likely than many other diaspora communities to foster the education of physicians and lawyers.

Both of these factors—money and professional connections—play an important part in successful lobbying, but it is also notable that U.S. policy toward Armenia has not been salient enough to attract much attention from non-Armenians. Presumably, most diaspora communities in the United States, if properly organized and funded, can exert substantial influence on U.S. foreign policy when the issues at hand do not overtly contradict other U.S. national interests. Watertown Armenians speak explicitly of the United States as a "host" country, and their allegiance to the homeland remains strong. One contributor to the *Armenian International Magazine* wrote in 1998, "We in the Armenian diaspora have a unique opportunity to exercise our dual allegiance to our host country and to Armenia. We should take advantage of our rights as citizens of the host country to gain its support of Armenia."[15] This raises potential problems for U.S. foreign policy toward any "home" country, because it is not often

---

15. Smith, *Foreign Attachments,* p. 14.

clear when the political interests of a diaspora are at odds with the long-term interests of the United States.

U.S. policy toward oil-rich Azerbaijan is a case in point. Before the territorial controversy over the post-Soviet status of Nagorno-Karabagh, a region within Azerbaijan predominantly populated by ethnic Armenians,[16] the Armenian-American diaspora was organized through lobbies and a cohort of supportive congressional lawmakers. Pro-Armenian members of Congress proved pivotal in securing an anti-Azerbaijan provision in the 1992 Freedom Support Act. The politics of that provision, known as Section 907, is discussed later in this article, and while the three-digit number meant little to most Americans, members of the Congressional Armenian Caucus came to view support for 907 as a litmus test signaling their friendship with Armenia.

Membership in the Congressional Armenian Caucus—formed by supportive lawmakers in 1995—like memberships in most issue-specific caucuses, is strongly related to the characteristics of a member's congressional district. According to the 2000 U. S. Census, 323,701 citizens identified themselves as Armenian-Americans. Armenian lobbying groups put the number closer to 1.5 million because many new immigrant ethnic Armenians were identified as Syrians or Lebanese.[17] (The census lacked a category for Azerbaijani-Americans, so they remain uncounted. Our estimates of Armenian-Americans in Watertown, Massachusetts comes from Father Davidian). Fifty-four percent of Armenian-Americans live in California, so it is no surprise that California is well represented in the Congressional Armenian Caucus with 27 of 107 members. Membership in the caucus was, according to aide Jon Lenicheck, a "no-brainer" for

---

16. The dispute between Armenia and Azerbaijan began in the late 1980s, prior to the breakup of the Soviet Union, as these two republics vied for control of the Nagorno-Karabagh region. Nagorno-Karabagh is situated within the legal boundaries of Azerbaijan. The majority of the enclave's population is ethnic Armenian, and a sizeable ethnic Azerbaijani community lived in Nagorno-Karabagh as well, which has since been expelled by Armenian forces. With the Soviet collapse, war erupted between Yerevan and Baku over Nagorno-Karabagh. By the time the two countries agreed on a cease-fire in 1994, the war had resulted in the deaths of more than 30,000 people and created large communities of refugees on both sides of the conflict—some 300,000 Armenians and 800,000 Azerbaijanis. Twenty percent of Azerbaijan's territory, including large areas of land outside of Nagorno-Karabagh, was occupied by Armenia. The leaders of the two antagonist states have meet frequently since 1994 and regularly conduct peace negotiations, but the sides have not yet succeeded in achieving a comprehensive settlement.

17. Emil Sanamyan, Research and Information Associate, Armenian Assembly of America, Correspondence with Eileen O'Connor, November 25, 2001. That number, however, is likely inflated to equal the number of Armenians claimed to have been killed during the genocide.

Congressman Michael Capuano when he entered the House in January 1999. With 28,393 Armenian-Americans living in Massachusetts, every member of the Massachusetts congressional delegation belongs to that caucus.

Eighty percent of the Congressional Armenian Caucus members come from just nine states, and those states hold 84 percent of the Armenians in the United States. With the Armenian-American population centered in a handful of states, and with no significant Azerbaijani presence in the United States, one would not be surprised that Section 907 has never figured in the local politics of Idaho, where the Census reports just thirty-seven Armenian-Americans. Idaho, however, is home to thirty-seven more Armenian-Americans than the total who were reported living in five other states *combined.*

Among the many nations within the Soviet Union, Armenia has long held a special place in the minds of members of Congress. Part of this was luck, because not every diaspora lands in a district that spawns a U.S. president and a Speaker of the House. Armenian-Americans were also more likely than those who remained in Armenia to embrace democratic values and to shun the Soviet Union, both of which served Armenian-Americans well in the Cold War era. As for a presence in Congress, no other Caspian nation came close to Armenia. Figure 6.1 shows the number of times that a member of Congress rose to talk about Armenia on the House or Senate floor. During the 98th Congress (1985–1986), Armenia was raised seventy-one times, which was twice as many times as the names of all of the other Caspian nations were uttered. The word "Turkmenistan" was said just seven times in five years (January 1985 through December 1989). While Azerbaijan did receive some attention, it was almost always in the context of conflicts with Armenia. These other Caspian nations had little representation in Congress because legislators had little reason to care about the links between their home districts and these far-off lands. Until U.S. petroleum companies rushed into the Caspian region after the Soviet collapse, no effective groups had lobbied Congress on behalf of anyone from the region but the Armenians.

In the decades leading up to the enactment of Section 907 in 1992, two Armenian-American groups had established offices in Washington to lobby the federal government on issues of concern to the community, particularly attempts to recognize the genocide. Their efforts had been spurred by the 1988 earthquake and by a 1988 decision in which the Armenian community in Azerbaijan's Nagorno-Karabagh region had called for independence from Baku. Azerbaijan's opposition to the secession of its territories (which were populated also by a sizeable Azerbaijani community) and the subsequent anti-Armenian riots in

Figure 6.1. U.S. Congressional Attention to Caspian Nations.

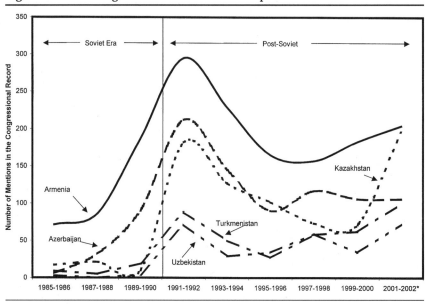

SOURCE: U.S. Congressional Record, January 1985–December 2001.
  *2000 estimate = twice the 2001 figure.

Azerbaijan were discussed in the diaspora in terms of the beginning of a "new genocide".

One of those lobbying groups, the Armenian National Committee of America (ANCA), traces its roots to 1918 and the American Committee for the Independence of Armenia, a group that resolutely urged a hard line against Moscow after Russia forcibly incorporated Armenia into the Soviet Union in the 1920s. In 1972, several prominent Armenian-Americans formed a new group, the Armenian Assembly of America (AAA), which was less dominated by anti-Soviet ideology and more willing to look for ways of cooperating with Moscow to help Armenia.

The AAA's less confrontational attitude toward Moscow allowed it to gain a foothold in Yerevan after the 1988 earthquake, where it helped distribute money from the Armenian diaspora to victims. Those ties grew as Armenia moved toward independence, with the Assembly serving as the main link between Yerevan and wealthy expatriates. Today, the assembly is so close to Yerevan that it boasts an office on the first floor of the Armenian Foreign Ministry.[18]

18. Interviews with Hirair Hovninian (AAA) and Aram Hamparian (ANCA), December 21 and 26, 2001.

The AAA had also been designed from the beginning as an elite organization designed to mobilize the Armenian-American community and its financial resources for national policy objectives with a "top-down" perspective. ANCA, on the other hand, was and remains largely a grass-roots organization; despite its long history, it wasn't until 1983 that it opened an office in Washington, and it still tends to look at issues from a "bottom-up perspective."

The policy differences between the two groups largely became moot after Armenia gained its independence following the breakup of the Soviet Union. Both groups focused on issues of widespread interest to Armenian-Americans, from enacting and retaining Section 907 to recognition of the genocide. Rather than weakening the community, many lawmakers and aides believe that having two lobbying groups has actually benefited Armenian-Americans.

As Heather S. Gregg noted in the fall 2001 issue of *Précis*, "competition between these two lobby groups has led to hyper-mobilization of this ethnic group's resources; their different approaches to lobbying have mobilized more Armenians and allies than one organization alone. The two lobbying groups have doubled outreach projects and resources on Armenian issues, magnifying the Armenian presence in the U.S."[19]

ARMENIA, AZERBAIJAN, AND SECTION 907

U.S. policy toward Azerbaijan has been dominated since 1992 by the discussion over Section 907 of the 1992 Freedom Support Act. This legislation had the effect of favoring newly independent and Christian Armenia in its territorial conflict over Nagorno-Karabagh with the newly independent, but Muslim, Azerbaijan.[20] Under Section 907, Congress directed that U.S. foreign assistance (with some exceptions) "may not be provided to the Government of Azerbaijan until the President determines, and so reports to the Congress, that the Government of Azerbaijan is taking demonstrable steps to cease all blockades and other offensive uses of force against Armenia and Nagorno-Karabakh."[21]

The one-paragraph provision came as part of a massive aid bill for the former Soviet Union, and Congress and the George H. W. Bush administration were far more concerned about ensuring that aid flowed to the fledgling government of Russian President Boris Yeltsin. Section 907

---

19. Heather S. Gregg, "Divided They Conquer: The Success of Armenian Ethnic Lobbies in the US," *Precis*, Vol. 11, No. 1 (Fall 2001), pp. 17–21.

20. Michael P. Croissant, *The Armenia-Azerbaijan Conflict* (Westport, Conn.: Praeger, 1998), chap. 4.

21. U.S. Public Law 102–511.

was little more than a footnote.[22] Supporters maintained the ban despite President William Clinton's objections as well. Following the September 11, 2001, terrorist attacks, however, President George W. Bush authorized Secretary of State Colin Powell to revise the restrictions against Azerbaijan, partly due to Azerbaijan's assistance in the war in Afghanistan. After months of negotiations, on January 11, 2002, President Bush officially waived the aid restrictions that had been imposed nearly a decade earlier.

News about Section 907 has been front-page material for *The Armenian Weekly* and other news outlets in the Armenian-American community, but few other Americans heard about it. Likewise, when Congress created Section 907 in 1992, few lawmakers paid much attention. Moreover, most lawmakers knew little about the conflict between Armenia and Azerbaijan or much about the other former Soviet republics only then beginning to break free of Moscow's domination. Those legislators who did follow the events in Yerevan were largely inclined to support Armenia's cause, since they hailed from states with significant Armenian-American populations. Armenian-American groups also counted on the power of a key supporter: Senate Minority Leader Robert Dole.

Only two years earlier, in 1990, Senator Dole had nearly shepherded legislation through Congress that would have defined the massacre of hundreds of thousands of Armenians by the Ottoman Empire as genocide. But Turkey, a North Atlantic Treaty Organization (NATO) ally and successor to the Ottoman Empire, raised strong objections, and the first Bush administration forced Dole to drop the issue. Ankara has consistently refused to recognize the massacres as genocide, insisting that they were the unfortunate by-products of war. The combined opposition of Turkey and the White House led a dozen senators to drop their support for the legislation. Two attempts by Dole to force an end to a weeklong filibuster by Senator Robert C. Byrd fell far short of the necessary sixty votes.[23]

Although Senator Dole's resolution failed, the debate contributed to a widespread sentiment on Capitol Hill that the Armenians had long been victimized and that the United States had not done enough to help them. Those feelings stretched as far back as the massacres themselves. The feelings were even stronger within the diaspora community. Armenian-Americans shared a collective sense of victimization, which had only

---

22. *1992 CQ Almanac* (Washington, D.C.: Congressional Quarterly, 1993), pp. 523–532.

23. *1990 CQ Almanac* (Washington, D.C.: Congressional Quarterly, 1991), pp. 807–808.

been hardened by their inability to win worldwide recognition of what they believed without question had been genocide. "I think if the genocide issue were to be taken care of, the air would go out of their tires politically. That is THE issue for them," said Representative Joe Knollenberg, Republican of Michigan., co-chair of the Congressional Armenian Caucus.[24]

The Image of the Caspian in Congress

When members of Congress have talked about Armenia and Azerbaijan since 1985, the themes have not focused on the religious culture of either country. Legislators talk about the Armenian Genocide, yet talk of the genocide rarely includes mention of Armenia's Christian background. (Christianity was more likely to be raised in Congress before the collapse of the Soviet Union, with Armenia contrasted against "Godless" communism.)

Likewise, the Muslim background of Azerbaijan was usually not mentioned in Congress, though this changed after the September 11, 2001, attacks. Before then, if Azerbaijan's predominant religion was cited at all, it was often pointed to as a reason that the United States should support Azerbaijan, not Armenia. Supporters of lifting Section 907 liked to raise the specter that Azerbaijan, secularized by decades of Soviet rule, could fall into the pattern of its fundamentalist neighbor, Iran, without U.S. assistance. Figure 6.2 shows the percentage of times that "Armenian" and "Christian" were mentioned in the same speech in Congress. Similar word combinations are shown for "Genocide," "Azerbaijan," and "Oil."

Over the last decade, talk of Azerbaijan's oil reserves dominated the conversation on Capitol Hill, and the religious cleavage that feels so important to both diaspora communities barely registered among members of Congress. Because congressional discussions about Armenia have long been framed around genocide, Armenia is more likely than not to be seen as a nation long victimized by its neighbors. Section 907 would seem to be a sympathetic gesture.

With 907 in place, all Armenian-American groups had to do was "play defense rather than offense," as ANCA's Aram Hamparian put it. James M. Lindsay noted recently in the *Brookings Review*, "The broader political factors that influence an ethnic lobby's effectiveness begin with whether it wants to preserve or overturn the status quo. Preserving it is

---

24. Interview with Representative Joe Knollenberg, Dec. 19, 2001.

Figure 6.2. Congressional "Frames" when Discussing Armenia & Azerbaijan.

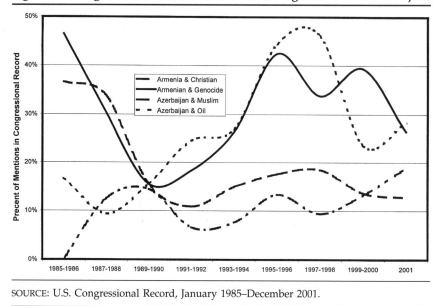

SOURCE: U.S. Congressional Record, January 1985–December 2001.

far easier—a lobby prevails if it wins at any step of the political process."[25] The Armenian-American lobby became skilled at cultivating gatekeepers, such as Dole and later Senator Mitch McConnell, Republican of Kentucky, who could help block efforts to overturn Section 907 at crucial steps in the legislative process.

Those gatekeepers became more important in the mid-1990s as energy companies sought to undo the law. Those companies became interested in the potential oil wealth of Azerbaijan and other countries bordering the Caspian Sea, just as Section 907 was signed into law. The political balance in Washington began to shift after Azerbaijani President Heydar Aliev signed "the deal of the century" in September 1994, with several U.S. oil companies, such as Amoco, Unocal, and Pennzoil, collectively holding the largest stake (40 percent) in a consortium to develop his country's oil and gas resources. As C. Frederick Starr of Johns Hopkins told an interviewer, "They secured their stakes in the region. Having done so, both the companies and the countries turned their attention to influencing Washington and other governments to protect their projects."

25. James M. Lindsay, "Getting Uncle Sam's Ear: Will Ethnic Lobbies Cramp America's Foreign Policy Style," *Brookings Review,* Vol. 20, No. 1 (Winter 2002), pp. 37–40.

One of the companies' initial moves was to establish a United States–Azerbaijan Chamber of Commerce, which also served to promote U.S. and Azerbaijani corporate interests in Washington.[26]

Competition between the energy companies and the Armenian-American lobby heated up after a cease-fire took effect between Azerbaijan and Armenia in 1994. Armenia and Armenians in Nagorno-Karabagh had emerged as military victors, holding not only that disputed region, but also many surrounding Azerbaijani provinces. Nonetheless, taking advantage of Congress's continuing perception of Armenia as victimized, its supporters on Capitol Hill still sought to convince other lawmakers that Armenia was the weaker party in the dispute and that the retention of Section 907 was necessary to bring Azerbaijan to the bargaining table.

Energy Secretary Spencer Abraham, former Republican Senator of Michigan, would articulate this defense of Section 907 several years later on the Senate floor:

"This is not the only time in this century that the people of Armenia have been victims of actions by military forces beyond their control. The treatment is simply unacceptable. I am not saying there are not arguments of sympathy toward all parties in this region, but the U.S. government made the right step when we instituted Section 907, that we expressed an appropriate level of sympathy, as well as support, and appropriately so, for the people of Armenia. It would be a tragic mistake for us today to reverse course and to set in motion what, in effect, would be a repeal of Section 907."[27]

Not coincidentally, Abraham's home state of Michigan has the fourth highest concentration of Armenian-Americans in the United States, behind California, Rhode Island, and Massachusetts.

The energy companies as lobbying organizations were hampered by not being able to claim any local constituencies on their behalf. The specter of the 1996 elections also made it difficult for them to diminish the scope of Section 907. Most crucially, Dole was expected to become the Republican presidential nominee in 1996, forcing both the Republican-led Congress and the Democratic White House to do all they could do to avoid the political hot potato. Indeed, one of Dole's Republican primary

---

26. Peter H. Stone, "Caspian Wells Come in for K Street," *National Journal*, Vol. 31, No. 11 (March 13, 1999), pp. 680–685; and Robert S. Greenberger and David Rogers, "Azerbaijan Pays Lobbyists $2.5 Million to Plug Its Image and Oil Potential," *Wall Street Journal*, June 23, 1995.

27. *Congressional Record*, June 30, 1999, S7871.

opponents, Senator Phil Gramm of Texas, went to great lengths to try and portray himself as the true champion of Armenian-Americans. For its part, the Clinton White House chose to reach out to Azerbaijan in other ways, issuing an invitation to President Heydar Aliev to visit the United States, but not until 1997, well after the 1996 elections.

The 1996 election—the first truly post–Cold War election—was a watershed for diaspora lobbies. With Congress and the White House no longer sharing a united view that foreign policy should be organized around the central principle of fighting communism, lawmakers were free to pay more attention to ethnic groups such as Indian-Americans, Cuban-Americans, and Armenian-Americans. At the same time, the post-Watergate reforms, which had diminished the power of political parties and the congressional leadership, meant that lawmakers sought out the fundraising opportunities offered by such prosperous ethnic groups.

As former House Foreign Affairs Committee Chairman Lee Hamilton, Democrat of Indiana, said, Armenian-Americans "established such a reputation for giving political contributions, that candidates would come to them seeking [financial] support. They became a stopping point for many congressional candidates."[28] Some candidates also came seeking votes, but since Armenian-Americans numbered less than a half million nationwide, they only constituted a significant presence in a handful of states.

"As an organized community, the Armenians have few peers. As a source of campaign funding help, they are clearly one of the most prodigious," New Jersey Democrat Robert Torricelli told *Congressional Quarterly*. Indeed, it hardly seemed a coincidence that some of the closest supporters of Armenian-Americans interests—Senators Torricelli, Gramm, and McConnell—served as heads of their parties' campaign fundraising arms.[29]

During his term as chairman of the Senate appropriations subcommittee that doles out foreign aid, Senator McConnell increased funds for Armenia every year, often well above what the Clinton administration requested, providing about $500 million U.S. for a country of little more than three million people. Although there are very few Armenian-Americans in Kentucky, Armenian-Americans raised nearly $200,000 U.S. for McConnell and the Republican Party in Kentucky. Considerably more money flowed to the National Republican Senatorial Committee, which

28. Interview with Representative Lee Hamilton, Dec. 26, 2001.

29. Carroll J. Doherty, "Foreign Aid and Favored Nations," *CQ Weekly*, Aug. 6, 1994, p. xx.

McConnell headed.[30] McConnell enjoyed a particularly close relationship with Hirair Hovninian, the founder and longtime head of the Armenian Assembly of America. Hovninian, a major New Jersey builder, cites his ties in the real estate community and his long-time efforts to cultivate a relationship with McConnell and other congressional leaders as keys to the community's success.[31]

An overwhelming 1996 House floor vote in favor of an amendment cutting off aid to Turkey, unless it agreed to trade with Armenia, served as a demonstration to opponents of Section 907 that a frontal challenge on the House floor would be suicidal. In the future, more successful challenges would take place in the Senate, where there was no Congressional Armenian Caucus and where the voting and fundraising power of Armenian-American groups was more diluted.

Lobbying on behalf of Armenia had a noticeable impact on U.S. foreign assistance to the former Soviet republic. In 1999, for instance, Armenia received $74.3 million U.S. in U.S. foreign assistance.[32] That was more than the combined total of all U.S. foreign assistance given to forty-three other states that also received American dollars in 1999. Officially, with a population of 3.8 million, U.S. foreign assistance to Armenia was $19.96 U.S. per man, woman, and child in the country in 1999, the seventh highest per-capita rate among all states receiving U.S. foreign aid that year.[33] In 1999 alone, that amounts to $229 U.S. per person identified as an Armenian-American in the U.S. census. In contrast, Azerbaijan, even with strong support from petroleum companies, brought in $3.63 U.S. per person in U.S. foreign aid in 1999. U.S. foreign aid is a useful proxy to demonstrate the strength of a diaspora community is in Congress, and Table 6.1 reports the total per capita aid to countries in the Caspian Sea region throughout the 1990s. Among all 151 states receiving some aid during the decade, Azerbaijan ranked 104th. Armenia came in eighteenth for the decade, despite receiving nothing until 1992, a year after independence.

---

30. Michael Dobbs, "Foreign Aid Shrinks, but Not for All: With Clout in Congress, Armenia's Share Grows," *Washington Post,* Jan. 24, 2001, p. A1.

31. Interviews with Hovninian, November and December 2001.

32. In fiscal year 2002 Armenia received $90.2 million U.S. in Freedom Support Act assistance.

33. U.S. Loans & Grants (Greenbook), USAID Center for Development Information and Evaluation (PPC/CDIE), 2001. The top ten per capita recipient nations in 1999 were: Israel, Jordan, Bosnia and Herzegovina, Egypt, West Bank and Gaza, Macedonia, Armenia, Cyprus, Georgia, and Honduras.

Table 6.1. Total Per Capita U.S. Foreign Assistance ($/Nation's Population) to Caspian Sea Nations 1990–1999.

	1990	1991	1992	1993	1994	1995	1996	1997	1998	1999	Decade Average
Armenia			6.77	20.66	25.59	14.86	19.76	4.63	20.23	19.96	13.25
Georgia			2.59	15.62	6.82	7.29	3.75	0.37	15.01	18.73	7.02
Turkey	8.65	14.63	8.99	11.38	6.92	8.25	5.78	3.17	0.13	0.08	6.80
Kyrgyz Republic			2.39	14.48	9.80	5.67	3.81	1.19	3.92	8.88	5.01
Turkmenistan				7.85	6.48	1.23	6.32	0.69	1.07	2.41	2.61
Tajikistan			1.86	2.65	8.30	1.49	0.59	1.82	1.95	4.28	2.29
Russia				1.17	9.11	2.31	1.18	0.44	0.93	4.68	1.98
Kazakhstan				0.30	6.27	2.46	1.87	0.64	2.00	3.21	1.67
Median, all nations receiving U.S. Assistance	**0.90**	**1.28**	**2.33**	**2.09**	**2.16**	**1.82**	**1.14**	**0.82**	**1.29**	**1.77**	**1.56**
Azerbaijan	0.77				2.77	1.27	0.72	0.27	3.12	3.63	1.18
Afghanistan		1.15	1.01	2.04	0.12	0.63	0.75	1.35		0.86	0.87
Uzbekistan				0.06	1.09	0.50	0.48	0.20	0.62	1.40	0.44

SOURCE: *USAID Loans & Grants Greenbook, 2001.*

UNDOING SECTION 907

Unable to mount a full-fledged challenge, House members sympathetic to Azerbaijan, such as then Appropriations Committee Chairman Bob Livingston, Republican of Louisiana, and Representative Charlie Wilson of Texas, then ranking Democrat on that panel's foreign aid subcommittee, used their committees and subcommittees to nibble away at the edges of Section 907, allowing Baku to participate in distributing humanitarian assistance and in democracy promotion programs. Congressman Livingston's interests in Azerbaijan probably had little to do with his concerns for international equity. He represented an "oil state," and he was one of the oil industry's strongest supporters in Washington. Oil was found in Louisiana in 1901, "followed by the huge Baton Rouge refinery that became the training ground for generations of top oil executives."[34] Once again, local politics was playing an important role in U.S. foreign policy in the Caspian basin.

With the 1996 presidential election over and Dole leaving politics, the White House could once again pay attention to oil in the Caspian region. Azerbaijani President Aliev's visit to Washington in 1997 marked the beginning of a new chapter in Azerbaijan's relationship with the United States, including the fate of Section 907.

Before coming to the United States, Aliev had agreed to support a U.S. effort to build multiple oil and gas pipelines out of the Caspian Sea region—including one to Turkey through Georgia—providing an alternative to the existing Soviet-built route to Russia. U.S. officials saw the new pipeline as a national security imperative, preventing Moscow from continuing its domination of its former republics through its control of their energy resources. After Aliev's commitment, the energy companies had a new and powerful weapon in their lobbying arsenal and an increasingly assertive White House as their ally.[35]

In 1997, the State Department issued a report estimating that oil deposits in the Caspian Sea were twice as large as previously estimated. "The Caspian Region could become the most important new player in world markets over the next decade," the report said. It also called for the United States to provide trade financing, saying that foreign competitors "benefit significantly from unrestricted political and financial support

34. Michael Barone, Richard E. Cohen, and Grant Ujifusa, *Almanac of American Politics, 2000* (Washington, D.C.: National Journal, 1999), p. 659.

35. Dan Morgan and David B. Ottaway, "Azerbaijan's Riches Alter the Chessboard," *Washington Post*, Oct. 4, 1998, p. A1.

from their governments."[36] Lawmakers acted quickly to address the oil companies' core interests. In 1997 and 1998, Congress approved legislation that allowed Azerbaijan to receive assistance from the Overseas Private Investment Corporation and the Trade Development Agency. Such trade financing was considered essential to building the proposed pipeline. The law continued to ban economic aid, but given Azerbaijan's energy wealth, Baku never hoped to win such assistance in any case. But the restrictions did prevent U.S. officials from fully participating in providing technical assistance to Baku, such as how to construct new commercial and tax codes. It also hampered military cooperation programs between the two countries.

Azerbaijani officials, locked in an authoritarian political culture, have found it difficult to explain to their public why the U.S. Congress could adopt a stance at odds with the White House's official desire for closer ties. Furthermore, as R.C. Longworth writes in the *Chicago Tribune,* "There is no cohesive Azeri diaspora in the United States. Azeri interests [are] represented by the Azerbaijan Embassy in Washington, staffed by diplomats with little skill in lobbying in the chaotic American political scene."[37] Azerbaijani officials repeatedly refer to U.S. policy—and the U.S. political system—as "incomprehensible."

In the Winter 2000 edition of *Azerbaijan International,* Agshin Mehdiyev, head of the foreign ministry's department charged with relations with the United States, said that, "To the average person, the U.S. government, the Congress and all other governmental and non-governmental structures are all the same—one entity. They don't differentiate between the branches of the U.S. government. They can't understand how it is that the U.S. government supports Azerbaijan while Congress votes against us. It's too complicated for the average person."[38]

Key members of the Azerbaijani government publicly blamed the existence and persistence of Section 907 on "corruption" in the United States and the deep pockets of Armenian-Americans. Husein Baghirov, the Azerbaijani Minister of Trade, complained that, "We cannot understand who governs America. Who is managing America? I'm not sure that small lobbies belonging to small minorities can shape the foreign

---

36. Carroll J. Doherty, "Armenia's Special Relationship with U.S. is Showing Strain," *CQ Weekly,* May 31, 1997.

37. R.C. Longworth, "Armenia's Angel of Karabakh: Armenians Acquire Roots of Power," *Chicago Tribune,* April 14, 1998.

38. Agshin Mehdiyev, "Quotable Quotes: Effects of US Law: No Peace," *Azerbaijan International,* Vol. 8, No. 4 (Winter 2000).

policy of this great country. I'm a fairly educated man, and to me this incomprehensible."[39] Azerbaijan's Ambassador to the United States, Hafiz Pashayev, wrote in 2000 that, "It is incomprehensible to us that the selfish, short-sighted interests of small ethnic groups can drive U.S. foreign policy, especially when such decisions run counter to America's long-term interests in the region."[40]

What Secretary Baghirov and Ambassador Pashayev failed to grasp is that geographically concentrated diaspora communities most certainly *can* exert disproportionate influence when U.S. short-term national interests are not plainly in danger. The U.S. Congress responds to local constituencies, not foreign dignitaries.

Oil companies only possessed a limited ability and interest in helping Azerbaijan communicate the geopolitical reasons for undoing Section 907. After trade financing restrictions were lifted, many lawmakers and White House and congressional aides concluded that the energy companies' real concerns had been met and that they were simply going through the motions of lobbying on Section 907 in order to please Baku. Indeed, since these restrictions seemed to carry little if any real domestic cost, many lawmakers were more than happy to support what appeared to be a "no-cost" means of pleasing the highly mobilized Armenian-American lobby. Those results were evident in a 1998 House vote, where an attempt to overturn Section 907 was defeated 231 to 182. The Senate, unwilling to risk the issue in an election year, did not even take up legislation that would have granted a presidential waiver.

As with membership in the Congressional Armenian Caucus, participation in House floor debates about Armenia is almost perfectly correlated with the number of Armenians in a legislator's home district. An examination of the *Congressional Record* finds several "extension of remarks" comments inserted into the record in support of Armenia. In 2001, a total of 6,897 words were inserted praising Armenia, while just 147 words were submitted praising Azerbaijan. The words on behalf of Armenia were inserted by representatives from just seven states,[41] which combined hold 82 percent of the Armenians in America.

After bungling efforts in the early 1990s and to make its case that lift-

---

39.   Husein Baghirov, "Who Governs America?" *Azerbaijan International,* Vol. 8, No. 4 (Winter 2000).

40.   Hafiz Pashayev, "Loss of Faith," *Azerbaijan International,* Vol. 8, No. 4 (Winter 2000).

41.   These states are: California, New York, New Jersey, Massachusetts, Michigan, Maryland, and Virginia.

ing the restrictions was in the U.S. national interest, Azerbaijan began turning to leading Americans with impeccable national security credentials. Amoco hired former National Security Advisor Zbignew Brzezinski; Texaco hired former Ambassador Richard Armitage. And in 1999, Azerbaijan retained two foreign policy heavyweights: former Secretary of State Lawrence Eagleburger and former Senate Majority Leader Howard Baker, Republican of Tennessee, when it signed a lobbying deal with Baker, Donelson, Bearman & Caldwell. Other former Reagan and George H. W. Bush administration officials, from former Defense Secretary Richard Cheney to former Secretaries of State Alexander Haig and James Baker, also weighed in on behalf of Baku.

These efforts won Azerbaijan a new hearing on Capitol Hill, particularly among Republican conservatives. It didn't hurt that these appeals coincided with a time of tension with Moscow over issues from Kosovo to the expansion of NATO. Republican lawmakers saw action to help Azerbaijan and punish Armenia as part of a broader scheme to prevent Russia from trying to reestablish its control of its former republics.

After the intervention of Republican heavyweight lobbyists, congressional voting on Section 907 began to split largely along partisan lines. In the 1998 House vote, 131 Republicans supported Baku's efforts to lift the restrictions, and only 88 opposed it. On the other hand, 142 Democrats supported retaining Section 907, and only 51 called for eliminating it. A similar pattern unfolded in the Senate the next year, with nearly three out of every four Democrats in favor of retaining the restrictions, while two out of three Republicans supported lifting them.

One official who epitomized this new view was Senator Sam Brownback, Republican of Kansas. It was a sign of diminished congressional interest in foreign policy that Brownback, a freshman senator, was given the chairmanship of the Foreign Relations Committee's Near Eastern and South Asian Affairs Subcommittee. Despite his junior status, Brownback was not shy about advancing his causes, which often involved efforts to check both Russia and Iran by supporting legislation to block missile sales between the two countries.

To Brownback, assistance to Azerbaijan and the other former Soviet republics in the Caucasus and Central Asia was a clear national security imperative; without U.S. aid, he argued, these newly independent countries, and their vast energy wealth, were in danger of once again falling under the sway of either Iran or Russia. "They desperately want to get out of the way of being under the thumb of Russia and don't want to get under the thumb of Iran," Brownback said of Baku. Harkening to a historical model for regional cooperation, Brownback called for "Silk Road" legislation, which would tie the region together economically through communications and transportation links. Retaining Section 907, he argued, was a clear impediment to such a vision.[42]

In 1999, the Senate Foreign Relations committee endorsed Brownback's vision on a party-line vote of ten to eight, and lawmakers braced for a crucial showdown on Section 907 on the Senate floor. His attempts foundered there, however, partly because of international developments. Azerbaijan had won support in 1997 and 1998 by endorsing a peace plan that was backed by the Organization for Security and Cooperation in Europe (OSCE) and eventually rejected by Armenia. It lost this diplomatic advantage the following year, however, by rebuffing a new OSCE peace plan backed by Armenia and the Armenian-led government in Nagorno-Karabagh. That allowed supporters of retaining Section 907 to argue that it needed to be maintained to induce Azerbaijan to come to the bargaining table. Azerbaijan's refusal of the peace offer also deterred what oil company officials and many congressional aides argued would be the most successful strategy for overturning Section 907.

George W. Bush's election seemed to augur well for those opposed to aid restrictions on Azerbaijan. Not only was Bush himself a former oil executive, but his cabinet was stocked with people who shared the worldview of the oil companies: from Vice President Richard Cheney to Deputy Secretary of State Richard Armitage. In his confirmation hearings, Secretary of State Colin Powell made it clear that he wanted to review all existing U.S. sanctions to see if they conformed to U.S. national interests.

Within months of taking office, an energy task force Cheney headed pointed to Azerbaijan as a key source for future oil and gas development.[43] With oil prices rising, it seemed a propitious time to push for lifting any restrictions that prevented development of overseas energy resources. As Representative Peter King, Republican of New York, a supporter of lifting Section 907 argued, "With the energy crunch in place, it would be insane to keep these restrictions."[44]

As a potential prelude, Bush and Powell decided to intervene in the conflict between Armenia and Azerbaijan in a more direct manner than any previous U.S. administration. Powell invited the presidents of Armenia and Azerbaijan, Robert Kocharian and Heydar Aliev, to Key

42. Miles A. Pomper, "Petro-Politics Greases the Way for A Different U.S. Approach to Nagorno-Karabakh Dispute," *CQ Weekly,* June 27, 1998.

43. National Energy Policy Group, *Report of the National Energy Policy Group* (Washington, D.C.: U.S. Government Printing Office, May 2001), pp. 12, 13, 19–20.

44. Miles A. Pomper, "Strong Feelings Fuel Debate on Aid to Azerbaijan," *CQ Weekly,* May 19, 2001, p. 1173.

West, Florida, in April 2001 for peace talks, followed by meetings with President Bush at the White House. That effort fell through, however. A follow-up meeting planned for June was postponed.

At the same time, the prospects of getting Congress to lift Section 907 appeared to dim. Overwhelming congressional support for retaining existing U.S. sanctions on Iran and Libya signaled that lawmakers were still more interested in paying attention to the concerns of ethnic groups (in this case, Jewish-Americans) than to pleadings from the White House or the oil companies.

ANTITERRORISM AS A UNIFYING PRINCIPLE IN U.S. FOREIGN POLICY
Then came the terrorist attacks of September 11, 2001. Suddenly, U.S. foreign policy, which had lacked an overarching rationale for the last decade, had a new focus: antiterrorism. Senator McConnell made clear that he would apply the new "Bush Doctrine" to foreign aid: "All of the legislation has to be viewed through the prism of the situation we find ourselves in," McConnell said on September 19. "We need to reward those countries that cooperate with us in fighting terrorism and punish those countries that don't."[45]

McConnell did not intend for the attacks to provide an excuse for the administration or Azerbaijan's supporters to lift Section 907. Indeed, he continued to fight against lifting the restrictions, arguing that "there's no relationship whatsoever" between lifting the sanctions and building an antiterrorist coalition. But Baku, determined to show its pro-U.S. orientation and to take advantage of the new thinking of the Bush administration, offered use of its airspace and military bases to serve as a potential air bridge to U.S. forces in Afghanistan and Central Asia. Brownback also made it clear that he would use Azerbaijan's actions as a new and forceful argument in the congressional debates.

Behind the scenes, both sides pressed their arguments with the Bush administration. Brownback lobbied administration officials either to take advantage of their existing authority to waive the restrictions or for Bush to call on Congress to provide him with new authority to waive Section 907 permanently. On October 1, twenty-nine members of the Congressional Armenian Caucus wrote to Powell asking him to maintain Section 907. Armitage and other administration officials began talking on Capitol Hill about the political reaction to lifting Section 907. Although McConnell publicly predicted that a floor debate would "split the Senate down the middle," the administration and the Armenian-American

---

45. Miles A. Pomper, "New Map of Friends and Foes," *CQ Weekly,* Sept. 22, 2001, p. 2191.

group soon came to the conclusion that the political winds had shifted, forcing groups like the Armenian Assembly to take a different approach. The final blow came to the Armenian-American groups when Powell urged Congress to grant Bush a waiver to lift the sanctions, pointing to Azerbaijan's help in the antiterrorism campaign, including granting the United States overflight rights, the use of its air bases, and intelligence support. Hoping to contain the damage, Hovninian from the Armenian Assembly worked closely with McConnell to craft a number of limitations to Brownback's proposed waiver as part of the fiscal year 2002 foreign operations appropriations bill.

Under the modified Brownback amendment, Section 907 could be waived through the end of 2002 if Bush made the following certifications. If he wished to continue the waiver after that date, these certifications would then have to be renewed on an annual basis:

- It is necessary to support counterterrorism;
- It is necessary in order to ensure operational readiness for the U.S. armed forces and those of our coalition partners;
- It is important for Azerbaijan's border security; and
- It will not undermine or hamper the Minsk Group (OSCE) peace talks between Armenia and Azerbaijan or be used for offensive purposes against Armenia.

As the Armenian Assembly's government relations director, Bryan Ardouny, explained in a press release:

"Our closest Congressional friends advised the Assembly that presidential waiver authority would be granted, in some form. In order to ensure the best possible outcome for Armenia and Karabagh, we advocated for a balanced and limited waiver of Section 907, suggesting such conditions as restricting its time and scope of activities, providing protection for Armenians, and ensuring that the United States maintains parity in its security relationship between Armenia and Azerbaijan."

To soften the blow to Armenia, the Senate agreed to support a separate McConnell amendment granting Armenia military assistance for the first time, including $4 million U.S. in military aid and $600,000 U.S. for International Military Education Training assistance to Armenia, which was also approved.

While the AAA and the Senate were satisfied with these changes, ANCA and the Congressional Armenian Caucus were not. In particular, they complained that although the legislation prevented U.S. aid from being used against Armenia, it did not block Azerbaijan from using such assistance against the separatist government in Nagorno-Karabagh. The administration finally agreed to a formula that prevented U.S. assistance from being used in such a way without inadvertently granting Karabagh any *de facto* recognition as an independent entity. Lawmakers, such as Congressional Armenian Caucus co-chairman Joe Knollenberg, vowed that they would revisit the waiver as part of the fiscal year 2003 budget cycle.

Even supporters acknowledged that they would have a hard time reinstating the restrictions now that they have been lifted. Massachusetts Senator John Kerry, who wrote the original restrictions, said Congress had to acknowledge that the war on terrorism had fundamentally changed Congress's view of Azerbaijan, "Obviously I am sensitive to the change," Kerry said. "But I completely understand the circumstances in which we find ourselves."[46]

Think Globally, Act Locally

Around the tables at Uncommon Grounds in Watertown, Massachusetts, however, patrons have the conviction that the waiver of Section 907 is a temporary setback—as if supporting a Muslim country over a Christian country would never be in the long-term interests of the United States. This sentiment ignores the newfound prominence of Section 907 in the minds of U.S. legislators and the importance of other Caspian Sea states in the fight against terrorism.

A diaspora's dominance of U.S. foreign policy can be maintained only when that policy fails to garner broader public attention. Armenian-Americans no longer have that luxury because U.S. policy toward the Caspian is no longer a purely "local" issue for a handful of legislators from Watertown, Glendale, and Fresno. In light of the war against terrorism and U.S. interests in supporting a moderate Azerbaijani government, the Armenian lobbying community finds itself on especially uncommon ground.

---

46. Miles A. Pomper, "Adversity for Ethnic Lobbies," *CQ Weekly*, Oct. 27, 2001, p. 2558.

Chapter 7

Domestic Politics, Bureaucratic Strategies, and Culture in Central Asia

Roger Kangas

After the collapse of the Soviet Union, references in both policy and academic circles to the newly independent states of Central Asia frequently used the term "Islamic republics"—despite the fact that the new states had not declared Islam to be the official state religion and that all had declared clear separation of religion and state. Many early assessors assumed that Islam would play a prominent role in the politics of the region and would be a basis for future alliances and coalitions that the new states would form—their assumption having been based on the fact that the overwhelmingly majority of most of the citizens of the Central Asian states are Muslims and that many are even observant. These assessments on the role of Islam in the new states' policies was further reinforced by most of the Central Asian leaders incorporating Islamic rituals into public ceremonies and making public displays of personal religious observance, such as the *Hajj* (a pilgrimage to Mecca), in order to further legitimize their regimes in the eyes of their Muslim publics.

Following the September 11, 2001, terrorist attacks on the United States and the subsequent U.S. military actions in Afghanistan and Iraq, the specter of "radical Islam," or "Islamic extremism," loomed large in international affairs discourse. Concurrent with this attention is the "new-found importance" of Central Asia to the rest of the world.[1] As a result of having permitted their territories to be used for bases of operations sup-

---

1. Scores of articles assess the strategic importance of Central Asia and the Caspian region to the United States, Russia, or other countries. Recent appraisals include Charles William Maynes, "America Discovers Central Asia," *Foreign Affairs,* Vol. 82, No. 2 (March/April 2003), pp. 120–132, and Rajan Menon, "The New Great Game in Central Asia," *Survival,* Vol. 45, No. 2 (June 1, 2003), pp. 187–204.

porting the military campaign in Afghanistan, the Central Asian states have been visited by international assistance organizations and foreign military representatives in record numbers. U.S. congressional delegations and top executive branch officials, such as the Secretary of Defense, Director of the Federal Bureau of Investigation (FBI), and others have visited Central Asia since 2001. Internationally, the European Bank of Reconstruction and Development (EBRD) held their annual meeting in Tashkent, Uzbekistan, in May 2003, partially to highlight that international financial institution's commitment to improving conditions in Central Asia. Not since the first years of independence (1991–1992) has so much attention been given to the region.

Having Muslim-majority populations, these states have also found themselves caught up in the discussions of the importance of Islam to societies and the potential dangers that it poses if radicalized. Indeed, the oft-quoted cases of Tajikistan's civil war, usually cast in the simplistic "Communist versus Muslim" dichotomy, and the recent developments of the Islamic Movement of Uzbekistan (also referred to as the Islamic Movement for Turkestan) are used to show that radical Islam is already a threat in the area.[2] At the same time, because Islam is such a prominent cultural feature of the region's population, the political leaders of Central Asia have often used their own adherence to the faith as a way to gain domestic credibility. Therefore, it is not surprising that "Islam" continues to be used as an explanation of events in Central Asia. This chapter will examine the impact of culture on the foreign policies of the Central Asian states and, in particular, will address the role of Islam in those foreign policies, considering that the overwhelming majority of the citizens of the area are Muslim and that many are observant.

This chapter will focus on a set of questions. First, do the leaders of the region "get trapped" in their own Islamic rhetoric? In other words, even if most of the leaders of the region are secular but use Islam to legiti-

---

2. Tajikistan's civil war took place during the period 1992–1997 and was more of a contest between regional rivals and political individuals than between any ideologies. See Muriel Atkin, "Thwarted Democratization in Tajikistan," in Karen Dawisha and Bruce Parrott, eds., *Conflict, Cleavage, and Change in Central Asia and the Caucasus* (Cambridge: Cambridge University Press, 1997), pp. 277–311, and Shirin Akiner, *Tajikistan: Disintegration or Reconciliation?* (London: Royal Institute of International Affairs [RIIA], 2002). In addition, groups such as *Hizb ut-Tahrir* are also being posited as threats to regional security and have become the subject of discussions by Western militaries in the region. See Roy Allison and Lena Jonson, eds., *Central Asian Security: The New International Context* (London: RIIA, 2001) and Olga Oliker and Thomas S. Szayna, eds., *Faultlines of Conflict in Central Asia and the South Caucasus: Implications for the U.S. Army* (Santa Monica, Calif.: RAND, 2003) for two recent examples of this sort of analysis.

mize their regimes, does this public use of Islam create expectations among their citizens that can constrain their foreign policy options? Second, how do additional local identities and histories and practices affect the foreign policy process? Third, is the Muslim background a factor in the coalition and alliance choices of the states of the region? In this discussion, the author will examine how indigenous and unique cultural factors in the region shape the local bureaucratic cultures and their subsequent impact on foreign policy choices. In this study, the author will also look at the specific cases of the new states' negotiations and decisions over energy pipeline routes, how the regimes contend with challenges from Islamic extremists, and their stances on various issues connected to support for the U.S.-led "Global War on Terrorism."

National Security Strategy Formulation: Is Islam the Key?

U.S. government policy analysts are trained to assume that culture has a major impact on the foreign policy of states. Take, for instance, how this is reflected in the major models used by the U.S. governmental analytical agencies to examine policy. Subsequently, policymakers tend to emphasize cultural factors in their policy analysis. For example, the U.S. Army War College uses the chart presented in Figure 7.1 in its core curriculum.

On the basis of these models, U.S. analysts are trained to assume that in addition to material interests, a country's "national interests" are shaped by what it considers to be its "national values." Such values are defined in these models as the national sentiments and characteristics that the population deems representative of the nation's belief system. These values are often cast in general, positive terms and reflect the views of the majority of citizens. Such notions as "individualism," "collectivism," "secularism," and "tolerance" are often cast as part of these "value systems." Other national interests are likewise generic and often focus on factors such as territorial integrity, safety of the population, ability to trade, and opportunities for material wealth. Most of the models in use suggest that this is accomplished through a careful reading of both the popular sentiment and the foreign policy elite.

These national values are presumably articulated in formal documents and statements issued by representatives of a ruling government; thus, it is assumed by these models that the regime's rhetoric about its policies indeed represents its actual policies. A "national policy" is something that most leaders in the world present with some ceremony and sense of importance. Often in the form of an "address to the nation" or a "presidential speech for the new year," this national policy should indicate the direction in which the ruling administration would like to go.

Figure 7.1. The Building Blocks for Strategy Formulation.

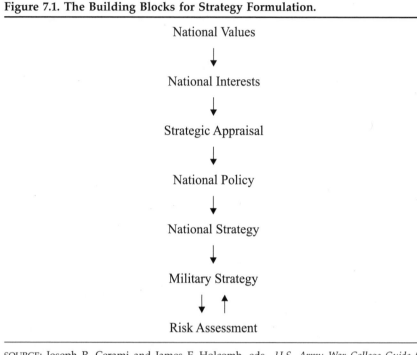

National Values

↓

National Interests

↓

Strategic Appraisal

↓

National Policy

↓

National Strategy

↓

Military Strategy

↓ ↑

Risk Assessment

SOURCE: Joseph R. Cerami and James F. Holcomb, eds., *U.S. Army War College Guide to Strategy* (Carlisle, Penn.: U.S. Army War College, 2001), p. 14.

Leadership is a quality highly valued at this level, for a strong national figure is crucial to the articulation of—and guidance for—a given national policy. The political system clearly affects which limits this leader may face. Even in systems run by autocrats, limits may exist, particularly if one factors in cultural elements. A leader may have to adhere to certain "rules" or "traditions" that are not necessarily apparent to an outside observer.[3] In addition, a state bureaucracy facilitates the translation of policy guidelines into actual actions. Actors on this level can potentially implement policy in such a way that it reflects local cultural preferences.

If the models employed by the U.S. government for analytical purposes are accurate, a review of national values and national interests of the states of Central Asia would provide a foundation on which actual policy decisions may be made. In countries where up to 90 percent of the

---

3. For a comparative evaluation of these pressures in Central Asia, see Sally Cummings, ed., *Power and Change in Central Asia* (London: Routledge, 2002).

population is deemed "Muslim"[4] and given that the political leaders of the states have elevated the status of Islam in their respective countries to gain the support and adoration of the general population, it is reasonable to assume that Islam is one of those national values and should have influence on foreign policy formulation. For instance, it would be a logical outcome that the Central Asian states would presumably have stronger ties with Muslim-populated states than with non-Muslim-populated states.

In Central Asia, Islam has indeed served for many generations as a "national value" and has played an important role in the legitimization processes of rulers in the area. In the past, the populations of the respective emirates and khanates of Central Asia felt a greater presence of Islam, largely because cities such as Bukhara and Samarqand were centers of Islamic learning and scholarship. More often than not, the existing leaders would use Islam as a means by which they could control their populations, much in the same manner that European leaders used Christianity to justify their positions *vis-à-vis* society. In his work on the Bukharan Emirate, Adeeb Khalid outlines the significance that Islam held for the ruling elite of that country. The interconnected leadership circles of politics and religion merged in the person of the emir.[5]

In light of the traditional importance of Islam as a legitimizing factor, the leaders of the region are in precarious positions. First, none of the Central Asian leaders are lifelong, devout Muslims. Whether one attributes this to their Soviet-era formative years or not, the leaders see themselves as being secular leaders first and foremost. Second, each walks a tightrope on his views of Islam in terms of regime stability. While condoning Islam can be viewed as a dangerous thing, the complete rejection of it can be deadly for the regime. Third, the region's ruling regimes perceive that threats to their regimes are supported by Muslim-populated states abroad, such as Iran, thus creating inherent antagonism with some Muslim-populated states. For example, when Iran suggests that the Economic Cooperation Organization (ECO) be transformed into a political

---

4. The percent of self-professed "Muslims" in each country is as follows: Tajikistan—90 percent; Turkmenistan—89 percent; Uzbekistan—88 percent; the Kyrgyz Republic—75 percent; and Kazakhstan—47 percent. Given the demographic trends in all five countries, one should expect to see these numbers increase over time. Indeed, the "Muslim" population in Kazakhstan is most likely over 50 percent as of this writing.

5. Adeeb Khalid, *The Politics of Muslim Cultural Reform: Jadidism in Central Asia.* (Berkeley: University of California Press, 1998); and Helene Carrere d'Encausse, *Reforme et revolution chez les musulmans de l'empire russe*, 2nd edition. (Paris: Presses de la Fondation nationale des sciences politiques, 1981).

entity and not just a trade organization, the Central Asian leaders balk. Accordingly, the regimes of Central Asia strike a balance through official interpretations of Islam that suit their policy preferences in both the domestic and foreign spheres. Moreover, in Central Asia, the debate on the role of Islam in the new states' foreign policy preferences is inextricably linked with policies toward the role of Islam in the domestic sphere, since many of the domestic Islamic political forces challenging the ruling regimes receive support from external Islamic forces and states. Moreover, since most of the ruling regimes face domestic political oppositions which are Islamic in nature, the leaders are careful to use Islam as a strong rallying call to boost their regimes.

Islam in Central Asia: The Domestic Arena

In 1991, many Central Asians suddenly found themselves in a situation where they could openly practice their faith after generations of Soviet oppression. The new regimes needed to decide: how to do it and where? Perhaps the most extreme example was in Tajikistan, where the Islamic Renaissance Party (IRP) established itself as a legitimate political force. When the IRP was excluded from the electoral process in December 1991, however, mass public protests ensued. In May 1992, this eventually led to outright violence in Dushanbe and the onset of the subsequent civil war. Perhaps one of the most significant accomplishments of the 1994–1997 peace negotiations was the willingness of the IRP to accept the notion of a secular state and the parallel acceptance of the government to allow religious-based political parties to function in the state.[6]

Other states have been much more restrictive in their legalization of political parties and organizations that have a strong Islamic foundation. Kazakhstan goes so far as to limit organizations that have a "nationalistic" focus—for fear of disrupting the political balance. The goal for all five states is simple: to create a system that is secular, while still utilizing the public discourse of Islam when referring to the cultural heritage of the populations. Within this system, it is nevertheless important to create a generic form of Islam that is culturally enticing, but ultimately politically neutered.[7] The rhetorical value of Islam is more important than the actual

---

6. For a concise discussion of Tajikistan's civil war and the role of Islam in it, see Kamoludin Abdullaev and Catherine Barnes, eds., *Politics of Compromise: The Tajikistan Peace Process,* Accord #10 (London: Conciliation Resources, 2001).

7. Andrew Mango, *Ataturk: The Biography of the Founder of Modern Turkey* (New York: Overlook, 2000). Mustafa Kemal Ataturk walked a fine line between celebrating the positive aspects of Turkish culture and creating a strong Turkish identity on one hand,

value of the faith as far as the leaders are concerned. Ultimately, this is critical to the success of the current leaders, for they are in the process of creating new states in images that they can control.

From a domestic perspective, Islam in Central Asia is used in positive ways: as a means of defining the cultural credentials of a given leader and as a way in which to justify certain policy decisions. On the other hand, Islam is also being used in a negative manner: as a justification for limiting opponents or even societal pressures, including the suppression of domestic Islamic political organizations. These organizations are termed by the governments in Central Asia as "Wahhabist" in order to stress that they are of foreign orientation and undermine the local culture and local Islamic values of Central Asia. Concluding that a particular organization or individual is linked to "Islamic extremism" is often a precursor to a campaign against that group or person.[8] Thus, the regimes interpret Islam in such a way as to justify their foreign policy choices. "Good Islam" is the locally-based and tolerant form promoted by the regime, while "bad Islam" is the foreign-based form, which is promoted by enemies of the regime.

In the early 1990s, each of the leaders felt it important to "establish their Islamic credentials." Whether this was in the form of public displays of piety, which included the *Hajj*, public displays of prayer, giving the oath of office with one hand on the *Qu'ran*, or declarations that Islam was now a permissible faith, the leaders all expressed strong support for Islam.[9] However, the political mechanisms by which Islam had been regulated during the Soviet era were not dismantled but rather assumed by the new leaders to co-opt the mainstream Islamic institutions. President Islam Karimov, for example, quickly used the issue of selecting the main "Spiritual Leader" of Uzbekistan's Muslims as a rallying point for ousting a potential rival and inserting a loyal supporter.[10] President

---

but limiting the power of what he believed to be an antiquated and stultifying caliphate on the other. He was not "anti-Islamic" as much as against an "Islamic establishment."

8.   This is a claim repeatedly made by groups such as Human Rights Watch and Amnesty International: that the various leaders are using the pretext of radical Islam to imprison or harass political opponents. For example, see *Uzbekistan: Progress on Paper Only* (New York: Human Rights Watch, June 3, 2003), which criticizes the United States for putting a positive spin on the current Uzbek human rights record—a record that singularly targets individuals suspected of being "radical Muslims."

9.   Roger Kangas, "State Building and Civil Society in Central Asia," in Vladimir Tismaneanu, ed., *Political Culture and Civil Society in Russia and the New States of Eurasia* (Armonk, N.Y.: M.E. Sharpe, 1995), pp. 271–291.

10.   See *RFE/RL Reports*, Summer 1993.

Saparmurad Niyazov has spent the past several years crafting a "legal code" for Turkmenistan that is partially based on a particular view of Turkmen values combined with some elements of Islam.[11] He maintains close control, however, of the religious organizations within the country. For all of these leaders, Islam can be seen as a positive force and a supporter of their particular power base.

The current generation of political actors thus understands both the logic of presenting Islam in a positive light (legitimacy), while having their own misgivings about the challenges to their regimes that actors speaking in the faith can present. Thus, after the initial shock of independence had worn off, the actual role of Islam in the policy process remained limited. The threats posed by the domestic Islamic oppositions actually encourage the ruling regimes to use Islamic rhetoric only in a very calculated, controlled fashion and to not foster Islamic-based ties to foreign states.

Islam in the Foreign Policy Sphere

As will be seen in the case studies to follow, the Central Asian states have not given preference to forging ties with Muslim-populated states. In fact, in their immediate vicinity, most possess more problematic relations with neighboring Muslim-majority states than with non-Muslim-majority states. These bilateral relations are further aggravated by the support that many of the groups that pose threats to regime stability receive from Muslim-majority states. Thus, despite the leaders' public displays of piety and respect for Islam, the case studies below show that the leaders of Central Asia, in the first ten years after attaining independence, have not been trapped by their own Islamic rhetoric and forced to forge alliances with Muslim-populated states in making their major foreign policy decisions. In fact, when looking at their threat perceptions, most of the states of the region view their Muslim-majority neighbors with more concern than neighboring non-Muslim-majority states such as Russia and China. Moreover, in many cases, Islam in used instrumentally to advance material and economic interests of the states.

---

11. The centerpiece of this campaign is the book *Ruhnama*, which was supposedly written by President Niyazov himself. The book's slogan is "The Golden Book for the Golden Age," and it outlines the president's vision of what Turkmen society should be like. It is currently required reading for all school and university grade levels and is prominently displayed throughout the country in banners and posters. See Saparmurad Niyazov, *Ruhnama* (Ashgabat, Turkmenistan: GosIzdatel'stvo, 2002).

Test Cases: The Role of Islam in Alliances and Partnerships

During their first ten years of independence, the most important foreign policy decisions of the Central Asian states concerned their respective national security strategies, and, consequently, alliances and coalition partners as well as threat definitions. For the energy producers in the region, energy pipeline networks were, and remain, crucial foreign policy and national security decisions. Presumably, if Islam, which is a well-established source of local values and an important component of the local culture, impacts the new states' foreign policy decisions, this impact would be evident or at least discernable in these major foreign policy decisions.

ENERGY PIPELINES

In choosing the pipeline routes for export of their oil or natural gas, the Central Asian states had a variety of options through both neighboring Muslim- and non-Muslim- populated countries. In all directions, various states attempted to court the other states to select their territory to transit their pipelines. Tehran, Moscow, and Washington were most actively wooing the new states to choose their preferred schemes. Many multinational companies were pushing the states to choose the Iranian route, which some companies initially viewed as the most commercially attractive option.

After the Soviet breakup, many of the Middle Eastern states were initially enthusiastic about the emergence of additional Muslim-populated energy-producing states—Azerbaijan, Kazakhstan, Turkmenistan, and Uzbekistan. A notion emerged that the power of the Islamic oil producing states and the Organization of Petroleum Exporting Countries (OPEC) cartel would increase. The expectations of the Middle Eastern states were, however, not met. Islamic values played no role in the energy pipeline decisions of the states of the region. In the debates on the various pipeline routes, the lack of reference to Islam was quite apparent. Were energy routes to be based on some "Islamic factor," one could imagine pipelines heading south—through Iran or Afghanistan. Indeed, officials from these countries have referred to the solidarity of Islamic states in justifying such routing. Kazakhstan and Turkmenistan have discussed this particular route from the multiple proposed pipeline options, but only out of economic necessity and never presented in Islamic terms.

Even the Baku-Tbilisi-Ceyhan (BTC) route chosen by Azerbaijan and Kazakhstan (for part of its oil) through Turkey has *not* been couched in Islamic terms, but rather in "pro-West" or "pro-U.S." language, obviating any Islamic connection.[12] While it would seem odd to have such business decisions made in terms of religion, past examinations of energy-rich states with Muslim populations show that they have, in fact, done so. The Middle Eastern states of OPEC saw their domination of the energy market as being a way in which the Muslim world could find a rightful place in the international sphere. Islamic solidarity was a key factor in their embargoes of the 1970s that targeted the West, and was couched in terms of their animosity towards Israel.[13] In addition to the decision to build most new pipeline routes to the West, the states of the region have not designated any special role or signed many serious contracts with national oil companies of Muslim-populated states such as Saudi Arabia.

ALLIANCES, COALITION PARTNERS, AND THREAT DESIGNATION

Following the Soviet breakup, many postulated that the Muslim states of Central Asia would align themselves with the states of the Middle East. After September 11, 2001, and the launching of the subsequent war on terrorism as well as the military operation in Iraq, many assumed that the Muslim populations of Central Asia would identify with the terrorist acts and Muslim rage expressed over the U.S. military actions. These phenomena were absent, however, and most of the area's regimes were among the states which joined the U.S.-led intervention in Afghanistan; some even supported the subsequent U.S.-led intervention in Iraq. U.S. military forces became based in Central Asia, especially in Uzbekistan. These bases in Central Asia were used to launch and support a large proportion of the operations in Afghanistan and beyond.

The U.S.-declared "Global War on Terrorism" has provided an important test for many states as to which coalitions they belong. It presents the countries of Central Asia with a particularly difficult conundrum, for many of the "sources" of terrorism in this current iteration are found in the Islamic world. Indeed, Arab states (and other Muslim-majority states) chafe at the notion that the West is somehow trying to blame Islam for contemporary international terrorism. Having significant Muslim populations, as previously noted, the Central Asian states could easily position themselves to be critics of the U.S.-led efforts in the name of protecting Islam from some new form of "neo-colonialism." To date, this has not been

---

12.   The Baku-Tbilisi-Ceyhan route, while it would benefit Turkey immensely, is cast as a "U.S.-route," in contrast to the Russian Caspian Pipeline Consortium (CPC), Iranian, and Chinese routes, to name several alternatives. This is largely because the U.S. government has been vocal in its support for this route.

13.   For a history of OPEC, see Jahongir Amuzegar, *Managing the Oil Wealth: OPEC's Windfalls and Pitfalls* (London: I.B.Tauris, 2001).

the case, as evidenced by the various stages of the effort to combat terrorism. The immediate aftermath of September 11, 2001, created the moral framework within which many states sought to act against local threats to their regimes, especially if they were Islamic-based. The Central Asian states viewed the military campaign in Afghanistan through the lens of direct security implications for the bordering states themselves—not in a global sense. Regarding the intervention in Iraq, the Central Asian states were more often than not focused on the security aspect of the campaign and only raised the notion of Islam with regards to fears of indigenous manifestations of Islamic extremism.

Immediately following the terrorist attacks on September 11, 2001, all five Central Asian countries expressed their deep condolences to the people of the United States. Whereas President George W. Bush was quick to point out that any retaliation should not be seen as an "anti-Islamic" campaign, the rhetoric in Central Asia did include direct references to Islam.[14] Each nation reaffirmed its secular foundation and decried any efforts to create "Islamic states" in Central Asia. More to the point, several, including Uzbekistan, Tajikistan, and the Kyrgyz Republic, couched their comments to the United States in an empathetic tone, citing that they, too, have been targets of terrorism. As a concept, the notion of the Global War on Terrorism held positive, political advantages for the respective leaders. They could use it to highlight their own secular credentials and discredit Islamic-oriented opponents. In addition, it was a new way in which to court the West for new forms of assistance.

These latter strategies were put to the test with the campaign in Afghanistan that began in October 2001, barely a month later. Four of the five Central Asian states viewed the Taliban as an illegitimate government and a direct threat to their own security interests.[15] Only Turkmenistan expressed some hesitation in any attack on the Taliban government. It advocated the continued use of the United Nations as a forum for conflict resolution and even offered its services to mediate the demands that the United States had placed on the Taliban regarding the turnover of al-Qaeda operatives and leaders. Ultimately, because the Central Asian leaders felt that the Taliban was an illegitimate govern-

---

14. As noted in the previous section, this included direct attacks against suspected groups within their own countries, even if the links to Islam were tenuous.

15. Repeatedly, Central Asian analysts repeatedly stressed that the most serious external threat to their countries originated from Afghanistan. Drug and weapons trafficking, Islamic radicalism, or even the potential for Taliban incursions northward were all expressed by Central Asian officials in documents, speeches, and conversations.

ment, the notion of state sovereignty was not in question. The concept of the Global War on Terrorism had been actualized in a manner acceptable and understandable to the Central Asians.

The demonstration of moral support a month prior turned into actual operational support during the conflict. Specifically, Uzbekistan, Tajikistan, and the Kyrgyz Republic all offered basing rights to U.S. and North Atlantic Treaty Organization (NATO) forces. In each, the question of how much information to disclose on the presence of foreign troops on their soil was debated in the government and eventually made clear to the populations.[16] In both instances, the necessity to be part of larger security arrangements was deemed too important to pass up. Uzbekistan was much more direct in its negotiations with the United States over use of the Karshi-Khanabad base in the southern part of the country.

Perhaps unusual was the fact that this component of the campaign—the bilateral agreements that each leader signed with the United States offering basing and fly-over rights—was almost absent from public discourse.[17] Given the leadership styles of the Central Asian presidents, it is evident as to why such secrecy existed. In Uzbekistan, the very location of Karshi-Khanabad base was not even revealed to the Uzbek population. Turkmenistan manifested the most extreme example of this secrecy, largely because of the awkward position it was in due to its previous relationship with the Taliban. While agreements for fly-over rights took place in October 2001, the Turkmen government kept this from public discussion. Furthermore, when the government offered basing rights in Turkmenistan for the delivery of humanitarian assistance, the news was again kept from the public eye. Indeed, over 80 percent of all humanitarian assistance passed through and often landed in Turkmenistan during the last months of 2001 and the early months of 2002, and yet none of this was made public.[18] The logic was clear: President Niyazov was, and remains, so beholden to his policy of "Positive Neutrality" that such direct violations of his own sacrosanct idea would be tantamount to heresy in the eyes of his people—or so he believes. At the same time, Turkmen

---

16. In all five countries, Standard of Forces Agreements (SOFAs) were signed by both sides. There was some controversy as to why the U.S.-Uzbek agreement was not made public—or even acknowledged in U.S. government statements for several months.

17. Given the state control over the media, this is not a surprise. Moreover, all actions related to the Global War on Terrorism were deemed extrajudicial in nature and therefore subject to additional scrutiny and censorship. Finally, this fits into the Soviet tradition of declaring even the location of military bases to be "state secrets."

18. This is unsubstantiated, but was noted by Turkmen officials in discussions with author in Ashgabat, December 2002.

officials are more than willing to discuss their country's contribution to the Global War on Terrorism with foreign officials, even publicizing such things at international conferences. Again, for domestic consumption, the culturally-based local leadership concept is the reason for how the Turkmen government presents its non-activity in the Global War on Terrorism.[19]

The positive material domestic ramifications of participating in the Global War on Terrorism were felt almost immediately. From a practical perspective, foreign assistance, especially from the United States, increased several times over. Military aid, economic assistance, loan deferrals, and even more favorable reporting of human rights records all occurred. For example, U.S. aid to Uzbekistan increased from over $30 million U.S. in 2000 to over $160 million U.S. in 2002.[20] In addition, just as some international financial institutions were debating the reduction of their presence in the region, the revived attention instead resulted in an increase of aid.

The increased visibility of the regional leaders and the concurrent attention given by outside powers was particularly beneficial domestically. It was not surprising, then, that in the ensuing months, the Central Asian states, especially Uzbekistan, used the pretext of the Afghan campaign as a reason to step up efforts against their own "Islamic radicals." Presidential speeches and daily news reports actually spent more time and effort on those issues than on the actual fighting that was taking place further south. The question of Islam is pertinent to the subsequent military action in Iraq and reflects the same logic of the campaign against internal opponents. In fact, the Global War on Terrorism maintained a local emphasis when discussed in Central Asia.

The reality is that such groups do exist in the region and are actively trying to recruit new members from the disaffected populations of these countries. For example, the ruling regimes have a deep concern that

19. By linking the foreign policy acumen of the president with nonalignment, it is logically impossible to raise the issue of alliances. Indeed, in that very year, the Turkmen legislature petitioned to have President Niyazov awarded the Nobel Peace Prize for his philosophical contributions to the concept of neutrality.

20. For U.S. assistance, see the 2002 and 2003 reports from the U.S. Agency for International Development and the Department of Defense. In addition, Human Rights Watch tracks these figures, and is particularly keen on linkages to human rights reporting in the region. There is a debate within the Central Asian countries, though, as to how beneficial the alliances with the United States and NATO powers are. See Jeffrey Donovan, "Central Asia: Verdict Still Out on U.S. Engagement Policy," *RFE/RL* (November 24, 2002) for a look at the danger of ignoring human rights records in foreign policies.

the young, unemployed, and frustrated residents of the Fergana Valley region of Uzbekistan, Tajikistan, and the Kyrgyz Republic may find the promises of radical groups appealing. The Islamic Movement of Uzbekistan (IMU) and *Hizb ut-Tahrir* are the region's primary radical groups. The activities of such groups strike at the central concern of government officials: they represent an independent quality that is outside the boundaries of their control. In the late 1990s, the Islamic Movement of Uzbekistan advocated the overthrow of the Karimov regime and the establishment of a caliphate in Central Asia. In addition, it is evident that they received external help from individuals from Saudi Arabia, Pakistan, and the Taliban government in neighboring Afghanistan.[21]

The IMU took new steps in 1999 and 2000 when it conducted a series of military raids into Tajikistan, the Kyrgyz Republic, and Uzbekistan. In each instance, the local military and militia forces held their own and, ultimately, defeated the IMU forces.[22] While militarily defeated, the IMU demonstrated that it could learn from its mistakes and seek out creative ways in which to support long-range operations within Uzbekistan and the Kyrgyz Republic, and many observers assumed that future campaigns would take place in 2002 or 2003. The IMU, however, opted to fight in Kunduz during the Afghan campaign and was consequently decimated as a fighting force.[23] During the peak years of the anti-IMU campaigns, the Uzbek government was able to associate this particular organization with the broader concepts of terrorism and radical Islam, both of which were gaining notoriety in the world. The effect in Uzbekistan, as well as in the other Central Asian states was immediate: certain types of Islam could be cast in a negative light.

Underlying the place of Islam in Central Asian policies is a rather instrumentalist view of the faith. At least from the regimes' perspectives, Is-

---

21. In retrospect, the primary provider of assistance—financial, training, and logistical—was al-Qaeda, while it was based in Afghanistan. There are numerous stories of IMU activity in the regional drug trade, which is most likely. The simplest and most direct discussion, however, has focused on how it and al-Qaeda had complimentary goals, hence the willingness of the latter to support the former. See Ahmed Rashid, *Jihad: The Rise of Militant Islam in Central Asia* (New Haven, Conn.: Yale University Press, 2002), for an excellent discussion of this relationship.

22. Indeed, casualty figures for the IMU detachments were nearly 100 percent. Often, these units of ten to thirty soldiers would be surrounded and fight to the death. Casualty figures of Kyrgyz and Uzbek troops are unknown. Report by Uzbek military official at the Uzbek Defense Academy, Tashkent, May 2003.

23. The leader of the IMU, Juma Namangani, was reportedly killed in November 2001 during a U.S. bombing raid over Kunduz. Tohir Yuldash, the political leader of the IMU, is supposedly still alive and hiding in the Pakistan's northwest territories.

lam is seen as something that can be controlled, shaped, and ultimately manipulated either to create conditions for stability or to forge ties with some outside states. Ironically, several of the Central Asian leaders have made parallels to Ataturk's legacy in Turkey. Unlike the founder of the modern Turkish state, they are not addressing Islam in the broader context of modernization, but rather in the hope of maintaining authority in their respective countries. Like the founder of modern Turkey, however, the current Central Asian leaders are concerned about the continued survival of their respective states and realize that both domestic policy considerations and foreign agreements and alliances should be designed to ultimately increase their respective state's—and regime's—chances of survival.

Thus, it is no surprise that Kazakhstan, for example, feels compelled to continue relations with Russia—its stronger neighbor to the north. That Russia is an Orthodox Christian–majority state and neighboring Uzbekistan, with which Kazakhstan has poorer relations, is a Muslim-majority state is immaterial. The same is true with Uzbekistan deciding to forge a strong security alliance with the United States—the very state often branded the "Great Satan" by Islamic extremists. Even Turkmenistan's relations with Iran are cast more in light of practical trade ties and less on anything related to a common Muslim heritage.[24] In order to promote economic and other material interests, however, common Muslim identity is often used as rhetoric to encourage economic cooperation with Middle Eastern states. Hence, the drive in the early 1990s to revive the moribund Economic Cooperation Organization was explained as a "Muslim way" of conducting business.[25] One can also cite the evolution of Saudi assistance programs to the region, particularly as they were, and remain, tied to rather generous contributions for the building of mosques and other religious institutions. However, during the past decade, the overall assistance from and trade with the Islamic world pales in com-

24. That Turkmen are Sunni Muslims and the majority of Iranians are Shi'a Muslims should be noted in this respect, although due to the minimal importance placed in religion in bilateral relations, ultimately, this is a non-issue.

25. This strategy was short-lived. The Economic Cooperation Organization includes the countries of Turkey, Iran, Afghanistan, Pakistan, Azerbaijan, and the five Central Asian countries. In spite of an initial optimism, the organization has failed to create conditions for favorable and easy trade; commerce among the countries remains modest, as compared to trade with states outside of the ECO. Iran sought to make it a political-strategic organization, but opposition from such countries as Uzbekistan and Azerbaijan quickly put an end to that ambition. For an early assessment of this strategy, see Daniel Pipes, "The Event of Our Era: Former Soviet Muslim Republics Change the Middle East," in Michael Mandelbaum, ed., *Central Asia and the World* (New York: CFR Press, 1994), pp. 47–93.

parison to that from the Christian West—the United States, Europe, and especially Russia.[26]

LOCAL TRADITIONS: STRONG LEADERSHIP AND BUREAUCRATIC INFORMATION FLOW

Islam, *per se*, is not a significant factor in the creation and shaping of foreign policy in Central Asia, but significant linkages do operate there between culture and policy decision-making. Local indigenous culture influences foreign policy preferences in Central Asia through the prevailing local political structures. Central Asian political culture leads to two trends that can influence foreign policy decision-making. The first is a tradition of strong, centralized political leadership. The second is a custom of selective reporting to superiors as part of a larger bureaucratic culture. Both of these influences suggest alternative ways in which one can examine the policy process in the respective Central Asian countries.

Time and again, references to the Central Asian states emphasize the states' leadership. It is often the case that articles and books on the political processes of the region barely mention names other than those of the sitting presidents, for few hold key roles in the decision-making process that are not directly linked to the respective presidents. Central Asians themselves consider "strong leaders" to be part of their political culture. The current generation of Central Asian leaders are products of the Soviet Union who spent their formative years working up through the ranks of the Communist Party of the Soviet Union (CPSU). While local authors have written much that downplays this influence, it is clear that there is at least a familiarity with the other former Soviet leaders and with the manner in which politics is conducted in former Soviet republics.

This leadership tradition has roots in the pre-Soviet period. The states in the region are typically based on clan, or regional, ties with certain elite families in charge. Politics was the "art of family ties and loyalties that occupied the upper classes." The majority of the population remained apolitical, in large part because they were preoccupied with subsistence living activities.[27] These conclusions are drawn from both studies of pre-

---

26. According to the World Bank and Economic Intelligence Unit reports, "Middle Eastern" countries barely register in trade and investment statistics. The exceptions are Iranian investments in Turkmenistan (under 10 percent of total foreign trade), and the United Arab Emirates' trade with the Kyrgyz Republic (under 8 percent). Turkey, a secular Muslim state, does play a more active role in the region with respect to international trade, but is likewise dwarfed by trade figures coming from Europe, Russia, and the United States.

27. The concept of "clans" itself is controversial and subject to numerous interpretations. Most scholars working on this issue agree that a fundamental relationship based

Soviet Central Asia and the impact of the Soviet era.[28] Political decisions tended to be made at the top, and the strength of the emir had been critical to the effective rule of the state. Because the political leader owned most of the property, the means of economic development and, indeed, the population, it was easy to descend to a level of nepotism and corruption. Entitlement, above all else, justified a ruler's action. Periodically there emerged emirs or khans who used their station for positive developments, but the overall mindset was one of ownership—of land, riches, and people. How these possessions fared seemed less important.[29]

It was in the Soviet era that the traditional notions of fealty and loyalty would merge with the intricate hierarchy of the CPSU. After the chaotic and blood-soaked era of the 1920s and 1930s, there emerged within Central Asia a generation of leaders who felt beholden to Moscow for their offices and yet acted as a buffer against radical changes in the new "republics."[30] Within another generation, "leadership" became defined as the ability to protect one's "people" and to represent a particular group in Moscow. Starting in the 1950s and leading up to the reforms of Soviet President Mikhail Gorbachev in the 1980s, key Central Asian leaders entrenched themselves in key positions of power, lasting for decades in high office. Sharaf Rashidov and Dinmukhammed Kunaev are just two of the leaders who were able to successfully merge the traditional notions of power with the political arena of the Soviet system.[31] They were responsive to the popular needs while using the rhetoric of the CPSU leadership.

---

on familiarity, lineage, and custom existed, and still exists, in Central Asia. Some, such as Olivier Roy, suggest that traditional notions of family ties have been replaced with spatial notions of association. The *kolkhoz*, for example, is one such modern manifestation of "clan." See Olivier Roy, *The New Central Asia: The Creation of Nations* (New York: NYU Press, 2000).

28. See Timothy J. Colton and Robert C. Tucker, eds., *Patterns in Post-Soviet Leadership* (Boulder, Colo.: Westview, 1995), and Sally Cummings, ed., *Power and Change in Central Asia* (London: Routledge, 2002), as two examples of this kind of analysis.

29. See Carrere d'Encausse, *Reforme et revolution*, chap. 1.

30. As a result of the National Delimitation of 1924–1925, the region of Central Asia was demarcated into "Union Republics." Through 1936, the entities went through several arrangements, until settling on the five existing Union Republics that turned into independent states in 1991.

31. Roy, *The New Central Asia*. Each country had leaders who remained in power for a long period of time. In the Kazakh Soviet Socialist Republic (SSR), D. Kunaev was First Secretary from 1959 to 1986; in the Uzbek SSR, S. Rashidov was in office from 1959 to 1983; meanwhile Tajik First Secretary Rasulov was in office from 1961 to 1982; Kyrgyz First Secretary Usulbaev was in power from 1961 to 1985; and Turkmen First Secretary Gapurov held office from 1969 to 1986.

In the post-Soviet period, the ruling regimes of the new states have national images based on a central role of the respective leaders and the contributions of their personal characteristics. Reserving a special role for the leader provides an opportunity for his cultural views to influence the foreign policy choices of the state. In addition, it allows for personal rivalries to play a role in regional foreign policies. In this, it is important to realize that the political leaders of each of the countries know each other quite well. They worked through the ranks of the CPSU apparatus together and emerged as prominent individuals at roughly the same time— the mid-to-late 1980s. All were hailed as "Gorbachev allies." It is in this light that intra-regional politics can be viewed: each sees himself as a prominent leader of his respective community and wants to assert some authority in the region writ large. The struggles for regional "authority" among the leaders have been legion, particularly the rivalry between Nursultan Nazarbaev of Kazakhstan and Islam Karimov of Uzbekistan.[32] Even President Askar Akaev of the Kyrgyz Republic had cast himself in a defined "role": that of regional broker between his two large neighbors. Interestingly, the only figure that was truly deemed "senior" by the Central Asian leaders was on the other side of the Caspian Sea: Heydar Aliev of Azerbaijan.

At the same time, the leader's policy options are limited in Central Asia by the prevalent bureaucratic tradition of not reporting bad news to one's superiors, which limits the information at the disposal of the leader, his ability to understand how the state's interests—both material and cultural—can be promoted, and consequently what the trade-offs will be. In this information vacuum, cultural factors may have more room to come into play. In the debate on culture and foreign policy, bureaucracies have a presence—both as representative of general, national values and as an arena within which specific cultural characteristics may be found. If, in fact, one takes culture to mean more than just the belief system of a people, but also the rules by which they function in a state, then the concept of bureaucratic behavior is critical. Officials are themselves part of the community, so it can be expected that they share common values and goals. More pointedly, they often feel proactive in putting such values into practice.

In this respect, Central Asia exhibits two competing traditions: much like the concept of leadership, the state administrations in the region are shaped by pre-Soviet and Soviet-era influences. Pre-Soviet bureaucratic

---

32. These rivalries are noted by analysts within Central Asia, but are rarely discussed in the local publications or media. *Res Publica*, a Kyrgyz publication, has had stories on this, but few others.

traditions center on the notions of "fealty and loyalty," as well as the code of behavior that exists among government officials. Specifically, this meant that officials, once in office, felt certain obligations to their family and clan. The notion of "protecting one's own group" is essential to understanding how offices may be staffed, but also how decisions could be influenced. Secondly, there is a strong sense of how and when one can challenge authority.[33] The traditional method of discussing issues was conducted in a highly ritualistic and orderly fashion. A specific culture of decision-making, which stresses the importance of age, seniority, rank, and familial relationships, still exists. Not only are there certain behavioral practices that one must exhibit, but also even word choices are affected.[34]

Paying fealty and demonstrating loyalty was, and remains, a very specific form of interaction among people within the Central Asian administrative system. It is expected that subordinates provide some financial renumeration for their position to their superior. Furthermore, if they benefit from their position, it is expected that they will continue to pay tribute to their superior who, after all, created the conditions through which such benefits arose. The concept of "loyalty" is colored by this relationship. Within a given clan structure, it is evident that loyalty remains a strong bond—for not only are there functional ties but also those of kinship.[35] In the impersonal atmosphere of an administration, the concept of kinship is weakened, and thus the notion of loyalty is also in doubt. Consequently, it is not surprising that one sees alliances shift and reform, with individuals opting out of one relationship to form another. This is not seen as being disingenuous or even treasonous, but rather a reality in the given arrangement. Indeed, even in military bureaucracies, it is not out of the ordinary for individual units to switch sides, or simply opt out of a conflict, if the conditions for fealty are unsatisfactory.[36]

---

33. See Gregory Gleason, "Fealty and Loyalty: Informal Loyalty Structures in Soviet Asia," *Soviet Studies*, Vol. 43, No. 4 (1991), pp. 628–631.

34. Simply put, one uses different suffixes on words depending upon whether you are speaking to a subordinate or superior.

35. Perhaps the most extensive study on this issue is a recent doctoral dissertation: Kathleen A. Collins, "Clans, Pacts, and Politics: Understanding Regime Transition in Central Asia" (Ph.D. dissertation, Stanford University, 1999). This remains an issue where there is much discussion, but little field research.

36. One saw this among Basmachi units in the 1910s and 1920s, and again in Afghanistan since the beginning of the recent period of violence in 1979. Tribal or clan leaders would switch sides, justifying their decision on what advantage could be gained for their particular subunit. This is not considered to be duplicitous or unexpected, for the strongest bond of loyalty remains the family and clan.

The Soviet era introduced a new framework within which these relationships were demonstrated and further cemented. A state bureaucracy existed within the Soviet Union, but the Communist Party's bureaucracy was even more important.[37] Within Central Asia, fealty arrangements were conveniently transferred into the CPSU mechanism, with the place of the "emir" being taken by the party headquarters in Moscow. In the post-Stalin Soviet Union, the First Secretaries of Central Asia masterfully balanced this arrangement, paying tribute to Moscow and deliberately shielding their own decision-making and staffing processes within the republics away from the eyes of the central party apparatus. In spite of periodic "reform" efforts from Moscow, the Central Asian bureaucracies were able to maintain their own power structures.

Within the system, some changes did occur. Particularly with the introduction of collectivization, one saw the creation of new relational groupings: *kolkhozes* and other functional or geographic entities. While some were simply co-opted by family groups, others became substitutes for these lineage-based structures. Thus, a sense of loyalty could now be applied to one's workplace or regional office. This created a more complex web of relationships that invariably led to multiple rivalries for positions and advancement.[38]

The bureaucratic legacy which has the greatest impact on contemporary foreign policymaking of the Central Asian states is the tendency for lower-level officials to couch their reports and advice to higher-level officials in ways in which they feel are necessary. Namely, subordinates are averse to informing their superiors of negative developments. This bureaucratic "survival mechanism" was important during the era of the centrally planned economy, for it required that mid-level and lower-level officials fabricate data to pass on to superiors in order to show "plan fulfillment." This was less a case of lying, but rather one of protecting one's position in the administration and in society as a whole. Much as in the Soviet era where planners forged numbers and kept two sets of books for economic units, the same things exist in present-day Central Asia. Statistics on economic development, oil production, social concerns, and the environment are often obfuscated in internal reports out of fear that reprisals could be felt.[39] The difficulties here, of course, are the real eco-

---

37. Claude Lefort, *The Political Forms of Modern Society: Bureaucracy, Democracy, Totalitarianism* (Cambridge, Mass.: MIT Press, 1986). Also, see Gordon B. Smith, ed., *Public Policy and Administration in the Soviet Union* (New York: Praeger, 1980).

38. See Roy, *The New Central Asia*.

39. Perhaps the most "famous" Soviet era case was the "Uzbek cotton scandal," in which scores of officials were arrested and convicted of various economic crimes in the

nomic and political repercussions that can arise if specific problems are left unsettled and complete information is withheld so that the ramifications of policy choices cannot be fully assessed.

The Role of History in Foreign Policy Choices

Traditional historical motifs are valued by many members of Central Asian societies and play an important role in legitimizing the foreign policy preferences of the ruling regimes of the region. Each regime has looked for symbols in its nation's history that could justify a current foreign policy preference. The choices were not dictated by past events, however, but the choice of which past to emphasize was dictated by current policy decisions. The policy choices evident in the region reflect an "inner drive": a need to justify things in domestic terms that are understandable to their own citizenry. For example, President Nursultan Nazarbaev, who had been a strong supporter of Mikhail Gorbachev during the late Soviet period and an advocate of continued "post-Soviet associations" (including his own "Eurasian Union") believes that Kazakhstan's future lies in its ability to placate the larger neighbors to provide viable trade routes and security shields. At the same time, he is quick to highlight his own connection to the traditional Kazakhstani past, even going so far as to allude to a Mongolian "white bone" heritage.[40]

President Islam Karimov sees Uzbekistan's destiny as that of being the leader of Central Asia. Consequently, Karimov points to historical experiences of past "Uzbek empires" and notes that the rightful place of his country is that of leader of the region. The Uzbek government displays itself as the logical "heir to the Timurid dynasty" in Central Asia and explains its policies on the continuation of that perceived supremacy. In addition, it would like to serve as a regional peacemaker and broker— playing an instrumental role in a number of meetings and conferences on regional security.[41] Such declarations are not always well received by Uzbekistan's neighbors. Uzbekistan's relationship with Tajikistan paral-

---

1980s relating to the fabrication of cotton harvest figures in the region. James Critchlow, *Nationalism in Uzbekistan: A Soviet Republic's Road to Sovereignty* (Boulder, Colo.: Westview, 1991).

40. This is a reference to the "white bone" and "black bone" dichotomy—the former represent the noble houses of the ancient nomadic tribes, while the latter represent the common folk.

41. Karimov alludes to this himself in several writings, including *Uzbekistan on the Threshold of the Twenty-First Century* (Tashkent: Uzbekistan, 1997). Such discourse has only increased with the Global War on Terrorism and the realization that as of 2005, Uzbekistan has the most developed military among the five Central Asian states.

lels that of the Russian Soviet Federated Socialist Republic to the other Union Republics during the Soviet era. This has affected trade relations with Tajikistan and even the periodic interference in intra-Tajik transportation, which, because of geography, must transit through Uzbekistan at times. The same can be said for Uzbekistan's attitudes and actions toward the Kyrgyz Republic. Uzbekistan strives to be the pivotal state in Central Asian politics.

In Turkmenistan, President Saparmurad Niyazov extols the value of a new Turkmen identity created out of a semi-Islamic, semi-national view of what his people should be. Early in his administration, Niyazov employed tactics standard for a Soviet Communist Party First Secretary. As time passed, he began to use images and measures more akin to that of a sultan or medieval potentate. At present, he is basing his leadership on the *Ruhnama,* a Turkmen spiritual guide ostensibly written by the president himself. In it, the concept of the "modern Turkmen" is explained with a focus on the "spiritual aspect" of Turkmen national values that are not evident in the other Turkic countries. In part, he is drawing on Turkmen mythology, ancient history, and his own interpretation of how clan and family relations among Turkmen ought to exist. Along with his 1995 declaration of "Positive Neutrality," Niyazov has ensured that Turkmenistan remains apart from the other states in the region—it is neither a leader nor a follower.[42]

Defunct President Askar Akaev of the Kyrgyz Republic and President Emomali Rakhmonov of Tajikistan, likewise, delved into their own countries' pasts to find symbols of legitimacy for their current actions. Interestingly, Rakhmonov began touting the Samanid lineage of modern-day Tajikistan in the late 1990s. In 1999, he led Tajikistan in a millennial celebration of the tenth century Samanid dynasty. This effort so upset neighboring President Karimov that the Uzbek leader petitioned the United Nations Educational, Scientific and Cultural Organization (UNESCO) to refrain from recognizing these events. Across the border in the Kyrgyz Republic, President Akaev harkened to the Manas, the legendary Kyrgyz folktale of the founding of the Kyrgyz people, as his source of inspiration.

In each of these examples, traditions do matter in the "packaging" of the respective regimes' images and legitimacy. These efforts are more

---

42. "Positive Neutrality" is a policy that was officially recognized by the United Nations in December 1995. In it, the Turkmen government pledges to not involve itself in alliances, security agreements, or other such compromising or potentially destabilizing situations. The reality is that Turkmenistan has become isolated in the region and in the world.

than empty gestures to placate the populations—they are also real efforts to consolidate authority. Perhaps couched in too instrumentalist of terms, it is nevertheless critical to underscore the linkages between culture and decision-making. It is likewise important to understand the limitations.

The Significance of Local Culture on Foreign Policy

To follow is an analysis of the foreign policy strategies adopted by the states of Central Asia in their first ten years after independence. As can be seen in each case, some traditional cultural values, such as the role of the leader and the bureaucratic traditions, seem to affect their foreign policy outcomes. At the same time, despite their open identification with Islam and the respect for the faith among large numbers of the population, it seems to play little role in these states' grand strategies. Advancement of material interests, especially regime stability, is important to the ruling regimes in Central Asia but does not explain all their foreign policy preferences, especially the problematic relations they have with one another. After all, were the countries to look for greater benefits, they would improve their international alliances and, more importantly, forge better regional associations. The logic exists which suggests that cooperative efforts will help expand economic development and increase stability in the region, but these have not been forthcoming in many cases.

KAZAKHSTAN. Kazakhstan's policy has vacillated between charting an "independent path" and becoming part of a larger alliance. Kazakhstani President Nursultan Nazarbaev has had no qualms about casting himself as a supporter of such alliances, even if he is sometimes perceived as being co-opted by Russia. He can do this, as he firmly believes that there are no real perceived external national threats—at least as directed by foreign governments. Russia, China, the Kyrgyz Republic, and Uzbekistan are four geographic neighbors, and relations with all four range from positive to benign. Outside of Russian nationalists, who are in the distinct minority, however, Kazakhstan has little to fear in the way of Russia attempting to "retake Southern Siberia," as the northern *oblasts* of Kazakhstan are sometimes called. Indeed, the one actual border dispute is with Uzbekistan—this neighbor to the south views parts of the Shymkent region as being "theirs."

The "real threats" are perceived as internal: maintaining Nazarbaev's leadership legitimacy, balancing competing groups, and creating a stable internal environment. President Nazarbaev considers energy exports to be the key aspect of his country's economic revival. In that respect, ensuring pipeline security and a steady flow of oil remain paramount to the country. This, then, affects how Kazakhstani officials will deal with counterparts in Russia, Iran, and the countries that support the Baku-Tbilisi-Ceyhan route. Indeed, it is this energy export demand that has dictated meeting schedules and the needs of the country's foreign policy staff.

Nazarbaev sees Kazakhstan's true security goal as only being reached through cooperation with others. Going it alone will only pit it against the larger states of China and Russia and put Kazakhstan in direct competition with Uzbekistan. An interconnected Kazakhstan addresses a major fear of Nazarbaev's: that his country will somehow become isolated from the global community and thus be marginalized by major economic powers. Kazakhstan has aggressively pursued relations within the Shanghai Cooperation Organization, the Quadripartite Security Agreement, and even the Commonwealth of Independent States (CIS).

The possibility of Kazakhstani energy prosperity and integration with larger neighboring states hints at one final issue of importance for President Nazarbaev. In the end, he views himself as the logical "leader" in the region, and Kazakhstan as the major country of Central Asia. While an academic debate as to whether Kazakhstan is actually "Central Asian" does exist as far as the geopolitical pecking order is concerned, Nazarbaev sees his country as such. Furthermore, President Nazarbaev has made enough statements that underscore his belief that Kazakhstan should be seen as the first among equals, given its territorial dimensions and economic potential. This is not idle chatter: it is logical if taken from the economic perspective.

UZBEKISTAN. Uzbekistan sees the role of regional leader as being its own. Uzbekistan's foreign policy agenda through the 1990s and into the current decade is one of establishing independence of agenda, economic autarky, and maintaining regional primacy. Immediately after independence, the Uzbek government established positive relations with European countries and the United States. Some pundits viewed this as an effort to pull away from Russia. Indeed, the rhetoric emanating from Tashkent was very "anti-Russian," with concerns raised periodically about fears of Russian hegemony and mistrust of the CIS. As already noted, Uzbek policy autonomy is part of a broader conceptualization of power in Uzbekistan: the need to assert the regional power of the country.

TURKMENISTAN. Under the leadership of President Saparmurad Niyazov, Turkmenistan espouses a policy of "Positive Neutrality." Any proactive policy is curtailed by President Niyazov's insistence on remaining noncommittal on regional agreements and basic policy trends. Turkmenistan's government (read: President Niyazov) feels that tying itself to the other states of Central Asia will only minimize the country's ability to address issues of specific concern, such as relations with Iran and Afghanistan.

The Turkmen-declared policy of "Positive Neutrality" is in fact a myth, as Turkmenistan must associate with other states. Trade relations have suffered as a result of an inability to complete business deals. This was especially evident when Turkmenistan failed to commit to an agreement on natural gas shipments to Turkey. When Azerbaijan discovered gas in the Shah Deniz region of the Caspian Sea, a deal was quickly struck between Azerbaijan and Turkey, leaving Turkmenistan out in the cold. The same can be said for pipelines southward into Iran or even Afghanistan. Turkmen foot-dragging and an inability to finalize agreements—due partly to the fact that Niyazov loathes being beholden to others, but also to the fact that he firmly believes "a better deal" exists out there—have caused great damage to his country's economy.

KYRGYZ REPUBLIC AND TAJIKISTAN. For both the Kyrgyz Republic and Tajikistan, the primary concerns relate to border viability and internal stability. As illegal product trafficking is conducted through their countries, they see these "international problems" as being close to home. Because they are relatively small states wedged between large neighbors—China to the east and Uzbekistan and Kazakhstan to the west and north—these two states tend to be reactive in policy decisions and open to participating in larger, multi-state organizations. It is no surprise that the Kyrgyz Republic was eager to join the Quadripartite Agreement with Kazakhstan, Russia, and Belarus in 1996 and that Tajikistan joined it in 1999. In addition, both are members of the Shanghai Cooperation Organization.

The push for defined geopolitical roles and regional alliances is evident among the Central Asian states of the Caspian region. They do not, however, provide explanations for how and why the policy decisions are actually made. After all, were the countries to look for greater benefits, they would increase these international alliances and, more importantly, forge better regional associations. The logic exists which suggests that cooperative efforts will help expand economic development and increase stability in the region.

However, this *Realpolitik* approach cannot be used to justify all decisions in the region, as it is thwarted time and again by how the leaders in the region opt for choices that alienate an outside power, be it Russia, the United States, or China. Leadership strategies and perceptions rooted in local culture are fundamental, and in systems where strong leaders dominate the policy process, decisions of that leader take on a greater role. After all, the possible failure of a decision could translate into a failed leadership legacy. In addition, while not as important, the limits that are imposed upon that leader from the administrative structure need to be considered. Ultimately, these are material interests that center on the internal dynamics of a country. It is even more important to underscore that, even in this environment, Islam does not play the role that one may have ascribed to it. Perhaps it is because Islam is either a force that the respective leaders cannot fully control or one that has become detached from the decision-making processes honed over the past several generations, this aspect of the region's culture remains detached from the political decision-making and policy processes of Central Asia.

Chapter 8

The Islamic Republic of Iran: Is It Really?

Brenda Shaffer

The Islamic Republic of Iran could conceivably be the poster child for the proponents of cultural explanations of foreign policy and of those who claim that Islam is the guiding force of foreign policy formation of Muslim-populated states. Few states in the international system today have so clearly articulated, as Iran has, an official religious creed and the view that the state should serve as an instrument of that belief system. In actuality, however, the foreign policy of the Islamic Republic of Iran challenges the culturalists' line. The material interests of the state and, specifically, of the ruling regime serve as the overwhelming determinates of Iran's foreign policy choices; cultural and ideological goals are rarely promoted at significant expense to those material interests.

The Iranian case illustrates that the struggle between material interests and cultural interests is particularly acute in states where the ruling regimes have identified themselves culturally with a wider or even universal community (such as all Muslims or the World Proletariat) beyond the borders of the state itself. This inherently brings into conflict the interests and the needs of the community within the borders of the state with those of the community abroad. Many times in its more than seventy years of existence, the Communist Soviet Union dealt with the dichotomy between its needs as a state and the goal of advancing the interests of the "World Proletariat." Dogmas such as "War Communism" and "Communism in One State" were the buckled attempts to reconcile these conflicts and provide some legitimacy to the pursuit of Soviet material interests in face of the official state ideology. Moreover, states with ethnical identities often face competition between the needs of the community living within the state's borders and co-ethnics abroad, which the state claims to represent. This type of dilemma has frequently emerged in policies and debates in Israel, Armenia, Russia, and Azerbaijan—all of which have large diaspora communities residing abroad.

The collapse of the Soviet Union and the subsequent independence of six Muslim-populated republics bordering on or close to Iran created tremendous opportunities for Iran to advance its official goal of exporting Islam and to demonstrate Muslim solidarity with the Muslims of the new states. At the same time, however, the establishment of the new states generated challenges for Iran that potentially threatened the stability of its ruling regime; thus, many policy dilemmas arose in which Iran's Islamic state interests were clearly pitted against Iran's material state interests. This chapter will examine those dilemmas by analyzing Iranian foreign policy toward Russia and the new states of Central Asia and the Caucasus in the first decade after the Soviet Union's breakup in 1991. The chapter will also examine Tehran's choices on the promotion of Islam in the region, its position on the independence of the new Muslim-populated republics, and its stances on the major conflicts in the region in which Muslims were embroiled (the Chechen conflict, the Nagorno-Karabagh war between Azerbaijan and Armenia, and the civil war in Tajikistan). Analysis of Iran's policy toward the neighboring states of Central Asia and the Caucasus can be especially informative on the question of culture and foreign policy because the region is populated with both Muslims and Christians, many of which engaged each other in conflicts in the post-independence period, and Tehran had to choose a side. In addition, these states were new states, and Iran had to create new policies toward them. In the period under analysis, one can view this foreign policy formation process. Moreover, one can most often view policy debates in Iran, especially in the post–Ayatollah Khomeini period, on the pages of the Iranian press: which policy debates took place in Iran, how various political forces there weighed material versus cultural—in this case, religious—interests, and which interests ultimately succeeded.

The chapter makes five major points: one, the officially proclaimed cultural identity of the state is not necessarily the one that has the greatest impact on foreign policy, and that a variety of identities held by the population of a state compete for influence. In addition, the content of the official identity is often ambiguous. Two, regimes do not necessarily get caught in their own rhetoric: they can make policy choices that contradict their official cultural rhetoric without serious repercussions. Three, states often use various and conflicting cultural explanations and messages in order to endow policies with legitimacy. Four, bureaucratic islands within the Iranian regime at times promote more ideologically pious policies. Five, rarely did common Islamic identity or solidarity serve as a basis for Tehran's alliance and cooperation partners in the Caspian region.

In the cases when it promoted Islam in the region, Iran often did it in an instrumental fashion in order to pursue material state interests.

States' Multiple Identities

States and their attendant societies often possess a multiplicity of cultural identities that can potentially impact an individual state's foreign policies, and often the identities of the state and the society are not congruent. States generally designate an official identity, but often even these identities are complex and may differ from the prominent cultural identities of the state's population. Therefore, it is not overtly apparent which culture, if any at all, within a state influences a state's foreign policy. In order to correctly assess how culture impacts a state's foreign policy, it is incumbent upon the researcher first to designate what the officially proclaimed culture of a state is, as well as to identify which cultural force, if any, within the state impacts foreign policy outcomes.

States identifying with trans-state cultures and ideologies (such as Islam) possess an inherent clash of interests between those of the state and the trans-state interests. In the case of Iran, even the name of the state itself is a clue as to the problematic nature of Iran's official identity. The name identifies the state as a republic, thus claiming that the state belongs to the populace and inherently its policies should reflect the populace's will; it refers to itself as Islamic, a universally-based religion that does not distinguish between ethnic or state boundaries, is a world-wide community of believers, and is potentially open to all; and finally, the state calls itself Iran—a recognized territorial unit and long-established state that promotes the interests of that defined territorial unit and its ruling regime. Thus, the name Islamic Republic of Iran identifies the state's three separate and often conflicting identities—the most obvious one being that between the universal Islamic identity of the state and that of Iran as a bounded territorial unit. These three identities are not monolithic, however, and further examination reveals additional factors. For instance, as a republic, the foreign policies of the Islamic Republic of Iran may be affected by the different cultures of its citizens, especially since Iran is a multi-ethnic polity.

Even within the framework of the officially articulated foreign policy of the Islamic Republic of Iran, a number of conflicting policy goals are apparent. In its Constitution, the Islamic Republic of Iran declares that: "The foreign policy of the Islamic Republic of Iran is based upon the rejection of all forms of domination, both the exertion of it and submission to it, the preservation of the independence of the country in all respects and its territorial integrity, the defence of the rights of all Muslims, nonalignment with respect to the hegemonist superpowers, and the maintenance of mutually peaceful relations with all non-belligerent states."[1]

At the same time, however, the Constitution states that the goals of the Islamic Republic are implemented through "framing the foreign policy of the country on the basis of Islamic criteria, fraternal commitment to all Muslims, and unsparing support to the mustad'afiin (freedom fighters) of the world."[2]

In this defined, official policy goal of the state, the potential for conflict is clear: Iran defines itself as committed to "the preservation of the independence of the country in all respects and its territorial integrity," while at the same time obligated to defend "the rights of all Muslims," including "unsparing support to Muslim freedom fighters." As will be seen in the next section, in many instances, Tehran has been challenged by policy dilemmas in which promoting the security of the state of Iran conflicts with "defense of the rights of all Muslims" and the goal of supporting Muslim "freedom fighters." Tehran has formally committed itself to exhibit Islamic solidarity with various Muslim factions and to support the expansion of Islamic influence and power in the world. At the same time, as Iran, the state must work for the preservation of its own resources, the good and security of the population of the state within those borders, and presumably the preservation of the ruling regime.

In some states, some of the major cultural forces can be further catagorized into subunits, and the interpretation of the content of those forces is not unanimous. In the case of multi-ethnic Iran, the cultural dictat of "Iranian" is subject to dispute. Some Iranians—especially many members of the ethnic minority communities—view Iranian identity as a supra-ethnic identity encompassing all the residents of the territory of Iran. Others, mainly those of Persian descent, equate Iranian culture with Persian culture. Iranian foreign policy institutions market a number of different cultural identities when attempting to build foreign ties and promote state interests. For instance, the Foreign Ministry promotes Persian culture and attempts to use it as a tool in hopes of fostering cooperative ties with Persian-speaking peoples in the region, especially in Central Asia and Afghanistan.[3] At the same time, the state was even willing to use the Turkic identity of Iran's large Azerbaijani minority in sup-

---

1. Article 152, Constitution, Islamic Republic of Iran.

2. Article 3, Constitution, Islamic Republic of Iran.

3. Iranian officials and press often used the idea of a common Persian identity to promote ties between Iran and Tajikistan. For instance, *Salam* (Iranian Newspaper) wrote, "The rightful struggle of the Tajikistan people enjoys the support of all Muslims, espe-

port of the state's interests. While serving as Deputy Foreign Minister responsible for Tehran's ties with the states of the former Soviet Union, 'Abbas Maleki commented on the need to use various "common" cultural ties with the peoples of Central Asia and the Caucasus to promote ties with Iran:

> In countries such as Afghanistan and Tajikistan the real language spoken by all is Persian. We see roots of this language in all the republics and Persian has its own special place in them. In Samarkand and Bukhara the people speak Persian and the language spoken in Ashghabad contains numerous Persian words.
>
> It is true that Turkish is spoken in Turkmenistan, Kazakhstan, and Azerbaijan, but the Turkish spoken in these republics is vastly different from Istanbuli Turkish. Much work has been done with the Turkish language in our country. Poetry has been written in this language."[4]

In addition to the impact of multiple cultures upon a state's policies, in its rhetoric, Iran is willing to apply messages from its various subcultures in order to promote its state interests. For instance, regarding Central Asia, Tehran often speaks of the shared Iranian civilization of the people of the region and promotes common celebration of pre-Islamic holidays such as the spring holiday Novruz. From an Islamic perspective, Ayatollah Khomeini had looked unfavorably on the celebration of Novruz, but bent to popular demand in Iran. The state's representatives were willing to go one step further and promote the Novruz holiday in the new republics as a way of spreading Iran's influence.

Iran's "Islamic Solidarity"

All regimes need legitimacy and need to legitimize their policies. Tehran is constantly stating its extensive commitment to "Islamic solidarity" and its support for Muslim forces around the world as a result of being an Islamic republic. The commitment to promoting Islam has been a constant theme in foreign policy statements by Iranian officials and, as pointed out, is clearly articulated in the state's Constitution and all major foreign policy documents. While serving as Minister of Culture and Islamic Guidance in 1992, Mohammed Khatami stated the importance of Iran's Islamic identity in its foreign relations: "In our belief, cultural ties

---

cially the Farsi-speaking people and the heroic people of Iran, who have a common history and culture with the Tajiks." July 19, 1993, p. 12 (FBIS-NES93-147).

4. Interview with former Deputy Foreign Minister 'Abbas Maleki, *Sorush* (Iranian journal), February 29–March 6, 1992, pp. 6–9.

are the basis for any kind of relations between states. Iran inspired movements in Muslim states following the victory of the Islamic Revolution (1979), drawing their attention and emerging as the focal point for the struggles against the common goals of Islam."[5]

Often foreign government analysts tend to assume that Tehran is automatically inclined to support both Muslim forces that are in confrontation with non-Muslims and religious Muslims in confrontation with secular forces as enumerated by Khatami above. The assumption that Iran would support Muslim forces over non-Muslim forces affected many of the early assessments of Iran's anticipated policies in Central Asia and the Caucasus following the Soviet Union's breakup.

The Iranian case illustrates the importance of distinguishing between a state's rhetoric about its policy decisions and the policies themselves. In the Caspian region, rarely was this declared Islamic solidarity reflected in the Iranian policy choices in the first ten years following the Soviet breakup, especially if there were any trade-offs in areas that could affect the security of the Iranian state, the preservation of the ruling regime, or other vital material interests. Moreover, the alliances which Iran has formed in the Caspian region have not been determined by shared religious affiliations. The propagation of Islam and advancement of the cause of other Muslim peoples is only a small facet of Tehran's activity in the region. In fact, in many cases, Iran uses Islam instrumentally to pursue material state interests as a way of contending with neighboring regimes or forcing changes in their policies. In this sense, culture serves the material interests of the Iranian state as opposed to being a factor shaping the policies of the state. In the Caspian region, Tehran has supported Islamic radicals and Islamist anti-regime movements almost exclusively in countries where its state-to-state relations are poor, such as in Uzbekistan or Azerbaijan. Iran does not work, however, to undermine very secular Muslim regimes, such as Turkmenistan, through the promotion of Islamic forces if the regime's relations with Tehran are good.

The following section will analyze Iran's major policy decisions relating to conflicts that raged in Central Asia and the Caucasus in the first ten years after the Soviet Union's breakup. In the adjacent area of Central Asia and the Caucasus, Tehran was faced with a number of policy dilemmas that often pitted "Islamic solidarity" against the material interests of the regime. Since a number of these conflicts emerged between Muslims and non-Muslims or between observant Muslims and secular forces, by analyzing Tehran's choices and alliance preferences, one can see if the

---

5. Islamic Republic News Agency (IRNA) in English, May 15, 1992.

common Muslim cultural identity played a role in its policy preferences. Four cases will be examined in which Iran had to choose sides in the adjacent Caspian region: therefore, one has a robust ability to test the impact of shared Muslim identity on policy choices. The analysis will concentrate on the following Iranian policy decisions: its support of continuation of the coercively secular Soviet Union versus promoting its breakup and establishment of independent Muslim-populated states; its stance toward the conflict between Chechnya and Moscow; its policy toward the Nagorno-Karabagh conflict between Azerbaijan and Armenia; and its actions with regard to the Tajikistani civil war. In this section, the analysis emphasizes the role or lack thereof of "Islamic solidarity" in Iran's foreign policy, as well as scrutinizing under which circumstances Tehran supports Islamic forces abroad in the Caspian region.

THE SOVIET UNION VERSUS THE INDEPENDENT MUSLIM STATES
On the eve of the Soviet breakup, Tehran was faced with an acute policy dilemma: whether to expand ties with the anti-religious Soviet Union and hope for its continued existence, or to lend support to the budding nationalist and Islamic movements in the Muslim-populated republics of the Soviet Union. Iran bordered on the Soviet Union, and in the late 1980s under Soviet President Mikhail Gorbachev's leadership, Tehran enjoyed excellent and expanding relations with the Soviet Union, especially in the economic and military spheres. As instability began to arise and movements in the Soviet Union's southern Muslim-populated republics were gaining strength and beginning to demand outside support, Iran's relationship with Moscow flourished. On the eve of his appointment as President of the Islamic Republic of Iran, Akbar Hashemi Rafsanjani conducted a landmark visit to the Soviet Union in June 1989, and during this visit, Russia signed its first commitment to cooperate with Iran in the civilian nuclear sphere, in addition to a number of military cooperation agreements.[6] At the same time, Moscow was violently engaged in attempts to quell nationalist and other movements in the Soviet Muslim-populated republics. In its official rhetoric, Tehran flagrantly condemned the Soviet actions against the Muslims of the Soviet Union. For instance, *Keyhan*, a Tehran-based newspaper, wrote:

---

6. Interview with Viktor Mikhailov, *Priroda*, No. 8 (August 1995), pp. 3–11. For more on Russian-Iranian cooperation and relations, see Brenda Shaffer, *Partners in Need: Russia and Iran's Strategic Relationship* (Washington, D.C.: Washington Institute for Near East Policy, 2001).

What answer will Mr. Gorbachev give to the population of over 60 million Muslims in the Muslim-inhabited Soviet republics? What answer does Mr. Gorbachev have about the calamitous killings of hundreds of Muslims in the Soviet cities and villages for the crime of wanting Islam and defending their fundamental rights, for the Islamic revolution and the revolutionary Islamic nations, as well as the 1 billion Muslims in the world. To lock horns with Islam and the Muslims is tantamount to playing with fire. The world of revolutionary Islam and the Hezbollah resistance forces are lying in wait for the enemies of Islam and the Muslims.[7]

In addition, after Moscow's massacre of 132 Azerbaijanis in Baku in January 1990 ("Black January"), Tehran publicly proclaimed its "Islamic solidarity" with the Shi'i Muslims of Azerbaijan. At the same time, however, it continued to accelerate its cooperation with Moscow:

The Soviet Government realizes, of course, that the Islamic Republic regime, which represents the focal point of the Islamic world, cannot ignore the unexpected events and developments which the Muslims of Soviet Azerbaijan are experiencing. The Soviet border guards who are stationed along borders with Iran saw with their own eyes how thousands of Azeris rushed to Iranian territories in the past few days. Such deep and human Islamic feelings and this sense of fraternity entail certain responsibilities. Officials in Moscow of course realize this fact. They realize that though borders should be respected, Muslim solidarity does not recognize geographic borders. . . . How can our people tolerate the fact that the conditions of Muslims in neighbouring Azerbaijan are totally ignored? It is not possible to ignore the question of religious, historical, linguistic, emotional and geographical solidarity.[8]

In actuality, in contradiction of this official statement, Tehran calculated that it would benefit more from a continued cooperative relationship with Moscow than from support to the secessionist movements and only provided those movements with rhetorical support. Iran's assessment may have been affected by the fact that it did not seem to view the Soviet collapse as either eminent or realistic, and Tehran actually seemed shocked and caught off guard policy-wise when the Soviet Union actually collapsed.

In contrast to the expectation of many Western assessors, Tehran did not greet the Soviet Union's breakup as a great opportunity for "export of Islam," but rather grasped that its once-stable northern border had been replaced by a conflict-ridden zone and that influences from the new

---

7. *Keyhan*, January 15, 1990, p. 14 (FBIS-NES-90-018).

8. Tehran International Service in Arabic, January 21, 1990 (FBIS-NES-90-015).

states could permeate into Iran. During the week of the Soviet Union's breakup, the official newspaper, *Tehran Times*, wrote:

The first ground for concern from the point of view in Tehran is the lack of political stability in the newly independent republics. The unstable conditions in those republics could be serious causes of insecurity along the lengthy borders (over 2000 kilometres) Iran shares with those countries. Already foreign hands can be felt at work in those republics, especially in Azerbaijan and Turkmenistan republics, with the ultimate objective of brewing discord among the Iranian Azeris and Turkmen by instigating ethnic and nationalistic sentiments.[9]

In addition, the Iranian press explicitly reported that it was not pleased with Gorbachev's exit from the Soviet Union.[10]

CHECHNYA

Throughout the post-Soviet period, the Chechen Muslims have been struggling for independence from Moscow. This conflict has been particularly acute during 1992–1994 and 1999–2000, when two all-out wars flared between Chechen and Russian forces. Many Chechen nationalist movement activists also came to identify strongly with Islam and supported many of the causes considered to be at the core of the Islamic agenda. Muslim symbols were frequently used by the Chechen forces, and the local government adopted *Shari'a* (Islamic law) in Chechnya. Despite the battles between Moscow and the Chechen Muslims, cooperation and relations between Russia and Iran had been excellent throughout the 1990s, and both have described these relations in many instances as "strategic." Surging conflicts between the Muslim Chechens and Moscow did not in anyway impede or retard the cooperation between Moscow and Tehran. Rather, they had the opposite effect. Tehran keenly discerned Moscow's potential vulnerability during the periods of heightened military conflict with the Chechens, and in these periods, the quantity of Iranian military and security delegations visiting Moscow increased significantly, and there they successfully elicited extensive, public commitments to military cooperation and assistance in the nuclear sphere.[11] In

---

9. *Tehran Times*, December 30, 1991, p. 2.

10. *Tehran Times*, August 18, 1991, p. 2; Statement of Deputy Foreign Minister 'Ali Mohammad Besharati in *Abrar* (Iranian newspaper), December 2, 1991, p. 2 (FBIS-NES-91-237); *Tehran Times*, December 30, 1991, p. 2.

11. For further information, see Shaffer, *Partners in Need: The Strategic Relationship of Russia and Iran.*

exchange, Iran was active in various forums of Muslim states in ensuring that no harsh condemnations of Russia were issued and in constraining any potential mass Muslim mobilization against Russia in response to its massive transgressions in Chechnya.[12] For example, in September 1999, at the height of Moscow's attacks on Grozny, Russia announced the signing of a contract worth $38 million U.S. to provide a necessary turbine to Iran's Bushehr nuclear power plant.[13] Concurrently, Moscow thanked Tehran for its efforts in explaining Russia's actions in Chechnya to the Organization of the Islamic Conference's member states.[14]

Iranian official statements on Russia's actions in Chechnya were actually much milder than those of either the United States or the European states. Iranian officials reiterated during both wars its "respect for the territorial integrity of Russia" and the fact that it regarded the "Chechen problem as a domestic one." At the height of Russia's bombings of Grozny, Tehran condoned the actions and stated that Moscow has the right to act in defense against terrorism.[15]

Through the example of Iran's policies regarding the Chechen conflict, one can see not only that "Islamic solidarity" had no significant impact in any way on its policies toward the Chechens, but Tehran was even willing to cynically use the Russian vulnerability arising from its attacks on the Chechen Muslims as a way to promote its bilateral agenda with Moscow. An article published in *Salam* was particularly revealing of the Iranian dilemma on Chechnya and its ultimate policy decision:

What should the Islamic Republic of Iran's stance be with regard to the crises? Support for Dudayev?[16] Condemnation of the Russian attacks against the Muslim people of Chechnya or . . . ? Whatever the decision, it is bound to have varied results. Some factors will affect such decisions.

Among these factors are the fact that the people of Chechnya are Muslim, the geographic proximity of the crisis to our land and sea borders, the nature of the Chechen leaders, Iran's economic interests in the Caspian Sea, particularly the issue of oil and gas in the region, and the strategic relations between Tehran and Moscow. In view of the unclear nature of the

---

12. Interfax, December 19, 1997.

13. ITAR-TASS, September 24, 1999.

14. Interfax in English, September 28, 1999.

15. See, for instance, the interview with Iranian Ambassador to Russia, quoted in IRNA in English, October 24, 1995; Tehran Voice of the Islamic Republic of Iran, November 28, 1999; and IRNA in English, November 29, 1999.

16. Dzhokhar Dudayev was elected president of the Chechnya Autonomous Republic in October 1991 on the eve of the Soviet collapse. Under his leadership, Chechnya declared independence from Moscow in 1992.

Chechen rulers and their future objectives in the region and the rumors about them, the benefits of categorically assisting the Grozny administration seem nebulous. On the other hand, silence in the fact of the massacre of the Chechen Muslims also seems inappropriate. It is certain however that support for the Chechen administration will certainly have concomitant repercussions on relations with Moscow.[17]

In other words, this is a recommendation for rhetorical "Islamic solidarity" with the Chechens but not for policy actions which could harm cooperation with Moscow. In the case of the Chechen conflict, cultural Islamic solidarity was clearly and consciously subordinated by Tehran to the pursuit of its material state interests.

AZERBAIJAN, ARMENIA, AND THE CONFLICT OVER NAGORNO-KARABAGH
Iran's policies toward the Caspian region are also influenced by domestic inputs and constraints, and one of Iran's chief goals has been to prevent trends from arising which could lead to destabilization in Iranian Azerbaijan and a rise in ethnical activity among the Azerbaijanis in Iran. Iran is a multi-ethnic state, and its domestic security can potentially be affected by developments in the Republic of Azerbaijan. Half of Iran's population comprises non-Persian ethnic minorities with the Azerbaijanis being the largest, representing almost a third of the population of Iran.[18] The majority of the residents of the northwest provinces of Iran, contiguous to the border with the Republic of Azerbaijan, are Azerbaijanis. In pursuit of precluding a rise in ethnical demands among Iranian Azerbaijanis, Tehran has declined support to the Republic of Azerbaijan (the majority of whose population is Shi'i Muslim) in its conflict with neighboring Christian-populated Armenia. Iran prefers Baku to be embroiled in a conflict and unable to serve as a source of attraction for the Azerbaijanis in Iran. In addition, Iran estimated early after the Soviet Union's breakup that Azerbaijan's independence had really created no opportunity for Iranian influence because of Baku's Western and specifically Turkish orientation, while Armenia was signaling for strong cooperation with Tehran and cool relations with the United States.[19]

The conflict between Armenia and Azerbaijan over Nagorno-Karabagh clearly pitted Tehran's material interests against its cultural interests, mainly Islamic solidarity. Armenia and Azerbaijan both border

17. *Salam*, December 25, 1994, p. 12 (FBIS-NES-95-002).

18. For more on questions of ethnicity in Iran, see Brenda Shaffer, *Borders and Brethren: Iran and the Challenge of Azerbaijani Identity* (Cambridge, Mass.: MIT Press, 2002).

19. *Jomhuri-ye Islami* (Iranian daily newspaper), March 4, 1992, p. 4.

Iran, and subordination of material interests to cultural interests would be much more costly in this proximity than in areas far away from Iran's borders. At the same time, the abandonment of both the only other state that is overwhelmingly populated by Shi'i Muslims and the more than 800,000 Azerbaijani Muslim refugees created by the conflict is difficult to reconcile with claiming to be a state promoting Islamic, and especially Shi'i, solidarity. Thus, when Tehran decided which side to support in the war between Azerbaijan and Armenia, both the trade-offs and implications of the decision were clear.

Since the 1988 eruption of the Nagorno-Karabagh conflict, Armenia has succeeded in capturing close to 20 percent of Azerbaijan's territory and almost 10 percent of the population of Azerbaijan has become refugees. Officially, Iran declared neutrality in the conflict—in itself inconsistent with the official ideology of a state that portrays itself as the protector and champion of the Shi'a. Despite its declared neutrality, Iran cooperated intensively with Armenia throughout most of the period of the war and its aftermath.

Tehran adopted anti-Armenian rhetoric only at the times when the conflict directly threatened Iranian state interests or when domestically pressured by political activities of Iranian Azerbaijanis. Considering that the Armenians were the force struggling for a change in the status quo and that they occupied a significant amount of territory within the internationally recognized borders of Azerbaijan, the lack of Iranian criticism and the adoption of a "balanced" approach has, in actuality, favored Armenia. Even when Armenian forces captured the strategic city of Shusha on May 9, 1992, during Iranian-sponsored peace talks held in Tehran, Iranian reference to the attack did not go beyond expression of "concern over the recent developments in Nagorno-Karabagh."[20]

In 1992, official statements of the Iranian Foreign Ministry continued to reflect a balanced approach toward the two belligerents, even following a new series of significant Armenian conquests in Azerbaijan. After Armenia had just overrun Shusha and Lachin and created tens of thousands of new Azerbaijani refugees, Deputy Minister Mahmud Va'ezi's restraint in his comment on the conflict was stunning: "The only thing that can solve the problem is political negotiation and a peaceful solution through any path that both sides accept."[21] Iran established diplomatic relations with Armenia in February 1992 and signed a number of eco-

---

20. IRNA in English, May 13, 1992.

21. Interview with Deputy Foreign Minister Mahmud Va'ezi, Tehran IRIB Television, May 21, 1992 (FBIS-NES-92-100).

nomic agreements at the height of one of the battles between Azerbaijan and Armenia. Iran has at times served as Yerevan's main route for supplies and energy and provided an outlet for its trade. In April 1992, at one of the most crucial points in the war between Azerbaijan and Armenia, Iran agreed to supply fuel to Armenia and improve transportation links.[22] These supplies to Armenia arrived at a crucial time in the war, and without Tehran's cooperation in this period when most supply routes had been cut by the war, Armenia's war effort probably could not have been sustained and escalated. Pointing out Tehran's role in helping Armenia circumvent its isolation, Armenian Prime Minister and Vice President Gagik Arutyunyan praised Iran in May 1992 at a ceremony commemorating the opening of a bridge over the Araz River linking Armenia and Iran and stated that the bridge to Iran will contribute to stabilizing the economic situation in the republic.[23] Some of the best indications of Iran's conciliatory position toward Armenia came from Yerevan and the Karabagh Armenians—their repeated praise of Iran's role in the negotiation process, the expression of their preference for Tehran over many other foreign representatives, and their call for the deployment of Iranian observers at the border between Azerbaijan and Armenia and in the Nakhchevan area, which was isolated from the rest of the Republic of Azerbaijan.[24] Armenia's President Levon Ter-Petrossian, stressing the importance of Iran's mission in settling the problem of Karabagh, stated: "The Iranians have proved their complete impartiality in this issue, respecting the rights of both sides and striving for a just solution, and therefore the sides trust Iran." In October 2002, Armenian Foreign Minister Vartan Oskanian stated, "Iran is the guarantor of stability in the Karabagh region."[25] At the close of the April 2003 visit of Iranian Foreign Minister Kamal Kharrazi in Yerevan, Armenian Foreign Minister Oskanian praised Iran's "balanced policy" in the South Caucasus and stated that "Iran's position is an example of wise and flexible policy pursued in the region."[26] In contrast, Azerbaijani leaders voiced critical statements regarding Iran's role in the negotiations, illustrating their perception that

---

22. Interfax (a private Russian news agency, in English), April 15, 1992.

23. Interfax (in English), May 7, 1992.

24. TASS, February 28, 1992 (FBIS-SOV-92-040); Moscow Programma Radio Odin, May 31, 1992 (FBIS-SOV-92-105); and Yerevan Armenia's Radio First Program, May 20, 1992 (FBIS-SOV-92-099).

25. IRNA, October 2, 2002.

26. Arminfo (an Armenian news agency, in Russian), April 30, 2003.

Tehran was not promoting their interests.[27] In addition, Tehran's lack of action on behalf of Azerbaijan in this period was so pronounced that hard-liners in Iran openly voiced criticism of the official policy, stating that Iran's policy toward the conflict and its cooperation with Armenia was not a proper reflection of Iran's "religious and ideological responsibilities."[28]

Iran's treatment of Azerbaijan is an important illustration of the need to distinguish between a state's rhetoric about its policies and the policies themselves. For instance, at the height of the Nagorno-Karabagh war, when Iran's cooperation with Armenia contributed to Yerevan's ability to sustain the war effort, Deputy Foreign Minister Va'ezi did not hesitate to publicly orate:

Calm and stability are most important in this region, not just for ourselves but for our neighbors, for the people of Azerbaijan, who are not separate from us. The common culture and history between us and the Azerbaijanis means that we cannot remain indifferent to Azerbaijan being ruined through war and the destruction of its people in this situation. Therefore, all our efforts, whether internally or through our influence in Armenia and Azerbaijan, must be used in order to stop the war from spreading.[29]

Tehran's rhetoric toward the Nagorno-Karabagh conflict changed in April 1993. This significant shift in Iran's rhetoric materialized as a result of pressure from Azerbaijanis in Iran and the escalation in the fighting that created massive amounts of refugees and threatened to spill over into Iran. Despite the discernible change in Iran's rhetoric, no significant modifications of its cooperation with Armenia took place in 1993. Iran continued to provide Armenia with energy and other supplies. High-level and cordial exchanges with Armenian officials were conducted regularly, and, in July 1993, direct flights between Tehran and Yerevan were inaugurated.[30]

Iran's specific positions on various proposals during the negotiation process between Azerbaijan and Armenia were often dictated by its inter-

---

27. *Komsomolskaya Pravda*, May 20, 1992, p. 1.

28. *Jomhuri-ye Islami*, March 2, 1992, p. 2.

29. Interview with Deputy Foreign Minister Mahmud Va'ezi, Tehran IRIB Television, May 21, 1992 (FBIS-NES-92-100).

30. See, for instance, Yerevan Armenia's Radio First Program Network, December 23, 1993 (FBIS-SOV-93-246) for early contacts on an agreement for construction of a gas pipeline between Iran and Armenia. On coal deliveries from Iran to Armenia, see ITAR-TASS, October 23, 1993 (FBIS-SOV-93-204).

nal Azerbaijani consideration. For instance, Tehran has fervently opposed propositions for the sides to trade land corridors linking Armenia to Karabagh and Azerbaijan to Nakhchevan, because these plans would result in a significant extension of the common border between the Republic of Azerbaijan and Iran, which Tehran strove to avoid.

Despite the fact that Armenia was engaged in a military struggle with a Shi'i Muslim–populated state, Iran and Armenia have frequently hosted visits of high-level representatives of their security and military establishments and conducted significant cooperation in these fields. During his March 2002 visit to Yerevan, Admiral 'Ali Shamkhani, Iranian Minister of Defense, signed a letter of understanding with his Armenian counterpart, Serzh Sarkisyan, on "bilateral military cooperation."[31] According to Arminfo News Agency, the agreement includes arms sales.[32] During his visit to Armenia, the Iranian Defense Minister stated that Iran does not maintain military cooperation with Azerbaijan and that "this was only a wish" of the Azerbaijani authorities.[33] Intelligence cooperation has been forged between the sides.[34]

Despite its concrete cooperation with Armenia throughout the post–Soviet period, Tehran still claims that what drives its policy is cultural solidarity with Azerbaijan: "Irano-Azeri relations, despite the two countries' common historical and cultural traditions, are sensitive. We should not forget that the Republic of Azerbaijan is one of the few states whose leaders belong to the Shi'i School of Islam and the common culture of the Shi'i School of Islam is a significant factor in the relations of the two countries."[35] At the same time, Tehran has often used the claim of common cultural ties to promote its relations with Armenia: "In view of the historical cultural ties between the two nations, the authorities in Tehran and Yerevan were in favour of political cooperation."[36] In tandem, Tehran openly stated that its cooperation with Armenia is driven by "national interests." Following a successful visit by Armenian President Robert

---

31. IRNA, March 6, 2002.

32. Arminfo, March 5, 2002.

33. Ibid.

34. This has been illustrated by the July 2001 visit of Hassan Rowhani, Secretary of Iran's Supreme National Security Council, who has served as key coordinator for Tehran on intelligence cooperation with foreign states.

35. Iran News (Tehrani, in English) March 4, 1996, p. 2.

36. Tehran Voice of the Islamic Republic of Iran Radio, March 4, 2002 (FBIS-NES-2002-0304).

Kocharian to Iran, the official Iranian daily *Tehran Times* reported in response to implied Azerbaijani criticism of the visit: "every country has the right to determine the extent of cooperation with another in line with its national interests. The expansion of Iran's ties with Armenia and Azerbaijan is the result of common national interests and geopolitical circumstances."[37]

In a discussion in the hard-liner newspaper *Jomhuri-ye Eslami*, an analyst pointed out that national interests guide Iranian policy, just like "every country": "Despite the fact that because of religious affinity the Azeri side expects us not to tilt, in the Karabagh crisis, toward Armenia as a Western country, we have established on the international level an appropriate balance with Armenia by taking into consideration the principle of national interests, which is the main concern of every country."[38]

TAJIKISTAN'S CIVIL WAR

In 1992, a civil war broke out in Tajikistan. The main combatants were organized by regional affiliations, but also formally identified themselves with an ideological grouping (the "Communists," the "Islamists"). At the beginning of the war, Russia and Iran found themselves supporting opposing forces in the conflict. Russia supported the old-guard grouping based in the Leninabad and Kulyob regions. Russian troops remained deployed in Tajikistan, especially along its border with Afghanistan, and were involved in the war. Iran gave support to insurgents affiliated with the Islamic Renaissance Party (IRP) of Tajikistan, who were engaged in direct combat with the Russian soldiers in Tajikistan, especially along the border with Afghanistan. Tehran provided most of this support to the IRP and their allies in Iranian strong-holds in Afghanistan, which served as Tajik rebel bases. Iran also provided sanctuaries in Tehran to IRP leaders. When opportunities arose in late 1993, however, to cement its cooperation with Moscow, Tehran decided to abandon its all-out support for the IRP and worked to integrate the forces into a peace process and broad-based coalition supporting the local Russian ally to lead Tajikistan. Tehran refrained from the promotion of the establishment of an Islamic state in Tajikistan and abandoned the goal of spreading Islam in Tajikistan, which had a chance of gaining ground in that republic. The modification in Iran's policy in Tajikistan was a turning point in its development of close political relations with Russia. In fact, Tehran has concentrated its cultural diplomacy in Tajikistan in the sphere of promoting their common

---

37. *Tehran Times,* quoted in IRNA, January 7, 2002.

38. *Jomhuri-ye Eslami,* September 26, 2002, p. 16.

Persian language roots and disseminating the use of the Perso-Arabic script in the republic.

It seems that the Iranian foreign ministry took the lead in this pragmatic policy toward Tajikistan. Hard-line groups in Iran were openly critical of the shift in the Iranian policy:

It is over 15 months since a virtual coup was staged and Russian puppets took over in the Muslim-inhabited Republic of Tajikistan. For months the Persian-speaking Tajik people witnessed the catastrophic crimes perpetrated by the Russian forces and antipopular government of Uzbekistan in the country.

It is being said that the Russian first deputy foreign minister has been in Iran for a few days and had had talks with the leaders of some Islamic national Tajik groups. Reports of these meetings were carried in some foreign media and in some Moscow publications. However, the officials of our Foreign Ministry have apparently not deemed it necessary to disseminate the news of these talks inside as well![39]

Some evidence exists that groups in Iran's Ministry of Intelligence and other agencies continued clandestine support for the IRP, despite the change in policy by the Iranian Foreign Ministry. This can serve as an example of a way in which cultural goals of certain elements of the regime can continue to be promoted even if the regime officially gives preferences to material interests.

Promotion of Islam in Central Asia and the Caucasus

In the first decade after the independence of the Muslim-populated states of the former Soviet Union, Tehran was very calculated in its use of the export of Islam and the development of Islamic political forces in those states. Iran views the states of Central Asia and the Caucasus as an important area for its influence, especially as areas bordering on Iran. The staffs of the Iranian embassies in these states are both numerically and relatively large, testifying to the expansive Iranian activity in the region.

Iran often uses Islam instrumentally to pursue material state interests.[40] It promotes Islamic radicals and anti-regime movements when its state-level relations with a country are poor, such as with Uzbekistan or Azerbaijan. Tehran refrains from activities aimed at undermining very secular Muslim regimes, such as Turkmenistan and Kazakhstan, where

---

39. *Salam*, March 8, 1994, p. 12 (FBIS-NES-94-050).

40. For comparison, see also an analysis of Pakistan's instrumental use of Islam to promote its security agenda *vis-à-vis* India in Jessica Stern, "Pakistan's Jihad Culture," *Foreign Affairs*, Vol. 79, No. 6 (November–December 2000), pp. 115–126.

Iran enjoys favorable state-to-state relations. Iran promoted and supported the Islamic element in Tajikistan until this activity clashed with its material interests, which were served by the improvement of cooperation with Moscow. Tehran was careful not to support Islamic elements in states close to its border if this could cause destabilization, because the implications of this support could be costly for Iran's ruling regime. In places where it wanted to use an internal lever to coerce a policy change, Tehran at times supported secular oppositional elements to regimes it was not friendly with, such as Islam Karimov's regime in Uzbekistan, even when it had the opportunity to assist Islamic forces. Tehran adamantly opposes the regime in Tashkent, due to its pro-U.S. orientation and its subsequent adoption of many anti-Iranian policies, such as support for the U.S. sanctions on Iran. Despite the lack of Islamic content in the party's political goals or messages, Iran grants Uzbekistan's opposition party ERK activists refuge and provides the movement and its leader Muhammad Solich with a platform for transmitting anti-regime broadcasts into Uzbekistan through the official Voice of the Islamic Republic of Iran station in Mashad. The ERK broadcasts fiercely attack the Karimov regime in Tashkent, yet contain little Islamic content. In addition, the Voice of the Islamic Republic in Mashad also broadcasts statements made by the Islamic Movement of Uzbekistan (IMU) into the republic. In these broadcasts, the IMU calls for observation of Islamic laws, the creation of an Islamic state in Uzbekistan, criticizes Tashkent's ties with the United States and Israel, and attacks the Karimov regime.[41]

In Central Asia and the Caucasus, Iran has continued to maintain limited ties with Islamic elements which are in friendly states. It seems as though Tehran continues to maintain these ties in reserve, however, so that it can activate these groups and possess a means of leverage if the state-to-state interests change. In addition, as seen in the case of Tajikistan, it seems that some Iranian ministries and agencies continue to develop and maintain ties with some Islamic elements, even when the chief foreign policy mechanism has formally decided to refrain from actively supporting these elements.

States may commit to a certain cultural policy, but domestic politics or bureaucratic interests can derail its implementation, or at least bureaucratic islands within regimes can disrupt these policies. In contrast, when states decide to give precedence to security of the state and regime or other material considerations at the expense of cultural loyalty, islands of cultural piety often derail the state policy and conduct some independent

---

41. See, for instance, Voice of the Islamic Republic of Iran (broadcast from Mashad) in Uzbek, March 19, 1999.

actions. The continued activities of unsanctioned elements in the Iranian regime in support of Islamic elements abroad in cases when the mainstream foreign policy apparatus had determined that this support conflicted with the promotion of the material interests of the state—such as Tajikistan—highlights a way that culture can come into play in the foreign policy of a state. Those elements that are not considering the overall strategy of the state or the ruling regime, or that even they themselves support their own vitality through pursuing their own mandate, promote cultural goals. In the case of Iran, these elements often promoted Islamic groups abroad, in places that the chief state apparatus had declined support. It seems, however, that dissenting agencies and domestic inputs do not always promote a more cultural agenda, but even at times sway a regime toward more material policies.

Conclusion

This analysis of the Islamic Republic of Iran's foreign policy choices toward the states of Central Asia, the Caucasus, and Russia in the first decade after the Soviet Union's breakup demonstrate that common Islamic culture with a number of the actors in the region played little role in determining Tehran's foreign policy priorities in the region. Islamic solidarity was confined primarily to the rhetorical level, and even on the rhetorical level, Tehran was willing to use a "common cultural" argument with a number of opposing forces (for instance, both Armenians and Azerbaijanis) and was willing to promote common cultural themes which ran counter to the Islamic creed of the state (such as common ethnic identity or pre-Islamic traditions), all in the service of promoting the goals of the Iranian state and regime.

The sphere where common Islamic culture played the most minimal role was in the formation of alliances and policies toward conflicts. Iran's declaration of Islam as its state culture and commitment to promoting Islamic goals and solidarity has not endowed the analyst with predictive power relating to Iran's choice of allies. The discussion of the case of Iran revealed that common religious affiliation has played no significant role in Iran's choice of ally partners in Central Asia and the Caucasus or the sides that it chose to support in the conflicts raging in the area. Among all the states in the region, Tehran maintained the best relations with Christian-populated Armenia and the very secular Republic of Turkmenistan. Iran has the most problematic relations with, of all states in the region, Azerbaijan, despite its shared Shi'i Muslim identity. In addition, the determination of who was declared the "enemy" was based on Iran's strategic interests and not on religious identity. Russia battled Chechen Muslims, the Soviet Union attacked Azerbaijani Shi'a, Armenian expelled hundreds of thousands of Azerbaijani Muslims, and each time Iran blamed the United States.[42]

In Tehran, policymakers and analysts were keenly aware of the challenges presented by its ideological allegiance versus its state material interests. Open statements in the Iranian press and in policy debates indicate that Iranian policymakers were often clearly alert to the trade-off between material interests and religious interests, and when they declared their material preferences, they were conscious that they stood in contradiction of their declared state ideology. For instance, the Qom Friday prayer leader Ayatollah Ebrahim Amini-Najafabadi, said, at a time that Iran chaired the Organization of the Islamic Conference, "we are witnessing the onslaught of Moscow's Red Army on the Chechen Muslims. This is very distressing. Unfortunately, the Muslims are silent and the Organization of the Islamic Conference is not performing as it should."[43]

Also in the case of Azerbaijan, Iranian decision-makers were aware of their lack of Islamic loyalty in their alliance choices. *Jomhuri-ye Islami* pointed out the inconsistency in Tehran's official policies toward Azerbaijan:

Simultaneous with the consecutive and ceaseless acts of aggression by the Armenian Armed Forces against the territory of the Republic of Azerbaijan, an exclusive exhibition devoted to the industries of Armenia was inaugurated in Tehran. This occurred when only last week the Iranian Foreign Ministry issued a statement warning Armenia against its continued aggression and declared that Iran would not remain indifferent in this regard.[44]

What is especially interesting, however, is that even the presumably pious hard-liners often took a "material" approach in criticizing the Iranian Foreign Ministry. At times, they expressed the view that what was objectionable was not the abandonment of Islamic solidarity, but the damage to Tehran's public image as a state that professes to be the "Islamic Republic" to support and cooperate openly with Armenia or Chechnya a time that it is in battle with Muslims. For instance, *Jomhuri-ye Islami* wrote:

---

42. See, for instance, Ayatollah Ahmad Jannati broadcast by Tehran Voice of the Islamic Republic of Iran, January 6, 1995 (FBIS-NES-95-005); *Tehran Times* (December 25, 1994), p. 2; and IRNA (in English), January 3, 1995 (FBIS-NES-95-002).

43. Quoted in A. William Samii, "Iran and the Moscow Hostage Crises," *RFE/RL,* October 25, 2002.

44. *Jomhuri-ye Islami,* August 23, 1993, p. 2.

Unfortunately, either because of our silence, or some incorrect statements by some of the officials from our Foreign Affairs Ministry, the foreign media are broadcasting news to the rest of the world that Islamic Iran is standing alongside Russia with regard to the war in Chechnya. This claim is very unpleasant for the Islamic Republic of Iran. In this great war, *the diplomatic authorities of the Islamic Republic of Iran should not speak in such a way that international public opinion may conclude Iran is standing alongside Russia in this war. Although we do not expect Islamic Iran to position itself alongside the resistance of the Caucasian Muslims,* we should not act in a way that benefits the Russians by suppressing the Caucasian Muslims. *This would be a heavy blow to the credibility of an Islamic Iran that supports the revolutionary Muslims of the world.* Hopefully, the officials of the Iranian Foreign Affairs Ministry will pay more attention in this regard.[45]

In many discussions in the Iranian press beyond the foreign policy sphere, Iranian leaders relate to the inherent tension between Iran's material interests and its self-declared cultural interests. In its deliberations, Tehran uses the term "national interest" to refer to material state interests versus its declared official religious ideology. Parviz Esmaeili, the managing editor of the state-sponsored *Tehran Times* newspaper, stated that "in the Islamic system of governance one can never claim that justice and judiciary are exempt from taking into consideration national interests." He suggested that the judicial system, which is based on Islamic law, should take Iranian national interest in to consideration when making its judgments, and that in this context, "maintaining calm and security are the most important national interests."[46]

---

45. *Jomhuri-ye Islami,* October 9, 1999, p. 12 (FBIS-NES-1999-1201). Emphasis in original.

46. IRNA, November 13, 2002.

Chapter 9

Civilizational Identity and Foreign Policy: The Case of Iran

Ali M. Ansari

"This spirit acts as a binding element for all of us despite any tendency, any ideas or any preference that we might have. If we are honest, if we are Iranian, what binding element could be better for all of us, despite all the differences that we have in our views and preferences, than to seek to create a distinguished Iran and a proud nation? Concern for our homeland is the binding element for all of us. And what is this homeland? In a material sense, homeland is manifested in a piece of land. But one piece of land is no more valuable than any other. What makes a homeland valuable is the fact that this piece of land is where people with a common historical memory have shared a common experience. In other words, motherland is in our hearts and minds, it is in our views and perspectives."[1]

Few would argue with the fact that Iran and the United States have shared a problematic relationship in the last quarter-century since the advent of Iran's Islamic Revolution in 1979. These problems have been accentuated and exaggerated by the perception of intimacy which colored the relationship prior to 1979 and, while forged through experience, have been emphatically institutionalized through a vigorous process of intellectual rationalization which has emphasized a sense of alienation and distinction.[2] Arguably, the reason few had been able to foresee the revolution which had transformed the position of the United States in the Middle East and removed an "island of stability"[3] from an otherwise troubled

---

1. President Mohammad Khatami's speech to Iranian expatriates in New York, September 20,1998, in BBC SWB ME/3339 MED/1–2, dated September 23, 1998.

2. See for example, Nikki R. Keddie, "Can Revolutions be predicted?" in Nikki R. Keddie, ed., *Iran and the Muslim World: Resistance and Revolution* (London: Macmillan, 1995), pp. 13–33.

3. The phrase "island of stability" had been a staple of Iranian foreign policy rhetoric

region was because it was so obviously the product of irrational forces (in this case, "fundamentalist" Islam).[4] In intellectual terms, the predictive quality of Western social scientific analysis could be excused because a rational and reasonable approach to foreign policy analysis had failed to accommodate the possibility of irrationality on the part of the other. In sum, this was an entirely "reasonable" mistake to have made. Henceforth, the dominant realist paradigm in international relations would come under increasing scrutiny, modification, and even transformation, so that the errors of the past could be avoided and culture would be examined as an important factor. The accommodation of new realities, however, has been a limited affair. While "irrationality" may have been redefined as "culture," many would hold that it remains, by and large, something which afflicts the other. Even, for example, where culture and civilizational factors are accepted as partially determining one's own foreign policy, an implicit assumption of superiority also exists; a rational culture in binary conflict with a culture of irrationality, emphasizing perhaps, the cultural (and ideological) foundations of the method.[5]

This essay will argue that such a dichotomous approach is misleading insofar as it tends to posit distinct and self-contained "cultures." On the contrary, "cultures" are neither indigenously homogenous nor quarantined within local environments. In short, cultural boundaries may be regarded as porous, and the tendency toward analytical categorization should not ignore the reality of continuous—dialectical—interaction.[6] At the same time, while the cultural determinants of foreign policymaking

---

for some years. However, it is most memorably associated with President Jimmy Carter's speech on the occasion of his New Year's Eve visit to Iran on December 31, 1977; For highlights of the speech, see James A. Bill, *The Eagle and the Lion: the Tragedy of American-Iranian Relations* (New Haven, Conn.: Yale University Press, 1988), p. 233.

4. Such reactions to revolution were not without precedent; see Alexis de Tocqueville, *The Old Regime and the Revolution,* Vol. 1, François Furet and Françoise Melonio, eds., Alan S. Kahan, trans. (Chicago: University of Chicago Press, 1998), p. 95.

5. Since September 11, 2001, numerous texts have emerged to try and explain the curious cultural inheritance of "Muslims," building on and arguably misreading Samuel Huntington's *The Clash of Civilizations and the Remaking of the World Order* (London: Simon and Schuster, 1996). At one end of the spectrum are the contributions of Bernard Lewis in *What Went Wrong?* (London: Phoenix, 2002), pp. 200, while at the other are offerings such as Oriana Fallaci's *Rage and the Pride* (New York: Rizzoli, 2002), p. 187, a work which discards any pretense to scholarly analysis. For an extremely useful antidote to such arguments, see Dale F. Eickelman and James P. Piscatori, *Muslim Politics* (Princeton, N.J.: Princeton University Press, 1996).

6. See, for example, Huntington, *Clash of Civilizations,* p. 43.

may be accepted, one should be careful not to assign rationality to one and irrationality to the other. All cultures and ideological paradigms contain within themselves the germs of both tendencies and, crucially, affect and influence each other. This is not to argue for cultural relativism, simply for an acceptance of the importance and pervasiveness of cultural (ideological) determinants in conjunction with material interests.[7] Indeed, there can be little doubt that culture informs and in many ways determines the priorities that a given state affords itself when defining its foreign policy objectives, but culture does not exist in a vacuum and is itself shaped by material experience. Interests may be shaped by cultural norms, but an ideological worldview is itself defined (and in many ways propelled) by the harsh realities of experience. At the same time, it will be argued that each foreign policy is determined and informed by competing cultures representing differing (though not necessarily exclusive) values, resulting often in a contradictory mix of policy applications. Iran provides a useful case study for analyzing the limits of culture because of the multiplicity of its constituent cultures and the porous, often ambiguous relationship between these cultural determinants and its material interests.

Iran and the Limits of Culture

Iran, especially after the revolution of 1979, offers an exceptional case study of the limits of culture in determining foreign policy directions. This is so because, in the eyes of many Western analysts, revolutionary Iran occupies a particular political space which places it beyond the rational pale of foreign policy actors and into the realm of "irrational fanaticism," which cannot be understood but must either be contained or confronted. In this way, Iran is the quintessential Other; a situation for which, arguably, the Iranians—or to use the more classical designation, the Persians—are well suited. For many analysts, bewildered by the dynamic of revolution, Iran fit the mold of what has been defined by the apposite term, a "martyr state." Indeed, the overthrow of Mohammad Reza Shah Pahlavi and the replacement of the ostensibly pro-Western authentically national Pahlavi state, with a distinctly Shi'a Islamic Republic, in which the virtues of martyrdom were being proclaimed, only seemed to confirm this assessment. Iranians, far from being the rational Persians of the Shah's era, had suddenly revealed themselves to be fanatical Muslims possessed of a martyr complex and devoid of rational judgement. As one

7. See Max Weber, *The Protestant Ethic and the Spirit of Capitalism* (London: Routledge, 1992), p. 183.

former Pahlavi technocrat argued, "Almost willfully, they suppressed their better judgment, refused to involve themselves in meaningful analysis, insisted on total denigration of the prevailing system, fabricated evidence of the nation's socio-economic destruction, exaggerated the reality of political tyranny, and clung to a utopian panacea that simply was not contained in the premises of the revolution."[8] Reports of human wave attacks during the brutal 1980–1988 Iran-Iraq War only served to compound this image and effectively institutionalize it.[9]

As this apparent transition indicates, another important factor for this essay's purposes is the cultural plurality of Iranian society. The notion of "culture" is an integral aspect of Iranian identity; this is particularly true following the revolution, when identity was defined in cultural terms to contrast it more explicitly with what was seen as the ethnochauvinism of the Pahlavis, which many considered to border on Persian racism. On the contrary, argued the intellectual heirs of the revolution, the exclusivity of Persianism was to be supplanted by an inclusive Iranian-ness, which, through the incorporation of the variety of ethnic groups that constituted the Iranian state, would be defined in cultural terms.[10] Their model for this was the *kultur-nation* of the German Romanticists. Culture, of course, is a difficult concept to define. In the Persian language, the word—*farhang*—encompasses a number of different meanings and associations, denoting not only culture, but education, and the arts. In other words, in Persian—as in English—the term for culture frequently denotes what in the West may be understood as "high culture," and as such its associations with the concept of civilization should be clear. Iranian culture is a vital ingredient in the composition of Iranian civilization, that totality of views and ideas which as Toynbee argued,

---

8.   Gholam R. Afkhami, *The Iranian Revolution: Thanatos on a National Scale* (Washington, D.C.: The Middle East Institute, 1985), p. 4. One should never forget that initial interpretations of the Islamic Revolution among Western observers derived much of its information from the "victims" rather than the "victors."

9.   The Iranians, however, with a surfeit of manpower over technology, were doing no different than the Soviets during the "Great Patriotic War" (1941–1945).

10.   The Iranian population is composed of a variety of different ethnic groups, including Persians, Azerbaijanis, Turkmen, Arabs, and Kurds, and while their integration has been facilitated through education and the modern mass media, differences undoubtedly persist. For details, see John W. Limbert, *Iran: At War with History;* (London: Croom Helm, 1987), pp. 19–28; and Brenda Shaffer, *Borders and Brethren: Iran and the Challenge of Azerbaijani Identity* (Cambridge, Mass.: MIT Press, 2002). It should be stressed that this paper relates to *ethnie* as fluid constructs; see Max Weber, *Economy & Society*, Vol. I, (London: University of California Press, 1978), pp. 387–393.

"comprehend without being comprehended by others." In this way, the concept of a civilization may be usefully related to that of hegemony, as defined by the Italian Marxist Antonio Gramsci.[11] Such an association would certainly permit a more rigorous political analysis and recognize the ideological (and hence political) dimension of culture and civilization.

While Huntington allocates Iranian (or Persian) civilization to a subset of a broader Islamic civilization, many Iranians would disagree and concur instead with Toynbee, who argued the case for an "Iranic" civilization, whose distinctive cultural contributions place it on a par, or in some cases beyond, the Islamic categorization.[12] In distinguishing an "Iranian Islamic" civilization, Iranians are not only appropriating the religion to the nation (the development in essence of a religious nationalism), they are highlighting the belief that Iran enjoys a privileged position among the world's cultures in possessing the characteristics of civilization.[13] It may be argued that this is simply a matter of preference and emphasis, but it does serve to highlight the existence of competing cultures within the modern polity of Iran. While Mohammad Reza Shah Pahlavi sought to drive his people toward the Great Civilization by emphasizing the splendors of Iran's ancient pre-Islamic Aryan past, many of his subjects disagreed and argued that Iranian civilization was in fact being denigrated by a willful ignorance of Islam and subservience to the West. This sin of omission had to be addressed, and in the aftermath of the Islamic

---

11. For further details see Chantal Mouffe, "Hegemony and Ideology in Gramsci", in Chantal Mouffe, ed., *Gramsci & Marxist Theory* (London: Routledge and Kegan Paul, 1979), pp. 168–204.

12. Arnold J. Toynbee, *A Study of History*, Vol. I (Oxford: Oxford University Press, 1934), p. 72, note 2. Toynbee explains his categorization thus: "'Iranic' is less cumbrous than 'Perso-Turkish,' and it is not really less accurate. 'Perso-Turkish' expresses the fact that most of the peoples in the original home of this society spoke either Persian or Turkish vernaculars (as one might coin the name 'Latino-Teutonic' to express a corresponding fact about Western Christendom). 'Iranic,' however, expresses the more significant fact that the vehicle of the new culture which was emerging in this region was the classical language and literature of Iran."

13. This view, which includes its own "myth of origin," was probably best expressed by President Khatami in his speech to Iranian expatriates in the United States in September 1998, when he referred to the mythology and "spirit" of Iran (see note 1 above); BBC SWB ME/3339 MED/1–2, dated September 23, 1998. For the localization of religion, see Anthony D. Smith, *The Ethnic Origins of Nations* (London: Blackwell, 1986), pp. 105–125. For an extreme example of this trend, see Houshang Tale, *Tarikhcheh-ye Maktab-e Pan-Iranism* (The history of the doctrine of Pan-Iranism), (Tehran: Samarkand, 1381/2002)

Revolution, Islamic Iran was emphasized at the expense of pre-Islamic Iran. Yet, as will be seen, this was not the replacement of one cultural paradigm by another, but a recognition that modern Iranian civilization was the fortunate heir of three particular and distinctive cultures. As the influential lay religious philosopher, Abdolkarim Soroush succinctly argued: "We Iranian Muslims are the inheritors and carriers of three cultures at once. As long as we ignore our links with the elements in our triple cultural heritage and our cultural geography, constructive social and cultural action will elude us. . . . The three cultures that form our common heritage are of national, religious, and Western origins."[14]

RELIGIOUS CULTURE

As Soroush argues further in the same article, "Islamic culture . . . is qualitatively and quantitatively the dominant culture of Iran."[15] While it is certainly true that religion has played a formative role in the defining of Iranian foreign policy objectives, it is important not to exaggerate its significance, not only because of the impact of experience (especially the Iran-Iraq War between two Muslim-populated states), but because the precise meaning of "Islam" (and specifically *Iranian* Shi'a Islam) was in a constant state of flux. Moreover, the interpretation of Islam as a factor of foreign policy varies, especially since Iran emphasizes Shi'a Islam, which can be more inimical with other Muslim sects than with non-Muslims. Also, Shi'a Islamic identity is often emphasized in Iran as a uniquely Iranian form of Islam and as a way of severing ties to the Arab-centric mainstream Islam. Perhaps the best way to observe this is to assess the process of Islamization which occurred as a reaction to the Pahlavi regime in the revolution's aftermath. Just as the Pahlavi regime was perceived as overtly secular, even laical in its approach to both domestic and foreign policy, so the revolutionary elite sought to emphasize in their policies everything that they perceived as having been rejected by the Shah. Principally, this entailed an intense injection of Islamic rhetoric into all policy discussions, non-alignment in the international arena, and, as with previous revolutions, a commitment to the oppressed and generally unenlightened of the world. This apparent transformation of Iranian policy from a secular to a religious world-view was confirmed both by Western policy analysts—anxious, as noted above, to inject a sense of irrationality into Iranian behavior—and traumatized emigres whose tales of chaos

14. Abdolkarim Soroush, "The Three Cultures," in Mahmoud Sadri and Ahmad Sadri, trans., *Reason, Freedom, and Democracy in Islam* (Oxford: Oxford University Press), p. 156.

15. Ibid, p. 162.

and fanaticism added fuel to the burgeoning fire.[16] The image of the Islamic Republic of Iran as a fundamentalist state—erratic, anarchic, and possessed of a dangerous tendency toward martyrdom that had been forged in the intense heat of revolution—has embedded itself within the Western mind-set and has become a staple of Western popular discourse.

For all its relevance—especially to the early period of the revolution—this revolutionary myth provides only part of the picture, and indeed, as one noted commentator has argued, "For all its apparent exceptionalism, the Iranian Revolution of 1979 followed, in many respects, the pattern of other modern revolutions."[17] Indeed, as Fred Halliday argues, for all the vaunted expressions of Islamic solidarity, there was much in the rhetoric (and actions) of the revolution which drew on anti-imperialism and left-wing ideologies.[18] The behavior of the Iranian state should have been recognized as revolutionary rather than as conveniently irrational and could arguably be better understood as having been drawn from different traditions of logic than from those of the West. Put simply, their interests were defined by different priorities, although even these priorities revealed more continuity with the last decade of Pahlavi rule than would at first appear. The notion of "neither east nor west" first entered official government discourse during the premiership of Iranian Prime Minister Amir Abbas Hoveyda in 1970 when he was attempting to explain the unique nature of the White Revolution (subsequently renamed the Shah-People Revolution).[19] Similarly, the official designation of casualties as martyrs, was not a novelty introduced at the time of the Islamic Revolution.[20]

Nevertheless, one should not underestimate the role of religious conviction in driving the actions of the early revolutionaries. Having successfully overthrown what many considered to be an omnipotent Shah and

16. It is worth noting that de Tocqueville considered the universalist pretensions of the French Revolution to qualify it as a "religious" revolution; Alexis de Tocqueville, *The Ancien Regime and The French Revolution* (Manchester: Fontana, 1966), p. 41.

17. Fred Halliday, *Revolution and World Politics* (London: Macmillan, 1999), p. 124.

18. See also Ervand Abrahamian, "Fundamentalism or Populism?" in Ervand Abrahamian, ed., *Khomeinism* (London: I. B. Tauris, 1993), pp. 13–38.

19. BBC SWB ME/3562/D/1, dated December 27, 1970—Hoveida's speech to the Central Committee of the Iran Novin Party, dated December 15, 1970. See also BBC SWB ME/3568/D/1, dated December 28, 1970—Hoveida's statement to Iran Novin Party meeting, dated December 22, 1970. The *Islamic* revolution was in many ways following a well-trodden tradition in modern Iranian politics.

20. See, for example, FO 248 1494, file 101/5, Summary of *Mardum,* File No. 1015/87/50, dated August 19, 1950; FO 371 180804 EP 1942/6, dated April 12, 1965; *Rastakhiz,* 6th Bahman 2535/1355 / January 22, 1977, p. 1.

humiliated his powerful patrons, an empowered generation of idealized Iranian youth felt that there was very little that they could not achieve. But a recognition of this righteous revolutionary fervor should not preclude an appreciation of the internal logic of many of their actions or indeed that other rationalizations had an input in the decision-making process. The seizure of the U.S. embassy on November 4, 1979, is regarded with some justification by observers as a supreme act of political folly rather than one of immediate political expediency that was supported by the embattled authorities, not only because of the perception that a foreign victory was essential if domestic anarchy was to be avoided, but also by the widespread (and cultivated) fear that the United States, after having admitted the ailing Shah for medical treatment (a reality viewed with suspicion), was preparing for a rerun of the 1953 coup orchestrated against Iranian Premier Dr. Mohammad Mosaddeq.

In other words, an act of illegality was justified and rationalized on the basis of a collective historical memory. Indeed, while many Iranians, soon to be preoccupied by other problems, considered the hostage crisis a detail of history justified by U.S. support for the Shah, it was for the American collective memory to be the definitive moment which was to define U.S. attitudes toward Iran and belie the neorealist fiction that U.S. material interests devoid of cultural (historical) determinants drove U.S. foreign policy toward Iran. Hawks on both sides, for instance, found it convenient to forget that diplomatic ties between the United States and Iran had not been severed with the overthrow of the Shah; that many thought the transition, while tense and undoubtedly antagonistic, could be managed; and that indeed the first occupation of the U.S. embassy in February 1979 had ended on the express authority of the Ayatollah Rouhollah Khomeini, who clearly did not interpret such an action as either legal or expedient.[21]

Similarly, the war against Iraq could not have been fought without a high level of religious fervor, and veterans testify that religious conviction played an important role in rationalizing the suffering that many undoubtedly endured. Yet the harsh experience of war is arguably the ultimate test of any ideological drive, and it was soon apparent that faith alone could not win the war against Iraq. The war clearly tempered the ideology, but it could not eliminate all its excesses; strategy was arguably

21. BBC SWB ME/6043/A/14, February 15, 1979—"Developments in Iran," Tehran Home Service, February 14, 1979. Also, BBC SWB ME/6044/A/4—"Developments in Iran," Tehran Home Service, February 14, 1979. The U.S. embassy was not the only embassy to be occupied during the year; both the Moroccan and British embassies had suffered the same fate, and the fact that all occupations had been ended arguably led to a sense of complacency on November 4.

sacrificed to the needs of mobilization, which dictated the continuation of grandiose rhetoric over the realities of military possibility. Thus, in order to excite the masses to war, the government portrayed it as a new Islamic conquest, although significantly with Iranians rather than Arabs in the lead role.[22] Still, the government was forced to use both religious and overtly national slogans (such as the call to defend the Holy Fatherland[23]), recognizing the need to draw on the other constituent cultures, while the necessities of war forced a review of a number of religious injunctions and their consequent modernization.

Two significant events in particular reveal the limits of culture in this period, although their consequences indicate the complexity of the reciprocal relationship between the notion of material interests and cultural interests in determining foreign policy. The first was the Iran-Contra Affair, the revelations of which probably caused more shock in the United States than in Iran, but an event which revealed a good deal more ruthless calculation in the pursuit of foreign policy. Suffering under the constraints of an arms embargo, Islamic Iran saw no contradiction in placing its immediate material interests over the dictates of revolutionary principle and purchasing arms from the United States via Israel. While the precise mechanics of the negotiations remain shrouded in secrecy, it seems highly unlikely that such an operation would have been initiated without the tacit approval of Ayatollah Khomeini. Similarly, for all of U.S. President Ronald Reagan's subsequent amnesia, his claim of being unaware of the generalities (if not the details) of this covert operation lacks credibility. That it proved disturbing to many Americans highlighted the gulf between the continuing *Realpolitik* of senior policymakers (who saw clear material gains in reaching out to Iran), and the attitudes of the U.S. public weaned on the memory of the hostage crisis. The lessons that each state derived from the experience were, however, diametrically opposed. Iranian politicians, epitomized by then Speaker of Parliament, Ali Akbar Hashemi Rafsanjani, became convinced that a ruthless realism dictated U.S. policy, and that culture was a secondary issue. U.S. policymakers, on the other hand, burnt by the public humiliation of failure, reasoned that culture could no longer be ignored.

Indeed, the realities of war resulted in one of Ayatollah Khomeini's more remarkable speeches, which, as with the Iran-Contra Affair, was both enormously significant and divergently interpreted. In January 1988, in a response to a somewhat verbose and meandering speech by

---

22. The belief in some circles that the Iranians were the heirs of true Islam (i.e., Iranian Shi'a Islam) could of course be supported by selected *hadith* of the Prophet.

23. The parallels with Soviet policy in World War II are striking.

then President Ali Khamene'i concerning the legal powers and preroga-
tives and Islamic Government, Ayatollah Khomeini outlined the following striking injunction:

I should state that the government which is part of the absolute vice-regency
of the Prophet of God . . . is one of the primary injunctions of Islam and has
priority over all other secondary injunctions, even prayers, fasting, and hajj
. . . the ruler is authorised to demolish a mosque or a house which is the path
of a road and to compensate the owner for his house. The ruler can close
down mosques if need be, or can even demolish a mosque which is the
source of harm if its harm cannot be remedied without demolition. The government is empowered to unilaterally revoke any Shari'ah agreements which
it has concluded with the people when those agreements are contrary to the
interests of the country or of Islam. It can also prevent any devotional or non-
devotional affair if it is opposed to the *interests* of Islam and for so long as it
is so."[24]

Khomeini seemed to signalling in no uncertain terms that the interests of
the state should have priority over Islamic law, and though controversial,
the Muslim ruler could either overturn or suspend Islamic injunctions (or
both), if the interests of the state were threatened. This was certainly
the way the interpretation was understood by Ali Akbar Hashemi
Rafsanjani, who, with an eye on the presidency, regarded Khomeini's
comments as official religious sanction for the politics of pragmatism that
he had hoped to emphasize.[25] Indeed, for Rafsanjani and his supporters,
the decree was a blow to those reactionary conservatives whose stubborn
adherence to dogmatism was adversely affecting the functioning of the
Islamic Republic. The conservatives, however, interpreted Khomeini's
comments in a radically different direction, noting the primacy of the
Islamic State and the use of the term absolute vice-regent. Khomeini, they
argued, was not enjoining the people to place the state above religion. On
the contrary, he was forcefully arguing for the suspension of all restrictions if the interests of the *Islamic* state were threatened. The definition of
interest was therefore very much beholden to one's understanding of the
state, and each side adhered to a different logic. Not surprisingly,
Khomeini practiced the ambiguity that he preached, showing characteristic pragmatism in making the decision to reverse years of official government policy and accept in 1988 the UN-sponsored cease-fire in the war

---

24. BBC SWB ME/0043 A/7, January 8, 1988; Tehran Home Service, January 7, 1988.
Emphasis added.

25. See BBC SWB ME/0043 A/8, January 8, 1988; Tehran Home Service, dated January 7, 1988.

against Iraq; he followed this with a dramatic *fatwa* condemning the British writer Salman Rushdie to death for allegedly insulting the Prophet Mohammad and, by extension, committing apostasy. If religion had its limits, so, quite clearly, had pragmatism.

NATIONAL CULTURE

If the first decade of the revolution can be characterized as the era of confrontation and counter-hegemony, in terms of identifying and reaffirming a cultural space between the West and Islamic Iran, the period of Rafsanjani's presidency—the era of reconstruction beginning in 1989—as the new president was to define it, sought to replace confrontation with mutually beneficial interest. Put another way, if the emphasis had been on the religious aspects of nationalism, Rafsanjani now sought to redress the imbalance by appealing to overtly national sentiment and justifying policies on the grounds of national interest. Indeed, the new president sought to present himself as nothing if not pragmatic with a keen eye on specifically national matters, although his interests were driven not only by a desire to leave a legacy of reconstruction, but, more importantly, by the search for commercial advantage. Rafsanjani was the merchant president with a strong populist streak, and he sought to drive reconstruction by cultivating the interests and expanding the opportunities for the mercantile bourgeoisie (as epitomized in his own person), whom he regarded as his quintessential constituency and the driving force behind reconstruction. Economic reconstruction, of course, required better relations with the outside world, and Rafsanjani seemed certain that mutual material interest would prevail over any cultural differences. Even disagreements with the United States would be overcome by the overwhelming temptations offered by economic advantage. After all, it was noted, the United States enjoyed buoyant economic relations with a host of countries with whom it shared little cultural affinity, or indeed, which held completely contrary values. In fact, Rafsanjani's administration arguably heralded a return to high *Realpolitik* in its understanding of international relations (although his administration singularly refused to recognize the reality of Iran's modest position within the international system), and a number of international relations institutes were inaugurated and staffed with eager academics, most of whom had been educated in the United States and were devotees of the school of pragmatism.[26]

---

26. This attempt to out-intellectualize and out-rationalize the West often took some striking turns. For example, one of the key proponents of this movement, Mohammad Javad Larijani, could offer the following assessment of the Islamic Republic: "While an Islamic society is not at ease with technical rationality, it finds itself quite in harmony

One of the ways in which this renewed affectation for pragmatism made itself felt was through a gradual reassertion of national interest.[27] Of course, the nation had never really gone away. The revolution, for all its Islamic rhetoric and pretensions about the unity of the *umma*,[28] had at its core a nationalist imperative that was reflected in the composition of the new constitution. Thus, for example, Khomeini himself instructed that all elected officials had to have been born in Iran.[29] Furthermore, in broad cultural terms, while there was every attempt to wipe away the excesses of the last Shah, the revolutionary administration did not attempt to substitute the Islamic calendar that is in common use in most Muslim-populated states in the world for the calendar introduced in 1924 under Reza Khan (who became Reza Shah Pahlavi in 1925), complete with months named after Persian mythological figures.[30] The onset of war, of course, simply confirmed this trend,[31] and after the war, the importance of the nation to Iranian identity could not be easily ignored. Rafsanjani actively played the patriotic card[32] in order to mobilize an exhausted population toward reconstruction and, above all, to attract investment—not only from the business elites within the country, but especially from the many thousands who had left the country. Regional changes were also forcing a reconception of policy, especially when the collapse of the Soviet Union reignited the "Great Game" in Central Asia and the Cauca-

with the authentic one. Therefore, Islamic modernity goes far beyond historical modernity and is basically a post-modern phenomenon." "Islamic Society & Modernism," in *The Iranian Journal for International Affairs*, Vol. 7, No 1 (Spring 1995), p. 58. See also the editorial in the *Tehran Times*, February 23, 1993, which boldly proclaimed now to be the time for "realism."

27. See, for example, Hossein Seifzadeh, *Estrateji-ye Melli va Siyasatgozari-ye khareji* (National Strategy and Foreign Policy-Making), *The Journal of Foreign Policy*, Vol. 7, (Winter 1994), pp. 705–722.

28. The *umma* is the greater nation of all believing Muslims.

29. Vanessa Martin, *Creating an Islamic State: Khomeini and the Making of a New Iran* (London: I. B. Tauris, 2000) p. 166; see also David Menashri, *Iran: A Decade of Revolution and War* (London: Holmes and Meier, 1990) p. 120.

30. See Marvin Zonis, *Majestic Failure: The Fall of the Shah* (London: The University of Chicago Press, 1991), pp. 81–83.

31. Significantly, "Persian" names were already dominating over "Islamic" names among newborn babies as early as 1982; see Nader Habibi, "Popularity of Islamic and Persian Names in Iran before and after the Islamic Revolution," *International Journal of Middle East Studies*, Vol. 24 (1992), pp. 253–260.

32. For example, he was the first post-revolutionary leader to pay a visit to Persepolis in April 1991. For further details of this process, see Shireen T. Hunter, *Iran after Khomeini* (New York: Center for Strategic and International Studies, 1992), pp. 92–100.

sus. The Islamic Republic suddenly found itself handicapped by its overt Shi'ism, while in contrast, Persian culture was very much in demand. Indeed, as some Central Asian states rediscovered their Persian cultural heritage with some enthusiasm,[33] as well as with a healthy dose of diplomatic tact,[34] Iran's national reticence seemed curiously out of place; some commentators argued for a vigorously nationalistic agenda in Central Asia, demanding that the two treaties of Gulestan (1813) and Turkmenchai (1829), through which Tsarist Russia had annexed Iran's Caucasian territories, be discarded as irrelevant. Such language was calculated to appeal to national emotions, since most Iranians were taught that Iran's great power status had been ended by these treaties. Even traditionally conservative newspapers were hard-pressed to disguise their nationalist indignation, with *Keyhan International* arguing that these states had suffered a mere "seventy years of artificial separation."[35] Consequently, it was not long before the national economic and cultural interests were being pursued.[36] At the same time, national zealotry was tempered by the new pragmatism that had been reinforced by the dramatic crushing of Iraq in the 1991 Gulf War. Iran's military vulnerability was apparent to all but the most ideologically committed.[37] A more consensual, cooperative, and constructive foreign policy was encouraged, with priorities firmly fixed on economic reconstruction.

Unfortunately, the enthusiasm which greeted the Rafsanjani administration, by both a domestic constituency exhausted by revolution and

---

33. President Rafsanjani, for example, made a point of noting in his New Year speech of March 1992 that Novruz was now being celebrated throughout Central Asia; see BBC SWB ME/1336 A/3–6, March 23, 1992, Vision of the Islamic Republic of Iran, March 20, 1992. For broader discussions see Farhard Kazemi and Zohreh Ajdari, "Ethnicity, Identity and Politics: Central Asia and Azerbaijan between Iran and Turkey," and Shireen T. Hunter, "Iran and Transcaucasia in the Post-Soviet Era," both in David Menashri, ed., *Central Asia Meets the Middle East* (London: Frank Cass, 1998), pp. 52–73, 98–128.

34. Initially, even Azerbaijani officials would proclaim their affection for Iran when diplomatic necessity required it; see Tamelan Karayev's comments on his visit to Iran in BBC SWB ME/1302 A/9, February 12, 1992, Voice of the Islamic Republic of Iran, February 9, 1992.

35. See BBC SWB ME 1334 A/10–11, dated May 26, 1993, IRNA, May 24, 1993.

36. See, for example, Edmund Herzig, *The New Caucasus: Armenia, Azerbaijan and Georgia* (London: RIIA, 1999), p. 111. Also Eric Hooglund, "Iran and Central Asia," in Anoushiravan Ehteshami, ed., *From the Gulf to Central Asia* (Exeter: University of Exeter Press, 1994), pp. 114–128.

37. It is difficult of course to distinguish between the religious and nationalist dimensions of commitment, and certainly in Iran's case, a combination of the two is better suited with any distinction resulting from emphasis.

war and an international business community intrigued by the apparent opening up of Iran, was to be misplaced. Fundamental to the failure was the inability of the two business communities to connect. Rafsanjani, with his crude understanding of interest, had believed that capital and commercial advantage would be sufficient to bridge the cultural gap. Quite apart from the fact that the Iranian mercantile community could not relate to the industrial capitalists of the West, the Iranian administration had clearly misunderstood the cultural dimensions of Western foreign policymaking. It was not enough to be counter-hegemonic and nonconfrontational; the West could not be enticed by economic interest alone. The double humiliation of the hostage crisis and the Iran-Contra Affair had hardened U.S. attitudes, while the Rushdie affair, increasingly regarded by Iranian officials as a trivial irrelevancy, had developed into a point of principle among Western elites. The cultural context was simply against the Islamic Republic, such that no major Western politician was prepared to take the domestic political risks.

In the aftermath of the Iran-Contra scandal and with threats of an investigation into the October Surprise, President George H. W. Bush simply was not going to risk his election prospects by responding positively to Rafsanjani's measures to encourage Hizbollah to free the Western hostages in Beirut. For the Iranians, this lack of response was taken as a sign of continuing bad faith. Other problems, however, compounded this situation. While Rafsanjani attempted to signal a more moderate Iranian position toward the Arab-Israeli conflict, continued hardline rhetoric, especially from Supreme Leader Ayatollah Khamene'i, continued support for Palestinian and Lebanese militants, in particular Hizbollah,[38] and an explicit policy of opposition to the Middle East peace process (which of course played well among ordinary Arabs, although increasingly less so with the Iranian population itself)[39], all served to make the bridge unsustainable. Any hopes Iran had for cooperation with Europe were rudely dashed when it became apparent that even economically pragmatic Eu-

---

38.   These groups were referred to as resistance fighters in Iran, and, of course, as terrorists by the United States. While support for Hizbollah, in large part because of the Shi'i affiliation, has remained consistent and popular, support for extreme Palestinian groups has enjoyed less popularity among ordinary Iranians and is occasionally justified on the purely *Realpolitik* grounds of antagonizing and ensuring the preoccupation of Israel. Interestingly, this is a view increasingly used to justify support for Hizbollah—that it has less to do with religious affiliation and more with a need to maintain a "deterrence" against Israel.

39.   The Iranian government was in the habit of holding alternative Palestinian conferences at times calculated to irritate the United States, for example in October 1991; BBC SWB ME/1193 A6–7, dated October 3, 1991, IRNA report October 1, 1991.

rope could not ignore the fact that Iranian dissidents were being murdered by the Iranian regime on European territory.[40] Again, the differences in attitudes were striking; some Iranian officials simply could not understand why an internal matter (the elimination of dissidents) should affect inter-state relations. The final nail in the coffin of this brief foray into pragmatism came in 1995, when the Iranian government authorized the awarding of an oil contract to Conoco, a U.S. company. As far as post-revolutionary Iran was concerned, this was an unprecedented and bold move that would provide the ultimate test for the realist theory of international relations. It proved to be a dramatic failure, and rather than help forge a consensus through interest, the dramatic declaration of extensive formal sanctions, along with secondary sanctions targeted against those companies seeking to invest in Iran's oil industry,[41] reversed any progress that might have been made and thrust U.S.-Iranian relations into their worst crisis since the seizure of the U.S. Embassy sixteen years earlier.

WESTERN CULTURE

The Conoco affair and its consequences marked the definitive end to a policy which was already coming under intense criticism within Iran, for the simple reason that many people considered the inherent, ideological antagonism to the West not only to be counterproductive and against Iran's interests, but in contradiction to Iran's own complex identity. Just as Rafsanjani had sought to build his foreign policy on a network of vested economic interests, so too had he sought to construct such a network domestically—and arguably with considerably more success. Those outside this loop—the vast majority of the population—were not impressed with Rafsanjani's economic policy, and the gross disparities in wealth that it seemed to encourage. They were even less impressed with the apparent alliance of convenience Rafsanjani had developed with hardline conservatives, which had not only hampered Iran's foreign relations but seemed to belie Rafsanjani's nationalist credentials. The hardliners, as noted above, drew a much more authoritarian interpretation from Khomeini's remarks about the interests of the state, and in the face of the apparent failure of pragmatism, saw the salvation of the Islamic state in the vigorous pursuit of such policies. Yet for many people, such policies

---

40. Relations were especially soured by the Mykonos trial, in which Iranian officials were convicted in Germany for the murder of dissidents at the Mykonos restaurant in Berlin. See David Menashri, *Post-Revolutionary Politics in Iran* (London: Frank Cass, 2001), pp. 103, 201–202.

41. For extensive detail of the sanctions policy, see Hossein Alikhani, *Sanctioning Iran: Anatomy of a Failed Policy* (London: I. B. Tauris, 2000).

seemed to contradict nationalist pretensions, since to be a genuine Iranian nationalist, it was argued, one had to appreciate and respect the will of the Iranian people; in sum you had to be a democrat (at least by inclination). Hard-line conservatives dismissed this notion as nothing less than the pollution of authentic Islam by Western ideas. What mattered was the Islamic State, in which sovereignty belonged to Allah and his divinely appointed and absolute vice-regent, in this case the Supreme Leader Ali Khamene'i. There was no place for a republic in the Islamic world view.[42]

Herein lies the most intriguing and much misunderstood aspect of Iran's civilizational identity: its relationship with the West. For Iran's foreign policy over the last quarter-century, in the very least, can be said to have been shaped and defined by the way in which its politicians have sought to navigate this relationship, in particular its relationship with the United States. As has been noted, for all the anti-imperialist rhetoric, Iran's relations with the West remained curiously ambivalent for most of the first year of the revolution. While governments may have been roundly criticized, individual Westerners visiting Iran discovered very little personal animosity.[43] On the contrary, there seemed to be an element of confusion insofar as many Iranians coveted (and continue to covet) visas for Western countries. The seizure of the U.S. embassy, however, changed the entire dynamic, and as one revolutionary leader noted with some irony, the United States was not only back at the top of the agenda, but became *the* priority for the revolution. Indeed, for all the success of the practical eviction, the Islamic Republic now found itself defined against the very foe it had sought to remove.[44] Arguably, it was the beginning of a mutual obsession.[45] The point to be made, and regularly overlooked, is that whether as friend or foe, Iran enjoyed an intimate relation-

42. For an excellent critique of this authoritarian tendency, see Abdollah Nuri, *Shokoran-e Eslah* (Hemlock of Reform), (Tehran: Tar-e No, 1378/1999–2000), pp. 117–121; see also Mohsen Kadivar, *Baha-ye Azadi: defa'at Mohsen Kadivar* (The Price of Freedom: the Defence of Mohsen Kadivar), (Tehran: Ghazal, 1378/1999–2000).

43. See, for example, John Simpson, *Strange Places, Questionable People* (London: Pan, 1999), pp. 219–220.

44. Discussions about the merits of relations with the United States were a staple of Iranian political life. See, for example, *Iran Focus*, June 1990, p. 1, which notes that factional fighting over the issue of direct talks with the United States were (yet again) gaining momentum. Note that this is before the Iraqi invasion of Kuwait. See also BBC SWB ME/1698 A/4, May 26, 1993, IRNA, May 24, 1993, during the presidential elections of that year.

45. On the Iranian side, this obsession was reflected in the print media and books; see for example, *Rabeteh?! (Relations?!) Salam*, Teheran, 1378/1999; *Nowruz,*

ship with the West and its epitome, the United States. The counter-hegemony that it had sought to construct was defined and hence related to the hegemonic challenge posed by the West.

The practical lessons of the war and the era of reconstruction encour-aged Iranian intellectuals to rethink their understanding of the philoso-phy of international relations which would also help resolve some of the many contradictions which continued in the Iranian worldview.[46] For a civilization that aimed to contrast itself with that of the West, it was strik-ing how much it had borrowed from the West; starting with the concept of a republic. Since Ayatollah Khomeini had been insistent on the use of the term, the desire to dismiss it on the part of conservatives proved to be problematic.[47] Furthermore, it was quite clear that many of the revolu-tion's highest officials had been educated in the West and felt none the worse for it, while more interestingly, the *narrative* of revolution which was being constructed (by mullah and layman alike), sought to situate Iran's Islamic Revolution within a historical pedigree of revolutionary movements that were sourced to the French Revolution and essentially European. No event better encapsulated this moment that President Khatami's visit to the Pantheon in Paris and his evocation of French En-lightenment philosopher Montesquieu. The intellectual consequence of all this was that hegemonies could neither be considered distinctive and inherently confrontational nor could they necessarily be conceived of as distinct but collaborative where mutual interest dictated; rather, the rela-tionship was far more integrated and intimate than either party would like to admit. History provided ample evidence: Islam (Persia) and the West (Christendom) were after all sister civilizations, and the Islamic Re-public was (in theory at least) the living embodiment of this ideal. Such were the ideas encapsulated by Soroush's argument and implicit in the introduction of the policy of "dialogue of civilizations."

The concept of a dialogue of civilizations, formally introduced by President Khatami during a speech to the Islamic Conference Organiza-tion, then being held in Tehran in December 1997, was more than a diplo-

---

19 Ordibehesht 1381 / May 9, 2002, p. 5; many articles of course dealt with the coup against Mosaddeq: Khordad 28 Mordad 1378 / August 19, 1999 p. 6; Neshat, 28 Mordad 1378 / August 19, 1999, pp. 8–9; Jame'eh, 28 Mordad 1377 / August 19, 1998, p. 6.

46.   See, for example, the interesting article by Mohammad Reza Dehshiri *"Charkhe-ye Armangerayi va Vaghegerayi dar siyasat-e khareji-e Jomhuri-ye Islami-ye Iran"* (Idealism and Realism Cycle in the Foreign Policy of the Islamic Republic of Iran), *The Journal of Foreign Policy*, Vol. 15 (Summer 2001), pp. 369–397.

47.   See Mehdi Karrubi's comments in *Salam*, 24 Aban 1376 / November 15, 1997, p. 1–2.

matic response to Samuel Huntington's *Clash of Civilizations* thesis.[48] It reflected more than a decade of intellectual inquiry within Iran on the nature of politics, its extension into the international arena, and represented a serious and genuine attempt to bridge the cultural gap.[49] Simultaneously in the domestic sphere, intellectuals were moving away from the absolutism of religious dogma toward a more interpretative framework in which diverse ideas were shown to be part of a related, integrated whole, rather than distinctive antagonisms: so too did this reflect Iran's more nuanced approach to its international relations. It was no longer simply a conjunction of interests, one now had to understand and relate to the Other, and this was to be achieved through dialogue, understood as a means of intellectual communication. In other words, "we must understand the peculiarities of our era and treat Western civilization as our era's ultimate manifestation and symbol. This means understanding the values and tenets of Western civilization."[50] In arguing for knowledge as a social construction, Khatami was shifting the emphasis from structure to meaning, and since the "West" was part of Iran's cultural heritage, there was no philosophical reason why Iranians could not come to know and relate to it. Indeed, Khatami's appreciation of the concept of dialogue was itself a product of his understanding of the Western, especially German, philosophical tradition, in particular Jurgen Habermas.[51] For a dialogue to be productive, it had to take place between intellectual equals, and it seemed as if Khatami felt that by 1998, Iranian intellectual life had developed enough to make this a realistic possibility.[52] The most intriguing aspect of this intellectual dialogue was the search for cultural com-

---

48. Such misreading was not limited to foreign observers. Many Iranian international relations specialists also viewed this move as simple pragmatic policy; see for example, the special issue of the Foreign Ministry's "Foreign Policy" journal, *Siyasat-e Khareji*, Vol. 12 (Summer 1998). The articles tend to focus on rebutting Huntington, discussing the notion of "civilization," or both.

49. It also reflected Iran's sense of its own identity; while President Khatami may talk of *Islamic* civilization, the evidence suggested a tendency toward *Iranian Islamic* civilization, in which "Islam," if referred to at all, was very much a junior partner.

50. Mohammad Khatami, "Observations on an Information World," in Mohammad Khatami, ed., *Islam, Liberty and Development*, Hossein Kamaly, trans., (Binghamton, N.Y.: Institute of Global Cultural Studies, Binghamton University, 1998), pp. 130–131. The speech was originally delivered in 1995.

51. Habermas visited Iran in May 2002, delivering a series of lectures and receiving a rapturous welcome from students as well as, significantly, a visit from a delegation of mullahs; *Nowruz*, 19 Ordibehesht 1381 / May 9, 2002, p. 9; *Nowruz*, 25 Ordibehesht 1381 / May 15, 2002, p. 1.

52. This sense of intellectual inadequacy in the face of Western civilization was well

mon ground between the United States and Iran, and it was found in the most unlikely of places: the relationship between religion and democracy. Some twenty years after the Islamic Revolution, a cultural synthesis that could bridge the apparent antagonisms of a generation appeared to be at hand. President Khatami stated:

"This civilization . . . is best described by the renowned French sociologist Alexis de Tocqueville who spent 18 months in the USA in the 19th century and wrote the valuable book entitled "Democracy in America." I hope most Americans have read this book, which reflects the virtuous and human side of this civilization. In his view, the significance of this civilization is in the fact that liberty found religion as a cradle for its growth and religion found the protection of liberty as its divine calling. Therefore in America, liberty and faith never clashed, and as we see, even today most Americans are religious peoples. There is less war against religion in America. Therefore the approach to religion, which was the foundation of Anglo-American civilization, relies on the principle that religion and liberty are consistent and compatible. I believe that if humanity is looking for happiness, it should combine religious spirituality with the virtues of liberty."[53]

Conclusion: A Monologue of Civilizations?

This paper has argued for the centrality of culture and civilizational identity to the formation of foreign policy, while at the same time indicating the limitations of these cultural factors and the importance of material experience in defining cultural parameters. The concept of culture must clearly be understood as heterogenous and multi-faceted, and while three distinct characteristics have been the focus of this paper, they should not be considered as exclusive. Policy is defined through the interaction of competing cultures and their interpretations of experience, providing the logic through which interests are rationalized and prioritized. In a multicultural polity such as Iran, this can often result in a contradictory experience at different levels of policymaking, a reality which can make any constructive international response problematic. This is not a circumstance unique to Iran, but given its geopolitical situation and the plurality of its revolutionary politics, the mechanics of policymaking are both relatively more visible and immensely consequential.

At the same time, Iran shows quite well the difficulties in demarcat-

---

expressed by Mojtahed Shabestari, quoted in Mehrzad Boroujerdi, *Iranian Intellectuals and the West: the Tormented Triumph of Nativism* (New York: Syracuse University Press, 1996), p. 168

53.   President Khatami, interviewed on CNN, BBC SWB ME/3210 MED/2, January 9, 1998, Iranian TV, January 8, 1998.

ing between material interest and culture and the ways in which different arguments may be brought to bear to justify a single policy. In accordance with Iran's diverse inheritance, it is not, for instance, unusual to see policies legitimized in diverse, apparently contradictory ways. For example, Iran's support of Hizbollah in Lebanon is frequently raised as an example of Islamic fraternity, while its seeming disinterest in the plight of the Chechens or, more interestingly, the Tajiks, is assumed to show the primacy of national interest. Yet, it can be shown, and is indeed argued, that support for Hizbollah has less to do with cultural loyalties and more with the realities of a grand strategy of bolstering Iran's role as an important regional power in the Middle East. At the same time, neither justification is proving satisfactory in convincing an increasingly skeptical and anti-Arab leaning population.[54] A similar logic has been expressed by some officials with respect to the 2003 war in Iraq. Here, the complexity of Iran's three cultures comes into its own, while also indicating the dynamic relationship between interest and cultural determinants. On the one hand, its Western sympathies have been expressed by the unprecedented popular support for the war against Saddam Hussein among the Iranian population, mirrored by the sympathetic approach to the U.S.-led coalition afforded by the Iranian government. While there was a clear affinity among some Iranians with Iraq's Shi'a, there was little sympathy as a whole for the Ba'athist state (defined broadly), and some Iranians went so far as to ascribe their own difficulties with the interference of "Iraqis" in Iranian politics (the key figure here was the Head of the Judiciary, Ayatollah Shahrudi, who many Iranians called 'al-Shahrudi' to emphasis his Arabness). On the other hand, some hard-liners sought to justify broad Muslim sympathies on the basis of national interest, in that as a part of the "axis of evil," Iran had an interest in preventing the United States from achieving stability in Iraq. This view would certainly not have carried any weight had U.S. policy since September 11, 2001, not turned definitively antagonistic and confrontational toward Iran. Indeed, the absence of an avenue for engagement of any sort has reduced the room for maneuvering among Iranian politicians, who are finding the logic of adopting a hard-line posture difficult to resist on grounds of religious, national, or, indeed, material interest.

Here, the importance of symmetry and reciprocity in international relations should be apparent. It has been argued that cultures are not lim-

---

54. When Special Police were placed on the streets of many Iranian cities in the summer of 2002, they were widely interpreted as "Arab mercenaries," a nice twist on the "Israeli mercenaries," which the Shah was meant to have imported into Iran to quell the revolution.

ited by national boundaries producing distinct hegemonies, but on the contrary, enjoy an international dimension which is both reciprocal and dialectical. The distinction between the "rational" Self and the "irrational" Other is unsustainable. While the balance of reciprocity remains to be defined and would clearly depend on the relationship being addressed, it would be fair to assume that the West will remain the dominant partner.[55] It is the principle of reciprocity which needs to be acknowledged. At the beginning of the Islamic Revolution, Iran's idealistic revolutionaries sought to construct a counter-hegemony which would ostensibly protect them from being "corrupted" by the West. Any form of dialogue was regarded as dangerous and the emphasis lay with confrontation. The onset of the war with Iraq provided practical fuel to this conception; while it remains a powerful influence in some quarters of Iranian political life, it was superseded in the aftermath of war by the pragmatism of cooperation defined through mutual interest. The cult of religious martyrdom gave way to the culture of national self-sacrifice, but this soon descended into the dogma of personal interest. Foreign policy was in many ways an extension of these domestic developments. Yet it was quite clear that these in turn were being influenced by the international arena (specifically the West), and Khatami's success on the international stage can largely be put down to his recognition of this reciprocity and his willingness to work within it. Khatami's logic and his understanding of regional politics dictated that, in redefining the cultural parameters of an international relationship, the particularities of an antagonism could in time be overcome.[56] The danger was that, in failing to tackle the details, these details would paradoxically undermine the grand strategy of cultural integration which was being pursued, especially if the proposed international partner has chosen a decidedly different path. Cultural dialogue obviously requires an interlocutor and must suffer as a credible option in its absence, providing succor for those who would seek to reinstate the culture of confrontation.[57]

It remains a supreme and distinctly cruel irony that 2001, the year

---

55. Reciprocity, however, is altering our conception of the "West," such that some philosophers now talk of the "decline of the West."

56. Iranian officials never tire of repeating, for example, that Iran's nuclear program had been initiated under the Shah with considerable support from the West, while it must be conceded that some U.S. allies in the region are certainly more active in the pursuit of weapons of mass destruction support for "Islamic terror," and consequent interference in the "Peace Process."

57. See, for example, Knut Royce and Timothy M. Phelps, "Secret Talks with Iranians," *Newsday*, August 8, 2003.

designated by the United Nations at the suggestion of the Iranian President to be that of "Dialogue of Civilizations," should have been marked by one of the most dramatic acts of terrorism to be committed against the West. Official messages of support and commiseration, along with widespread public sympathy for the United States among ordinary Iranians, showed how far the environment had changed from 1979—and to what extent the Islamic Republic was willing to work with (and in some cases within) U.S. hegemony. For the United States, however, dialogue was no longer a politically acceptable option domestically. A generation after the Islamic Revolution, the United States had rediscovered Iran's revolutionary credentials. Comprehending without being comprehended by others, a new political culture was rationalizing a new worldview with different priorities and a radical interpretation of U.S. interests. Indeed, as the war on terrorism extended toward the war on Iraq, justified through a doctrine of pre-emptive idealism, and the United States castigated its critics for placing material interest over principle, it appeared as if culture, which never really had gone away, had returned with a vengeance.

Chapter 10

Taliban Afghanistan: A True Islamic State?

Svante E. Cornell

"The Taliban appeared as rigid, blissfully egoistic and self-righteous rulers ready to go to any length to pursue their Islamic agenda."[1]

The short-lived Taliban government in Afghanistan could at first sight be the best contemporary approximation of a "Samson state": one that makes policy decisions that imperil its own viability or even harm its material interests in order to satisfy the perceived dictates of culture.[2] In practically all journalistic and academic depictions of that now-defunct regime, it appears as an extreme Islamic fundamentalist group that sought to force a particular and austere model of societal and individual life onto the inhabitants of the areas that it controlled. The decisions made by the Taliban government often seemed to lack rational justification, and to be based on cultural rather than material interests. The refusal to mollify the repression and seclusion of women against a unified world opinion and alienation is one example. The decision to destroy the ancient giant Buddhas of Bamiyan in March 2001 in the face of an international outcry, including that from the entire Islamic world, is another example. So is the refusal of the Taliban to surrender Osama bin Laden in the aftermath of September 11, 2001, in the face of certain military defeat at the hands of the U.S. military. Moreover, the decision to ban and eradicate opium production in Afghanistan in 2001 was equally damaging to both the country's—and the leadership's—economic interests, given that it was the major source of income in the country, and nothing replaced it.

---

1. Imtiaz Gul, *The Unholy Nexus: Pak-Afghan Relations under the Taliban* (Lahore, Pakistan: Vanguard, 2002), p. 30.

2. The phrase "Samson State" was coined by Brenda Shaffer in the conceptualization of this book.

Just a mention of these events and the decisions that led to them may appear to be enough evidence that Taliban Afghanistan was, indeed, a true ideological Islamic state, and that many of the foreign policy decisions taken by the Taliban regime had been influenced by religious motives. A closer analysis of the Taliban's key decisions, however, indicates a need to qualify the definition of Taliban Afghanistan as a state where culture and ideology took precedence over material interests. In fact, most policy decisions of the Taliban stemmed from a perception of an overlap of the religious agenda with material interests of the state. Moreover, this chapter argues that a variety of cultural factors influenced the policy choices of the Taliban, of which Islam was only one among several.

The Taliban's policies were also greatly affected by the codes of Pashtun tribal society, *Pashtunwali,* and even the form of Islam practiced by them should not be interpreted as being universal, but as a specific product of the mixing of Islam with *Pashtunwali.* In the case of the Taliban, it is difficult to separate Pashtun culture from Islamic culture, and the version of Islam that they practice is unique. Hence, this chapter raises the point that even when a regime acts in the name of a professed culture or ideology, this does not necessarily endow analysts with the ability to predict their policies, because their interpretation of that culture or ideology can be quite rarefied. In addition, cultural influences had a high impact on the Taliban, due to the nature of its decision-making process and the composition of its decision-makers. The Taliban was never a monolithic bloc, and it had wings that emphasized more material policies. With the progressive growth of the power of Mullah Mohammad Omar over the movement, the impact of culture on the movement's and later the regime's decisions grew. Moreover, since the Taliban leadership was extremely uneducated and operated in an information vacuum, many of its decisions were made without an ability to calculate the material trade-offs of these decisions accurately.

Before it can truly be determined whether Taliban Afghanistan can be classified as the exception to the rule, a true "Samson state" in a world where most—even ideologically- founded—states in fact act primarily to satisfy their material self-interest, the first question that needs to be addressed is whether or not Taliban Afghanistan was in fact, a state, in the sense that it had a government possessing sovereign powers over a defined territory. Did this group of religious students really install a government in Afghanistan, or were they simply a ragtag gang that took over the country during the anarchy that had existed, merely controlling but never ruling the country, only to evaporate when the U.S. military came in to take over? Alternatively, was Taliban Afghanistan not a state in its own right but a puppet regime put in place by Pakistan's intelligence services to provide stability in Afghanistan and strategic depth to the Pakistani military? Or was the Taliban hijacked by al-Qaeda and used toward the narrow purposes of that non-state organization? These questions are important, as it would be pointless to discuss the Taliban's policies if one assumes that it were not a genuine state regime but the puppet or instrument of foreign or alien powers. Answering this question requires a thorough analysis of the Taliban movement's emergence, arrival to power, rule, and demise. In particular, the role of Pakistan in its creation and al-Qaeda's manifestly increasing role inside Afghanistan are crucial elements in understanding the Taliban.

A problem with the study of the Taliban is the mystery that surrounds the entire movement's emergence, its nature, its leader, and its links to the outside. Afghanistan under the Taliban was isolated, ostracized, and practically cut off from the outside world. Very few journalists or academics were given access to the Taliban leadership or had a thorough understanding of the regime's inner structure, power relations, and policies; information on the organization is still deficient. In this context, no study of the movement and subsequent regime is likely to give a completely correct perspective on its character and nature. This study will be organized around several main elements. The first is the emergence of the movement—including its roots, its ideology, and foreign powers' role in the process—in order to evaluate whether or not Taliban Afghanistan was a state at all. Second, an attempt will be made to understand the character of the Taliban by studying its internal politics and the politics of some key decisions. Among these, the eradication of opium in 2001 and the destruction of the Buddha statues of Bamiyan are particularly important, given their apparently illogical character as far as the material interests of the Taliban were concerned. Likewise, at the end, abandoned by their few allies, the Taliban refused to remand Osama bin Laden to the United States, pledging rather to die than to surrender their "guests." This discussion will also highlight the Taliban's relationship with al-Qaeda, in order to investigate if and when the regime was hijacked by al-Qaeda and therefore not in the true sense an independent government anymore.

Was Taliban Afghanistan a State?

THE EMERGENCE OF THE TALIBAN MOVEMENT

The roots of the Taliban movement are shrouded in mystery. The movement is widely seen as a creation of the Pakistani intelligence service, but evidence shows that while Pakistan's role was important in the movement's growth, it was an indigenous and genuine movement of protest against the anarchy that had taken over large parts of southern Afghanistan after the civil war in the early 1990s. According to the official version favored by the Taliban, their movement was a spontaneous reaction by religious students in the spring and summer of 1994 to the anarchy and decadence under the *mujahideen* commanders that had established their fiefdoms all over the country, especially in the Pashtun-majority south around Kandahar.[3] In the spring of 1994, two teenage girls were kidnapped by *mujahideen* in the Sang Hesar village in Kandahar Province, taken to a local commander, and repeatedly raped. Mullah Mohammad Omar, a teacher at a local *madrasa,* assembled some thirty students or *Talibs,* who took over the local commander's base and hanged him from the barrel of a tank.[4] Another favorite tale in the Taliban mythology is of an incident in Kandahar, a city that had different areas controlled by different commanders. Two commanders were fighting over the right to sodomize a boy and conducted a minor tank battle in the city, resulting in the death of over a dozen people. Omar's *Talibs* intervened and freed the boy, again hanging the rival commanders.[5] As news of this spread, Omar's ragtag group of students was asked by ever-growing numbers of people in an increasingly wider region to help restore law and order. The movement grew quickly as young Afghans, primarily Pashtuns, from the entire Kandahar region and from refugee camps in Pakistani Baluchistan joined the movement. It then uncovered a major arms depot near the Pakistani border and, having armed itself, began spreading its influence over southwestern Afghanistan. Again, according to the mythology, people welcomed the *Talibs* as their liberators, and the religious zeal of the movement's adherents made most *mujahideen* fighters submit to them. The movement gradually became organized militarily, eventually spreading into the Pashtun areas of eastern Afghanistan, where the Nangarhar Shura and Gulbuddin Hekmatyar's *Hizb-i-Islami* controlled pockets of territory, and finally also to Herat in the west before taking Kabul and Mazar-i-Sharif, becoming the rulers of Afghanistan, save some areas in

---

3. See Kamal Matinuddin, *The Taliban Phenomenon* (Karachi, Pakistan: Oxford University Press, 1999), pp. 25–27.

4. See Michael Griffin, *Reaping the Whirlwind: The Taliban Movement in Afghanistan* (London: Pluto Press, 2001), p. 35; Ahmed Rashid, *Taliban: Militant Islam, Oil and Fundamentalism in Central Asia* (New Haven, Conn.: Yale Nota Bene, 2001), p. 25; and Presentation by Sayid Rahmatullah Hashimi, Taliban Foreign Ministry, Washington, D.C., April 12, 2001.

5. John F. Burns and Steve LeVine, "How Afghans' Stern Rulers Took Hold," *New York Times,* December 31, 1996.

the central Hazarajat and the northeast that they never managed to conquer or control.

Indigenous Heroes or Foreign Puppets?

This idealized picture of the Taliban as pure-minded heroes liberating the people and sweeping through most of Afghanistan welcomed by locals is nevertheless fiercely rejected by its opponents, including representatives of the non-Pashtun ethnic groups in Afghanistan and neighboring powers such as Iran, Russia, India, and Central Asian states—as well as by a large number of foreign observers. They see the Taliban movement as conjured up by Pakistan's powerful Inter-Services Intelligence (ISI), variously seen as created from scratch either in cooperation with Saudi Arabia, the United States, or both.[6] Pakistani involvement in "creating" the Taliban movement is nevertheless seen as central. A typical statement is that "with Pakistan's support, the Taliban (Islamic Student) movement emerged in 1994."[7] This view is often backed up by reports of the sighting of Pakistani military officers, either disguised as Taliban or even in uniform, claims that are often less than well substantiated. The first evidence of Pakistan's involvement is often cited as the Taliban seizure in October 1994 of a large arms cache near Spin Boldak on Afghanistan's border with Pakistan.[8] Only weeks later, a test convoy trying to open up a land trade route between Pakistan and Central Asia via Kandahar and Herat was held hostage by a local commander, but was soon freed by a Taliban attack on the forces of this commander.[9] Within days, the Taliban captured Kandahar, apparently by bribing commanders to surrender and enlisting their soldiers into their own forces—setting the precedent of the Taliban way of warfare. In fact, most of southern Afghanistan was taken without much fighting, especially as *mujahideen* forces were often disillusioned with their leaders and saw the Taliban as the more promising force in the region. When the Taliban first captured Jalalabad and then Kabul in the early fall of 1996, the Afghan government under Burhanuddin Rabbani

---

6. See, e.g., Bhure Lala, *Terrorism Inc.: The Lethal Cocktail of ISI, Taliban and Al-Qaida* (New Delhi, India: Siddharth, 2002); Jean-Charles Brisard et al., *Forbidden Truth: U.S.-Taliban Secret Oil Diplomacy, Saudi Arabia and the Failed Search for Bin Laden* (New York: Thunder's Mouth, 2002); and John Elliott, "A Game of Smoke and Mirrors," *New Statesman*, October 1, 2001.

7. Zalmay Khalilzad, "Afghanistan: The Consolidation of a Rogue State," *Washington Quarterly*, Vol. 23, No. 1 (1999), p. 67.

8. Matinuddin, *The Taliban Phenomenon*, pp. 60–61; Rashid, *Taliban*, pp. 27–29.

9. Rashid, *Taliban*, p. 28.

and his legendary military leader, Ahmad Shah Massoud, and its allies blamed Pakistan for providing the military leadership, logistics, and troops to the Taliban. Should this be the case—that the Taliban was a mere creation that Pakistan with some assistance from Saudi Arabia and, initially and even more covertly, the United States, utilized as a puppet to enforce its interests in Afghanistan, it would be difficult to speak of a independent government that makes decisions based on either ideology or material self-interest. Such a puppet regime would only execute the decisions made elsewhere. In this sense, the entire question of an Islamic state would be irrelevant, because Taliban Afghanistan would not be a state at all.

Reality is more complex, however, than either the mythical version of the purely indigenous movement that swept through and conquered Afghanistan like a whirlwind or the depiction of a simple Pakistani creation. In fact, the Taliban seemingly emerged as an indigenous movement at an auspicious moment. In a sense, there had been a considerable and increasingly anarchic vacuum, especially in southern Afghanistan, since the fall of President Mohammad Najibullah's regime in 1992.[10] By mid-1994, the security situation had deteriorated so badly that the population of southwestern Afghanistan desperately clung to any force that would restore law and order and disarm the region. The Taliban promised to do that, and wherever they established their rule, they indeed successfully curtailed crime through their draconian punishments and repressive rule. Their initial successes can be explained with relative plausibility through this factor. Yet the ease with which they assumed control over areas strongly suggested that they had financial and perhaps political and military backing from elsewhere. Many indications do indeed point in the direction of Pakistan. Several important elements, however, lend important nuances to Pakistan's role. First of all, the Pakistani leadership was by no means unanimous in its support for the Taliban. Second, it is highly doubtful that Pakistan in any real sense ever controlled the Taliban. Pakistan may have been the state that had the most influence over the Taliban, but in key issues often failed to influence the Taliban to make decisions in Pakistan's national interest—indicating that the Taliban was nobody's puppet.

PAKISTAN AND THE TALIBAN

Neighboring Pakistan had an important role in the establishment of the Taliban, and it attempted to influence its policy decisions. The Taliban was, however, an independent actor. Pakistan's role in the creation of the

10. Griffin, *Reaping the Whirlwind*.

Taliban movement was complex, with the involvement of different governmental agencies and private forces acting independently and sometimes in contradiction with one another. During the Afghan resistance or *jihad* against the Soviet Union in the 1980s, Pakistan extended support to the *mujahideen* factions that had fought against Soviet forces. Most, if not all of them, were at one or another point in time receiving funds, arms, or training from Pakistan's ISI, which was distributing Saudi and U.S. funds that had been earmarked for the *jihad*. Ideologically, Pakistan favored the groups that had espoused a radical Islamist agenda, with an ideology akin to the Pakistani *Jamaat-e-Islami* and the Egyptian Muslim League, mainly to counteract Afghan nationalist groups, which had territorial pretensions on Pakistan and, it was feared, potentially entertained good relations with India. The ISI's favorite was Gulbuddin Hekmatyar, who was a Pashtun from Kunduz in northern Afghanistan; Hekmatyar's *Hizb-e-Islami* received the lion's share of the funds that had been distributed by the ISI. It also had an efficient organizational structure. Hekmatyar's religious views, similar to those of the Pakistani *Jamaat-e-Islami*, were radical and relatively progressive, unlike the purist, ultra-Orthodox Deobandi views of the Taliban. Hekmatyar's close relationship with Pakistan's ISI continued after the Soviet military's withdrawal of 1989, and he increasingly became Pakistan's horse in the struggle for the government of Afghanistan. Through the bewildering shifting alliances among Afghan factions in the early 1990s, the ISI stuck with Hekmatyar in all major decisions. When the Taliban emerged in 1994, the ISI was still cozy with Hekmatyar. Even when the Taliban approached Kabul in 1995 and later on when they were fighting *Hizb-e-Islami* in mid-1996—routing Hekmatyar's forces in August—a steady flow of weapons supplied *Hizb-e-Islami* forces from across the Pakistani border.[11] The leader of Pakistan's *Jamaat-e-Islami*, Qazi Hussain Ahmad, a long time ally of the ISI, was mediating fervently in May 1996 between Hekmatyar and Massoud, in order to avert a Taliban take-over of Kabul. This would hardly seem to fit with the picture of a well-oiled Pakistani plot to impose its puppet Taliban regime on the country. As Griffin puts the question, "depleted of resources and political muscle as it was after the death of Zia and the end of U.S. funding, could the ISI also have created the force which was to drive its long-standing ally in Afghanistan from the field?"[12]

Within and outside Pakistan, there are those who subscribe to the theory that the ISI is a nefarious state-within-a-state that practically runs

11. *The News International*, August 25, 1996.
12. Griffin, *Reaping the Whirlwind*, p. 70.

the country and pursues a clearly defined, radical Islamic agenda geared to destabilize India, Afghanistan, and even Central Asia. Seeing that the Hekmatyar option was leading nowhere, the ISI, accordingly, created the Taliban, helped organize its military structure, channeled Saudi funds to the movement, and armed it. Good grounds exist, however, to doubt that the ISI possesses the capacity so often ascribed to it. First of all, a study of the structure of the ISI's members shows that it is unlikely to have an institutional agenda of its own in the long run: the ISI is a military organization. Three quarters of its staff, including the totality of its senior operatives and decision-makers, are military personnel. They are rotated from and to military staff and field positions on a three- to five-year basis. As a result, hardly anyone serves in the ISI for more than five years at a time. In other words, no consistent ISI leadership cadre is in place with the possibility to develop an agenda of its own. However, organizations, particularly, intelligence organizations, often have a specific organizational culture, and ever since Zia ul-Haq's regime, Pakistan's intelligence agencies certainly have been influenced by Islamic ideology, a trend that continues to this day, but not one that is impermeable to the changes in the military hierarchy that controls the organization. This casts doubt on the theory that the ISI under Zia ul-Haq had become an organization with a radical Islamic agenda, which remains untouched to this day. In fact, the ISI's grip on Pakistan's foreign and security policies has waned since the early 1990s. In any case, the ISI, if at all married to any religious agenda, was attached to the radical strain of the Jamaat-i-Islami, certainly not the purist Deobandi views of the Jamaat-e-Ulema-e-Islam.

Commentators on Pakistan's policy toward Afghanistan frequently fail to note the internal conflicts that existed between the civilian government under Prime Minister Benazir Bhutto and the military, particularly the ISI, and that the civilian government itself had a very clear foreign policy agenda geared toward Central Asia. Benazir Bhutto's relationship with the military was deeply colored by the fact that a military ruler, Zia ul-Haq, had executed her father, Zulfiqar Ali Bhutto. With this background and her fear of the military's ambitions to curtail her power, Bhutto's relationship with the ISI was hostile. Indeed, she saw the ISI as one of the major internal threats to her power. In her first administration in 1988–1991, ISI General Hamid Gul had widely been thought to conspire with her main rival, Nawaz Sharif, to undermine her position. From that experience, she had good reasons to fear and distrust the ISI.[13] Bhutto herself, however, had a considerable interest in Central Asia.

---

13. Lawrence Ziring, *Pakistan in the Twentieth Century: A Political History* (Karachi, Pakistan: Oxford University Press, 1997), pp. 516–517.

Influenced by long-time Afghanistan specialist and Interior Minister General Nasirullah Babar, her government pursued an ambitious agenda of broadening Pakistan's foreign relations by linking it with the former Soviet republics of Central Asia, in hopes of turning Pakistan into a regional power and a major trade hub. In retrospect, it seems as though the force in Pakistan that had supported the Taliban early on had been Babar himself.

In September 1994, Babar had traveled the road from Quetta to the Turkmen border, receiving a promise of safe passage for his convoy. The test convoy left Quetta in October and was supposed to take supplies to Ashgabad to prove the viability of Pakistan's position as a hub for Central Asia's trade links to the world. When the convoy was held by a local Afghan commander, however, Babar had Mullah Omar rescue his convoy rather than Pakistani special forces—indicating that a relationship between the two already existed at this point. In fact, the ISI's support for Hekmatyar to the bitter end, when the Taliban had turned against Hekmatyar's forces, and Bhutto's and Babar's ambitious project of linking Pakistan to Central Asia indicate that Pakistani state involvement in Afghanistan is much more complex and contradictory than often depicted—and that if anyone had supported the emergence of the Taliban movement, it was not the ISI but Interior Minister Babar and through him the popularly elected government, possibly in cooperation with alternative intelligence forces such as the Intelligence Bureau (IB) with whom Babar had links. In this sense, there may be some truth to the statement that "the rise of the Taliban came as a surprise to the Pakistani establishment"—or at least to parts of it.[14]

Of course, Pakistan's relationship with the emergence of the Taliban was much deeper than the simple operations of one or another branch of the government. Understanding the Taliban's emergence requires understanding the movement's singular and probably unique social origins. The Taliban stands out in Afghanistan's history by being rulers that arose from the have-nots of the country—they lacked titles and pedigrees, be they royal or religious. The Taliban was formed of young men, some of whom had fought the Soviet Union, but most of whom were too young to have done so for any significant period of time. All were, however, children of the war against the Soviet Union in the 1980s: all but a few of the Taliban were in their early twenties when the movement emerged and as such had all been children when the Soviet Union invaded Afghanistan in 1979. Their entire lives had been marked by the devastation and suffering of war. Indeed, much of the Taliban's manpower came from refugee

14. Gul, *The Unholy Nexus*.

camps in Pakistani Baluchistan, where the refugee children grew up in a shattered society. The traditional frame of reference of a Pashtun village in southern Afghanistan, where most of the refugees came from, was absent. The sheer size of the refugee population—over three million—made it impossible for the Pakistani government to provide them with health care and education. Instead, this task was taken up by the radical religious groups that had grown strong during the *jihad* against the Soviet Union with ample funding from their patrons in Saudi Arabia. Groups like the Jamaat-e-Ulema-e-Islam (JUI) established religious schools (*madrasas*) for the refugees.[15] They offered some form of education and often also food and shelter to the refugee boys; hence, they were warmly welcomed by the refugee community.

The JUI's Deobandi version of Islam, which it inculcated into its students, was—and remains—extremely austere. Established in India in the 1860s, the Deobandi school was a purist form of reform within Islam, nominally within the majority and normally tolerant Hanafi school of thought, but with much influence from the rising orthodoxy of Wahhabism in Saudi Arabia. Like Wahhabism, Deobandi Islam rejects the concept of *ijtehad*, or interpretation of religious tenets according to context and circumstance. Where Hanafi Islam, not to speak of Sufism, leaves the details of everyday life to the interpretation of the individual believer and only providing general guidelines for personal behavior, stricter schools like the Shafi'i and the Hanbali, from which Wahhabism is derived, to a much larger extent codify and enumerate the details of individual life through thousands of religious orders or *fatwas*. Driven by an urge to define every aspect of everyday life, Deobandism developed a strict orthodox and literalist interpretation of Islam. Moreover, just like Wahhabism, Deobandism accepts only a very limited number of *hadith*—the accounts of the sayings and life of the Prophet Mohammad. The result is a very restrictive sect that leaves the individual little discretion in defining his or her own lifestyle. This strict form of Islam only comprises approximately 10 percent of Pakistan's population. Its relative proximity to Saudi Arabia's Wahhabism, however, made it a leading candidate for Saudi money; its ability to train and indoctrinate fighters made it an asset to all powers involved in the war against the Soviet Union. Ideologically, the Deobandi *madrasas* played an important role in the creation of the Taliban. It would be an exaggeration, however, to say that the JUI had organizationally created the Taliban.

Both Pakistan's state and society have, clearly, not been strangers in the Taliban's creation and assent to power. The narrative above makes it

---

15. Gul, *Unholy Nexus*, p. 87.

possible to conclude with relative certainty that Pakistan and its ISI did not create the Taliban. The Taliban movement with reasonable likelihood *did* emerge at first as a spontaneous reaction to the anarchy and chaos in southwestern Afghanistan. While clearly in more ways than one a creation of the civil war in Afghanistan, the Taliban's religious ideology was heavily determined by the JUI's ability to take advantage of the misery of Afghan refugees in order to create an army of indoctrinated souls.

Meanwhile, the Pakistani government was looking for a way to stabilize Afghanistan in order to pursue its role as a regional power in Central Asia. Interior Minister Babar clearly saw that Hekmatyar, while fulfilling short-term and limited tactical goals in Afghanistan, was not going to be the instrument to help Pakistan pursue this larger strategic objective. The discovery of the Taliban movement, on the other hand, provided Babar with a new option. This option at first proved immensely successful, for several reasons: the war-weariness of Afghanistan's population, the relative acceptance in Pashtun tribal society of the ideology that the Taliban had brought; and the financial help that they had received from Saudi Arabia, which—when combined with tactical advice from Pakistan—enabled the Taliban to form a serious military power while conquering territory through deception and bribery rather than battle. The ISI did not turn into a backer of the Taliban until its own favorite, Hekmatyar, had been routed by the new force. For a short while, different branches of the Pakistani state were supporting different and opposing armed factions in Afghanistan. Pakistan then neither created nor controlled the Taliban, though it was undoubtedly the foreign power with the largest level of influence over the movement.

Like most Afghan factions, however, the Taliban was never anyone's stooge. Perhaps the most obvious example is the way in which their relationship with Saudi Arabia—which had played an extremely important role in bankrolling the movement's emergence—came undone. Saudi Arabia had played a major role in financing the Taliban movement and sending large numbers of the white Toyota pick-up trucks that became the trademark Taliban mode of transportation. The first high-level contacts had been made through the JUI, with princely hunting trips to Kandahar by senior princes of the Saudi Royal family. Later, Prince Turki Bin Faisal, head of the *Mukhabarat*, the Saudi intelligence agency, visited the Taliban leadership regularly. By early 1996, Saudi Arabia had facilitated the Taliban move on Kabul through provisions of money, vehicles, and fuel supplies.[16] Saudi oil companies as well as the Wahhabi religious hierarchy both formed powerful lobbies that urged the state to support

16. Rashid, *Taliban*, p. 201.

the Taliban. Saudi Arabia's enthusiastic support for the Taliban was itself ended by a personal insult—a more emotional than *Realpolitik* factor. In August 1998, Prince Turki visited Kandahar and asked Mullah Mohammad Omar, who by now had proclaimed himself Amir-ul-Momineen, or Commander of the Faithful, to extradite Osama bin Laden; the prince was called an envoy of the United States. Mullah Omar reportedly took off his turban and asked to be doused with a bucket of water, telling his erstwhile benefactor that he had done so to calm his anger and then asked the Saudi visitor to leave.[17]

Pakistan may have benefited strategically from the Taliban, because it provided a safe border and a government that harbored no pro-Indian ambitions, as both the preceding and successive governments to the Taliban have done. Of course, what Pakistan gained in this way, it arguably lost in international prestige by its close affiliation with a pariah state. Pakistan's support for the Taliban made perfect sense given that Afghanistan was a neighbor of Pakistan's and crucial for its security and its strategic balance with India. As such, Pakistan was forced to engage and try to influence the Taliban. As Pakistani officials have long argued, had the entire world engaged the Taliban and sought to mollify and influence the regime instead of isolating, ostracizing, and imposing sanctions upon it, Taliban Afghanistan may have developed in another, more benign direction and not become dependent on al-Qaeda.[18]

Pakistan never managed to coerce the Taliban to change its policies, even when it was crucial to Pakistan's interests. One of Pakistan's foremost policy concerns is to have Afghanistan recognize the Durand Line, the border between the two countries that was drawn by the British in November 1893. No Afghan government has recognized this border, and the Taliban was no exception, in spite of persistent Pakistani efforts. Had Pakistan controlled or even exercised a dominant influence over the Taliban, recognition of the Durand Line would surely have been one of the first steps that the Taliban would have taken. Likewise, in the first two months of 1996, Pakistan tried to forge an alliance between the Taliban and other factions, including Hekmatyar's, which opposed the government of Burhanuddin Rabbani. The Taliban, despite pleas by Interior Minister Babar and by JUI leader Fazl-ur-Rehman, refused to join this

---

17. Jeffrey Bartholet, "Inside the Mullah's Mind," *Newsweek*, October 1, 2001.

18. See, e.g., "Taliban Cannot be Wished Away, Says Musharraf," *IRNA*, February 26, 2001. This view was shared by high figures in the U.S. government, including then Assistant Secretary of State for South Asia Robin Raphel. See Mushahid Hussain, "Afghanistan's Myths," *Asia Times*, November 30, 2001.

alliance that had been very much engineered by Pakistan and which other groups had already agreed to join.[19] Pakistan also put pressure on Mullah Omar to cut links with bin Laden, particularly after the U.S. embassy bombings in Kenya and Tanzania in 1998. More blatantly, the Taliban ignored Pakistan's strongly voiced opposition to the destruction of the giant Buddhas of Bamiyan in March 2001. Pakistani delegations to Kandahar and Kabul, public appeals, statements of religious authorities, and the like were all made in vain.[20] The final proof of Pakistan's inability to influence the Taliban came after September 11, 2001, when Pakistan cut all links with the Taliban and eventually withdrew diplomatic recognition, demanding that bin Laden and al-Qaeda be handed over. The Taliban refused.

The Taliban government was, hence, a government. It came to power partly through the assistance it received—just like any other Afghan faction or group—from abroad, in this case Pakistan and Saudi Arabia, with a benevolent nod, at first, from Washington.[21]

The Taliban Mindset

The policies that the Taliban had implemented once in power shocked not only the West, but also most of the Muslim world. In fact, many Muslims were more upset than Westerners at the Taliban, given that the movement gave Islam an even worse name than it already had in the West. The Taliban in fact represented a unique blend of Deobandi Islam, Saudi Wahhabism, and, most importantly tribal, Pashtun beliefs and values. Culture played a progressively more important role in Taliban Afghanistan's decisions, due to the structure of the decision-making and background of the decision-makers in the movement and the growing strength of the less pragmatic wing of the Taliban.

The Taliban was not a monolithic movement and was comprised of activists possessing different primary motivations for their policies. The researcher Neamatollah Nojumi divides them into three, though at later stages such varied characters joined the movement for personal gain and

19. Rashid, *Taliban*, p. 44.

20. Nasim Zehra, "Why the Buddha Bashing?" *The News International* (Islamabad), March 15, 2001.

21. Nafeez Mosaddeq Ahmed, *Afghanistan, the Taliban, and the United States* (Brighton: Institute for Policy Research and Development, 2001); "U.S. Policy Toward Afghanistan," Statement prepared by Congressman Dana Rohrbacher, Senate Foreign Relations Subcommittee on South Asia, April 14, 1999.

out of opportunism that it is nearly impossible to map their origins in any meaningful way.[22] The original groups, however, made their mark on the movement, which would stay till the end. The leaders were typically local mullahs in Afghanistan who were in their thirties in the early 1990s. They had become part of the resistance against the Soviet Union. Many of the would-be Taliban had moved away from the mujahideen in the infighting of the early 1990s, as had Mullah Omar himself. Some still fought, primarily those of the more Orthodox, often Saudi-oriented groups such as the Ittehad-i-Islami of Abdul Rasul Sayyaf, the Hizb-i-Islami splinter group of Yunus Khalis, and the Harkat-Inqilabi-i-Islami of Mohammed Nabi Mohammadi. Mullah Omar himself had been a commander in the latter group. These commanders had joined the Taliban movement promptly when it was sweeping through southern Afghanistan in 1994 and 1995. A second group who later became part of the Taliban had been abroad, especially in Pakistan, along with a disproportionate number of senior Taliban who came from JUI-run *madrasas* like the Jamiat-ul-Uloom-al-Islamiyyah in Karachi. Three of six members of the inner *shura* (council) of the Taliban had come from this *madrasa*.[23] Another part of this category, and perhaps the bulk of the original Taliban movement, was composed of the young refugee men who had grown up primarily in Pakistani Baluchistan and been trained in the JUI *madrasas*. Their social origin is of crucial importance in understanding the peculiar character of the Taliban's views, attitudes, and policies. As Nojumi writes, "becoming refugees in Pakistan for long periods of time caused these students to be disconnected from their social, cultural, and economic bond with Afghanistan. Many of them were young men when they arrived in Pakistan, and they had not experienced the historical and national pattern in which their ancestors lived for hundreds of years. These young Afghan boys . . . were like a fertile land for those who wanted to plant the seeds of their political ideologies."[24]

Competing cultural influences impacted the policies of Afghanistan under the Taliban regime. It is unclear which culture most affected the Taliban. A specific form of Islamic extremist subculture certainly shaped their views, as did a skewed understanding of the tribal codes of Pashtun society—*Pashtunwali*. The Taliban mindset stands on two major foundations—in particular their combination: Deobandi Islam and

22. See Neamatollah Nojumi, *The Rise of the Taliban in Afghanistan: Mass Mobilization, Civil War and the Future of the Region* (New York: Palgrave MacMillan, 2002).

23. Nojumi, *The Rise of the Taliban in Afghanistan,* p. 120.

24. Nojumi, *The Rise of the Taliban in Afghanistan,* p. 122.

Pashtunwali.[25] The ideological origin of the Taliban's widely condemned suppression of women came from the Deobandi school, which argues that the education of a girl after the age of eight is pointless. As the spokesman of the Dar-ul Uloom Haqqani Deobandi Seminary in Akora Khattak, Maulana Adil Siddiqui, phrases it, "It is biologically, religiously and prophetically proven that men are superior to women. Women can be educated and improved, but not to the extent of a man."[26]

The Taliban's mindset is, however, equally if not more defined by *Pashtunwali. Pashtunwali* coexists with Islam in regulating the societal and private life of the tribal Pashtuns. *Pashtunwali* contains several key elements. Perhaps its main rule is hospitality, together with the upholding of honor or *nang. Nang* being a dominant principle in customary law, other principles follow from it, most importantly the blood feud, which, as in many other acephalous societies, is a brutal but relatively effective way of preserving self-restraint and order in society. In particular, female honor is a central matter in *Pashtunwali* and is defined mainly in terms of the protection of the chastity of women. Women are at a very early age kept away from the male population, except for the immediate family. The practice of covering women in the all-enveloping burkha when they are outside the women's quarters of their homes is a custom found in all Pashtun areas. It is hence more a Pashtun than an Islamic tradition, as it is not widely practiced among neighboring peoples such as Punjabis, Tajiks, or Uzbeks and is not explainable through *Quranic* injunctions. While the practice is carried out in the name of religion, it is more correctly understood as resulting from a peculiarly Pashtun interpretation of Islam through the prism of *Pashtunwali.* Punishments for breaking *nang* are severe, and the burden of proof required is relatively weak. Whereas *shari'a,* or Islamic law, requires four witnesses to an act of adultery to punish the perpetrators, simple suspicion has at times been sufficient in the Pashtun tribal context to execute swift and lethal punishment. *Pashtunwali* also pays great importance to hospitality. A guest is close to sacred in Pashtun society, and the host is responsible for the safety and life of the host, failing which honor is lost.[27]

To many tribal Pashtuns, *Pashtunwali* and Islam are not understood

25. See Barbara D. Metcalf, *Islamic Revival in British India: Deoband, 1860–1900* (Princeton, N.J.: Princeton University Press, 1982).

26. Kathy Gannon and Richard N. Ostling, "Who are the Taliban and how Do Other Muslims See Them?" *Associated Press,* March 18, 2001.

27. See, e.g., James W. Spain, *Pathans of the Latter Day* (Karachi, Pakistan: Oxford University Press, 1995), pp. 39–49; Ghani Khan, *The Pathans* (Islamabad, Pakistan: Pushto Adabi Society, 1947).

as separate or complimentary codes, but as one and the same. The Taliban movement's policies very much reflect this union of tribal custom with a specific understanding of religion that is, in itself, very much determined by Pashtun culture. Of course, while the separate though overlapping roots of *Pashtunwali* and Islam can be defined by outsiders, the two concepts are virtually synonymous and inseparable to the tribal Pashtuns. Many practices of the Taliban, in fact, are poorly understood by Muslims unfamiliar with tribal Pashtun society. Deobandism was a purist religious movement from the outset, but as Ahmad Rashid puts it, "the Taliban were to take these beliefs to an extreme which the original Deobandis would never have recognized."[28] In fact, *Ulema* at the *Darul Uloom Deoband* have said as much, arguing the Taliban interpretations go beyond the spirit of Deobandi Islam.[29]

Two factors distinguished the Taliban from the rest of Pashtun society and from the rest of the Muslim world—their remarkable ignorance of Islam as a religion and their link to Pashtun tribal society, which was more abstract than concrete. The Taliban phenomenon is inexorably related to the societal destruction to which the Soviet Union's invasion and the subsequent civil war contributed; this is crucial to understanding the peculiarity of the Taliban mindset. The teachers who trained many of the young *Talibs* were by no means authorities on Islamic law or theology. In fact, the religious credentials of the movement were dubious, including those of its leader, Mullah Omar, who actually does not possess the adequate Islamic training to be called a "Mullah" and was hence ill-suited to take up the ambitious position of Amir-ul-Momineen, or Commander of the Faithful. Taliban officials do not hide that "many people know more of Islam than Mullah Omar."[30] Likewise, the Taliban were socially uprooted from traditional Afghan society by the war. As such, the strict traditions of *Pashtunwali*—applicable to most Taliban since the overwhelming majority of them were Pashtuns—were known to them in a patchy way and in the abstract, rather than concretely through experience. This combination of poor knowledge both of the religion and of their social traditions; their near total lack of other training in science or letters; and the added factor of their self-righteous conviction that they possessed the truth made for a peculiar combination that was particular to the situation in Afghanistan and would be difficult to replicate elsewhere.

---

28. Rashid, *Taliban*, p. 88.

29. Kenneth Cooper, "Taliban Islamic-Code," *Washington Post*, March 11, 1998.

30. Griffin, *Reaping the Whirlwind*.

Taliban: Internal Politics and Structure Affected Policies

An important and often overlooked factor in the study of the Taliban is the level of internal cohesion of the movement. To the outside, the Taliban appeared as a monolithic bloc, moving in unison and led by its all-powerful leader, Mullah Omar. Representatives indeed went to great lengths to deny any internal conflicts or disagreements, claiming there were no factions within the Taliban, who were all united in a single movement intent on creating the ideal Islamic state.[31] This idealized picture does not, however, hold up to closer scrutiny. In fact, given the varying origins of the Taliban and the schisms that have affected most Afghan political factions in the modern era, the movement must be said to have managed its internal divisions relatively well. Until the bitter end, the movement showed no external signs of divisions, and the authority and leadership of Mullah Omar was respected until the very fall of both Kabul and Kandahar. Yet it is possible to discern at least two main factions within the Taliban. One was the Kandahar-based group under Omar's leadership, which retained a dominant position in the entire span of Taliban rule. This was a conservative and ideologically uncompromising group. The second was the Kabul-based group that ran the day-to-day affairs of the government, apparently of a more nationalist Afghan and pragmatic orientation, which sought the mollification of the implementation of religious edicts and the integration of Taliban Afghanistan into the world community.[32] The leader of the latter group was the Taliban second-in-charge and Chairman of the Council of Ministers, Mullah Mohammad Rabbani. The Kandahar-based group found an additional power base in the Department for the Promotion of Virtue and the Elimination of Vice, the Taliban religious police. This grouping was most indulgent in religious zealotry, patrolling streets to ensure that no part of a woman's body could be seen, measuring men's beards, forcing men into mosques to pray, etc.[33] Their existence often tilted the balance in favor of the conservatives. In the development of these differences, the geographical difference was likely of importance. In the provincial backwater of Kandahar, Mullah Omar, who never visited Kabul, continued his hard-line, ideologically-based policies. By contrast, the leadership in

31. Interview with Seyed Rahmatullah Hashimi, Foreign Ministry of the Islamic Emirate of Afghanistan, Washington, D.C., April 10, 2001.

32. Nojumi, *The Rise of the Taliban in Afghanistan*, pp. 179–181. Interviews with Pakistani academics and Afghan exiles in Islamabad and Peshawar, July 2001.

33. Peter Marsden, *The Taliban: War, Religion, and the New Order in Afghanistan* (New York: Zed Books, 1998), p. 45, 63, 73.

Kabul, the more worldly capital of the country, faced the challenge of actually ruling a country of which the Taliban now controlled over three quarters by the late 1990s. The realities of this challenge put many pragmatically-minded Taliban in the trap that all religious fundamentalists face when they actually assume power: that the simple truths they believe will create an ideal society are, in fact, far from sufficient to run a country, let alone rebuild a devastated Afghanistan. The understanding of the need for external support and reconstruction aid forced part of the movement to reconsider the feasibility of their ideologically-driven agenda and veer toward moderation. Taliban Ministers in Kabul, such as Mullah Rabbani and Health Minister Mullah Mohammad Abbas, on the one hand engaged in diplomatic activities, seeking to restore diplomatic ties to the world, while by 1999–2000, also worked on easing the harsh restrictions on individual freedoms in society. The zeal of upholding revolutionary principles had dissipated—similar to the case of Iran. The religious police were less stringent in enforcing dress and beard codes, women were allowed to work in World Food Program–operated bakeries, and dozens of schools for girls had been opened by the Swedish committee for Afghanistan and the few other relief organizations still operating in Afghanistan.[34] Mullahs Rabbani and Abbas even reportedly accepted a U.S. peace plan that would have foreseen the return of King Zahir Shah and a peace with Massoud.[35] Rabbani was later reprimanded by Mullah Omar for having exceeded his authority, and Mullah Omar repudiated the agreement that Rabbani had made with visiting U.S. diplomats.[36]

Hence, the Taliban was no ideologically united bastion, but a regime riven by internal differences. Yet there was no question that the supreme authority always remained with Mullah Omar. Neither Rabbani nor reformist Taliban officials could ever challenge him. Moreover, whereas the late 1990s saw a gradual softening of the Taliban, the last one to two years of the movement saw a renewed radicalization and downgrading of relations with the world. This development is intimately linked with the eradication of opium and the activities of al-Qaeda. An additional important element is that for much of the Taliban movement's time in power, its decision-making mechanism was very non-transparent, characterized by

34. Peter L. Bergen, *Holy War Inc.* (New York: Touchstone, 2002), pp. 160–161; Nasim Zehra, "Taliban Afghanistan: Image and Governance," *Himal Magazine*, April 2000.

35. Nojumi, *The Rise of the Taliban in Afghanistan*, p. 180.

36. B. Raman, "Osama Bin Laden: Rumblings in Afghanistan," *SAPRA*, December 22, 1998.

the dominance of one person, whose access to information and advice is very unclear. Such settings are well-suited for personal idiosyncrasies, including cultural ones, to have a large influence on the making of decisions.

Zeal or Miscalculations?

In the aftermath of the September 11, 2001, terrorist attacks, the Taliban refused to hand over Osama bin Laden to the United States in spite of enormous pressures from the international community, then steadfastly stuck to their refusal and faced obliteration. Was this the logical end result of a Samson state? On the surface, this assertion would seem to be justified: the Taliban chose to die rather than to compromise with their principles—be it the *Pashtunwali* core concept of compulsory hospitality, *melmastia,* or the Islamic injunction not to give up any fellow Muslim to infidels.

The Taliban had previously made an apparently self-destructive decision. In spring 2001, two unrelated events testified to the regime's erratic character. In March, Mullah Omar decided to raze the giant Buddha statues of Bamiyan, since they were considered idolatrous in the rigid Islamic understanding of the Taliban—never mind that the prohibition on picturing living beings is not *Quranic,* but extrapolated from a *hadith,* or saying of the Prophet Mohammad. This move, implemented in the face of immense condemnation from the Muslim and Western worlds, effectively killed remaining hopes for the normalization and integration of the Taliban in the world community. This trend was further reinforced by the death in this same period of Mullah Rabbani, the apparent leader of the "moderates," leading to the removal of a faction promoting more material policies within the Taliban.

Whereas this picture of the Taliban as a self-destructive movement disinterested in material realities is conceivably true, it does not fit with the apparent gradual opening of the Taliban that took place in the late 1990s—which would seem similar to the increasingly lax and pragmatic attitude of the Iranian revolution. In all likelihood, it is related to an interaction between a failed Taliban gambit for recognition and the utilization of this failure by al-Qaeda. A short overview of the landmark decisions of the period follows.

OPIUM ERADICATION

In 1999, Afghanistan produced a record crop of opium, estimated by the United Nations Drug Control Program (UNDCP) at 4,565 metric tons, or over 75 percent of the world's production of opium.[37] While the opium produced in Afghanistan in the late 1990s was worth about $30–40 billion U.S. in the form of heroin on European or U.S. streets, Afghan farmers are collectively thought to have earned some $100 million U.S. on the trade— significant in Afghanistan but a minuscule sum in comparison to the profits of the retailers in the West. The opium issue is by nature equally a domestic Afghan issue but also a foreign policy issue, given that one of the world's largest grievances with Afghanistan concerned illicit narcotics, and conversely, much of the Taliban's contact with international organizations was through international drug control agencies. Decisions on opium directly had a bearing on Afghanistan's relations with the world and were very well understood as a negotiating chip in the Taliban's foreign relations.

The Taliban government taxed the growth and sale of opium like any other agricultural product. The Taliban is variously estimated to have reaped between $10 and $50 million U.S. from the opium trade through taxes, and likely much more through individual commanders' involvement.[38] In the absence of a functioning economy, the opium trade was by far the most significant economic activity in Afghanistan and the largest revenue source of the Taliban government. Yet Mullah Omar in 2000 issued a *fatwa* which forced the eradication of opium on all Taliban-controlled territories. Omar's attitude toward opium had never been lenient; when the Taliban came to power in 1995, the areas under opium cultivation in Afghanistan, which in any case were primarily the southern, Pashtun areas, decreased from approximately 70,000 hectares to 54,000 hectares.[39] In 1998, he had offered the eradication of opium in exchange for internatonal recognition, but was not taken seriously.[40] This time around, Western observers were stunned when UNDCP and U.S. officials concluded that the efforts to eradicate opium in one year had, in fact, been successful. The UNDCP estimated that whereas 3,276 tons of opium had been harvested in 2000, the figure for 2001 had fallen by 94 percent to 185 tons. Factoring in that the Badakhshan region which was controlled by the Northern Alliance at this time saw an *increase* in output of 158 percent, the Taliban areas saw a decrease of over 97 percent.[41] In

---

37. United Nations Drug Control Program (UNDCP), *Afghanistan Opium Survey 2000;* UNDCP, *Global Illicit Drug Trends 2001.*

38. Rashid, *Taliban,* p. 119, Griffin, *Reaping the Whirlwind,* p. 154.

39. UNDCP, *Global Illicit Drugs Trends 2001,* p. 39.

40. Griffin, *Reaping the Whirlwind,* p. 220.

41. UNDCP, *Afghanistan: Annual Opium Poppy Survey 2001* (Islamabad, Pakistan: UNDCP, 2002).

Helmand Province, which itself had produced approximately 40 percent of the world's opium in 1999 and 2000, total eradication was reported. Only patches of land in Nangarhar Province still cultivated opium.

Why did the Taliban eradicate opium? During 1996–1999, Omar had seemingly reversed his principled aversion to the drug trade, given that the effects of opium harmed, allegedly, non-believers—ignoring the millions of heroin addicts in Pakistan and Iran. In economic terms, Omar may have seen little choice; in the middle of a war of attrition with the Northern Alliance, in a dire economic situation especially after the break with Saudi Arabia, and with only spotty assistance from Pakistan, opium was the factor that was keeping Taliban Afghanistan from starving. Yet in July 2000, Omar reversed his opinion and ordered the eradication, which was swiftly implemented. According to UN reports, it affected the livelihood of 530,000 farmers only in the south of Afghanistan. Over a million people were thought to be dependent on the opium business in all.[42] This move would seem to conform with the view of the Taliban as an Islamic-based state, which suddenly makes an ideologically determined decision that significantly harmed its economic basis and, certainly, affected its popularity tremendously in some of its core areas. Unused to thinking in terms of ideological states, analysts groped for a material explanation of the eradication of opium and readily found one: the Taliban had large stockpiles of heroin from bumper harvests of previous years and simply wanted to drive up the price. This argument even gained some popularity in a UN panel that had assessed the eradication of opium in Afghanistan.[43] Yet a closer analysis of the Taliban's policies toward opium production and trade disputes this explanation—but suggests not the workings of an Islamic-driven state, but rather another material explanation.

In fact, the Taliban had all along and with increasing vigor been building its effort to eradicate opium, failing to implement it for simple economic reasons—that it would devastate Afghanistan's economy. In November 1996, shortly after taking Kabul, Taliban Foreign Minister Mullah Mohammad Ghaus sent a letter to the UNDCP, asking for international help for the struggle against illicit drugs and stated this could not be done without international support. The Taliban also publicly declared their opposition to the production, processing, trafficking, and

42. Gul, *The Unholy Nexus*, p. 221.

43. *Daily Press Briefing by the Office of the Spokesman for the Secretary-General*, United Nations, May 25, 2001, <http://www.un.org/News/briefings/docs/2001/db052501.doc.htm>.

abuse of opiates.[44] Interestingly, UNDCP representative Giovanni Quaglia expressed his view as follows: "We have told them, 'We give you one, and you give us one back'. This is the language of business. Taliban are Afghans, and all Afghans are traders. This is the language they understand."[45] By September 1997, the Taliban issued a declaration banning the production and trade in opium. In October, the UNDCP formalized a written agreement with the Taliban in the matter, while it drew up a crop substitution plan for Afghan farmers.[46] Only a month later, the UNDCP's Executive Director Pino Arlacchi offered the Taliban $250 million U.S. in aid over ten years if they successfully eradicated opium production.[47] In May 1998, a U.S. Drug Enforcement Agency official visited Kabul and discussed cooperation in combatting illicit drugs.[48] By June, however, the Taliban threatened to cut their cooperation with UNDCP as very little had been done to boost crop substitution.[49] In spite of this impasse, Taliban authorities in February 1999 issued a ban on heroin production and destroyed thirty-four laboratories in Nangarhar Province.[50] By September, after the international community had made few efforts, the Taliban asked all farmers to cut their production by one third, as a step toward actual eradication.[51] In November, apparently frustrated by the lack of aid, Taliban leaders said they would cooperate in drug eradication efforts if their regime were recognized as a legitimate government.[52] A UN official was quoted as saying that "they [the Taliban] were interested in financial assistance only, but we told them that will come only if they could demonstrate a firm resolve for cracking down on opium growers."[53]

As is clear from the brief and incomplete chronology above, the Taliban had followed a relatively clear and consistent line ever since tak-

44. Geopolitical Drug Watch, *The World Geopolitics of Drugs, 1995/96, Annual Report.*

45. Transnational Institute, *Merging Wars: Afghanistan, Drugs and Terrorism,* Drugs and Conflict Debate Paper No. 3, November 2001.

46. *BBC News,* October 26, 1997.

47. Transnational Institute, *Merging Wars: Afghanistan, Drugs and Terrorism,* p. 11.

48. International Narcotics Control Strategy Report, 1998, Bureau for International Narcotics and Law Enforcement Affairs, U.S. Department of State, Washington, D.C., February 1999, <http://usembassy.state.gov/afghanistan/ wwwhnr98.html>.

49. "South Asia: Taliban Angry with UN," *BBC News,* June 10, 1998.

50. "Afghanistan's Taliban Bans Heroin," *Associated Press,* February 29, 1999.

51. UNDCP, *Global Illicit Drug Trends 2001,* p. 35.

52. PRNewswire (New York), November 29, 1999.

53. Gul, *The Unholy Nexus,* p. 220.

ing Kabul in 1996: they had offered to cooperate on opium eradication and taken both symbolic and concrete steps toward this end. They later did not follow up their decisions, as they had been expecting a similar step from the West—either in the form of assistance or in the form of recognition. Thus, it is likely that in the rapport between the Taliban and the UNDCP, a more or less explicit *quid pro quo* had existed all along: eradication of opium by the Taliban would be a step toward the integration of their country into the world and lead to assistance and recognition. This is the framework in which the Taliban authorities in early 2000 actually moved ahead with the eradication of opium. In March, they banned the levying of taxes on opium; in April, they publicly plowed under a number of opium fields; and in May, visiting U.S. narcotics experts stated that "the ban seems to have taken effect."[54] The Taliban's understanding that there had been a *quid pro quo* is unmistakable: As a Taliban official put it, "we have done what needed to be done, putting our people and our farmers through immense difficulties. We expected to be rewarded for our actions, but instead were punished with additional sanctions."

If the Taliban believed that a *quid pro quo* existed—that they would receive either assistance or recognition in exchange for eradicating opium production—there are two possibilities: either that they had completely misread vague statements by visiting UN officials and there never was a *quid pro quo*, or that there had been one, but the West reneged. The former interpretation is possible but implausible, given that the Taliban had earlier failed to vigorously eradicate opium when given vague promises by UNDCP officials Arlacchi and Quaglia, as described above. The second explanation would raise the question: why had the West changed its mind? In retrospect, the al-Qaeda bombing of the *USS Cole* in Yemen in October 2000 may have sealed the fate of attempts to engage the Taliban instead of ostracizing it. Although the United States still disbursed $43 million U.S. in humanitarian aid to Afghanistan several months later, the Cole bombing increased the hostile U.S. attitude to the Taliban as the bin Laden link to that terrorist act became apparent. This strengthened the hand of those that had supported the international isolation of the regime. In December 2000, the United States joined Russia in pushing through expanded sanctions against Taliban Afghanistan in the UN Security Council.

In retrospect, it cannot be said with confidence that the Taliban's eradication of opium was an ideologically motivated act contradicting

---

54. "U.N. Official Happy with Taliban Drug Enforcement," *Kyodo News Service*, February 21, 2001; Barbara Crossette, "Taliban's Ban on Growing Opium Poppies is Called a Success," *New York Times*, May 20, 2000.

the material interests of the regime and the state of Afghanistan. In fact, an equally plausible argument can be made that the decision was, while religiously motivated in part, a desperate gambit to gain integration into the world community and to receive international recognition. But only three months later, the Taliban demolished the Buddhas of Bamiyan, thoroughly ending talk of engagement of the movement.

BUDDHAS

The destruction of the Buddhas of Bamiyan seems to be the Taliban act that, short of the endgame in October–November 2001, fits best into the ideal type of an ideologically-driven state. Oblivious of global outrage from the Western and Islamic worlds, Mullah Omar had decided to raze the Buddhas and, ignoring all pleas and threats of consequences should he proceed, did just that. The report provided by the *Christian Science Monitor* conforms to this picture: when a Pakistani official visiting Mullah Omar tried to dissuade him from destroying the Buddhas, "Mullah Omar replied by describing a dream he'd had about 'a mountain falling down on him.' Before it hit him, Allah appeared, asking Omar why he did nothing to get rid of the false idols. The diplomat recalls, 'I closed my attaché case. There was nothing left to say'."[55] Other Taliban officials have put forward a more down-to-earth version of the decision. According to Sayed Rahmatullah Hashimi, an official of the Taliban foreign ministry sent to the United States on a diplomatic mission at the time of the destruction of the Buddhas, the decision was taken in a fit of rage. Just as Afghanistan was facing a harsh winter with the risk of hundreds of thousand of people starving, incidentally due in part to the loss of income after the eradication of opium, a United Nations Educational, Scientific, and Cultural Organization (UNESCO) delegation visited Afghanistan and offered money to restore the statues in Bamiyan. The Taliban then asked the European delegates if the money that they were intending to spend on statues could not be spent instead to save Afghan children dying from malnutrition. They were told this money was only for statues. As the Taliban were hardly experienced enough to grasp the separation of accounts common for Western enterprises and government agencies, this seemed to be the ultimate insult to them, leading them to decide to destroy the statues, which had now become "harmful."[56]

Whether or not this version of events is true—and it has not been de-

---

55. Robert Marquand, "The Reclusive Ruler Who Runs the Taliban", *Christian Science Monitor*, October 10, 2001.

56. Interview with Sayed Rahmatullah Hashimi, Taliban Envoy to the United States,

nied by UNESCO—either way the Taliban decision was harmful to the national interests of Afghanistan, as it led to even further isolation of the regime. Moreover, it was followed by half-hearted attempts to destroy museum pieces deemed idolatrous. This illustrates how the Buddhas were intimately tied to the decision-making structure of the Taliban and the dominant personal role of Mullah Omar, and thereby in a deeper sense how single-person decision-making structures allow for cultural and other idiosyncratic factors to take up a more important role in decision-making.

After the eradication of opium, the Taliban found itself in a situation of extreme economic crisis. The largest source of income in the country had been destroyed, leading to dire conditions for most of the population, but also to a decrease in state income as the tax revenue from the cultivation and transportation of opium was lost. Meanwhile, the Taliban's sheltering of bin Laden had led to several setbacks that now had begun to pose large economic and political problems. First of all, the Taliban's relations with Saudi Arabia had been severed, eliminating a major source of income as all Saudi assistance ceased.[57] Moreover, the October 2000 bombing of the *USS Cole* had been traced back to bin Laden and intensified the international, especially U.S., pressures on the Taliban to hand over bin Laden. This killed hopes for a normalization of the Taliban's relations with the West and the possibility of receiving badly needed assistance to replace lost income in order to keep the country functioning.

With this lack of finances becoming acute, the regime was forced to turn to the only remaining source of funding available to them—bin Laden himself. Though information on the actual amount of funding that the Taliban received from bin Laden is unknown, it is clear that by 2001 a substantial portion of Afghanistan's modest budget was being covered by al-Qaeda. Already by late 2000, reports had intensified that bin Laden was bankrolling the Taliban and providing his own elite troops, including the "055 brigade," to the Taliban's efforts to finally defeat the Northern Alliance, led by Ahmad Shah Massoud.[58] This meant that while relations between the Taliban and bin Laden had been frosty in the late 1990s, the

Washington, D.C., March 22, 2001. Also Barbara Crossette, "Taliban Explains Buddha Demolition," *New York Times,* March 19, 2001.

57. Rashid, *Taliban,* p. 139.

58. Luke Harding, "Bin Laden: The Question Facing the Next U.S. President," *Guardian,* November 13, 2000; Robert O'Harrow Jr., et al., "Bin Laden's Money Takes Hidden Paths to Agents of Terror," *Washington Post,* September 21, 2001.

drying up of Taliban tax revenue and bin Laden's ability to provide the two things the Taliban needed—cash and a serious fighting unit—tipped the balance, and the regime now became increasingly beholden to bin Laden. In some ways, bin Laden was at once a major reason for the Taliban's alienation from the international community, but also the main beneficiary of this alienation as it enabled him, perhaps consciously, to hijack the Taliban regime and thereby Afghanistan.

Conclusion

Determining whether Taliban Afghanistan was a true Islamic-driven ideological state has proven to be more difficult than the question seemed to warrant at first glance. It is clear that a "Samsonite" trend was present all along in the Taliban. Having made a decision, the Taliban seldom reconsidered; their worldview was simple, divided into black and white and guided by very concrete obligations and codes of conduct. Islamic and *Pashtunwali* principles were important to them and may on many occasions have weighed heavily in their decision-making process. Compared, for example, to the highly educated and informed Iranian leadership, the Taliban was far truer to their original Islamic agenda in the way that they had formulated and tried to implement it. But to see the Taliban as impermeable zealots heading toward their own destruction at full speed would be misleading. The Taliban was not monolithic, containing a relatively moderate and pragmatic faction that grew in strength until the death of its leader, Mullah Rabbani—an event that may very well have helped remove the last obstacle to bin Laden's influence over Mullah Omar. But though this moderate faction failed to dominate the Taliban movement and government, closer analysis shows that even some of the most apparently ideological decisions of the Taliban were conditioned by some sort of material logic, as flawed and inaccurate as this logic may have been. Opium was eradicated partly, it is true, for religious reasons, but the Taliban clearly had the expectation of a material *quid pro quo;* the Bamiyan Buddhas are harder to justify in terms of material interests, but may conceivably have been a reactive deed to a perceived injustice by the world community. Likewise, the refusal to hand over bin Laden had a strong cultural element in the obligation to observe *melmastia,* or hospitality. Yet it may very well have been partly conditioned by a failure to grasp the difference in military capacity between the Soviet Union in the 1980s and the United States in 2001. After the defeat of the Soviet Union, the Taliban felt that Afghanistan could defeat any superpower that tried to invade its territory. Moreover, the Taliban's economic dependency on bin Laden in 2001 created a strong material motivation not to eject him from Afghanistan.

In sum, culture mattered strongly in the decisions of the Taliban. But whereas culture was a leading explanatory factor of their decisions, there are limits to the influence of culture even in the case of the Taliban. In many ways, they sought, in their own very culturally conditioned worldview, to integrate with the Western world to secure the material interest of their country. As important as culture was, the greater factor impinging on the foreign policy decision-making process was the inexperience and lack of education and exposure of the leaders of the Islamic Emirate of Afghanistan. These leaders were, at the end of the day, semi-literate mullahs and field commanders with little or no understanding of the world, of the consequences of their actions, and of the wider geopolitical game of which they were on center stage.

Chapter 11

Pakistan's Foreign Policy: Islamic or Pragmatic?

Svante E. Cornell

Since the late 1970s, discussions on Islamic precepts have come to play a prominent public role in Pakistan's foreign policy formation. With the advent of General Zia ul-Haq's regime in 1977 and the Soviet invasion of Afghanistan, a wave of Islamization swept through Pakistani society and came to influence the government and its domestic and foreign policies. Since the late 1980s, Pakistan has continuously supported Islamic movements in Kashmir and Afghanistan, helping them to dominate their respective political spheres over more secular and nationalist-oriented forces. This chapter explores the proposition that Pakistan's foreign policymaking has been dominated by Islamic ideology, arguing that the main reason for the Islamic component of its foreign policy has been pragmatic and instrumental—support for Islamic causes has served the material national interests of Pakistan.

Islam In Pakistan's State and Society

At its founding in 1947, Pakistan was a unique state. As a homeland for the Muslims of British India, Pakistan stood out in the community of nation-states as being a state formed solely on the basis of religious identity—with neither ethnic nor territorial identity. The Muslims of India, embodied and led by the Muslim League, had concluded that their collective rights could not be exercised as a minority in a Hindu-majority India; therefore, the only way to safeguard the rights of Muslims on the Indian subcontinent was to establish a separate state for Muslims. Additionally, Pakistan had the territorial distinction of having three thousand miles of Indian territory divide its two parts (East and West Pakistan) and was the most populous Muslim-majority country in the world—and therefore an actor in the politics of the Middle East, South Asia, and Southeast Asia.

From even before the creation of the state of Pakistan, a debate had flared and still continues on the implications of this Islamic identity for the structure of the state of Pakistan as well as, significantly, for the foreign policy that the state of Pakistan should pursue. Was Pakistan, whose existence was justified on the basis of Islam, meant to be an Islamic state—a theocracy? Was it meant to be a state guided by Islamic principles? Was it simply established in order to save Muslims from persecution by Hindus—with no direct implications for the governance of the country?

Despite occasional historical revisionism, it is clear beyond doubt that Muhammad Ali Jinnah, the founder of Pakistan, had envisaged nothing like the creation of an Islamic state. Quite to the contrary, Jinnah, a British-educated lawyer, saw Pakistan as a modern state allowing for the religious beliefs of its citizens, including minorities, to be protected. Jinnah spearheaded the creation of Pakistan as a state *for* Muslims, not as a state run by the Muslim clergy.[1] Many of Jinnah's colleagues and followers, however, did not draw the sophisticated and delicate line between a state for Muslims and an Islamic state. Devotion to Islam, while genuine among much of the leadership, was also a useful way for politicians to buttress public support. For example, the introduction of religious laws in Pakistan (such as the prohibitions on gambling and alcohol) began not with the pious military ruler Zia ul-Haq in the 1980s, but with his self-avowed socialist predecessor Zulfikar Ali Bhutto when the latter's position was weakened in the late 1970s.

Pakistan's foreign policy has likewise seen a vivid debate, both within and outside the country. From the earliest days, forces in Pakistan gave preference to Islamic agendas in the foreign policy of the country, including advocacy for Muslim causes such as a Palestinian state and the liberation of Indonesia from Dutch colonial rule, immediately following the creation of Pakistan itself. Meanwhile, a strong pragmatic strain has always run through Pakistan's foreign policy. Mainly due to its conflict with India, Pakistan has constantly been in an acutely vulnerable situation. Its search for security has pushed it to seek alliances with larger powers. While Islamabad always sought support from Muslim-majority countries, with questionable success, Pakistan's most important allies

---

1. For biographies of Jinnah, see Akbar S. Ahmed, *Jinnah, Pakistan and Islamic Identity: The Search for Saladin* (London: Routledge, 1997); Stanley Wolpert, *Jinnah of Pakistan* (New York: Oxford University Press, 1984).

have been neither Islamic nor Muslim-majority: the United States, especially in the 1950s and 1980s, and China since the 1970s.

However, Pakistan's foreign policy in the post–Cold War era has appeared on the surface to turn toward a zealous advocacy of Islamic causes. Already before the end of the Cold War, Pakistan's Islamic-minded military ruler Zia ul-Haq had played a most central role in organizing support for the Afghan resistance to the Soviet Union in the 1980s. Moreover, Zia had been the driving force that ensured that the bulk of foreign support for Afghanistan went to Islamic radical formations—not to traditional or nationalist forces within the resistance. Essentially, thanks to Pakistan, the Afghan resistance acquired a radical religious character that had by no means been a foregone conclusion in 1980. By the late 1980s, an indigenous rebellion had emerged in Indian-held Kashmir. Pakistan, laying claim—just like India—to this entire, disputed territory since the partition of the subcontinent in 1947, actively supported the rebellion in Kashmir by funneling funds and arms to the Kashmiri freedom fighters, offering bases in Pakistan and support on the international scene to them. As in Afghanistan, Pakistan increasingly extended support to organizations sprouting a religious ideology such as *Harkat-ul-Mujahideen,* while gradually decreasing its support for secular nationalist Kashmiri groups such as the Jammu and Kashmir Liberation Front (JKLF). Again, Pakistan in the early 1990s supported Gulbuddin Hekmatyar in Afghanistan, one of the most radical-minded *mujahideen* leaders. This support was then shifted to an even more puritanical movement, the Taliban, which originated in great part in the Afghan refugee camps in Pakistan's Northwest Frontier Province (NWFP) and Baluchistan Province. While the terrorist acts of September 11, 2001, forced Pakistan to realign its Afghan policies, accusations still abound, as of 2005, that Pakistan is allowing Taliban remnants to base themselves in the Tribal Areas of the Northwest Frontier and is continuing to support "cross-border terrorism" in Kashmir by not cracking down on Kashmiri *mujahideen* groups that are based in Pakistan. This foreign policy is taking place against the backdrop of a military government that allowed free elections in October 2002, only to see a coalition of religious parties increase their representation significantly.

If this were the case, it would seem at first sight that Pakistan's foreign policy is indeed endowed with an increasingly strong Islamic inclination, which the avowedly secular leadership of General Pervez Musharraf has not been able or willing to stem. This chapter will seek to challenge this proposition by investigating whether key axes of Pakistani foreign policy are determined by religious imperatives or by considerations of material national interests, as defined by the leadership of the country.

At first, a short overview of the gradual "Islamization" of Pakistan's state and society will provide a necessary backdrop for studying Pakistan's foreign policies. Then important foreign policy issues will be studied, including Afghanistan in the 1980s, Kashmir as well as Afghanistan in the 1990s, and the evolution of Pakistan's foreign policy since September 11, 2001.

The Islamization of Pakistani Society

While Pakistan's society has been subjected to state-sponsored Islamization, this trend should not be overstated. Zia's policies did have an effect and lingered on through 2005, but the support for radicalism among the Pakistani public remains, in spite of the results of the 2002 elections, very low. Yet, only with the advent of the regime of General Pervez Musharraf did the state begin to roll back the advances made by the few but loud and influential radical Islamists.

Pakistani society is a deeply religious society; the population consists of a Sunni majority of roughly 80 percent and a Shi'i minority of roughly 15 percent—mainly Jafar'i, the "twelver" sect of Shi'i Islam practiced in Iran, but also a smaller Ismaili community. Minorities include the Hindus, Christians, and Sikhs as well as the Qadiani, a sect that was declared non-Islamic by the Zulfikar Ali Bhutto government in 1977. The Sunni majority is in turn subdivided into a large majority influenced by the Barelvi School and a minority belonging to the Deobandi School. This difference is significant, because the Barelvi interpretation of Islam is more tolerant of other religions and divergent interpretations of Islam and is accepting of the mystical Sufi orders in Islam. Deobandi Islam, on the other hand, is more orthodox, more intolerant of deviations in interpretation, and more intolerant of Sufism and the veneration of shrines.[2]

ISLAM IN THE CREATION OF PAKISTAN

While the Islamic faith was the common denominator of the citizens of the emerging state of Pakistan, the Pakistan movement was by no means a movement to create an Islamic state. In fact, the struggle over the role of

---

2. Annemarie Schimmel, *Islam in the Indian Subcontinent* (Leiden, Germany: Brill Academic Publishers, 1997); Usha Sanyal, *Devotional Islam and Politics in British India: Ahmed Riza Khan Barelvi and His Movement, 1870–1920* (New York: Oxford University Press, 2000); and Barbara Daly Metcalf, *Islamic Revival in British India: Deoband, 1860–1900* (Princeton, N.J.: Princeton University Press, 1982).

Islam in the state of Pakistan has been a major issue since its inception and remains a major point of contention in the country.

A secular political movement, the Muslim League, established Pakistan with a clearly secular leader, Muhammad Ali Jinnah. Documents make it clear that the demand for Pakistan was made on the basis of creating a homeland for Muslims, with little consideration for the character of the state that would follow. It is clear, however, that it was never the intention of the Muslim League to create an Islamic state. As Lawrence Ziring notes,

Jinnah discounted the notion of Pakistan as a theocratic state and by his actions promoted and encouraged the idea of secular nationalism. Jinnah did not share the vision of other subcontinent Muslims who postulated a rigid Islamic ideology. Jinnah was a pragmatist, a lawyer, and a constitutionalist. His conviction was that Muslim minorities could best be protected if states where Muslims were in a majority displayed tolerance for other creeds and embraced those whose traditions and values were different from their own. Such a posture did not in any way impede the Muslims of Pakistan from realizing their dream of a country where they were free to pursue and develop their religious traditions and social values. In effect, Jinnah practiced a strict separation between religious experience and political development.[3]

Jinnah also famously noted that "religion, caste or creed . . . will have nothing to do with the business of the State."[4] The leadership of the Muslim League, while appealing to the Muslim identity of its constituency, only much later tried to include religious figures in its leadership. This religious leadership, in turn, was overwhelmingly opposed to the very creation of the state of Pakistan—on the grounds that it would divide Indian Muslims, which was considered impermissible as it forged borders across lands inhabited by Muslims.[5] In fact, given its character, the Muslim League was not well situated to support an Islamic state: "The Westernized leadership was modern and therefore capable of creating a viable state, but it was not religious and therefore incapable of creating an Islamic state."[6] Also, the identity of the people of what came to be Pakistan was not exclusively Islamic. As Nasir Islam has noted,

---

3. Lawrence Ziring, "From Islamic Republic to Islamic State in Pakistan," *Asian Survey*, Vol. 24, No. 9 (September 1984), pp. 933–934.

4. Quaid-I-Azam Muhammad Ali Jinnah, *Speeches as Governor General of Pakistan, 1947–1948* (Karachi: Pakistan Publications).

5. See the writings of Maulana Mawdudi, for example.

6. Wilfred C. Smith, *Islam in Modern History* (Princeton, N.J.: Princeton University Press, 1957).

Pakistan was born with a temporary sense of national identity, developed as a reaction to militant Hindu nationalism. Various Muslim groups in the subcontinent were able to suspend their regional, ethnic, and linguistic identities . . . but this certainly did not mean that regional and other ethnic identities had been assimilated by this newfound sense of Muslim nationhood.[7]

Nevertheless, Pakistan soon saw a debate flourishing on the nature of the state and its relationship to Islam and Islamic law that was especially articulate during the debates over the constitutions of Pakistan. Pakistan's first constitution, adopted in 1956, referred to the country as an Islamic state, yet it retained a parliamentary political system and merely stated that the Head of State had to be a Muslim. The Constitution of 1962, imposed by the military ruler Field Marshal Ayub Khan, was significantly more authoritarian and sought to abolish political parties by adopting a system of grassroots democracy called "Basic Democracies." It even omitted, however, the phrase defining Pakistan as an Islamic Republic, although this was rapidly reinstated by the National Assembly—in a sense an early example of the constant policy of Pakistan's rulers to cave in to demands from the religious forces to bolster legitimacy. Ayub's regime, in fact, sought to elevate the mystical strain of Islam, Sufism, in the country.[8]

THE RETURN TO ISLAM: THE LEGACY OF ZIA UL-HAQ

The Pakistan People's Party (PPP), a clearly secular party with socialist inclinations, dominated the 1970s. Yet by the early 1980s, the pendulum had swung to a determined government advocacy of Islamization, in part due to a perceived need to strengthen the common bond uniting the disparate ethnic and cultural groups in Pakistan after the loss of East Pakistan. The PPP's leader, Zulfikar Ali Bhutto, was a wealthy Sindhi landlord belonging to the minority Shi'i faction. Bhutto's rise to power was based on a populist rhetoric of *roti, kapra aur makan* (bread, clothing, and shelter) that sought to attract the votes of the less privileged masses in Pakistan. Bhutto even termed Islam irrelevant to the politics of the country, as both oppressed and oppressors were Muslim, and publicly acknowledged his drinking of alcohol.[9] In fact, the victory of the PPP in

---

7. Nasir Islam, "Islam and National Identity: The Case of Pakistan and Bangladesh," *International Journal of Middle Eastern Studies,* Vol. 13, No. 1 (February 1981), p. 57.

8. Katherine Ewing, "The Politics of Sufism: Redefining the Saints of Pakistan," *Journal of Asian Studies,* Vol. 42, No. 2 (February 1983), pp. 251–267.

9. Bhutto's famous phrase was "mein sharab peeta huun, awam ka khun to naheen peeta" (I drink wine, but not the blood of the masses). See, e.g., Eqbal Ahmed, "Islam as a Refuge from Failure," *Dawn* (Pakistani newspaper), September 6, 1998.

West Pakistan in the elections of 1970 has been interpreted as a challenge to the forces seeing Islam as being central to Pakistan's politics. As Muhammad Ayoob notes, the elections of 1970 "were important because . . . for the first time, they demonstrated convincingly that the political slogan of Islam could no longer be used to perpetuate an extremely unjust social and political order in Pakistan."[10]

Within a few years, Bhutto and the PPP had nevertheless failed to deliver. Bhutto provoked a bloody rebellion in Baluchistan by choosing repression to curtail forces there that were perceived as separatist; he also developed an intolerant attitude toward the increasing opposition to the PPP government. He went to the extent of creating a paramilitary structure loyal only to himself, the Federal Security Force, perhaps fearing the army's independent role. Moreover, far from combatting feudalism as he had promised, he soon found himself courting the feudal leaders in a search for an alternative power base. In Ziring's words, "the promise that was the People's Party in 1972 proved to be a harsh burden by 1975."[11] As opposition grew, Bhutto engineered elections in 1977 that were in no sense fair. As the opposition coalition campaigned on a defense of Islam platform against the socialist PPP that it had accused of threatening Pakistan's Islamic character, Bhutto placated his opponents, and the electoral campaigning degenerated into a contest for Islamic credentials. Bhutto, upon being elected, then announced the prohibition of alcohol, gambling, horse racing, bars, and nightclubs. He also changed the weekly holiday from Sunday to Friday. It was, however, too late: a July coup deposed Bhutto and brought General Zia ul-Haq, the Chief of Army Staff, to power.[12] While the political opposition to Bhutto had clearly used Islam instrumentally, General Zia was a devout Sunni Muslim who seemed to see Bhutto's deviance from Islamic principles as a threat to Pakistan. In fact, the loss of East Pakistan was seen in military circles as a result of the failure to integrate the different ethnic groups of Pakistan into a cohesive national identity. The salience of ethnic nationalism in all provinces of Pakistan outside the dominating Punjab—among Sindhis, Baluchis, and Pashtuns alike—also contributed to a perceived necessity to emphasize Islam as the dominant identity of the country. Whether Zia's emphasis on Islam was determined mainly on this pragmatic basis or mainly on a personal religious conviction is debatable; most likely, it was a combination

---

10. Mohammed Ayoob, "The Two Faces of Political Islam: Iran and Pakistan Compared," *Asian Survey*, Vol. 19, No. 6 (June 1979), p. 537.

11. Ziring, "From Islamic Republic to Islamic State in Pakistan," p. 940.

12. Lawrence Ziring, *Pakistan in the Twentieth Century: A Political History* (Karachi, Pakistan: Oxford University Press, 1997), p. 418.

of both. Zia's vision of Pakistan articulated in a July 1977 speech was indicative of the former tendency: "Pakistan, which was created in the name of Islam, will continue to survive only if it sticks to Islam. That is why I consider the introduction of an Islamic system as an essential prerequisite for the country."[13] Within days, Islamic penalties for theft and other crimes, including flogging and amputations, were announced.

By the early 1980s, Zia began to implement his vision of Pakistan, seriously redirecting society and state to the teachings of the *Quran* and the *Sunna*, to create a *Nizam-i-Mustafa*, or prophetic order, in the country. Practically, Zia's government introduced Islamic principles into the judicial and political system of the country. These included *zakat* (alms), and *ushr*, a tax on agriculture, introduced in 1980. This generated great protests among the Shi'a, as according to Shi'i jurisprudence, compulsory collection of *zakat* can be ordained only by governments that are legitimate successors to the Prophet—which Zia's military regime had doubtful credentials to claim, to say the least.[14] As a result of strong and public Shi'i opposition, the community was exempted from the *zakat* ordinance.[15] *Shari'a* courts were also introduced in parallel to the existing common law–based judicial system, and the *hudood* ordinances[16] entrenched Islamic penalties for un-Islamic behavior. Islamic principles of evidence (*diyat*) were also introduced.[17] Finally, a blasphemy law was imposed in 1985, which foresaw the death penalty for an intentional act of defamation of the Prophet. Zia's policies were sometimes more declaratory than practical, and far more than affecting the functioning of Pakistani society in general, it fueled the dormant sectarian divisions in the country. In fact, Zia faced the problem that all attempts to institutionalize Islamic statehood face: the need to select one among the many competing schools of Islamic jurisprudence as the leading one. Zia's favor for the Sunni Hanafi *fiqh* or jurisprudence was clear, hence the difficulties with others, especially the Shi'a.

Zia's Islamization process had its strongest consequences on the criminal justice system, as described above, and on the situation of mi-

---

13. *Pakistan Times*, July 7, 1977, as quoted by William Richter, "The Political Dynamics of Islamic Resurgence in Pakistan," *Asian Survey*, Vol. 19, No. 6 (June 1979), p. 555.

14. Smruti Pattanaik, "Islam and the Ideology of Pakistan," *Strategic Analysis*, Vol. 22, No. 9 (December 1998), pp. 1273–1295.

15. Ziring, *Pakistan*, pp. 466–467.

16. The *hudood* ordinances especially on the laws concerning adultery and rape and making fornication a crime.

17. Ziring, *Pakistan*, p. 444.

norities and women in Pakistan, whose gradually improving situation over the preceding thirty years was overturned.[18] In particular, a discriminatory blasphemy law was introduced that still is predominantly used to persecute minorities. The change was most obvious in the urban areas and for the Westernized elite as well as for minorities, whereas the impact of Islamization in the predominant rural areas of the country was, according to observers, limited.[19]

THE 1990S: "SHAM DEMOCRACY" AND MUSHARRAF'S COUP

The death of Zia in 1988 led to a slowdown of the process of Islamization in Pakistan. No Pakistani political leader was, however, prepared to press actively for rolling back the reforms made by Zia. Attachment to Islam being strong among the population, such moves could easily be exploited by political opponents to brand any politician as un-Islamic, or worse, an unbeliever. Moreover, the growth of the radical religious parties throughout the Afghan war made them potent and potentially violent opponents of secular initiatives that any politician, whether in opposition or in power, had to take seriously.

Benazir Bhutto's electoral victory over the Muslim League in 1988 was a clear sign of the Pakistani electorate's dissatisfaction with Zia's authoritarianism and Islamization program—not only because it brought a woman to power in a deeply Islamic country, but because her Pakistan People's Party campaigned on a decidedly modernist and progressive agenda.[20] As Human Rights Watch notes, however, "the protection of women's rights [under Benazir Bhutto] had been subordinated to the need to maintain a delicate balance between various political forces, including those representing conservative religious values."[21] Her successor, Nawaz Sharif, was less immune to toying with religion for political purposes. In fact, he introduced a fifteenth constitutional amendment that would make *Sharia* the supreme law of Pakistan.[22] The fact was that Sharif did this very much due to his weakening position in the country—

18. Human Rights Watch, *Crime or Custom? Violence Against Women in Pakistan* (New York: Human Rights Watch, August 1999).

19. Richard Kurin, "Islamization in Pakistan: A View from the Countryside," *Asian Survey*, Vol. 25, No. 8 (August 1985), pp. 852–862.

20. Christina Lamb, *Waiting For Allah: Pakistan's Struggle for Democracy* (London: Hamish Hamilton, 1991).

21. Human Rights Watch, *Crime or Custom?*

22. Tim McGirk, "Can Nawaz Sharif Live On a Prayer?" *Time*, Vol. 152, No. 12 (September 28, 1998).

proving, as Eqbal Ahmed noted, that "in Pakistan Islam has been a refuge of troubled and weak leaders."[23] Sharif's move was less a religiously motivated one than an attempt to change the state structure in Pakistan with a view to concentrate power in his own hands—Sharif seemingly calculated that Islamic rule would, unlike democratic rule, spare him the problem of securing re-election and enable him to curtail the power of the opposition.[24]

Sharif was nevertheless unable to pull through his plan of changing his office into a religiously legitimized and therefore more secure position, as General Pervez Musharraf's October 12, 1999, coup dissolved the Pakistani parliament and suspended the constitution.

As will be seen below, only Pervez Musharraf was to challenge the religious parties and organizations openly. The lingering and largely unopposed effects of Zia's Islamization program, however, characterized the foreign policy of Pakistan between Zia's 1977 coup and Musharraf's 1999 coup. After the death of Zia, the lingering effects of the policies of Islamization remained, though the government did not actively pursue them—although rulers such as Nawaz Sharif during both his tenures as Prime Minister have occasionally followed Zulfikar Ali Bhutto's example in appealing to religion to strengthen legitimacy.[25] Religious radicals were allowed great leeway in developing religious schools, securing funding from abroad, proselytizing, and agitating against secular forces, without considerable interference by state authorities—and indeed in many cases with the willing participation or support of various parts of the bureaucracy.

MUSHARRAF'S COUP AND THE CHANGE OF STATE ATTITUDE

While widely condemned in principle in the West, Chief of Army Staff General Pervez Musharraf's coup in October 1999 was seen as a hope for slowing of the Islamization of Pakistan.[26] Indeed, Musharraf consciously portrayed himself as a moderate and secular leader and openly expressed his admiration for Kemal Atatürk, founder of the Turkish Republic and the perhaps most prominent secularizing figure in the history of the

---

23. Eqbal Ahmed, "Islam as Refuge from Failure," *Dawn*, September 6, 1998.

24. See, e.g., B. Chengappa, "Pakistan: Insight into Islamization," *Strategic Analysis*, Vol. 22, No. 11 (February 1999), pp. 1695–1712.

25. Bidanda Chengappa, "Pakistan: Insight into Islamisation," *Strategic Analysis*, Vol. 22, No. 11 (February 1999), pp. 1695–1712.

26. Musharraf's coup is best described in Owen Bennett Jones, *Pakistan—Eye of the Storm* (Islamabad, Pakistan: Vanguard, 2002).

Muslim world.[27] From the outset, Musharraf openly opposed the legitimacy of the radicals, urging for Pakistan to be a "progressive Islamic state"—though he only gradually built enough of a power base and determination to confront the radicals. In his first speech on October 17, 1999, Musharraf stated that "Islam teaches tolerance, not hatred; universal brotherhood, not enmity; peace, and not violence. . . . I urge [the Ulema] to curb elements which are exploiting religion for vested interests and bringing a bad name to our faith."[28] Musharraf spoke out against the "Kalashnikov culture" that had spread in Pakistan since the civil war in Afghanistan in the early 1990s and opposed the radical agenda of the Islamist parties, arguing that the overwhelming majority of Pakistanis are moderate and harbor no wish to be ruled by zealots. Musharraf then announced a series of measures to limit the influence of radical groups in the country. This included the highly symbolic measure of the blasphemy law, which Musharraf wanted amended; however, in the face of strong protests by the Islamic clergy, he was forced to backtrack on this point, thereby gravely damaging the perception of a strong and determined reformer.[29] During the almost two-year-long interval between Musharraf's coup and the terrorist attacks of September 11, 2001, Musharraf's government initiated a series of steps against radical Islamic groups. These steps neither succeeded in decimating the radical religious forces in Pakistan, nor managed to significantly influence the Saudi-funded *madrasas* or Islamic schools across the country, which train thousands of students in religious education—and in many cases, nothing else, creating halfliterate and brainwashed students unable to compete in the regular job market in the country. In the words of the International Crisis Group, "Musharraf's government has . . . relied mostly on cosmetic measures to advance its stated goal to crack down on militants and reform madrasas."[30]

Musharraf capitalized upon the September 11, 2001, terrorist attacks to give a new boost to his crackdown on the radicals. Musharraf's reversal of policy toward the Taliban resulted in U.S. support that helped Pakistan come out of isolation in world politics and produced significant inflows of money into the economy, strengthening Musharraf's position

27. See, e.g., Musharraf's statements on Turkish Television, *Channel NTV,* October 14, 1999.

28. Text of President Musharraf's Address to the Nation, *Dawn,* January 12, 2002.

29. See Owen Bennett Jones, "Pakistan Blasphemy U-Turn," *BBC News,* May 17, 2000.

30. International Crisis Group (ICP), *Pakistan: Madrasas, Extremism and the Military* (Brussels, Belgium: ICP, July 29, 2002).

greatly. The benefits of siding with the United States were very tangible: within four months of September 11, 2001, Pakistan had secured pledges of $1.5 billion U.S. in direct assistance or grants, signed debt rescheduling agreements with fifteen countries, and a number of new loans from international financial institutions.[31] Pakistan's macro-economic situation completely turned around, and its previously hemorrhaging economy was stabilized. In fact, Pakistan was "enjoying a measure of economic stability it hasn't seen for decades."[32] All these developments greatly strengthened Musharraf's own position at the helm and allowed him to initiate a severe crackdown on the sectarian terrorist groups operating inside Pakistan. The death toll in sectarian violence in the country decreased by half from 2001 to 2002, while the most vicious sectarian groups suffered large blows. The *Lashkar-i-Jhangvi* and *Sipah-i-Muhammad* had both been outlawed on August 14, 2001, and were targeted in the following months. Over fifty leading members of *Lashkar-i-Jhangvi* were either killed or apprehended.[33] While the state showed its ability to crack down effectively on these organizations that were vehemently opposed to the state and thoroughly unpopular inside Pakistan, the same was not true for extremists whose agenda coincided with that of the state, especially in Indian-occupied Kashmir. Given the increasingly hostile position of New Delhi, which sought to portray Pakistan as a terrorist state, Islamabad seemed to follow a two-pronged policy of closing down activities of some groups inside Pakistan, while being reluctant to destroy them in the absence of any signs of Indian willingness to compromise on Kashmir, as will be seen below.

The aftermath of September 11, 2001, also showed Musharraf that his room for maneuvering *vis-à-vis* the religious extremists was greater than he had thought. Whereas pictures of anti-U.S. protests in Pakistan spread around the world, the demonstrations were, by Pakistani standards, much smaller than expected and soon petered out, illustrating the low level of support of the radicals among the Pakistani population as a whole. The radicals' purported "street power" had turned out to be a bluff.[34]

On January 12, 2002, Musharraf delivered a historic address to the

---

31. Moinuddin Ahmed, "Assistance, Loans and Rescheduling Pacts after 9/11," *Dawn*, September 11, 2002.

32. Naveen A. Mangi, "Pakistan: It Pays to be Uncle Sam's Pal," *BusinessWeek*, April 7, 2003.

33. See Kanchan Lakshman, "Deep Roots to Pakistan's Sectarian Terror," *Asia Times*, July 9, 2003.

34. See Jones, *Pakistan: Eye of the Storm*, p. 26.

Pakistani nation, attacking religious extremism in terms unheard of in that country's recent history. Echoing his own words from October 1999, he stressed the damage done to Pakistan by the religious extremists, accused them of only sowing the seeds of hatred, and forming a "state within a state that has challenged the writ of the government."[35] Putting his agenda for Pakistan more clearly, Musharraf said: "The day of reckoning has come. Do we want Pakistan to become a theocratic state? Do we believe that religious education alone is enough for governance or do we want Pakistan to emerge as a progressive and dynamic Islamic welfare state? The verdict of the masses is in favor of a progressive Islamic state."[36] Simultaneously, five further groups were outlawed, the *Lashkar-e-Taiba* and the *Jaish-e-Mohammad*, both accused of involvement in the December 13, 2001, terrorist attack on the Indian parliament; as well as the *Sipah-i-Sahaba*, the *Tehrik-i-Nafaz-i-Shariat-i-Mohammadi*, and the Shi'i group *Tehrik-e-Jafria* in the crackdown that began two weeks before the speech.[37]

While implementation of the ban has been less than exemplary, the ability of these groups to operate inside Pakistan has been constrained. Another of Musharraf's main targets has been the *madrasas*. Legislation was passed to broaden the curriculum of *madrasas*. Moreover, Musharraf also made significant reforms in electoral law. Before the October 2002 elections, the government abolished the separate electorates, which Zia had introduced in 1985 to segregate the religious minorities in Pakistan from the Muslim majority. The issue was comparable to the blasphemy law in its symbolic importance, loathed by minorities as a sign of being treated as second-class citizens and upheld by religious extremists. In January 2002, Musharraf simply announced that the elections would be held on one universal electorate, with Muslims as well as non-Muslims contesting and voting on the same ballots, showing his increased confidence in confronting the radicals.

On a political level, the tone and the steps initiated by Musharraf signify a sea change in the political development of Pakistan. Before Musharraf, radical Islam was allowed an ideological monopoly of sorts—little opposition to the views voiced by the radicals were heard, except among courageous moderate intellectuals and clerics, which the well financed, determined, and often violent radicals could easily outstrip.

---

35. Text of President Musharraf's Address to the Nation, *Dawn*, January 12, 2002.

36. Ibid., see also Uwe Parpart, "Musharraf: Can this Man Change Pakistan?" *Asia Times*, January 18, 2002.

37. "Pakistan Crackdown Gathers Pace," *CNN International*, January 14, 2002; Muzamil Jaleel, "Crackdown Offers Hopes of Peace," *The Observer*, January 6, 2002.

Musharraf, however, forcibly, publicly, and consistently has proclaimed the unsuitability and extremism of the ideas of the religious radicals. The significance of Musharraf's statements was that since the Zia regime, no Pakistani leader had dared challenge the Islamist forces directly, instead following a policy of appeasement toward them—whether reluctantly as in the case of Benazir Bhutto or willingly as in the case of Nawaz Sharif.

Musharraf's failure to effectively curb all religious extremists has led to some disillusionment, as well as lingering accusations that he had never desired to curb them, instead keeping them in place for various reasons, either because they are useful for Pakistan in Kashmir, providing a proxy army that fights Indian rule without directly implicating Pakistan,[38] or because the government, Musharraf himself, or both remain inclined to the Islamization of the country.[39]

What this type of analysis ignores are the constraints on the Musharraf regime. Assuming that Musharraf's position as a military ruler gives him unlimited power implies a fundamental misunderstanding of Pakistan's politics and Musharraf's form of government. Pakistan is not a totalitarian state, and Musharraf's government has always kept violence as a last resort, realizing that the use of violence and repression is counterproductive to the type of society that Musharraf aspires to build. In this context, the government's ability to push forward reforms is dependent on its ability to have the civilian and military bureaucracy implement its policies. Additionally, the international environment and the widespread condemnation of Musharraf's military coup also meant a need to abstain from the use of force to seek political goals. As Pamela Constable argues, Musharraf's consistent strategy has been to portray himself as a leader and not as a dictator.[40]

Unlike Zia ul-Haq, who concentrated power in his own hands, Musharraf established a collegial form of government in Pakistan, bordering on consensus decision-making. Before major policy decisions, Musharraf made a practice of meeting with major political leaders, jour-

38. See Jessica Stern, "Pakistan's Jihad Culture," *Foreign Affairs*, Vol. 79, No. 6 (November/December 2000).

39. See, e.g., Howard W. French, "Pakistani Militants' Ties to Military Make Radicals Hard to Dislodge," *New York Times*, May 27, 2002; Selig Harrison, "Bush Needs to Attach Strings to Pakistan Aid," *USA Today*, June 23, 2003; and Ali Ahmed Rind, "Pervez Musharraf: What the West Doesn't Know—or Doesn't Want to Know," *Baltimore Chronicle*, August 7, 2002;

40. Pamela Constable, "Pakistan's Predicament," *Journal of Democracy*, Vol. 12, No. 1 (January 2001), pp. 22–23.

nalists, and religious figures;[41] in addition, Musharraf's relationship with the military leadership was one of consensus rather than of one-way decision-making, implying that Musharraf needs the consent of leading generals to implement policy, especially in the foreign policy sphere. To sum up, Musharraf's intentions have undoubtedly been to reduce the strength of the religious extremists in Pakistan. His resolve to implement such wide-ranging reforms, however, has been compromised by constraints upon his regime that stem partly from the need for consensus within the top brass and partly from a deliberate strategy to avoid the use of repression, the capacity for which the military nevertheless clearly possesses. Musharraf, in other words, has stemmed the growth of religious extremism in Pakistan, whereas the rollback of extremist forces is likely to be long and arduous. Far from staying on the defensive, however, Musharraf has moved to enunciate the concept of "enlightened moderation" as a guiding doctrine in Pakistan's foreign policy, stressing the virtue of coexistence and understanding between religions and civilizations.[42]

THE OCTOBER 2002 ELECTIONS

The results of the October 2002 elections appeared to have been a large setback for Musharraf's policies of curtailing the power of religious extremists. The Islamist coalition *Muttahida Majlis-e-Amal* (MMA)[43] came in third in the national elections, with fifty-three seats, short of the seventy-seven seats gathered by the Pakistan Muslim League—*Quaid-e-Azam* (PML-Q)—and the sixty-two seats of the Pakistan People's Party Parliamentarians (PPPP). In addition, it was able to form a government of its own in the Northwest Frontier Province. This result was interpreted by various sources as a great victory for Islamist parties, as a protest vote against Musharraf's pro-U.S. policies, and as a further sign of the

---

41. See, e.g., "Consensus on Reforms: Musharraf to Meet Leaders of All Parties," *Dawn*, July 3, 2000; "Musharraf to Hold All-Party Meet on Summit," *The Hindu*, June 24, 2001.

42. Pervez Musharraf, "A Plea for Enlightened Moderation," *Washington Post*, June 1, 2004.

43. The MMA consists of the *Jamaat-i-Islami* Pakistan (JI), a relatively orthodox but modernist movement based in the urban areas of Pakistan; the two wings of the *Jamaat-i-Ulema-Pakistan* (JUI), a purist, Deobandi movement, led respectively by Maulana Sami ul-Haq and Maulana Fazl-ur-Rahman; the *Jamiat-Ulema-e-Pakistan*, a Barelvi organization representing the more traditionalist and Sufi-oriented population; the *Jamiat-Ahl-e-Tahriq Pakistan*, a small Wahhabi-oriented party; and the *Islami-Tehrik-Pakistan*, a Shi'i party.

Islamization of Pakistan. *Newsweek* even termed the election "A Big Vote for Jihad."[44] While it is irrefutable that the elections led to a greater influence of political Islam through their simple numbers, the origin of this phenomenon, beyond the surface, is to be found not in a process of Islamization but rather in a series of circumstances that contributed to the salience of the MMA party.

First of all, the religious parties may have made a great jump in terms of the number of seats that they had been allotted in the National Assembly, but their electoral support was basically stagnant at 11 percent of the vote. Eleven percent of the vote in the 1997 elections had resulted only in a handful of parliamentary seats, whereas it had meant 20 percent of the seats in 2002. The reason is the unprecedented alliance of six religious parties with highly diverging interpretations of Islam that constituted the MMA.[45] In earlier elections, these parties have often fielded different candidates for the same seats in Pakistan's British-modeled first-past-the-post electoral system, and hence, through their fragmentation, undermined the electoral strength of political Islam by competing with one another. The alliance that created the MMA nevertheless led to so-called seat adjustments, with the MMA carefully selecting single candidates for individual constituencies, thereby maximizing their electoral capacity.

Second, whereas the MMA was united and had optimized its ability to gain seats, the mainstream political parties were discredited, fragmented, and obstructed by the government. The Pakistan People's Party and the Muslim League had served in government twice each in the 1990s, and their time in government had been characterized by rampant corruption, economic stagnation, and a general failure even to try to fulfill their electoral promises. They were also both led by the same politicians who had been in power and failed, Benazir Bhutto and Nawaz Sharif, respectively. This ensured three things: first, popular dissatisfaction with these parties led by widely discredited leaders; second, government obstruction, because the Musharraf government adamantly persisted in denying both Bhutto and Sharif the opportunity to return to Pakistan and run in the elections and went out of its way to level the playing field in favor of the PML-Q, thereby also benefiting the MMA; and third, by extension, the disadvantage of party leaders being in exile and therefore not being able to campaign effectively for their respective party's candidates. This weakened and divided the mainstream parties,

---

44. Ron Moreau and Zahid Hussain, "Pakistan: A Big Vote for Jihad," *Newsweek,* October 16, 2002.

45. See, e.g., ICG, *Pakistan: The Mullahs and the Military* (Brussels, Belgium: ICG, March 2003), pp. 5–18.

given that detractors from Sharif and Bhutto had established their own separate wings of the parties. Most significant was the split within the Muslim League, with the government actively cultivating a group of detractors from Nawaz Sharif, which turned into the dominant faction of the Muslim League, receiving 25 percent of the vote and sixty-two of the directly elected seats.[46] The PML-N loyal to Sharif received 11.23 percent and only fourteen seats, compared to the MMA's four times as many seats with fewer number of votes of 11 percent, or 3.19 million votes—the PML-N losing most seats to the PML-Q. Two other factions of the PML similarly stole five seats. The PPP had smaller problems with detractors and managed to receive sixty-seven seats, thereby becoming the main opposition to the PML-Q government. The weakening of the mainstream parties had benefited the MMA greatly, as their unified candidates could defeat the multitude of candidates fielded by the mainstream parties in many constituencies.[47]

A third factor was the regional bias in the electoral results of the MMA. It won practically all its seats in the NWFP and in Baluchistan, as well as in the metropolis of Karachi. The MMA was basically irrelevant in the provincial assemblies of the Sindh and the Punjab. This reflected two things. First, that if one could speak of an Islamic wind sweeping through the country, the electoral aspect of it could be witnessed only in the Pashtun-populated areas of the northwest of the country. In turn, there is reason to question whether the advances of the MMA are due to an Islamic wind or to other factors. First of all, while the Pashtun-populated areas are the most strictly Islamic of Pakistan, Pashtun nationalist parties, especially the Awami National Party, had dominated them earlier. Its failure in provincial government and corruption scandals had led to widespread dissatisfaction, which favored the MMA. Moreover, the 2002 elections were the first in which the Tribal Areas had been allowed to vote. These most orthodox Islamic regions were carried by the MMA, which often was the only party seriously campaigning in these areas, tipping the balance in its favor. Finally, economic concerns were also very likely involved. The U.S.-led military campaign in Afghanistan had severely crippled the cross-border trade—both legal and smuggling—that had previously taken place along the extensive Pakistani-Afghan border. Increased military surveillance on both sides and tighter border controls

---

46. Sixty seats in the National Assembly were reserved for women, and ten were reserved for minorities; these were allocated according to the proportion of votes that parties received in the general election. The MMA received fourteen additional seats of these seventy.

47. ICG, *Pakistan: The Mullahs and the Military*, p. 16.

caused trade to plummet in regions where little other economic livelihood was possible, leading to a very real economic sting from the war for
many people. This, as much as Islamic ideology, pushed many Pashtuns
closer to the anti-government and anti-U.S. views of the MMA.[48]

In sum, good reasons exist to take issue with the argument that Pakistan is gradually succumbing to a wave of religious zealotry. In fact, there
is also good reason to claim that Pakistan's wave of Islamization,
launched by Zia ul-Haq in the late 1970s, continued on its own momentum during the years of elected rule in the 1990s, but has been stemmed
by the change of governmental attitude toward extremism after
Musharraf's coup. The pace of the government's reforms remains slow,
chiefly due to internal constraints on a government that is unwilling to
use repression. A clear change in the Pakistani state's attitude to religious
extremism is visible, with the population of the country seeming to support Musharraf's vision of a moderate and progressive Pakistan. This
does not mean that the danger of Islamic radicalism is over; extremist
groups remain well financed, assertive, and armed and therefore a significant force in the politics and society of Pakistan. Their ability to
influence policy, however, has been sharply reduced.

Pakistan's Foreign Policy

Pressures for Islamization have undoubtedly been present in Pakistan
since its inception and have gradually strengthened in society, especially
in the 1980s, with lingering effects to this day. Several questions remain:
to what extent has this Islamization affected Pakistan's foreign policy?
Has Islamization injected an ideological element in the making of foreign
policy? Has Pakistan made decisions on Islamic grounds that have run
counter to its material, national interests? Ideological elements in the society and politics of a country do not necessarily translate into the foreign
relations of a country. In Pakistan's case, however, several elements of its
foreign policy seem to indicate the possibility that, in retrospect, decisions with an Islamic slant carried the day and had negative material consequences for Pakistan. The support for Islamic extremists in the Kashmiri conflict, and perhaps even more blatantly, the support for the
Taliban are examples of this. Both ended up harming Pakistan's interests,
both its international standing and the physical security of the country,
while failing to achieve stated objectives. But were these decisions taken
on Islamic grounds or based on material considerations of interest?

---

48. This section is based on the author's travels in Pakistan during September 2002,
especially in the Northwest Frontier Province.

ISLAM IN PAKISTAN'S EARLY FOREIGN POLICY

Pakistan has struggled with the role of Islam in its foreign policy formulation since the state's creation. Pakistan has continuously voiced support for Islamic causes, partly rhetorically, but also often in deeds as well as in words, especially where this carried little risk. The main and dominating foreign policy goals of Pakistan have, however, always been taken on the basis of material interests—it has always sought support wherever it was available among great powers that are neither Islamic nor Muslim-majority. As a state founded to safeguard the interests of Muslims, Pakistan, in its early years, made a number of Muslim causes its own and has, over the ensuing years, continued to identify with the plight of Muslims who are perceived to be oppressed elsewhere. From 1947 to 1954, Pakistan tried to make use of its position as the fifth largest country in the world and the world's largest Muslim state to develop closer ties with other Muslim countries. The liberation of Indonesia was an example, and Pakistan tried from the outset to develop close ties with Turkey and Iran.[49] Likewise, Pakistan's attachment to Islamic causes also explains its strong support for the Palestinian cause, as well as its support for Azerbaijan in its war with Armenia and its relatively strong positions on Bosnia, Kosovo, and Chechnya. Yet, these elements are not exclusive to Pakistan. Secular Turkey shares most of these priorities; indeed, despite the close common strategic interests of Turkey and Israel, it was only the Oslo agreement of 1993 that allowed Turkish leaders to develop and publicize the close extent of their relations with Israel—the public cherishing of the Palestinian cause would have prevented such a move before that date. Turkey's support for Azerbaijan and concern for Chechnya have been even more marked than Pakistan's. Muslim constituents, whether in a secular state like Turkey or an Islamic one like Pakistan, tend to feel a strong sense of solidarity with Muslims under siege or attack elsewhere, and this creates public opinion pressure that secular and Islamic governments alike must take into account.

While such popular opinion generates a need mainly for rhetorical support for Islamic causes, Pakistani leaders to a certain extent have followed policies supporting them as well, such as sending fighter jets to Syria to fight Israel in the 1973 war or arranging for hundreds of *mujahideen* to be sent to Azerbaijan to fight in the war against Armenia in 1993. Clearly, rhetoric and genuine policy is always somewhat mixed, and the reason for support may vary: in Turkey's case, support for Chechnya was based on the ethnic ties between large sections of Turkey's population with Chechnya, and in the case of Azerbaijan, on a mixture of

49. Burke, *The Foreign Policy of Pakistan*, pp. 68–69.

ethnic proximity and strategic interests. In Pakistan's case, a similar mix between material interests and genuine solidarity can be seen; support for Muslim causes generated goodwill that helped Pakistan secure financial support from Saudi Arabia and other Gulf states, while policy-makers in many cases supported causes, such as Chechnya and Azerbaijan, where few material benefits—yet also few costs—could be found for either Pakistan or the individual decision-makers.

On another level, Pakistan's foreign relations in the security sphere have never had a strong Islamic component. Pakistan's efforts to attract support from the Muslim world in its conflict with India met with very little success. Given India's leading role in the Non-Aligned Movement and the membership of most Muslim states in this movement, Pakistan saw little more than declarations of solidarity from Islamic countries on the matter, and it never fully succeeded in activating the Organization of the Islamic Conference on the Kashmir issue. Instead, Pakistan's vulnerable security situation *vis-à-vis* India led it to seek help where it was available—with the great powers. In the 1950s, Pakistan turned toward the United States, especially under Field Marshal Ayub Khan's rule. It willingly occupied a crucial place in U.S. efforts to contain the Soviet Union, seeing this as the best way to improve its military capacity and international standing with regard to India. The 1970s, especially under Zulfikar Ali Bhutto, saw a booming of the Sino-Pakistani relationship.[50] While U.S.-Pakistani relations worsened mainly as a result of Pakistan's striving for a nuclear capability, the Afghan war enabled General Zia to again enlist the United States, while the renewed deterioration in U.S.-Pakistani relations in the 1990s, especially under the Clinton administration, again led to a strengthening and deepening of Pakistan's alliance with China. In sum, Pakistan's foreign policy was simply to seek support wherever it was available. The September 11, 2001, terrorist attacks reflected a shift in Pakistan's strategic orientation, where relations with Washington were not the highest priority, especially when compared to those with China: it was made clear from the outset that Washington's warming up to Islamabad would not be permitted to upset Chinese interests. While the United States is clearly understood to be the greater power of the two, Pakistanis have, especially since the U.S. withdrawal from Afghanistan in 1989, concluded that the United States can not be trusted as a reliable strategic ally. China, on the other hand, is understood

---

50. John Garver, "The Future of the Sino-Pakistani Entente Cordiale," in Michael R. Chambers, *South Asia in 2020: Future Strategic Balances and Alliances* (Carlisle, Pa.: U.S. Army War College, 2002), pp. 385–387.

to have much more stable and long-term interests in the region, and is therefore a more predictable and reliable ally for Islamabad.

REALPOLITIK IN PAKISTAN'S AFGHANISTAN POLICY, 1980–2003
The Soviet invasion of Afghanistan immediately aggravated Pakistan's security situation. Its relations with Afghanistan had never been rosy, with a thorny border conflict and the issue of "Pakhtunistan" dividing them. Because Afghan governments have challenged the legitimacy of the Durand Line that divided the two countries and Pakistan's sovereignity over the Pashtun-populated Northwest Frontier Province, Pakistan's relations with its closest Muslim-majority neighbor had been chilly from the start. Yet Afghanistan hardly posed a direct military threat to Pakistan. This changed with the entry of the Soviet military forces into Afghanistan, which was interpreted by Pakistani and Western observers alike as a step in achieving what imperial Russia had always lacked, access to the warm seas.[51]

REACTING TO THE SOVIET INVASION. Faced with this imminent threat, already in a defensive posture toward the growing might of India, and disturbed by the overthrow of the Shah of Iran, Pakistan was hard-pressed to shore up its security. The invasion of Afghanistan—it was widely believed—would be followed by a Soviet push to the Arabian Sea through Pakistani Baluchistan, and it also rekindled fears of externally inspired unrest among Pakistan's Pashtun population. The question was how to bolster security; in fact, while Pakistan eventually opted for full-scale and covert aid to the Afghan rebels, this was by no means a foregone conclusion in 1979. In fact, one option that was explored was to mend fences with India in view of the advancing Soviet threat.[52] Indian officials did not, however, see the looming Soviet threat over the subcontinent as Islamabad did. Quite to the contrary, New Delhi's initial reaction was to term the invasion a defensive response to the activities of "certain foreign powers."[53] Though some change in the Indian view occurred later, India's ties with the Soviet Union were close, and it did not see any reason to challenge Moscow over Afghanistan. Moreover, India showed much more concern at signs of a U.S. return to the subcontinent through assistance to Pakistan than at Moscow's presence in Afghani-

51. Selig Harrison, *In Afghanistan's Shadow: Baluch Nationalism and Soviet Temptations* (New York: Carnegie Endowment for International Peace, 1981).

52. W. Howard Wriggins, "Pakistan's Search for a Foreign Policy After the Invasion of Afghanistan," *Pacific Affairs*, Vol. 57, No. 2 (Summer 1984), pp. 289–290.

53. Wriggins, p. 289.

stan. While both sides had some interest in having a dialogue, especially because India did not want Pakistan to once again bring the United States into the South Asian arena, this did not lead to any breakthrough.

Zia also sought support from Middle Eastern allies, who were recently enriched by the aftermath of the 1973 oil crisis. It is likely that Saudi Arabia had already pledged some money at this stage, but Zia was well aware that the kingdom could do little more than provide funds— desirable, but by no means sufficient for Pakistan in its struggle to determine whether to seek to appease the Soviet Union or confront it, even covertly. Pakistan's ability to find support in the Middle East also faced the problem that Iran, which had been a major supporter of Pakistan under the Shah's rule, was now not only promoting a form of Islam very different from the one favored by Zia, but was also in the middle of a war with Iraq that was extremely bloody and ensured that Iran had no time or energy to spare supporting Pakistan. An "Islamic" way to solve the Soviet dilemma was simply not there. Likewise, Pakistan could expect quiet support from China, but Beijing showed no intentions of directly challenging the Soviet Union over Afghanistan.

Instead, Zia's fortunes were improved by the victory of Ronald Reagan in the November 1980 U.S. presidential election. Compared to the Jimmy Carter administration, Reagan was much less concerned with Pakistan's human rights record, military rule, and nuclear weapons program. Reagan was convinced of the need to address the threat posed by the Soviet Union and of Pakistan's importance as an ally. For Zia, of course, the war in Afghanistan enabled Pakistan to have a new beginning in its relations with the United States, damaged as they had been by a U.S. arms embargo on Pakistan for its nuclear weapons program and a refusal to restructure Pakistan's large debt. In establishing a new strategy against the Soviet Union, Zia famously labeled an initial U.S. offer of $300 million U.S. in assistance "peanuts."[54] Reagan later offered Pakistan much more; eventually an estimated $4 billion U.S. in assistance was channeled to Pakistan. Zia, however, was well aware of the risks involved in confronting the Soviet Union, something many observers at the time thought futile. His decision to go ahead with the plan to arm the Afghan *mujahideen* was only taken on the advice of Akhtar Khan, his chief of Inter-Services Intelligence (ISI), who argued that a guerrilla war in Afghanistan, as leading U.S. "cold warriors" were advocating, could actually be won.[55] Nevertheless, acquiescing to cooperation with Wash-

---

54. Shahid Javed Burki, "Pakistan Comes Full Circle," *Dawn,* October 2, 2001.

55. Mohammad Youssaf and Mark Adkin, *The Bear Trap: Afghanistan's Untold Story* (London: Cooper, 1992), p. 25.

ington, Zia ensured that *all* financing, training, and arming of the *mujahideen* should be channeled through Pakistan and not directly through the Central Intelligence Agency (CIA).[56] In this sense, Pakistan's support for the Afghan *mujahideen* may have included a limited cultural component, as Pakistani foreign policy had always tended to support Muslim causes abroad. On the other hand, the policy, once U.S. involvement was secured, was completely coterminous with Pakistan's material national interests: countering what was perceived as a direct threat to its national security—recalling that Pakistanis widely believed that Baluchistan, with a recent legacy of a bloody rebellion in the 1970s, was next on the agenda of Moscow's ambitions to reach the Gulf. A. Z. Hilali has termed the U.S.-Pakistani cooperation "an opportunistic partnership between two unequal powers," a correct assessment in the sense that both shared a narrow and short-term objective—the defeat of the Soviet Union in Afghanistan and a check on Soviet expansion into South Asia.[57]

SUPPORT FOR RADICAL GROUPINGS. The Afghan *mujahideen* was, however, divided into numerous and very different groups. Among these groups, Pakistan consistently nurtured the Islamic radical components. While providing assistance to all of the Peshawar-based factions, Pakistan stifled the flow of funds to the moderate organizations such as Pir Gailani's National Islamic Front and Sibghatullah Mojaddidi's National Salvation Front, and secular organizations were never accorded any support in the war. Instead, Zia systematically channeled funds to the radical forces, especially Gulbuddin Hekmatyar's *Hizb-e-Islami*. This was not only because it was the best organized of the movements, as ISI support for the splinter faction of *Hizb-e-Islami* headed by Yunis Khales shows. These two groups, in fact, were the most internationalist—as opposed to Afghan nationalist—of the factions, among other being the ones to draw in foreign fighters, the so-called "Arab Afghans." This policy fulfilled a very pragmatic policy goal for the Pakistani state, the one that Pakistan had always pursued in its relationship with Afghanistan: to counter the risk of Afghan territorial claims on Pakistan, the so-called question of "Pakhtunistan" that had poisoned Pakistani-Afghan relations from the outset.[58] Even from before the creation of the state of Pakistan, the Afghan government had campaigned for the Pashtun areas of Pakistan,

---

56. John K. Cooley, *Unholy Wars: Afghanistan, America and International Terrorism* (London: Pluto, 2000), p. 88.

57. A. Z. Hilali, "The Costs and Benefits of the Afghan War for Pakistan," *Contemporary South Asia*, Vol. 11, No. 3 (November 2002), p. 291.

58. See, e.g., Erland Jansson, *India, Pakistan or Pakhtunistan?* Studia Historica Upsaliensia, No. 119 (Uppsala, Sweden: Uppsala University, 1981).

especially the tribal areas, to be included in Afghanistan. These claims persisted and were argued vigorously by the former King of Afghanistan, Zahir Shah; Afghanistan never recognized the Durand Line, which forms the border between the two countries.[59] While Hafizullah Amin, during his brief tenure in Kabul in 1979, had offered Afghanistan's acceptance of the Durand Line in return for Pakistani support, the Soviet-controlled regime again took up the issue.[60] Hence, Pashtun nationalism was a major threat that Zia in no sense would have liked to see strengthened, but which the Soviet Union saw as an instrument both to keep Pashtuns of Afghanistan happy and to counteract and undermine Pakistan.

Pakistan's logical allies in Afghanistan were the Islamic forces, who in the name of Islamic internationalism had a higher degree of solidarity with Islamic Pakistan than they had with Pashtun nationalism. In this sense, the Islamization of the Afghan resistance not only offered an attractive rallying cry inside Afghanistan while it attracted Muslim volunteers and support from the outside; it also, from Islamabad's vantage point, increased Pakistan's national security vis-à-vis Afghanistan as it strengthened, in Afghanistan's domestic politics, the previously weak forces that were friendly to Pakistan. Thus, the urge to support radical Islamic groups in the Afghan resistance had constituted a thoroughly pragmatic and self-serving interest of the state of Pakistan. Hilali has gone so far as to argue that "the paramount objective of Pakistan's policymakers in supporting the Afghan War was to block the revival of Afghan nationalism and persuade a friendly government in Kabul to recognize the Durand Line as an international border so as to stifle any resurgence of transborder Pakhtun nationalism."[61]

THE CIVIL WAR AND THE TALIBAN. Pakistan's Afghanistan policy was guided by three major policy goals: its first and major concern remained the stability of Pakistan's Northwest Frontier Province, implying an absolute priority to avoid the ascendancy of Pashtun nationalism in Kabul and possible territorial demands on Pakistan. Ideally, Pakistan sought to have the Durand Line recognized by the Afghan government. It should be noted that Islamabad's worries regarding ethnic nationalism in general and Pashtun separatism in particular have decreased during the 1990s. While ethnic tensions still exist, the political forces in Sindh,

59. See Azmat Hayat Khan, *The Durand Line* (Peshawar, Pakistan: Area Study Centre, University of Peshawar, 2000), pp. 179–211.

60. See Hafeez Malik, *Soviet-Pakistan Relations and Post-Soviet Dynamics* (London: MacMillan, 1994).

61. Hilali, "The Costs and Benefits of the Afghan War for Pakistan," p. 296.

Baluchistan, and the NWFP that have pursued separatist agendas have been weakened considerably, partly as a result of governmental policies against them, but mainly due to public disenchantment with separatist politicians. The gradual decline of the Awami National Party in the NWFP is an example of this, which has calmed Islamabad's worries somewhat. Pakistan's acceptance of ex-King Zahir Shah of Afghanistan as a major political player in the post-Taliban period, in spite of the anti-Pakistani stance that he had followed while in power, is a clear example of this.[62]

Second, Pakistan desired a government dominated by pro-Pakistani forces in Kabul. Islamabad was determined to avoid the return of a pro-Indian government in Afghanistan, which would aggravate Pakistan's strategic vulnerability *vis-à-vis* India.

Third, the primary additional factor since the 1980s was that Afghanistan's economic and geopolitical importance for Pakistan had skyrocketed because of the independence of the former Soviet republics in Central Asia. Pakistan therefore required stability in Afghanistan—without which Pakistan would neither be able to function as a major trade corridor nor to project influence in Central Asia.

The logical conclusions stemming from these policy goals left Pakistan with few options, at a time when geopolitical competition over Afghanistan had increased through the roles of Iran, Russia, and India; therefore, a *laissez-faire* policy of not intervening in Afghanistan was interpreted in Islamabad as a non-option, which could only have worsened Pakistan's predicament. The Tajik- or Uzbek-dominated political factions in Afghanistan had entertained close relations with Iran and India, as well as Russia, and were therefore ill suited to Pakistan's ambitions. Moreover, these factions, together with most Pashtun-dominated ones, had, during the civil war of the early 1990s, proved their inability to secure Afghanistan's territory and enable the country to function as a trade corridor. This dictated the need for a new cast of characters. Finally, among the Pashtun forces, Pakistan still preferred the Islamic-oriented ones to secular forces, given their solidarity with Pakistan on the basis of Islamic identity. The Taliban movement, in this sense, was at first sight an excellent candidate to answer to Pakistan's blueprint for Afghanistan. Ethnically, it was mainly Pashtun, and more importantly had close ties with Pakistan, as most of the members had lived in refugee camps in Pakistan and been trained by the JUI's Deobandi *madrasas* in the NWFP

---

62. See, e.g., "Zahir Shah Sends Team to Pakistan," *Dawn*, October 15, 2001.

and northern Baluchistan. This Pakistani link made Islamabad's planners believe that the Taliban would remain loyal to Pakistan.[63]

After the Soviet withdrawal from Afghanistan, Pakistani policy-makers felt that this policy had been successful. The victory against the Soviet Union, however, for which Pakistan and the United States deserve a significant part of the credit had not stabilized Afghanistan. Quite to the contrary, the failure of the *mujahideen* groups to compromise on power-sharing in Kabul had grave consequences for Pakistan as well as Afghanistan's other neighbors, especially Iran. Pakistan had averted the Soviet threat, but the fallout of the war on Pakistan was severe. It had a refugee problem of immense proportions to handle, topping off at over three million refugees who profoundly altered the demography, economy, and even ecology of Pakistan's already arid and poor border areas with Afghanistan. The unrest on the border also exacerbated the problems of consumer goods smuggling, armament of the population, and the production, smuggling, and abuse of opium and heroin. Likewise, the inflow of major amounts of U.S. aid into the military intelligence structures greatly increased the domestic power of the ISI and increased corruption within the bureaucracy and the armed forces. As if all of this were not enough, the infighting between *mujahideen* groups from 1989–1996 sent wave after wave of refugees fleeing to Pakistan. Clearly, the fallout of the Afghan war was becoming threatening to the very security of Pakistan.

In 1991, when the five former Soviet republics of Kazakhstan, the Kyrgyz Republic, Tajikistan, Turkmenistan, and Uzbekistan became independent, Pakistan under Prime Minister Benazir Bhutto was poised to position itself as the logical trade corridor to Central Asia. The civil war in Afghanistan, however, made such a prospect impossible to realize, perpetuating Central Asia's dependence on Russia because trade southward remained practically impossible given the insecurity and destruction in Afghanistan. The Afghan government under Burhanuddin Rabbani, while unable to control the country, was Tajik-dominated and entertained good relations with India, while being cold toward Pakistan. Meanwhile, Pakistan's perspectives on Afghanistan had not changed significantly.

As discussed in the chapter on Afghanistan in this volume, the Taliban soon showed their potential to arrest the anarchy and lawlessness in southwestern Afghanistan, which further convinced Pakistani policy-makers of its capacity to stabilize Afghanistan—policymakers who had

---

63. See, e.g., Imtiaz Gul, *The Unholy Nexus: Pak-Afghan Relations under the Taliban* (Lahore, Pakistan: Vanguard, 2002).

not initially joined Interior Minister General Nasirullah Babar in supporting the nascent movement.

In other words, studied on its merits, the policy decision taken by
Islamabad to sponsor the Taliban movement makes sense from the point
of view of the material interests of Pakistan; a secular analysis of national
interest, rather than Islamic radicalism, had conditioned Pakistan's support for the movement. The sponsorship of the Taliban has nevertheless
often been portrayed as a decision taken by radicalized officers in the ISI
leadership. This culturalist view, however, makes little sense if one accounts for the doctrinal differences that existed at the time between the
modernist Islamic radicals of the *Jamaat-e-Islami* and the Deobandi puritans of the *Jamaat-e-Ulema-e-Islam*. Zia ul-Haq had been close to the
Jamaat-e-Islami views and promoted cadres close to that community in the
military, including the ISI. This also explains the fact that long after
General Babar had launched his support for the Taliban, ISI support for
Hekmatyar still continued. In other words, the Islamist cadres of Pakistan
were not the first to support the Taliban; quite to the contrary, the secular
leadership of Benazir Bhutto and her Interior Minister had launched this
policy, which the Islamist cadres started to comply with only in early
1995, when the Taliban had grown into a significant force in the
Kandahar area. Babar himself is hardly a man guided by ideological principles alone. In fact, while working under Zulfikar Ali Bhutto in the
1970s, he was instrumental in organizing a proactive Pakistani policy toward Afghanistan as early as 1973, after the overthrow of King Zahir
Shah. In General Babar's own words, Pakistan "had a permanent geopolitical interest in Afghanistan and we should groom people from inside
Afghanistan to guard that interest."[64] That policy led to the grooming of
the main leaders of the resistance, who at the time were mainly students
in Pakistan including Gulbuddin Hekmatyar and Ahmad Shah Massoud.
As these players, almost twenty years later, were no longer serving Pakistan's interests, Babar repeated the procedure and helped to groom a new
movement that could provide security and access to Central Asia for Pakistan. To argue that religious zeal was the reason for Pakistan's support
for the Taliban is hence misplaced. This, of course, does not imply that individual officers or bureaucrats did not support this policy with enthusiasm born out of religious conviction. Certainly, high ranking army
officers such as former ISI Directors Generals Hamid Gul and Mehmood
Ahmed, who Musharraf dismissed in October 2001, held this orientation.
These Islamist elements may have been an important constituency supporting the Pakistani alliance with the Taliban; however, little ground ex-

---

64. See Gul, *The Unholy Nexus*, pp. 10–15.

ists on which to conclude that they had been instrumental in making these decisions.

INDIA AND KASHMIR. Pakistan's policy of supporting radical groups in Kashmir since its 1989 insurrection against Indian rule is an additional example of how Islam was used instrumentally to promote the state's material interests.

The Kashmir dispute has been the main bone of contention between India and Pakistan since 1947; in fact, Kashmir remains an unfinished remnant of the partition of the Indian subcontinent.[65] India and Pakistan fought their first war in 1948 over Kashmir, as Pashtun tribesmen from the NWFP with some support from the nascent Pakistani army descended on Kashmir to support the overwhelmingly Muslim Kashmiri population's uprising against the Hindu ruler of that state. Pakistan managed to secure one-third of Kashmir's original territory while India secured the remaining two-thirds, including the prized Vale of Kashmir. A second war was fought in 1965, when Pakistan again tried to infiltrate Indian-held Kashmir by sending infiltrators across the Line of Control, which separated Pakistani-held Kashmir from Indian-held Kashmir, in order to stir up a popular uprising.[66] Pakistan nevertheless calculated that India would not expand the war outside of Kashmir, which proved to be a serious mistake, as the Indian army crossed the international border and moved toward Lahore.[67] The 1971 war, in which the Indian military helped Bangladesh to secure its independence, thereby dismembering Pakistan, led to a long period of decreased tensions in and around Kashmir. Many leading policymakers in Pakistan had lost hope on ever wresting Kashmir from Indian rule, due to the simple military imbalance between the two states.[68] Indeed, the 1980s saw great increases in tourism to Kashmir. Mishandling of Indian-controlled Kashmir, however, led to a mushrooming of frustration with Indian rule.

In 1989, this frustration exploded into an indigenous revolt. India immediately blamed the unrest in Kashmir on Pakistan, but in reality Pakistan's role in fomenting the trouble was minimal. As Victoria Schofield puts it, "the alleged 'foreign hand' was . . . a convenient scapegoat which

65. Alastair Lamb, *Birth of a Tragedy: Kashmir, 1947* (Hertingfordbury, UK: Roxton, 1994).

66. See, e.g., Shahid M. Amin, *Pakistan's Foreign Policy: A Reappraisal* (London: Ashgate, 2002), p. 51.

67. Victoria Schofield, *Kashmir in Conflict: India, Pakistan, and the Unfinished War* (New York: I.B. Tauris, 2000), p. 110.

68. Robert Wirsing, *India, Pakistan and the Kashmir Dispute* (New York: St. Martin's Press, 1994) p. 121.

prevented the Indian government from seeing the internal trauma within the valley."[69] The emergence of a strong, indigenous uprising against Indian rule in 1989 surprised even Pakistani observers and led them to conclude that India's inability to withstand the many separatist rebellions that it faced would make it possible, at some point, for Kashmir to be separated from India. Pakistan hence began to support the Kashmiri liberation movement from the outset in 1989. At the beginning, this included a multitude of groups, dominated by the secular and Kashmiri nationalist Jammu and Kashmir Liberation Front (JKLF), and the more Islamic-minded *Hizb-ul Mujahideen*, an offshoot of the *Jamaat-e-Islami* political party. Very soon, however, Pakistani support for Kashmiri liberation movements began to discriminate between the pro-independence and pro-Pakistan groups. In fact, secular Kashmiri nationalist movements, while seeking separation from India, were in no hurry to accede to Pakistan—instead favoring the independence of Kashmir from both India and Pakistan. Pakistan's claim since 1947 has been that Kashmir, as a Muslim-majority state in British India at partition, was to become a constituent part of Pakistan. In fact, part of the problem in Kashmir stems from the region's importance to the national idea of both India and Pakistan. As a state created for protecting the Muslims of South Asia, the very justification for the existence of Pakistan would be challenged by Kashmir's belonging to India. On the other hand, the grave human rights violations carried out by Indian forces in Kashmir vindicate Pakistan's claim that Muslims need a separate state to be safe. But likewise, Kashmir, as the only would-be Muslim-majority state in India, is crucial for New Delhi's attempts to portray India as a secular, multi-ethnic, and multi-religious democracy. In fact, Kashmir's secession from India would boost secessionist tendencies in other Indian states, especially in Northeastern India.

In this context, Pakistan moved toward cutting off the JKLF from its support and tried to reorient the fighting forces to strengthen the pro-Pakistani factions. In this sense, Islamabad faced a situation similar to the one in Afghanistan: secular and nationalist forces did not share crucial interests with Pakistan. Secular Kashmiri nationalists did not pose the same threat to Pakistan as Pashtun nationalists in Afghanistan did, being in no sense hostile to Pakistan at the time. Neither, however, did they fit with Pakistan's policy goals of securing Kashmir's accession to Pakistan. The religious forces in Kashmir did, however, support accession to Pakistan. As Schofield notes, "After the JKLFs early successes, its leaders found that the Hizb-ul Mujaheddin was finding more support in Pakistan at

---

69. Schofield, *Kashmir in Conflict*, p. 142.

their expense . . . [and leaders] complained that recruits were being co-
erced to join the Hizb and other groups."[70]

Indeed, in a further indication that Pakistani leaders had been unpre-
pared for the popular *Azadi* (freedom) movement in Kashmir, a conscious
decision was taken to curb the *Azadi* movements, fearing that a movement for Kashmiri independence could eventually reach Azad Kashmir,
the Pakistani-administered areas of Kashmir, and thereby threaten Pakistan's security.[71] Pakistan then threw its support behind the *Hizb-ul
Mujahideen*. This organization was, like the JKLF, ethnically over 80 percent Kashmiri, but much less popular in Kashmir, due to the relatively
moderate form of Islam dominating the region. Support from Pakistan as
well as heavy-handed Indian repression, however, increased the popularity of the group among some sectors of the Kashmiri population, while
other sectors grew wary of the agenda of the militants, who targeted not
only Indian security forces but also tried to alter the ways of life of
Kashmiri Muslims in line with more extremist interpretations of Islam.[72]

The Soviet withdrawal from Afghanistan suddenly provided Pakistan's intelligence bodies with an ample and willing source of manpower
to fight the jihad in Kashmir. Moreover, this source of manpower—
mainly Afghan or Pakistani members of the *Hizb-e-Islami*—was even
more amenable to Pakistani control than the *Hizb-ul Mujahideen*. Pakistani
intelligence followed the example that the CIA and the ISI had set in
Afghanistan of supporting several smaller groups rather than one strong
and united one, in order to preserve greater ability to control the resistance.[73] These groups included the *Lashkar-e-Taiba, Jaish-e-Mohammad,* and
other extremist groups that were deeply unpopular in Kashmir itself. But
these groups served Pakistan's interests, as became clear during the brief
Kargil war in 1999. In fact, Pakistan was well aware that a direct Pakistani
military intervention in Kashmir was politically impossible and would
lead to Pakistan's being ostracized in the international community. Pakistan still aspired to use force in Kashmir, however, and could use the
Islamist guerrillas as proxies in this sense, portraying the Kargil offensive
as an indigenous uprising by Kashmiri militants.[74]

Of course, support for Islamic radical groups in both Kashmir and

---

70. Schofield, *Kashmir in Conflict*, p. 157.

71. See Wirsing, *India, Pakistan and the Kashmir Dispute*, p. 122.

72. See, e.g., Schofield, *Kashmir in Conflict*, p. 173.

73. Gul, *The Unholy Nexus*, p. 69.

74. See, e.g., Ashley J. Tellis et al., *Limited Conflict Under the Nuclear Umbrella: Indian
and Pakistani Lessons from the Kargil Crisis* (Santa Monica, Calif.: Rand, 2001).

Afghanistan has, with the benefit of hindsight, been damaging to the international standing as well as some of the national interests of Pakistan. In Afghanistan, the pro-Taliban policies brought Pakistan close to being ostracized internationally and increased the perceptions of Pakistan as an adventurous state on a downward slope of Islamic radicalism. Pakistan also failed to control the Taliban—a movement that, once in power, neither recognized the Durand Line as an international border nor handed over Pakistani radicals who were wanted by authorities in Islamabad, to name only two examples. In Kashmir, the damage was possibly even greater. Internationally, Pakistan's support for the cause of Kashmiri independence from India had substantial legitimacy as a policy based on international law and UN Security Council resolutions. India was on the defensive, disallowing the holding of a referendum on Kashmir's status. As the struggle for Kashmir has taken on a radical Islamic color and involved the increased use of terrorist tactics, however, the Kashmiri cause has lost much of its international legitimacy. In both Afghanistan and Kashmir, Pakistan has lost much of the goodwill that it had enjoyed among those respective populations due to these policies. Therefore, in retrospect Pakistan suffered from these policies. That they had been perceived as serving Pakistani short-term interests is obvious; whether the considerations leading to their adoption included a long-term perspective of Pakistan's interests in another matter. Irrespective of these considerations, Pakistan's support for Islamic radicals in Kashmir, just as in the case of Afghanistan, served a clear political purpose defined in terms of the national interests of Pakistan, in which Kashmir has always held a crucial importance.

The End of the Instrumental Use of Islam?

As a result of material national interests Pakistani foreign policy has used Islamic radicalism as an instrument. Evidence of the material factors overriding the cultural is the fact that whenever radical Islamic groups have been deemed not to serve the interests of the Pakistani state, they have not been supported. Most obviously, the sectarian groups wreaking havoc inside Pakistan were practically eliminated as soon as Musharraf got an opportunity to do so. On the other hand, Pakistani policymakers have often seen radical Islamic groups as useful instruments in their foreign-policy goals.

In this context, it is useful to reflect on the rapid change of global political attitudes to radical Islam. In the 1980s, the Afghan *mujahideen* were admired by world leaders and public opinion alike as heroic liberators. The United States was itself deeply involved in the joint effort with Pakistan, Egypt, Saudi Arabia, France, China, and other states to use holy warriors against the Soviet Union—a policy that continued up until 1989, when U.S. goals had been achieved and the United States hurriedly left the scene. The thinking of the Pakistani elite, in this context, was fully logical: the game in town in the 1980s was to use Islamic radicals for political purposes, and the United States itself was indulging in this practice. While Pakistan's enthusiasm had an influence on the U.S. decision to support the radicals, U.S. policymakers had little difficulty in sharing Islamabad's view that the radicals were the most motivated and reliable forces available in the fight against the Soviet Union. In addition, if these radicals could be used to defeat the might of the Soviet superpower and drive it out of Afghanistan, then may they not now, equally successfully, be used to drive India out of Kashmir? The same logic was then again applied to Afghanistan in the mid-1990s: Islamic radicals had been useful in Afghanistan once, they may be useful again. The only problem with the Pakistani thinking was that it had been bypassed by events in the world. With the collapse of communism, radical Islam in the early 1990s gradually grew to be perceived as a threat to peace and stability and to the security of the West. Hence, the global context in which Pakistan's foreign policy instrument had been both successful and acceptable had been the Cold War context. In the post–Cold War context, these same practices very rapidly became unacceptable in the new threat perceptions that emerged, as Pakistan later learned with the Taliban and again with the Kargil episode.

It is clear that the aftermath of September 11, 2001, taught Pakistani leaders a very serious lesson: the use of radical Islam for political purposes is simply not permissible in the global politics of today. Islamabad adopted the lesson and subsequently altered its policies. While Pakistani leaders may initially have believed that the U.S. need for Pakistan in the war on terrorism would translate into increased lenience toward Pakistan as far as Kashmir was concerned, the aftermath of the December 13, 2001, terrorist attack on the Indian parliament proved that this was not the case. U.S. policymakers have continuously exerted strong pressures on Musharraf's government to curb the insurgents' bases in Pakistan and discontinue state support for these groups. It has become clear that under current circumstances, armed Islamic groups are practically equated with terrorists. This has certainly shaped Musharraf's decision to ban the major extremist outfits and to claim, as he did in his landmark January 12, 2002, speech, that no one will be allowed to use terrorism in the name of Kashmir.

Whether Pakistani foreign policy will continue to use political Islam for its own purposes is dependent on several factors. First, Pakistan is not a one-man dictatorship, and changes to the current functioning of the state and the implementation of new rules of the game are likely to take time. It is also important to note that state patronage over radical groups allows the state a modicum of control over these groups, preventing them from turning against the state. In this sense, it could be dangerous for Pakistan to simply cut them off, without having contemplated the consequences of the loose cannons that would be generated in Pakistan and in the region. Second, the Indian attitude toward Pakistan will be crucial. At present, the Hindu nationalist government of India and its virulent anti-Pakistani policies has convinced the Musharraf government and most of the elite in Islamabad that India will accept no normalization of relations with Pakistan on equal terms.[75] India's posture is hence taken as a threat to Pakistan irrespective of what Pakistan does in Kashmir. From this standpoint, Pakistani policymakers are extremely reluctant to voluntarily destroy the only sizeable leverage they still maintain on India: the ability to inflict serious damage on India's ability to control Kashmir. This implies that Pakistan would be even more vulnerable to India if it completely abandoned its ambitions in Kashmir, including the support for radical groups.

---

75. Interviews in Islamabad and Washington with Pakistani officials, September 2002 and June 2003.

Chapter 12

Conclusion

Brenda Shaffer

This study examined the foreign policies of the states of the greater Caspian region throughout the first decade after the Soviet Union's demise and attempted to identify the role of culture in the foreign policy decisions of these states. Analysis of a decade's worth of policy decisions discovered few concrete cases in which vital material interests were sacrificed for the pursuit of cultural interests, including, the foreign policies of the some of the most culturally-ideologically visible regimes—the self-proclaimed "Islamic republics" of Iran, Taliban Afghanistan, and Pakistan.

The contributing authors of this volume presented different approaches to the question of the impact of culture on foreign policy. Some of the proponents of the significance of culture in foreign policy outcomes claimed that culture played a role in the articulation of interests. Even those proponents stated, however, that when cultural interests conflicted with material interests, cultural ones rarely trumped material ones. Some proponents claimed that once the cultural identity of a state has been articulated, constraints are set on the policy options that a state may utilize. The cases presented here, however, showed that, in some cases, states are not constrained by their articulated culture and can act in defiance of official cultural dictates, such as seen in the policy preferences of the Islamic Republic of Iran.

The key to understanding when culture is most likely to impact upon foreign policy decisions is, in most cases, the anticipated degree of the material cost trade-off. When it is cost-free, or close to it, regimes will spew rhetoric in support of and pursue policies that are culturally congruent to their officially articulated culture and conceivably that of the state's polity—at least for the sake of strengthening the legitimacy of the regime. When confronted with significant material costs, however, the pursuit of cultural interests rarely prevails. In states where cultural interests did prevail over material considerations for an extended period of time, serious consequences emerged and often brought about the demise of the state.[1]

An illustrative example of the significance of the degree of the material cost of pursuing cultural-ideological interests is Iran's support for Shi'a and other radical Muslim movements in different arenas. Iran tends to demonstrate "Islamic solidarity" in regions that are far from its borders; thus, Tehran's chances of experiencing material consequences, especially in the security sphere, are relatively small. In areas bordering Iran, Tehran is very cautious in implementing potentially destabilizing policies that could either spillover into Iran or could cause bordering states to retaliate against it. In order to prevent crises of legitimacy and satisfy the demands of the more religious elements in the regime, the Islamic Republic of Iran displays more Islamic solidarity in the Arab-Israeli arena, where the material costs and risks of its actions are minimal. Tehran pays neither in terms of retribution on Iranian territory nor by damage to the vital interests of either the state or the regime's policymakers for its support of the Hizbollah movement in Lebanon and Palestinian terrorists. In addition, this policy projects an image of strong Islamic loyalty both abroad and throughout the Muslim world, connoting a special role for Iran, which translates into material value. Thus, Iran can gain legitimacy and power through its support for terror, both internally and in the broader Middle East, relatively cost-free.

Where Culture Matters

As stated, cultural interests are promoted in cases where the material costs are few. A corollary conclusion to the centrality of the degree of material cost is that cultural interests will at times be promoted when the material trade-offs are unknown to the decision-makers. The amount of information that the decision-makers possess on the consequences of policy actions in terms of material trade-offs impacts the degree to which culture can influence foreign policy. If the decision-maker is unaware of

---

1. As Yekezkel Dror pointed out, while the number of states that pursue materially illogical policies is low, and their longevity is limited, these states have great capacity to impose great harm during their short-lived periods of action and thus should be monitored carefully. Yehezkel Dror, *Crazy States: A Counterconventional Strategic Problem* (Lexington, Mass.: Heath Books, 1971), p. xiii.

the possible or probable material costs of the cultural policies, their pursuit will then appear to be relatively free of negative consequences and therefore be likelier. This point was made by Svante Cornell in his analysis of the foreign policy decisions of Taliban Afghanistan. Lack of information on potential material trade-offs could result from the structure of the policymaking process itself, from cultural practices that restrict flow of information (as was shown to be prevalent in the policymaking process in Central Asia), or through the actions of islands within a state apparatus that may purposely deny information to the decision-makers in order to bring about a certain policy outcome (e.g., reporting by ambassadors in the field, reports or actions taken by military units abroad). Lack of information on the material costs may arise from cultural factors that impact upon the interpretation of information, such as signals from other actors, and this sphere of research warrants further study.

An additional situation that is more conducive to cultural influence on the policy process is the existence of domestic political constraints that do not allow the leader to pursue a material agenda. For instance, as was illustrated by David King and Miles Pomper, legislation enacted by the U.S. Congress in the foreign policy sphere is at times based on local, cultural interests and does not take into consideration the overall material interest of either the United States or that of its current administration. In addition, domestic political situations can deprive the leader of the ability politically to pursue worthy material policies due to anticipated domestic repercussions (fear of not being re-elected, domestic strife, fall of government in parliamentary regimes) and can force implementation of materially costly policies in order to ensure political survival. It seems, however, that the implementation of materially costly policies over an extended period of time may be very dangerous to the state and its regime.

As was shown here, regimes do not necessarily get trapped in their own rhetoric. They often act in defiance of their officially articulated cultural and ideological rhetoric or publicly interpret their culture as a way of having the culture conform to their policies. As Roger Kangas showed, the leaders of all the Central Asian states used Islamic symbols and rituals to legitimize their regimes. These trappings did not, however, force the regimes in any way to implement more Islamic-based policies or to exhibit Islamic solidarity with other Muslim-populated states. Even in the case of Iran, where the hard-line Islamic press was quick to point out the discrepancies in the regime's policy choices (Armenia over Azerbaijan, Russia over Chechnya) with its professed commitment to Islamic solidarity, little action was taken by the decision-makers to modify these policies in light of the criticism.

The number of cases in this study is not large enough to draw conclusions regarding the impact of regime type on the propensity of cultural influences upon foreign policy. This sphere does, however, warrant further research, and the information presented in this book challenges the widely held perception that in "one-man regimes," culture—especially in the form of religion—has an opportunity to determine foreign policy outcomes in contrast to open democratic systems. In the cases analyzed in this book, the democratic political structure of the United States, in which the locally-elected legislature has tremendous sway over foreign policy outcomes, permits locally-based cultural groups (and other local factors) to impact upon U.S. foreign policy. In contrast, authoritarian regimes, such as the Islamic Republic of Iran, were shown to cope easily with straying from and even contradicting their declared affinity with Islam and Islamic forces—with neither constraint nor domestic or international repercussions.

Preliminary research conducted here indicates that regime type may influence the impact of culture on the outcome of peace negotiations that entail territorial concessions. In the case of Uzbekistan and Kazakhstan, the lack of powerful domestic oppositions that could have incited public sentiments and rallied the public to oppose territorial concessions certainly eased the conclusion of the border delimitation agreement between the two republics in 2002 that entailed hundreds of territorial concessions from each side. Domestic political oppositions, especially in parliamentary democracies, clearly have a political incentive to mobilize cultural sentiments to attack a ruling government's intent to negotiate away territory. While in political opposition, the material consequences of pursuing cultural policies may not always be taken into consideration, due to the goal of achieving political power. The connection between regime type and the role of culture on the outcome of peace negotiations should be explored in further research.

In the Caspian region, at times, cultural agendas of actors within a state have succeeded in creating facts on the ground and forcing a policy on the state that it may not have initiated. Units of the Russian army stationed abroad in the former Soviet republics in the early 1990s often acted independently of Moscow, and imposed policies from the field on their resident states without concern for the overall material consequences for Russia. Domestic ethnic lobbies in the United States have been able to impose a cultural agenda on Washington, often in contradiction to the state's material interests as viewed by the executive branch. In cases where states have significant numbers of co-religionists, co-ethnics, or former citizens abroad that are active in that state's political process, conditions are more conducive to the pursuit of cultural policies at the expense of material ones. Diasporas and other communities abroad often have a huge impact on the foreign policy choices of their "homeland" states, especially by means of the financial resources that they can wield and the subsequent strength of the various political forces there that they support, and even through direct participation in elections in states they do not reside in.[2] Ethnic or religious diasporas and other extra-territorial members of a given state's identity community do not bear the brunt of various policy decisions, such as war or economic ruin, and often promote more cultural policies in the homeland state in which they do not reside. The involvement of the diaspora in the foreign policy of the kin state is seen in the case of the Republic of Armenia. The Armenian diaspora worked intensively to undermine the government of the first president of the Republic of Armenia, Levon Ter-Petrossian, who attempted to build ties with the Republic of Turkey and negotiate a peace agreement with Azerbaijan over Nagorno-Karabagh that would have entailed territorial concessions from Yerevan.

Culture can also impact foreign policy outcomes when foreign states take another state's rhetoric seriously and craft policies in reaction to it. While culture and cultural rhetoric are frequently and cynically used by regimes to endow their foreign policy decisions with legitimacy, they often stray from the cultural dictates of their official ideologies. This rhetoric does seem, however, to impact other states' perceptions of these rhetoric-wielding states. As shown in the Kangas chapter, models used to train analysts in the U.S. governmental policymaking community assign a significant role to culture ("national values") in shaping foreign policy outcomes of other states. This training and approach seems to permeate the way in which many U.S. policymakers assume that policy is conducted outside the trans-Atlantic world. Also in this volume, Ali Ansari points out that U.S. policies toward the Islamic Republic of Iran were highly influenced by the fact that Washington took Tehran's revolutionary rhetoric seriously. Washington was willing to accept at face value Iran's martyrdom rhetoric, thus assuming that Tehran was willing to preclude material interests and even survivability in order to promote its cultural-ideological goals. Iranians have often been surprised by the extent to which the regime's rhetoric is taken seriously and how its domestic practices, such as the murder of dissidents and the threat to assassinate novelist Salman Rushdie, impacted the way that the United States,

---

2. A rising number of states allow members of their diasporas to vote from abroad in elections in states they do not reside in. Iraq, Russia, and Georgia are among the states that sanction voting from abroad. This allows people who do not directly bear the material costs of the states' decisions to directly influence the states' policies, which may create more pressure for cultural policies.

and to a certain extent Europe, viewed the potential for cooperation with Iran.

Alliances and Coalitions

Based on the cases examined in this book, the foreign policy sphere in which culture had the smallest impact was coalition and alliance choices. The states under study forged their alliances and selected cooperation partners mostly on the basis of contemporary material interests, and common cultural affiliations, or lack thereof, rarely impinged on coalition formation. The coalitions formed in the Caspian region were not determined by shared cultural or religious affiliations, and cultural differences did not prevent the creation of the most interesting bedfellows.

Cultural proximity does not necessarily determine strategic alliances. Most of the states and peoples of Central Asia enthusiastically identify with their common Turkic identity, but this has not translated into shared identity with the Republic of Turkey. Likewise, the common celebration and primacy attributed to the Iranian pre-Islamic holiday of Novruz did not serve to unify Central Asians with the Islamic Republic of Iran. In fact, when political forces differ, cultural proximity can be used to explain the conflict and competition over the leadership of a certain bloc of states. Thus, in similar cultures, there are often more elements of contention than in cultures that are poles apart. Examples of this are the disputes among the Christian Orthodox churches and competition between the Shi'i centers of Najaf and Qom.

It is significant that there has been no serious "Muslim" mobilization around the world in support of the Muslims in Chechnya and Azerbaijan, despite the fact that tens of thousands have become refugees and thousands have been killed as a result of their conflicts with non-Muslims. Russia and Armenia continue to maintain excellent relations with Muslim-populated states, and Russian and Armenian diplomats can move around Muslim-populated countries without any particular fear. Neither Russia nor Armenia has been a special focus of Muslim public campaigns or grievances, and the Muslim refugees created by these conflicts have not been of any special concern to Muslim-populated states. This can be explained by the good bilateral ties and cooperation maintained by prominent Muslim-populated states with Russia and the subsequent lack of desire to disrupt these ties on behalf of the Chechen Muslims. Likewise, the Republic of Azerbaijan's pro-Western orientation and secular regime inhibits sympathy in other Muslim-populated states, such as Iran, toward the plight of over 800,000 Azerbaijani refugees.

This lack of Muslim mobilization on behalf of the plight of the

Chechens and Azerbaijanis can lead us to approach the Muslim public response in an instrumental fashion, instead of the belief that Muslim reactions to certain political and social phenomena are inherent and connected to cultural and religious solidarity. Rather, the cases of Azerbaijan and Chechnya can lead to the conclusion that the response of the public is often selective and organized around varying interests and agendas of political and other forces.

Authors in this volume presented diverse views as to the causal direction of conflict and coalition partners. Douglas Blum stated that at times, culture follows coalitions, not the other way around. Blum cited the examples of the states of Central Asia and the Caucasus who adopted democratic and liberal laws and instituted democratic rituals in hopes of joining the U.S.-led camp. In contrast, Ido Oren claimed that, in the cases that he had analyzed, cultural views changed incrementally and were connected to changes in the nature of coalitions. Blum further stated that enthusiasm for a common cultural identity does not necessarily translate into alliances.

While examining the impact of common culture on alliance and coalition choices, this volume did not discuss whether or not common culture contributes to the successful functioning of those alliances. This should be a direction of further study.

Which Culture Influences Foreign Policy Is Not Clear

The examination of the impact of culture on foreign policy in this book not only confirmed in the case of the Caspian states that cultural interests rarely trumped material ones, but also showed that the cultural forces that potentially impact foreign policy are not always apparent. First and foremost, a variety of collective cultural identities operates on different levels and in different spheres within a state. People possess multiple identities, including those of region, family, ethnicity, state, religion, and religious sect, and it is not always clear which identity is primary and under which circumstances it fulfills the primary role. In different parts of the world, different primary identities are often more prominent and politically relevant. It is not evident that the professed religion of a population of a state or even the primary language spoken there determines the primary identity of a collective. In many areas of the world, various identities play an important political role—especially in domestic politics—such as regional, tribal, and family identities, and in many cases, they have much more bearing on political processes than either ethnic or religious identities. This is true, for instance, in Central Asia. In attempting to assess the role of culture in foreign policy, the researcher should not presume that either religion or ethnicity is the primary cultural factor that can influence policy formation.

Moreover, language is not a clear indicator of cultural identity. Often there is a huge gap between language proficiency and vitality of self-identification based on language. A large disparity between the primary language of a group and its cherished language can exist, with the cherished language being the basis for primary identity designation. Large groups of peoples in the region—such as Azerbaijanis in Iran, Kazakhs in Kazakhstan, and diaspora Armenians may not possess fluency in their titular languages, but these languages are cherished by them, and they act politically to promote their status, often at the expense of the status of their own primary functional languages (Persian, Russian, French, or English).

Another factor complicating the impact of culture on foreign policy is: not only is the official culture not the only one that can impact policy determinations, but often those cultural influences which do sway policy are neither overt nor clear markers of ethnic or religious groupings. For instance, as Roger Kangas showed, the cultural practice in Central Asia of not reporting bad news to one's superiors has significant impact on the foreign policy outcomes by denying the leaders information on the potential outcomes of their policies or the need to make new policies. In the Caucasus and Iran, another prominent cultural tendency is viewing one's rivals as being very sophisticated in their policymaking and assuming the existence of elaborate policy conspiracies. This cultural habit seems to have bearing on the policies of these states. It is, however, a cultural habit that an analyst would have difficulty recognizing on the basis of the religious, ethnic, or officially designated culture of a state. Thus, the cultural habits that may have the most bearing on foreign policymaking are often not connected with common cultural groupings or official designations.

In the case of Muslim-populated states, Western analysts too often presuppose that Islam serves as the primary collective identity of the residents of a state, and as such, is often the determinant of policy choices and coalition preferences. As clearly illustrated in this book, common Muslim identity played no role in the choice of coalition partners of the states of the region or their overall security orientations. By assuming that the Islamic element was primary, the United States and other Western states have often missed policy opportunities or come to develop them late because of the assumption that the Islamic identity of a state's citizens could preclude cooperation. This was the case in the initial period following the Soviet Union's dissolution. In the South Caucasus, for instance, the United States was initially cautious in its relations with

Muslim Azerbaijan relative to its active pursuit of cooperation and ties with Georgia and Armenia, assuming that there were strong chances that Muslim Azerbaijan would fall into either Iran's or another Muslim-populated state's orbit.

The impact of religion on policy is also complicated, since interpretations of religious texts often vary from region to region, and many regions are home to a number of competing sects that may view themselves as being more in conflict than unified. An important example of this is the difference of Islamic interpretation between two bordering "Islamic Republics": the Islamic Republic of Iran and the Taliban in Afghanistan. The two neighboring states viewed each other as enemies and came close to war. Moreover, in examining the policies of Muslim-populated states, researchers often focus on the letter of the law in formal religious texts as being the guide to a state' policies, erroneously ignoring the complex realties that affect choices and the varying interpretation of texts, even within a cultural grouping. This leads to difficulty in defining what the cultural dictates on policy are exactly.

Even in cases when Islam seems to be a primary motivating factor in policies, interpretations can vary and disputes can arise within confessions. As Svante Cornell maintained, Taliban Afghanistan's policy choices were influenced by a mix of Islamic and Pashto cultural directives that the Taliban and their supporters had interpreted as being one insepa-rable element that they had also perceived as being Islamic. Roger Kangas pointed out that how a regime interprets what is Islamic is highly discretionary and often in service of current policy agendas. He cites the insightful example of how the regimes in Central Asia often refer to "good Islam" or "real Islam" and "bad Islam" or "false Islam." "Good Islam," and therefore the true one, is one of tolerance to foreigners and other religions and locally rooted, incorporating local (non-Arab) traditions. In contrast, "bad Islam," as interpreted by the Central Asian leaders (and their foreign policy orientations), is led by foreign Muslims and is intolerant toward non-Muslims.

The Caspian Region

In addition to its theoretical contributions, this book sheds light on the Caspian region itself. A region that is so often interpreted as being ruled by "ancient hatreds" and religious and ethnic divides turns out, in many cases, to be a flagship of *Realpolitik* and material interests. Many opportunities for good policies toward the region have been squandered due to these misinterpretations. Further research on this region can enhance political studies. Research based on cases from Central Asia and the Caucasus, and even Iran, is surprising scarce in the major journals of international relations and political science. Inclusion of these cases could enhance political studies in general and the pursuit to better understand the role of religion and Islam in politics and foreign policy specifically.

The Caspian region, which is a landbridge between Europe and Asia, is re-emerging as a region of major geopolitical significance. U.S. military basing and deployment in this region is growing, and the area has become a major route for U.S. transport and transit into major theaters of operation in Afghanistan and the Middle East. In this region, the military forces of Russia, China, and the United States are in close proximity, and in some of the states even overlap, with basing of both Russian and U.S. forces (Tajikistan, Georgia, and the Kyrgyz Republic). Growing energy demands from Asian states, especially China and India, will lead to the Asian powers' greater involvement and presence in the region in the near future. In the Caspian region, significant economic activity and interests of a number of world powers overlap: the United States, Europe, Russia, and China.

Energy security will be at the forefront of the world policy agenda in the coming decades. While the proven oil and natural gas reserves in Azerbaijan and Kazakhstan are not immense, a source outside the Organization of Petroleum Exporting Countries (OPEC) cartel is significant because diversity of sources can contribute to energy security. Moreover, small amounts of additional oil on the world market can have a disproportionate impact on global oil price trends. In addition, the extent of the Caspian region's reserves, especially those of Kazakhstan, is unknown, and significant discoveries may be in store. This makes the Caspian region attractive to investment.

Policy Implications

The analysis in this volume holds a number of policy implications. First of all, the U.S. governmental policy community should rethink the training models used for the analysts who assign a prominent role to culture in forming the foreign policy choices of states. Culture should be considered one among a number of factors that have varying impact on foreign policy outcomes, but it should not be approached as a constant and necessarily prominent factor. Analysts should be trained to approach the impact of culture on a case-by-case basis and to assess its impact. Analysts should also be taught that the official collective identities in a state, and other prominent cultural factors, such as religion and ethnicity, are not necessarily the cultural factors that constrain policy outcomes, and that when researching, they need to probe deeply to find the essence of those factors. This is actually the nexus of regional studies and international relations in policy assessment: tasking regional specialists to look for the cultural influences that are beyond the prominent cultural identity categories, such as religion and ethnicity, and can impact upon foreign policy formation.

Furthermore, the "Islamic Republics" in the international system should be viewed as actors that often have material interests as guiding forces in their foreign policy and are thus deterrable and enticeable like other states in the system. Viewing these states in this manner will create a wider range of policy options, and subsequently, appropriate policies can be crafted *vis-à-vis* these states. Previous assumptions that most of these states were driven by religious belief and passion and were thus willing to take on detrimental policies added to both their deterrence ability and their perception as being beyond engagement and undeterrable. A new look at the material foundations of many of their policies will create an opportunity for a wider range of policy options toward them and potentially toward other culturally articulate states.

The lack of correlation between cultural affinity and alliance formation can lead to a new understanding of many of the unfolding relationships in the Middle East and beyond. Iran does not necessarily sway the support of Shi'i forces and states in the region. Just as Tehran does not champion the cause of the Shi'a of Azerbaijan, it may not necessarily champion that of the Shi'a of Iraq and is not unmovable in its support for Hizbollah in Lebanon. Moreover, there is not necessarily an affinity of interests between all the Shi'a in the Middle East. Shi'i identity is not necessarily the major identity of the Shi'a, many of whom are secular. Even in the cases where Shi'i identity is prominent, it is not necessarily the factor that will determine the political and strategic alliances of the Shi'i group or state. The response of the Muslim public should not be perceived as a given, but as an outcome that is both selective and often directed by various political factors.

In recent years, many comments have been made on the perceived stances and actions of "the Muslim world." The lack of impact that common Muslim identity had on the coalition lines, and the lack of Muslim-led mobilization for and world Muslim apathy toward the Muslims of the Caucasus that have suffered in the region's conflicts, lead one to question thinking in terms of the existence of a Muslim world. This study shows that in the case of the Muslim-populated states of the Caspian region, there are huge divides in the actions and attitudes of Muslims. Just as one cannot easily speak of a "Christian world" as a variable in foreign policy attitudes, one must view Muslim-populated states in a nuanced fashion, and not as a monolithic bloc of states and actors.

About the Authors

Ali M. Ansari is Reader in Modern History with reference to the Middle East at the University of St. Andrews and Associate Fellow of the Middle East Programme at Chatham House, London. He is the author of *Iran, Islam and Democracy: the Politics of Managing Change* (Royal Institute of International Affairs, 2000), and *Modern Iran Since 1921: the Pahlavis and After* (Longman, 2003). He has published in a number of journals including *Middle Eastern Studies* and *The Washington Quarterly*. He is also a contributor to the *New Cambridge History of Islam*.

Douglas W. Blum is Professor of Political Science at Providence College in Providence, Rhode Island, and Adjunct Professor of International Studies at the Thomas J. Watson, Jr., Institute of International Studies at Brown University. His general research interests include cultural globalization, the politics of energy development in the Caspian Sea, and the international relations of post-Soviet Central Asia. Much of his recent work has focused on the Caspian region, and he has published and spoken on a number of related themes including Russian and U.S. policy, energy geopolitics, and environmental security in the Caspian basin. He is currently working on a monograph entitled *Globalization, State-Society Relations, and the Construction of National Identity in Post-Soviet Space*.

Svante E. Cornell is the Deputy Director of the Central Asia–Caucasus Institute of the Paul H. Nitze School of Advanced International Studies, Johns Hopkins University. He is the Editor of the Institute's bi-weekly publication, the *Central Asia–Caucasus Analyst*. He co-founded the Silk Road Studies Program of Uppsala University, Sweden, and serves as Research Director there. He holds a Ph.D. degree from the department of Peace and Conflict Research of Uppsala University and a degree in international relations from the Middle East Technical University, Ankara, Turkey. His books include *Small Na-*

tions and Great Powers: A Study of Ethnopolitical Conflict in the Caucasus (Routledge, 2001), and Autonomy and Conflict: Ethnoterritoriality and Separatism in the South Caucasus (Uppsala University, 2002), and he has published numerous academic and policy articles in World Politics, Washington Quarterly, Current History, Journal of Democracy, Foreign Service Journal, Orbis, and other journals. His commentaries occasionally appear in the U.S., Swedish, Turkish, and Pakistani daily press.

Markus Fischer is an Assistant Professor at California State University, Fullerton. His research straddles political theory and international relations. He has published on the political thought of Machiavelli and the foreign affairs of feudal Europe. His current work compares the ideas of the legalist tradition of ancient China to those of political realism in the West.

Roger D. Kangas is the Professor of Central Asian Studies at the George C. Marshall European Center for Strategic Studies in Garmisch-Partenkirchen, Germany, and is a specialist on the politics of, and regional security in, Central Asia and the Caspian Sea basin. Prior to joining the Marshall Center in 1999, Dr. Kangas held positions at the U.S. Department of State's Foreign Service Institute, Georgetown University; Johns Hopkins University's the Paul H. Nitze School of Advanced International Studies (SAIS), the Open Media Research Institute, and the University of Mississippi. Dr. Kangas has written numerous articles and book chapters on Central Asian politics and society.

Robert Kauffman is a graduate of the University of Florida, where he majored in finance and political science.

David C. King is Lecturer in Public Policy and Associate Director of the Institute of Politics at Harvard's John F. Kennedy School of Government, where he teaches about the U.S. Congress, interest groups, and political parties. He is the author, coauthor, and co-editor of three books focusing on Congress and on public confidence in government. He chairs Harvard's Program for Newly Elected Members of the U.S. Congress. In the wake of the 2000 presidential elections, he chaired the Task Force on Election Administration on behalf of former presidents Gerald Ford and Jimmy Carter. King oversees several large national surveys that explore youth attitudes about politics, and his current research is on political polarization.

Ido Oren is Associate Professor of Political Science at the University of Florida. He is the author of Our Enemies and US: America's Rivalries and the Making of Political Science (Cornell University Press, 2003). His articles have appeared in International Security, the European Journal of International Relations, Journal of Conflict Resolution, and other professional journals.

Miles A. Pomper is the editor of *Arms Control Today,* a journal focusing on global security and the proliferation of weapons of mass destruction. Previously, he served as the lead foreign policy reporter for *Congressional Quarterly* and covered national security issues for *Legi-Slate News Service.* Before turning to professional journalism, he served as a foreign service officer with the U.S. Information Agency and holds master's degrees in both international affairs and journalism. He has written extensively on the Caucasus and U.S. policy toward the region.

Brenda Shaffer is a faculty member of the School of Political Sciences and the Department of East Asian Studies at the University of Haifa and Research Director of the Caspian Studies Project at Harvard University. Her research focuses on the Caucasus, Central Asia, Iran, Russian-Iranian relations, theoretical issues of collective identity, energy and politics, and the link between culture and foreign policy. Shaffer takes a special interest in Caspian energy issues, ethnic politics in Iran, and the Nagorno-Karabagh conflict. She is the author of *Borders and Brethren: Iran and the Challenge of Azerbaijani Identity* (MIT Press, 2002) which was formally recognized by the Azerbaijan Academy of Sciences in 2004. Shaffer has also published *Partners in Need: Russian-Iranian Strategic Cooperation and Relations* (Washington Institute for Near East Policy, 2001) and a number of journal articles. She serves as a lecturer and consultant to a number of government fora and regional security organizations regarding their policy toward the Caspian region.

Ronald Grigor Suny is Professor of Political Science and History at the University of Chicago. Formerly the Alex Manoogian Professor of Modern Armenian History at the University of Michigan, he is the author of *The Revenge of the Past: Nationalism, Revolution, and the Collapse of the Soviet Union* (Stanford University Press, 1993); *Looking Toward Ararat: Armenia in Modern History* (Indiana University Press, 1993); *The Making of the Georgian Nation* (Indiana University Press, 1988, 1994); and *The Soviet Experiment: Russia, the USSR, and the Successor States* (Oxford University Press, 1998). He is currently working on a biography of the young Stalin and a collection of essays on empire and nation.

Index

BCSIA Studies in International Security
Published by The MIT Press

Sean M. Lynn-Jones and Steven E. Miller, series editors
Karen Motley, executive editor
Belfer Center for Science and International Affairs (BCSIA)
John F. Kennedy School of Government, Harvard University

Agha, Hussein, Shai Feldman, Ahmad Khalidi, and Zeev Schiff, *Track-II Diplomacy: Lessons from the Middle East* (2003)

Allison, Graham T., Owen R. Coté, Jr., Richard A. Falkenrath, and Steven E. Miller, *Avoiding Nuclear Anarchy: Containing the Threat of Loose Russian Nuclear Weapons and Fissile Material* (1996)

Allison, Graham T., and Kalypso Nicolaïdis, eds., *The Greek Paradox: Promise vs. Performance* (1996)

Arbatov, Alexei, Abram Chayes, Antonia Handler Chayes, and Lara Olson, eds., *Managing Conflict in the Former Soviet Union: Russian and American Perspectives* (1997)

Bennett, Andrew, *Condemned to Repetition? The Rise, Fall, and Reprise of Soviet-Russian Military Interventionism, 1973–1996* (1999)

Blackwill, Robert D., and Michael Stürmer, eds., *Allies Divided: Transatlantic Policies for the Greater Middle East* (1997)

Blackwill, Robert D., and Paul Dibb, eds., *America's Asian Alliances* (2000)

Brom, Shlomo, and Yiftah Shapir, eds., *The Middle East Military Balance, 1999–2000* (1999)

Brom, Shlomo, and Yiftah Shapir, eds., *The Middle East Military Balance, 2001–2002* (2002)

Brown, Michael E., ed., *The International Dimensions of Internal Conflict* (1996)

Brown, Michael E., and Šumit Ganguly, eds., *Government Policies and Ethnic Relations in Asia and the Pacific* (1997)

Brown, Michael E., and Šumit Ganguly, eds., *Fighting Words: Language Policy and Ethnic Relations in Asia* (2003)

Carter, Ashton B., and John P. White, eds., *Keeping the Edge: Managing Defense for the Future* (2001)

de Nevers, Renée, *Comrades No More: The Seeds of Political Change in Eastern Europe* (2003)

Elman, Colin, and Miriam Fendius Elman, eds., *Bridges and Boundaries: Historians, Political Scientists, and the Study of International Relations* (2001)

Elman, Colin, and Miriam Fendius Elman, eds., *Progress in International Relations Theory: Appraising the Field* (2003)

Elman, Miriam Fendius, ed., *Paths to Peace: Is Democracy the Answer?* (1997)

Falkenrath, Richard A., *Shaping Europe's Military Order: The Origins and Consequences of the CFE Treaty* (1994)

Falkenrath, Richard A., Robert D. Newman, and Bradley A. Thayer, *America's Achilles' Heel: Nuclear, Biological, and Chemical Terrorism and Covert Attack* (1998)

Feaver, Peter D., and Richard H. Kohn, eds., *Soldiers and Civilians: The Civil-Military Gap and American National Security* (2001)

Feldman, Shai, *Nuclear Weapons and Arms Control in the Middle East* (1996)

Feldman, Shai, and Yiftah Shapir, eds., *The Middle East Military Balance 2000–2001* (2001)

Forsberg, Randall, ed., *The Arms Production Dilemma: Contraction and Restraint in the World Combat Aircraft Industry* (1994)

George, Alexander L., and Andrew Bennett, *Case Studies and Theory Development in the Social Sciences* (2005)

Hagerty, Devin T., *The Consequences of Nuclear Proliferation: Lessons from South Asia* (1998)

Heymann, Philip B., *Terrorism and America: A Commonsense Strategy for a Democratic Society* (1998)

Heymann, Philip B., *Terrorism, Freedom, and Security: Winning without War* (2003)

Heymann, Philip B., and Juliette N. Kayyem, *Protecting Liberty in an Age of Terror* (2005)

Howitt, Arnold M., and Robyn L. Pangi, eds., *Countering Terrorism: Dimensions of Preparedness* (2003)

Hudson, Valerie M., and Andrea M. den Boer, *Bare Branches: The Security Implications of Asia's Surplus Male Population* (2004)

Kayyem, Juliette N., and Robyn L. Pangi, eds., *First to Arrive: State and Local Responses to Terrorism* (2003)

Kokoshin, Andrei A., *Soviet Strategic Thought, 1917–91* (1998)

Lederberg, Joshua, ed., *Biological Weapons: Limiting the Threat* (1999)

Mansfield, Edward D., and Jack Snyder, *Electing to Fight: Why Emerging Democracies Go to War* (2005)

Martin, Lenore G., and Dimitris Keridis, eds., *The Future of Turkish Foreign Policy* (2004)

Shaffer, Brenda, *Borders and Brethren: Iran and the Challenge of Azerbaijani Identity* (2002)

Shaffer, Brenda, ed., *The Limits of Culture: Islam and Foreign Policy* (2006)

Shields, John M., and William C. Potter, eds., *Dismantling the Cold War: U.S. and NIS Perspectives on the Nunn-Lugar Cooperative Threat Reduction Program* (1997)

Tucker, Jonathan B., ed., *Toxic Terror: Assessing Terrorist Use of Chemical and Biological Weapons* (2000)

Utgoff, Victor A., ed., *The Coming Crisis: Nuclear Proliferation, U.S. Interests, and World Order* (2000)

Williams, Cindy, ed., *Holding the Line: U.S. Defense Alternatives for the Early 21st Century* (2001)

Williams, Cindy, ed., *Filling the Ranks: Transforming the U.S. Military Personnel System* (2004)

The Robert and Renée Belfer Center for Science and International Affairs

Graham Allison, Director
John F. Kennedy School of Government
Harvard University
79 JFK Street, Cambridge MA 02138
Tel: (617) 495–1400; Fax: (617) 495–8963
http://www.ksg.harvard.edu/bcsia   bcsia_ksg@harvard.edu

The Belfer Center for Science and International Affairs (BCSIA) is the hub of research, teaching and training in international security affairs, environmental and resource issues, science and technology policy, human rights, and conflict studies at Harvard's John F. Kennedy School of Government. The Center's mission is to provide leadership in advancing policy-relevant knowledge about the most important challenges of international security and other critical issues where science, technology and international affairs intersect.

BCSIA's leadership begins with the recognition of science and technology as driving forces transforming international affairs. The Center integrates insights of social scientists, natural scientists, technologists, and practitioners with experience in government, diplomacy, the military, and business to address these challenges. The Center pursues its mission in four complementary research programs:

- The **International Security Program** (ISP) addresses the most pressing threats to U.S. national interests and international security.

- The **Environment and Natural Resources Program** (ENRP) is the locus of Harvard's interdisciplinary research on resource and environmental problems and policy responses.

- The **Science, Technology, and Public Policy Program** (STPP) analyzes ways in which science and technology policy influence international security, resources, environment, and development, and such cross-cutting issues as technological innovation and information infrastructure.

- The **Program on Intrastate Conflict** analyzes the causes of ethnic, religious, and other conflicts, and seeks to identify practical ways to prevent and limit such conflicts.

The heart of the Center is its resident research community of more than 140 scholars: Harvard faculty, analysts, practitioners, and each year a new, interdisciplinary group of research fellows. BCSIA sponsors frequent seminars, workshops and conferences, maintains a substantial specialized library, and publishes books, monographs, and discussion papers.

The Center's International Security Program, directed by Steven E. Miller, publishes the BCSIA Studies in International Security, and sponsors and edits the quarterly journal *International Security*.

The Center is supported by an endowment established with funds from Robert and Renée Belfer, the Ford Foundation and Harvard University, by foundation grants, by individual gifts, and by occasional government contracts.